15/2/17

麦克·贝茨勋爵

Andrew,

Best wishes,

Michael

2013年麦克·贝茨勋爵夫妇在英国国会开议大典上

2011年"为奥林匹克休战徒步"期间,麦克·贝茨勋爵夫妇受到联合国秘书长潘基文的接见

2015年8月30日枣庄,全国人大常务委员会副委员长、中国红十字会会长陈竺看望徒步途中的麦克·贝茨勋爵

2015年"为和平徒步"

1. 贝茨勋爵在议会大厦前与前来商谈在华徒步事宜的中国红十字会常务副会长徐科合影
2. 勋爵夫妇邀请志愿者团队到上议院做客并一起讨论徒步方案
3. 勋爵夫妇和中英舞蹈夏令营的孩子们同游颐和园
4. 2015年英国大选的当晚勋爵夫妇在保守党总部电话助选

7月27日:"为和平徒步"启程仪式在天坛公园举行,中国红十字会副会长郝林娜(雪琳右侧)主持并讲话,国务院侨办主任裘援平(勋爵左侧)出席仪式并宣布徒步开始

7月27日:国务院侨办主任裘援平为贝茨勋爵送行

7月27日:浙江省外事侨务办公室主任金永辉(右二)专程来京参加徒步启程仪式

1. 7月29日：走进河北省廊坊市
2. 7月30日：参观"天下第一城"
3. 7月30日：在酒店大堂有WiFi的地方，贝茨勋爵借用值班经理的桌子写博客
4. 7月31日：贝茨勋爵在路边小憩
5. 7月31日：第一个100公里里程碑

7月29日：大城县至沧州市的路上

7月31日：经过村镇

8月1日：途中

8月1日：因为是周末，更多人加入了徒步行列

8月1日：在廊坊

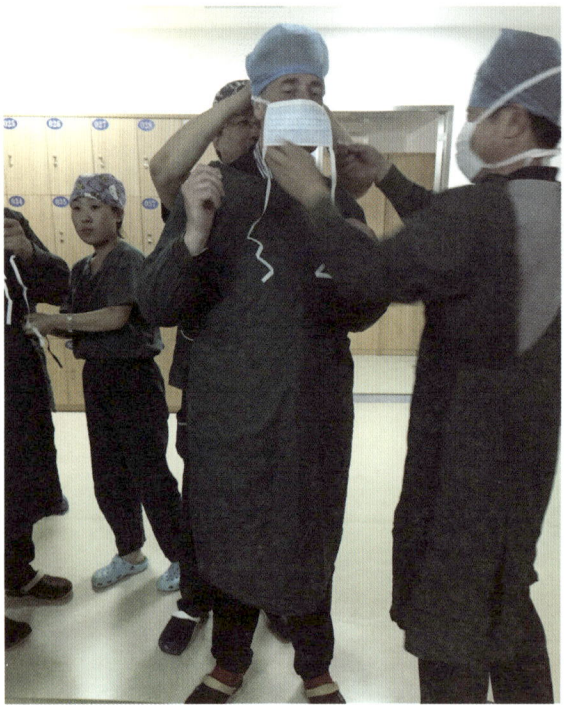

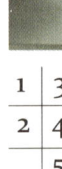

1. 8月3日：贝茨勋爵夫妇在沧州接受媒体采访
2. 8月3日：抵达沧州第一天，参观青县人民医院
3. 8月4日：五名训练有素的红十字救援队志愿者加入徒步行列
4. 8月4日：走过华北平原一望无际的青纱帐
5. 8月4日：枣园小憩

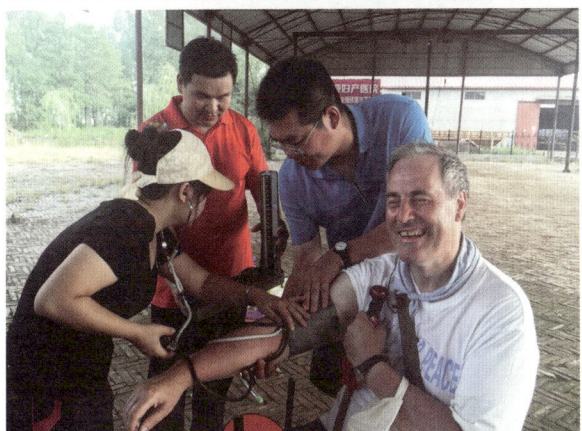
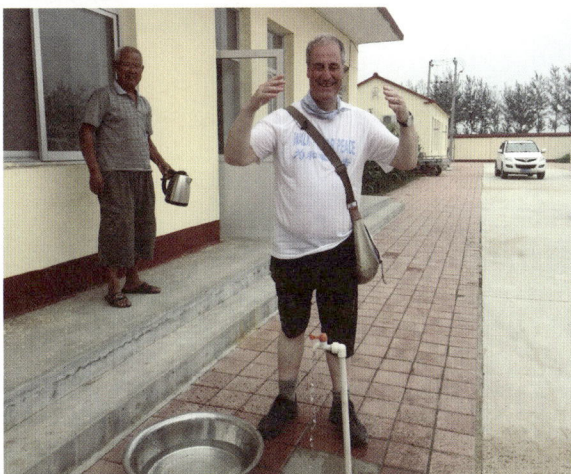

1. 8月5日：在河北境内的最后一天
2. 8月5日：红十字会随行人员时时关注勋爵的健康状况
3. 8月5日：徒步途中在村委会休息
4-5. 8月5日：徒步中愉快的瞬间

1	2
3	4
5	

1. 8月6日：在路边与卖水果的小贩交谈
2. 8月6日：在路上与勤劳的护路工人们合影
3. 8月6日：前往山东德州途中与村民合影
4. 8月7日：在宁津新城受邀下一盘中国象棋
5. 8月7日：热情好客的山东人为勋爵一行人送上冷饮

8月10日：返京出席"美丽中国"手机摄影大赛开幕活动，贝茨勋爵第一次乘坐传说中的高铁

8月10日：出席"美丽中国"手机摄影大赛启动仪式

8月10日：接受《中国日报》采访

8月10日：在京与英国驻中国大使吴百纳交流

8月10日：勋爵夫妇与全国侨联副主席乔卫

8月12日：重返山东继续前行，从德州走出正在修路的地段，抵达济南界

8月13日:跨过黄河大桥

8月14日:中国红十字会副会长王汝鹏(左一)与贝茨勋爵一同行走济南

8月14日:山东省副省长王随莲(右三)亲切会见贝茨勋爵夫妇

8月16日:途经高而乡红十字幸福苑

8月16日:前往泰安途中,到访邢家村。村中700年历史的老井,仍然清水充盈

8月18日：行走在环泰山景观路上

8月17日：休整日，参观泰山太庙

8月18日：从泰安到宁阳，途中驻足于孔子像前。同行的人问勋爵"你是在与孔子对话吗？""不，我是在聆听。"

8月21日：在孔子诞生的地方阅读《论语》

8月21日：行至曲阜阙里

1. 8月24日：从滕州走到枣庄市中心薛城区，一路上是壮观的水杉大道、千亩梨园，以及大片的试验田
2. 8月26日：在美丽的枣庄市中心广场，庆祝走过800公里
3. 8月27日：朋友李少林、薛建君专程从北京来到枣庄与勋爵夫妇共走一程
4. 8月27日：从薛城到峄城，沿途是延绵不绝的万亩石榴园，举目皆是美好的乡村风光
5. 8月30日：在台儿庄大战纪念馆前

1	2
3	4
5	6

1. 8月30日：贝茨勋爵夫妇在台儿庄古城中"大运河"标识前
2. 8月30日：在中国大运河边欣赏古城美景
3. 8月30日：古城文化气息浓厚
4. 8月30日：中国的大部分景区都建有红十字救护站
5. 8月31日：途中遇到村民排演当地的民间艺术竹马戏
6. 8月31日：走过运河大桥，告别山东到江苏

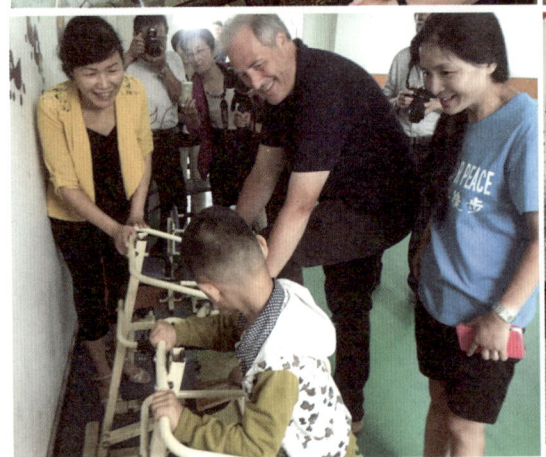

1-5. 9月1日：贝茨勋爵夫妇到访邳州红十字会"希望之家"

1. 9月3日：在宿迁。宿迁的城市发展口号是"我能、我行、我成功"
2. 9月3日：勋爵夫人雪琳作为华侨代表，受邀赴京出席阅兵观礼
3. 9月3日：在蔡集镇观看大阅兵直播
4. 9月4日：大雨中的41.9公里
5. 9月4日：抵达1000公里时的喜悦

9月5日：贝茨勋爵夫妇出席宿迁"国际生态四项精英赛"

9月5日：巧遇曾经横渡英吉利海峡的中国游泳健将张健

9月6日：在宿迁项王故里向大师学习中国书法

9月6日：参观宿迁儿童福利院

9月6日：在项王故里观赏以项羽故事为主题的歌舞表演

1. 9月7日：清晨与宿迁市委书记魏国强（右五）、市长王天琪（左四）一同种下两棵桂花树
2. 9月8日：徒步进入淮安境内
3. 9月9日：参观周恩来纪念馆
4. 9月13日：参观黄花塘新四军军部

9月10日：在和平镇，贝茨勋爵与中共淮安市委书记姚晓东一起徒步

9月13日：与盱眙县村民合影

9月13日：走过1200公里

9月13日：盱眙的黄昏。这是一个通过发展小龙虾产业走向繁荣的县城

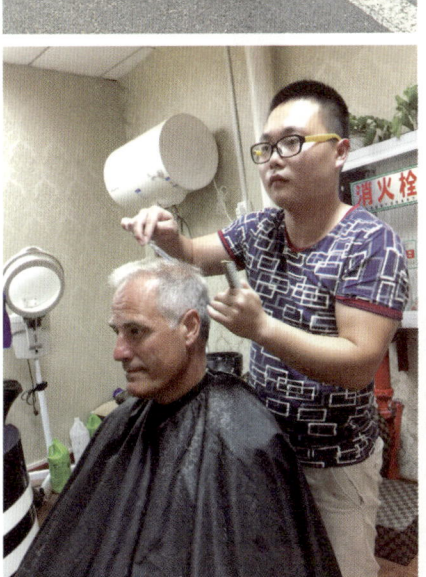

1. 9月14日：大步向南京走去，此程最重要的一站南京，就要到了
2. 9月14日：南京市红十字会的工作人员前来迎接
3. 9月15日：休整日，洗去征尘理理发
4. 9月15日：外出散步，走进一家民办教育中心和补习功课的孩子们交谈
5. 9月15日：刚刚走进南京，进入酒店时翻阅中国书籍

1. 9月17日：抵达南京长江大桥北，庆祝走过1300公里
2. 9月18日：走过南京长江大桥
3. 9月18日：中国红十字会副会长郝林娜和凤凰卫视执行董事王纪言专程来到南京加入到徒步中
4. 9月18日：参观拉贝与国际安全区纪念馆
5. 9月18日：千里征程完成大半的喜悦

9月19日：参观侵华日军南京大屠杀遇难同胞纪念馆

9月19日：30名中学生与贝茨勋爵夫妇一同参观了侵华日军南京大屠杀遇难同胞纪念馆。学生们参加了"为和平徒步"的"慈善学徒"活动，筹得善款3万多元

9月19日：江苏省副省长张雷亲切会见贝茨勋爵

9月19日：在古老的南京城墙上与浙江大学校友会的同学们度过愉快的一天

9月21日：国际和平日，贝茨勋爵在南京金陵中学演讲，题目为"文化在构建和平中的作用"

9月21日：贝茨勋爵与南京红十字会组成"为和平徒步队"，和金陵中学校足球队进行了一场快乐的友谊赛

9月23日：从南京溧水到常州溧阳

9月24日：勋爵夫妇在京拜访中国侨联主席林军

9月25日：做客凤凰卫视

9月26日：贝茨勋爵夫妇在京出席"为和平摇滚"慈善典礼时，受邀与万科集团创始人、董事会主席王石进行赛艇比赛

1. 9月31日：抵达浙江省，与前来欢迎的浙江省红十字会工作人员在一起

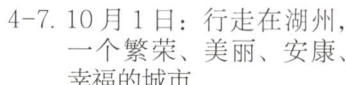

2. 10月1日：全天沿着太湖行走
3. 10月1日：贝茨勋爵在路边吃午餐

4-7. 10月1日：行走在湖州，一个繁荣、美丽、安康、幸福的城市

10月5日：1702.7公里，历时71天，"为和平徒步"胜利抵达终点浙江大学

10月5日：贝茨勋爵夫妇在浙江大学校门口与众人合影

10月5日："为和平徒步"结束仪式在浙江大学图书馆举行。中国红十字会副会长郝林娜，浙江省政协副主席、省侨联主席吴晶（第二排左六），浙江省政府副秘书长、省红十字会副会长李云林（第二排左五），省红十字会常务副会长王冬梅（第二排左四）以及浙江省外事侨务办公室、浙江大学的领导和同学们出席了徒步结束仪式

1-5. 10月5日：在"为和平徒步"结束仪式上捐赠善款。受赠方为：江苏省徐州市邳州红十字会"希望之家"、山东省德州市临邑县光荣院关爱抗战老兵项目、浙江省红十字会抗战老兵慰问项目、江苏省宿迁市儿童福利院、河北省沧州市红十字会青县流沙中学助学项目

10月5日：时任浙江大学党委副书记任少波（右三）和校长助理、浙大校友总会副会长张美凤（左二）及校友总会秘书长胡炜（右二）等与勋爵夫妇在庆祝徒步结束的仪式上合影

10月5日：任少波向勋爵夫人雪琳赠送当年就读浙江大学时的成绩单

10月10日：回到伦敦受到侨界欢迎。中国驻英国大使馆总领事费明星向贝茨勋爵夫妇祝贺徒步取得圆满成功

10月10日：伦敦，英国浙江联谊会举办活动，祝贺勋爵夫妇"徒步中国"活动圆满成功

2016年"为奥林匹克休战徒步"

1	2
3	4
5	

1. 徒步开始之前,贝茨勋爵夫妇拜访里约奥组委,在残奥会的标志前留影
2. 4月23日:勋爵庆贺当天徒步里程数超过48.30公里
3. 结束了当天的徒步,贝茨勋爵的衣服已被汗水浸湿
4. 6月3日:庆祝走过1500公里里程碑
5. 在巴西的路上,勋爵一直在国道上行走

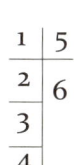

1. 7月27日：抵达里约奥运场馆，正好是徒步走过3000公里里程碑
2. 7月29日：徒步结束之日，贝茨勋爵夫妇受到国际奥委会主席托马斯·巴赫的接见
3. 7月29日：2016年"为奥林匹克休战徒步"结束仪式
4. 7月29日：贝茨勋爵夫妇向联合国儿童基金会捐赠徒步筹得的善款
5. 7月29日：向基督山山顶进发
6. 7月29日：抵达基督山山顶，宣告2016年徒步活动圆满完成

国际奥委会主席巴赫邀请贝茨勋爵夫人雪琳在 2016 年 8 月 4 日担任里约奥运火炬手

贝茨勋爵夫妇受到国际奥委会主席巴赫的邀请观看里约奥运会开幕式

徒步结束回到伦敦,贝茨勋爵为夫人雪琳的家乡杭州送上 G20 寄语

WALK FOR PEACE

徒步中国
爱与和平的信仰征途

［英］麦克·贝茨勋爵　著
（The Rt. Hon. Lord Michael Bates）

李雪琳·贝茨勋爵夫人 等　译
（Lady Xuelin Li Bates）

新世界出版社
NEW WORLD PRESS

First Edition 2016

By The Rt. Hon. Lord Michael Bates
Translated by Lady Xuelin Li Bates, et al.
Edited by Li Shasha
Book Design by He Yuting
Copyright by New World Press, Beijing, China
All rights reserved. No part of this book may be reproduced in any form or by any means without permission in writing from the publisher.

ISBN 978-7-5104-6029-6

Published by
NEW WORLD PRESS
24 Baiwanzhuang Street, Beijing 100037, China

Distributed by
NEW WORLD PRESS
24 Baiwanzhuang Street, Beijing 100037, China
Tel: 86-10-68995968
Fax: 86-10-68998705
Website: www.nwp.com.cn
E-mail: nwpcd@sina.com

Printed in the People's Republic of China

致中国读者

亲爱的中国旅伴：

"生命是一段旅程而不是一个目的地。"

去年我有幸在中国进行了一段从北京到杭州的难忘旅程，这是有关这段旅程的故事。

在71天的徒步行走中，

我遇到了一些真正令人惊奇的地方，

但最令人赞叹的是我沿途遇到的人们。

我邀请你加入我们的这段不可思议的旅程，一起感受真正的中国。

致以最好的祝愿！

麦 克

> Dear Chinese Fellow Traveller,
>
> 'Life is a journey, not just a destination'. This is the story of a remarkable journey I was privileged to undertake in China last year from Beijing to Hangzhou. During the seventy one days of walking I encountered some truly amazing places, but the most amazing were the people I met along the way.
>
> I invite you to join me on this incredible journey and experience the real China.
>
> With all good wishes
>
> Michael

最近英国议会上院议员贝茨勋爵在中国开展了为期两个多月的慈善徒步行走，他顶着烈日步行约1700公里，将募捐来的善款投入中国慈善事业，并呼吁人们珍爱和平。正是得益于无数中英友好人士的辛勤付出，中英关系才能跨越重洋、发扬光大。

——摘自习近平主席在英国议会的演讲
2015年10月

目 录

i　序
v　前　言　千里之行，始于足下

为和平徒步　中文篇
1
3　　中英准备就绪
5　　7月27日　　第1天　　启程
7　　7月28日　　第2天　　在京郊
9　　7月30日　　第4天　　"天下第一城"
11　　7月31日　　第5天　　冬奥会与个人佳绩
13　　8月1日　　　第6天　　来自陌生人的温暖
15　　8月2日　　　第7天　　一起走
17　　8月3日　　　第8天　　医院和媒体
20　　8月4日　　　第9天　　以人为上
22　　8月6日　　　第11天　向劳动人民致敬
25　　8月8日　　　第13天　优秀的管理者
29　　8月9日　　　第14天　山东公路
31　　8月10日　　第15天　"美丽中国"手机摄影大赛
33　　8月11日　　第16天　在北京的文化交流
35　　8月12日　　第17天　重返山东公路
37　　8月13日　　第18天　紧急事件中的红十字会
39　　8月15日　　第20天　与我同行走过济南
41　　8月16日　　第21天　会有"这样的日子"
44　　8月19日　　第24天　宁阳县的友谊盛宴

I

46	8月20日	第25天	追寻孔子的足迹
48	8月21日	第26天	行至曲阜
51	8月23日	第28天	邹城和奥运理念
53	8月24日	第29天	雷德格雷夫与前赛艇运动员
55	8月26日	第31天	孟子和理雅各
57	8月27日	第32天	纯真年代
59	8月29日	第34天	台儿庄战役
61	8月30日	第35天	前往台儿庄
63	8月31日	第36天	你好，江苏
65	9月1日	第37天	邳州的"希望之家"
68	9月2日	第38天	体育与和平
71	9月3日	第39天	9·3大阅兵
73	9月4日	第40天	走过1000公里
75	9月5日	第41天	国际生态四项精英赛
77	9月6日	第42天	笃信人性本善
79	9月7日	第43天	令人感慨的"宿迁速度"
81	9月9日	第45天	小小淮安，大大世界
83	9月10日	第46天	市委书记在和平村
85	9月11日	第47天	准备在南京金陵中学的演讲稿
88	9月12日	第48天	"为和平徒步"的十万个为什么
91	9月13日	第49天	时尚盱眙
93	9月14日	第50天	中石化、1200公里和简·奥斯汀
95	9月16日	第52天	走进南京
97	9月17日	第53天	南京长江大桥
99	9月19日	第55天	穿过黑暗，走向光明
102	9月20日	第56天	捐款大突破

104	9月21日	第57天	我的"南京宣言"
108	9月23日	第59天	中国少年之声
110	9月24日	第60天	北京活动日
112	9月25日	第61天	交流的重要性
114	9月26日	第62天	与王石赛艇
117	9月29日	第65天	中国梦与英国梦
120	9月30日	第66天	越来越强大而有深度的中国
122	10月1日	第67天	小小世界之湖州篇
124	10月3日	第69天	关于"人身安全"
127	10月4日	第70天	雪琳母亲的问题——徒步的意义
130	10月5日	第71天	跨越终点线
134	10月9日		回家、回顾

为和平徒步 英文篇

137			
139	Preparations		Red Cross Society of China & HM Government of the UK
143	July 27	Day 1	Departure
147	July 28	Day 2	In the Suburbs of Beijing
150	July 29	Day 3	Misunderstandings
153	July 30	Day 4	Tourist (Human) Potential
156	July 31	Day 5	Winter Olympics & Personal Best
159	August 1	Day 6	The Kindness of Strangers
162	August 2	Day 7	Travelling Together
165	August 3	Day 8	Hospitals & the Press
168	August 4	Day 9	Human First
170	August 5	Day 10	Milestones
173	August 6	Day 11	'Up the Workers'
176	August 7	Day 12	Healthy Living

Page	Date	Day	Title
178	August 8	Day 13	The Good Manager
183	August 9	Day 14	Shandong Highway
186	August 10	Day 15	Back in Beijing & Yao Chen
189	August 11	Day 16	Cultural Exchanges in Beijing
191	August 12	Day 17	Back on the Road in Shandong
194	August 13	Day 18	Thoughts with Tianjin
196	August 14	Day 19	Rest Day in Jinan City
199	August 15	Day 20	Across Jinan and Fellow Walkers
202	August 16	Day 21	There Will Be Days Like This
205	August 17	Day 22	Charity Appeal
208	August 18	Day 23	Through Tai'an
210	August 19	Day 24	Feast of Friendship in Ningyang County
212	August 20	Day 25	In the Footsteps of Confucius—Part I
215	August 21	Day 26	Walk to Qufu
218	August 22	Day 27	Confucius—Part II
220	August 23	Day 28	Zoucheng and Mo Farah
223	August 24	Day 29	Zaozhuang
225	August 25	Day 30	Reflections on 500 Miles (800 km)
228	August 26	Day 31	Mencius and Legge
231	August 27	Day 32	Age of Innocence
234	August 28	Day 33	Somewhere in Zaozhuang?
236	August 29	Day 34	The Battle of Tai'erzhuang
238	August 30	Day 35	The Road to Tai'erzhuang
241	August 31	Day 36	Jiangsu Province
244	September 1	Day 37	Hope House—Pizhou
247	September 2	Day 38	Peace & Sport
249	September 3	Day 39	The Big Parade
252	September 4	Day 40	1,000 km in Suqian

255	September 5	Day 41	International Eco-Quadrathlon Classic
258	September 6	Day 42	Whatever You Do for the Least …
261	September 7	Day 43	Lightning Speed in Suqian
263	September 8	Day 44	Red Nails
265	September 9	Day 45	It's a Small World in Huai'an
267	September 10	Day 46	Secretary of the Party Committee in 'Peacetown'
270	September 11	Day 47	Address to Students in Jinling Middle School
273	September 12	Day 48	*Wei Shen Mo*—Walk for Peace
277	September 13	Day 49	'In Vogue' Xuyi
280	September 14	Day 50	Sinopec, 1,200 km and Jane Austen
282	September 15	Day 51	Hope, Haircuts and Singing Horses
285	September 16	Day 52	Nanjing in Sight
287	September 17	Day 53	'Bridge Over the River Yangtze'
290	September 18	Day 54	Crossing a Bridge of History
293	September 19	Day 55	Walking Through the Darkness into the Light
297	September 20	Day 56	Donations Breakthrough
300	September 21	Day 57	Nanjing Declaration
305	September 22	Day 58	Thoughts on Professor Bates
308	September 23	Day 59	The Voice of Youth
311	September 24	Day 60	Back to Beijing
314	September 25	Day 61	The Importance of Communication
316	September 26	Day 62	Rock the Boat
320	September 27	Day 63	Moon Festival
322	September 28	Day 64	Route Perspectives and Teapots in Yixing
324	September 29	Day 65	A Tale of Two Dreams
328	September 30	Day 66	China Growing Taller and Getting Deeper
330	October 1	Day 67	It's a Small, Small World in Zhejiang
332	October 2	Day 68	It's not the Critic that Counts + PS & PPS

336	October 3	Day 69	Personal Safety?
340	October 4	Day 70	Mrs. Wu's Question Goes to the Heart of the Matter
344	October 5	Day 71	Crossing the Finishing Line
349	Homecoming Reflection		

353　附录一　麦克·贝茨勋爵 2011—2016 年徒步回顾

367　附录二　2015 年"为和平徒步"捐款名单（部分）

373　后　记

379　Conclusion

序

衷心祝贺《徒步中国——爱与和平的信仰征途》一书，即麦克·贝茨勋爵"为和平徒步"日记出版。

这是一本不同寻常的日记。

一根竹杖一个布包，新中国成立以来第一位英国终身贵族和国务大臣，一位现任部长级官员以徒步方式行走千里，深入中国城镇乡村，用亲身经历书写了关于中国的故事。

71天，71篇文字，写就于风尘仆仆的征途，完成在每天几十公里疲劳困乏的徒步之后。或风趣幽默，或思考深沉的每一篇，都凝聚了作者的顽强毅力和澎湃于心中的热烈情感。

2015年7月至10月，为纪念世界反法西斯战争胜利70周年和第一届中英文化交流年，英国内政部国务大臣麦克·贝茨勋爵来到中国，开展了北京—南京—杭州"为和平徒步"的主题活动，中国红十字会作为"为和平徒步"在华实施的协助单位，为贝茨勋爵在体能允许的情况下完成徒步里程提供技术支持和后勤保障，而我作为这个项目的负责人，则有幸全程随同勋爵到终点，成为这个神奇之旅的参与者和见证者。

贝茨勋爵的"为和平徒步"始于2012年伦敦奥运会前，从希腊古奥林匹亚行至奥运会举办地伦敦，历时10个月，途经14个国家，行程4693公里，沿途宣传奥林匹克休战。贝茨勋爵不是运动员，甚至都不能说是徒步爱好者，在这之前他的日徒步最高纪录不超过16公里。作为一个长期忙碌于议会大厦办公桌前，五十多岁已经做了爷爷且体重超标的人，他以挑战个人体能极限的方式追求自己的理想、为呼吁世界和平奔走的壮举感动众人。联合国秘书长潘基文、时任国际奥委会主席雅克·罗格以及罗马教皇本笃十六世在与之会见时都对他表示由衷的赞佩。之后，贝茨勋爵坚持利用国会每年的假期"为和平徒步"，并沿途开展慈善募捐以帮助战争受害者，5年累计行走10000多公里。选择来中国徒步与他的妻子李雪琳女士有关，雪琳女士是浙江杭州人，毕业于浙江大学建筑系，是一位成功的建筑师和企业家。虽旅居英国27年，但爱国是她一生的情怀，2015年"为和平徒步"，勋爵接受了夫人的建议来到中国。

"北京—南京—杭州，为和平徒步"2015年7月27日自北京启程，途经河北、山东、江苏、安徽、浙江5省，历时71天，行程1702.7公里，于10月5日胜利到达终点！徒步期间正值中国暑季，贝茨勋爵经历了酷热高温、蚊虫叮咬、水土不服、满脚水疱以及部分地区交通流量巨大的道路环境的考验，平均每个徒步日行走40多公里。为了保护书包里那两个对勋爵极为重要的记录徒步里程的手机不因汗水浸湿而"罢工"，他不得不用塑料袋将手机包上。从清晨出发时的精神饱满，到日暮时分的步履蹒跚，他几次中暑虚脱，仍始终坚韧不拔一步步向前，让我们深深感到，对勋爵来说，"为和平徒步"靠的不仅仅是体能，更是执着于伟大目标的坚定信念和百折不回的顽强毅力，是梦想的力量鼓舞他向前，正如他在日记中所说："我不是在走，我是在用双腿追逐心中的目标。"

阅读勋爵的日记，展现在读者面前的是用英国人特有的幽默感描绘出的一个充满喜悦的旅程，而徒步所经历的艰难却鲜有提及。跨越黄河、淮河、长江，行走在大运河、洪泽湖、太湖边，从辽阔的华北大平原到秀美的江南水乡，热闹的集市、宁静的村庄、待收的果实、芬芳的田野、初升的朝阳和远山的落日，1700公里徒步路在勋爵面前展开一幅绚丽的画卷！大自然的壮美，每一天不同的景色，让勋爵深深为美丽中国赞叹，他在日记中热情洋溢地引用简·奥斯汀华丽的语言描述那种美好的感觉。

对贝茨勋爵来说，"为和平徒步"是一场中国文化的巡礼，他的日记中许多篇幅谈到中英历史和文化异同的绝妙之处。流连在孔子、孟子、墨子故里，经过五岳之首泰山，买一本英文版的《论语》，"在圣贤诞生的地方思考如何把他们的思想运用到实际中去"，热爱中国文化的勋爵热切地探究中国文化之源。

"为和平徒步"，带领勋爵走进中国人民抗日战争的峥嵘岁月。在曾经烽烟滚滚的抗日战争主战场台儿庄，他在纪念馆认真抄写下令其感悟的解说词；在曾经的新四军总部黄花塘，在侵华日军南京大屠杀遇难同胞纪念馆，在保护完好的约翰·拉贝故居，他仔细倾听讲解介绍……饱受战争摧残、奋起抗争、英雄辈出的民族，中国人民在"二战"期间付出的巨大牺牲以及为"二战"胜利做出的巨大贡献令勋爵动容、赞叹。

北京—南京—杭州，贝茨勋爵走过大江南北，深入中国腹地，一路行走一路播撒和平理念和中英友好，也一路追寻探访一个真实的中国，她的昨天与未来，她苦难辉煌的经历，以及她的人民和深沉的情感。行走中遇到过辛勤劳作的养路人，忙碌的枣园主人和牧羊的老者，朝气蓬勃的青年学生，随行的红十字志愿者和在红十字"希望之家"默默奉献的人们，还有意气风发带领当地群众改革开放求发展的基层官员……他心怀尊敬地记下了他们的面容和名字，把他们写入日记中。中国人民的勤劳朴实、真诚善良，多姿多彩的民俗风情和热气腾腾的生活，令人惊讶的"宿迁速度"，人们对过去 30 年取得的伟大成就的自豪和对更加美好未来的"中国梦"的憧憬，给勋爵留下了深刻的印象。在他眼中，这是中国奇迹背后的故事，劳动者们和各行各业敬业的群体是国家的脊梁，正在以一种西方人难以理解的拼搏精神，创造出让亿万人摆脱贫穷的奇迹。他在每天十分疲劳的情况下坚持撰写日记，并由其夫人和志愿者团队连夜翻译成中文，及时传递徒步途中的见闻和感想，客观地向世界展示一个他亲眼所见的真实的中国。

以追求世界和平、维护人类尊严为崇高使命的中国红十字会为贝茨勋爵提供了最真诚的帮助。一批又一批红十字志愿者，以接力的方式随行、护送勋爵到终点。他们中有工人、农民、教师、学生、家庭主妇、救援队员，也有外科医生和职业画家，其中最大的 60 多岁，最小的只有 17 岁。徒步路上他们是向导，是医护人员，是勋爵了解当地情况的顾问。休息的时候，勋爵喜欢与大家促膝谈心，而他们也在与勋爵共走一程的经历中获得鼓舞和激励。勋爵在日记中充满感情地写下："感谢为徒步活动辛勤付出的每一位红十字会工作人员和志愿者，你们饱满的激情以及对工作的热忱，每天激励着我按时启程并坚持完成目标。""此次徒步活动，正是因为有了你们，我才能坚持到底，并最终成功，这是我们团队的胜利。"

"因为了解，我更爱中国！"是贝茨勋爵在徒步结束启程返英时留给我们的临别赠言。返回英国后他多次发表关于中国的文章，在英国国会和许多场合介绍在中国的经历，"你不能站在中国之外看中国、评论中国，而必须亲身体验才能真正了解她。"正如他在日记中所写："这段美好的经历会永远留在我心中，而我也会继续向世界讲述中国故事：一个真实的中国、美丽的中国。"习近平主席 2015 年 10 月访问英国时在英国议会大厦的演讲中，专门讲到了勋爵的故事，赞扬勋爵是中英友好的使者。我们希望勋爵能多来中国看看，并把不断更新版的中国故事带到世界。

感谢新世界出版社，特别要感谢张海鸥总编辑的努力，在贝茨勋爵徒步中国一周年之际将勋爵的徒步日记集结出版。当本书付梓之际，传来贝茨勋爵夫妇再次完成2016年里约奥运会"为奥林匹克休战徒步"壮举的消息！本次徒步2016年4月初自阿根廷首都布宜诺斯艾利斯启程，在没有任何当地支持的情况下，在偏僻寂寞的南美荒原上、丛林中、群山里，顽强跋涉115天，麦克·贝茨勋爵以超人毅力，在其夫人雪琳的支持下，胜利抵达终点巴西里约基督山山顶，全程3025公里。距徒步中国仅仅不到一年，他们就创造了新的纪录！他们追求世界和平的精神以及在此过程中表现的雄心、毅力和忘我的坚持，凝聚成一种鼓舞人心的力量，越来越多的追随者加入到声援贝茨勋爵的行列中，加入到呼吁休战呼吁世界和平的行列中。

"为和平徒步"是一个伟大的壮举，它让我们珍惜得来不易的和平环境，也提醒我们和平理想的最终实现仍然路途遥远。放眼望去，战争和局部冲突、恐怖主义的威胁、有史以来最大的难民潮正在冲击欧洲……这一切都告诉我们，真正的和平时代，还远远没有到来。保护人的生命，维护人的尊严，不让战争的悲剧重演，要靠一代又一代人对和平理念的不懈追求，要靠国家和民族之间的理解和尊重。我们向身体力行传播和平理念的贝茨勋爵及全程支持勋爵完成2016年里约奥运年"为奥林匹克休战徒步"壮举而荣耀当选里约奥运会火炬手的雪琳·贝茨勋爵夫人致以崇高敬意！祝贺麦克·贝茨勋爵以连续五年挑战身体极限，徒步23个国家、累计行走12000公里"为奥林匹克休战徒步""为和平徒步"，为慈善事业筹集善款，身体力行呼吁世界和平的壮举，以及多年担任英国政府高级官员的政治影响力，荣任国际奥委会休战委员会成员。

北京—南京—杭州"为和平徒步"之旅虽然结束了，但人类和平的光辉理念将永存人心，其光芒必将照耀整个世界。

张明

原中国红十字会总会联络部部长

2016年10月10日

前言

千里之行，始于足下

2015年7月27日星期一，我将从北京天坛公园开启中国徒步之旅。此次徒步，将用时两个多月时间，从北京经南京到达终点杭州，行程1700公里，从北到南穿行半个中国。

为什么我要徒步中国？

首先，2015年是首届中英文化交流年。中英两国之间将通过举办许多丰富多彩的活动向两国民众展示彼此的优秀文化。我的夫人是中国人，我们对彼此耳濡目染的文化相互尊重并很欣赏。文化无国界，它对于人类起到的互联作用非他物所能比拟：音乐、电影、诗歌、绘画、舞蹈、文学、教育、美食、宗教、语言、传统习俗、对美的欣赏、对大自然的好奇和对运动的热爱，是人类最简单的共同要素，却有着无可衡量的价值。我们越看重彼此的共同之处，我们的关系就越亲密。事实上，"文化"一词的拉丁语和法语词根就是"抚育"与"成长"之意。

其次，2015年正值第二次世界大战胜利70周年。在"二战"中，英国与中国同仇敌忾，1941年至战争结束期间建立了同盟关系。"二战"时期中国战场的战火爆发于1937年，英国也于两年后投身于欧洲战场。第二次世界大战结束后，中国、美国、英国、法国和当时的苏联以创始国的身份携手建立了联合国，并成为联合国安全理事会的常任理事国。中国在反法西斯战争中付出了巨大代价，2000多万人因战争和饥荒失去了生命。我们需要牢记昔日反法西斯同盟精神，并时刻敲响警钟，继续通力合作，在国际社会共同的努力下维护这来之不易的和平，杜绝战争再次发生。

再次，2015年7月27日是2012年伦敦奥运会开幕式三周年纪念日。伦敦从北京接过了奥运会主办城市的接力棒。两国奥运会的独特之处在于，均从本国博大精深的历史文化中汲取灵感，进一步丰富和发展了奥林匹克精神。超越时空传承至今的"奥林匹克休战"理念，远远超越了传统意义上的体育比赛，它激发我迈出人生为这崇高目标长途行走的第一步。2012年，我从希腊的奥林匹亚启程，单人徒步4693.10公里、历时10个月走回伦敦。2013年，为了帮助战乱中的叙利亚儿童，我为"拯救儿童基金会"募捐而行走，从伦敦出发，徒步834.90公里，抵达英国的德里。2014年夏天，为纪念"一战"爆发100周年，我为德国儿童慈善机构"国际和平村"筹集善款，从伦敦走到柏林，徒步1697.50公里。

最后，我想通过徒步方式来支持红十字会的人道事业。红十字会的宗旨是为战争和武装暴力的受害者提供人道保护和援助。我对战争带来的影响深恶痛绝；恐怖主义和暴力行为通过24小时新闻和社交媒体源源不断地侵入我们的生活，并且以娱乐的方式在电影和电脑游戏中呈现。过去的战争对峙大多发生于人烟稀少的地区，而如今，一些城市沦为主战场，多少手无缚鸡之力的妇女儿童、老弱病残被推上战乱的风口浪尖，无辜地卷入其中。我这次中国徒步之行的重要一站是南京，一座曾经见证了1937年人类历史浩劫的城市；在那场臭名昭著的惨案中，30万中国无辜百姓惨遭屠杀。提到战争，英国作家威尔斯曾简明扼要地指出："如果人类不终结战争，那么必被战争所终结。"纵观20世纪历史不难发现，战争使人性几近毁灭。

综上原因，我决定再次踏上征途。感谢我的夫人一如既往地支持我，为我计划徒步行程并支付所有费用。我已经是54岁做爷爷的人了，体重超标且并不健硕，每天在35摄氏度至40摄氏度高温的户外行走30多公里，对我来说将是极大的挑战。但倘若你问我为什么还要这么做，那是因为我内心坚定的信念足以克服所有的障碍，我希望徒步之旅所留下的每个脚印都能够成为英中文化交流的友好见证；我希望募集善款，为那些在这个充满冲突与苦难的世界中寻找和平的人带来帮助与支持；我希望能证明我们并非无能为力而是可以非常强大；我希望展示理想主义和梦想并不只是年轻人的专利；我希望向世人宣告我们不该桎梏自己于内心的阴影或是他人的嘲讽之中。

在人生这场伟大的游戏中，我们不应是旁观者，我们是竞技者，我们要在梦想的赛场上做最棒的自己。

中文篇

为和平徒步

WALK
FOR
PEACE

中英准备就绪

在为徒步中国做准备的时候，我还不确定这一活动能否顺利进行。首先是英国大选的不确定性。2015年5月7日的选举结果无疑将决定我此次徒步行走的时长。如果我所在的保守党赢得选举，我便要拿出时间协助上议院立法工作；卡梅伦首相还可能会留任我为政府大臣。当然，如果我们输给工党的话，也罢，那就是上天给我机会在未来五年去实现我小时候想走遍世界的梦想。然而最后结果是对方输掉了竞选，我也很荣幸地被卡梅伦首相再次任命为内政部国务大臣。

英国的国会体制决定了议员们每年都会有一个很长的暑期休假，一般是两个半月。这样做是为了让下议院的议员们能有时间去倾听、了解所属选区选民们的意见和建议。由于上议院的议员是由首相提名、女王任命产生，而不是被选民选举出来的，所以对我们这些上议院议员来说，暑期就变成了一个很长的假期。身负重任的议员们，可以不需要把时间花在每天的议会工作和辩论投票上，这段时间是他们专注于自己其他工作的好时机。而我是全职从政，没有其他副业，所以我从2009年开始，就利用这段时间去追求我的理想——"为和平徒步"，并在途中为需要帮助的人做慈善筹款。因此大选一尘埃落定，我就开始着手寻求另一段徒步的许可。而徒步的地点，我定在了中国。

经过两个月的努力，我终于得到负责内政部的内阁大臣（我的直属上级）、英国外交部当然还有卡梅伦首相的许可。他们不但批准了我的徒步，还同意安排其他人暂时代替我的相关工作。对于他们的支持，我非常感谢。而2015年是第一届中英文化交流年，且中国的习近平主席将于这年10月访问英国，这也为我到中国徒步获得批准起到巨大的推动作用。

"为和平徒步"，雪琳和我是彼此的搭档。我负责拿到英方的批准，她则去争取中方的许可。令我们高兴的是，中国驻英大使馆和中国外交部对我徒步中国的想法非常支持，为了使我顺利达成目标，它们还联系到拥有200多万志愿者的中国红十字会全程为我提供协助。起源于战场救护的红十字运动已经有150多年历史，她的宗旨是拯救人的生命、维护人的尊严，推动建设一个和平与和谐的世界。这与我"为和平徒步"的理念十分契合，能与中国红十字会合作我感到非常高兴。雪琳与红十字会的沟通非常顺利，当我们从英国启程之际，我们得到的已经不止是中方的许可，而是一份详细周密的计划书，包括完美的路线设计、每天的里程安排、餐饮住宿等后勤保障，还包括让我非常感兴趣的一些参观项目。而专门写给我的长达三页纸的在华徒步指南，则就天气和道路交通情况、途经地民俗习惯以及可能遇到的挑战等都做了详尽的说明。看来我可以没有后顾之忧地大步走了。这让我感到，有了这个好的计划，我已经成功一半了。

最后一项工作，就是我们需要建立一个后方团队承担我每天撰写博客的翻译工作和社交媒体维护工作。中英相隔遥远，受到时差的影响，我们面临的交流和技术上的挑战比以往任何一次徒步都多，我希望有更多人参与，以使每个志愿者不要因为工作量太大而耽误学业。出乎意料的是，招聘消息一发出去，就收到了许多杰出青年的响应。被选拔出来的志愿者是（按姓氏拼音首字母排列）：黄樆、轷则喁、刘家彤、李泳萱、马理唯奇、马婉青、肖梦、肖晓。在我和雪琳就要出发去中国的前一天，我们邀请整个团队来到英国国会一起交流，喝下午茶，以表示我们对他们的感谢。就这样，我们成功地拿到了伦敦和北京方面的许可。双方各项准备工作也已就位，徒步指日可待。

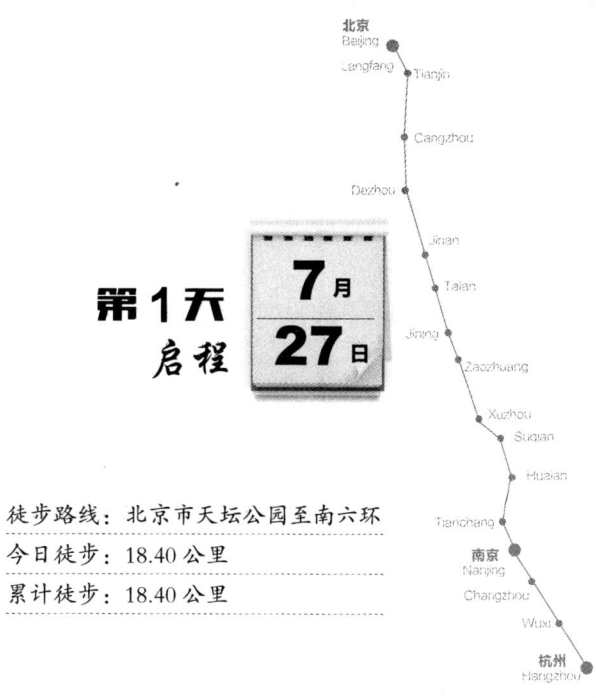

第1天
启程

7月27日

徒步路线：北京市天坛公园至南六环
今日徒步：18.40公里
累计徒步：18.40公里

  千里征程，今天迈出了第一步。

  中国红十字会在位于北京城南的天坛公园为我举行了起步仪式。天坛被认为是中国首都北京的象征，这个美丽庄严的古老建筑群已有800年历史，园内有几百年树龄的苍松翠柏，中央是中国古代皇帝祭天的圣坛。1865年英法联军发起第二次鸦片战争之后曾将此处作为营地，我始终无法理解他们为什么要驻扎在这么一个神圣的地方。试想如果当初是中国两次入侵英国，并把圣保罗大教堂当作军事基地，英国人也会有一样强烈的感受吧。

  仪式下午2点钟开始，大约有150多人顶着酷暑前来为我壮行。大家非常热情，我收获了大束的鲜花、"千里之行，始于足下"的书法作品，还有两个铜铃。一位女士把两个铜铃挂在我的书包上寓意保佑我一路平安。红十字会副会长郝林娜发表了精彩演讲，国务院侨务办公室裘援平主任宣布"为和平徒步"开始。启程之前我被告知七、八月份是北京最热的季节，但身临其境，我还是发现炎热的程度远远超出我的想象。滚滚热浪袭来，我觉得自己几乎有点站不稳，开始担心即将要走的20公里。幸好为了保证首日徒步顺利，红十字会特意安排了两位来自中国徒步网的徒步健将陪我走上一段，为此他们还事先勘察了路线。见到他们，我顿时感觉信心增加了许多。

　　简短仪式后正式起步，裴援平主任陪我走到南护城河，而郝林娜副会长则和我一起走到了南五环，几乎有5公里。郝林娜副会长曾在英国卡迪夫大学进修，讲得一口地道的英语。我们天南海北地聊了许多，尤其讨论了社会流动、财富和"富二代"越来越多的现象。我们俩一个来自保守党，一个来自共产党，但在这几个普遍关注的社会问题上有着一致的观点。

　　下午6点的时候我已经浑身湿透了，并不时觉得头晕目眩，但我仍被今天收到的祝福鼓舞着，庆幸千里之行有了一个好的开始。

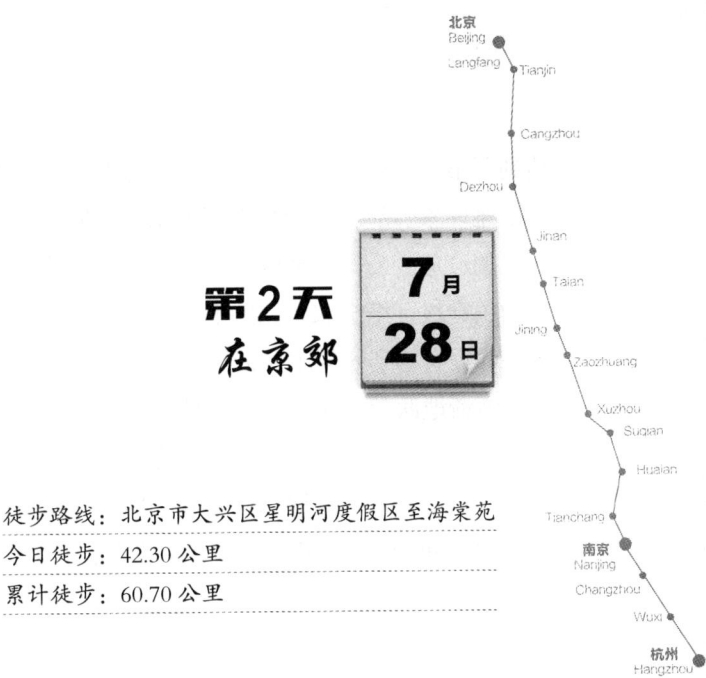

第2天 在京郊　7月28日

徒步路线：北京市大兴区星明河度假区至海棠苑

今日徒步：42.30公里

累计徒步：60.70公里

　　第一天徒步由于大量出汗造成脱水，我的双腿出现了痉挛的症状。今天这种痉挛感更加严重。今天的既定里程是30公里，因昨天只走了半天，我希望今天可以超额完成任务。我服用了一些布洛芬试图缓解疼痛的感觉，启程出发。

　　此刻，手机里的定位依旧显示在北京城郊，离我们计划中的河北省边界还有很远的距离。坦白说，在40摄氏度的湿热天气下沿着滚烫的公路行走真是一件苦差事。当地人把这样的天气称作桑拿天，想象一下在桑拿房里连续在跑步机上跑上10个钟头就可以体会我的感受了。

　　北京近郊与我所去过的其他大城市的郊区非常相像，一眼望去，贫富差距不像市区之间那么显著。一路见到许多崭新的公寓住宅区。据了解，一套两室的公寓的售价折算后大约为10万英镑，这和许多英国城市诸如利兹、伯明翰、曼彻斯特和纽卡斯尔郊区相同配置公寓的房价相当。但不同的是，中国人均GDP约为7500美元（2014年数据），而英国的人均GDP约为45000美元。我想说的是，中国有很多地方的富裕程度已经和英国差不多了，达到了第一世界水平，但还有大部分地区仍然处在第二、第三世界水平。尽管上述现象容易出现社会内部不稳定，但我眼前所看到的景象却没有任何不稳定的迹象。公寓住宅区门口的小贩在货摊上叫卖各式食物，衣着入时的年轻白领穿梭于满载农贸品的三轮车以及光着膀子的农民之间，对于眼前的景象，我没有感到任何不和谐。

  渐渐地两旁鳞次栉比的高楼变成了翠绿的林荫大道和乡村景色，匆匆的行人变成了悠闲的绵羊，空气里弥漫着莲花的芳香。河岸旁的人们或是惬意地看护羊群或是怡然地垂钓，好一幅宁静祥和的画面。我陶醉在这和谐的美景之中，同时不禁自问道："这就是我心心念念想见到的那个真实的中国吧？"

第4天
"天下第一城"

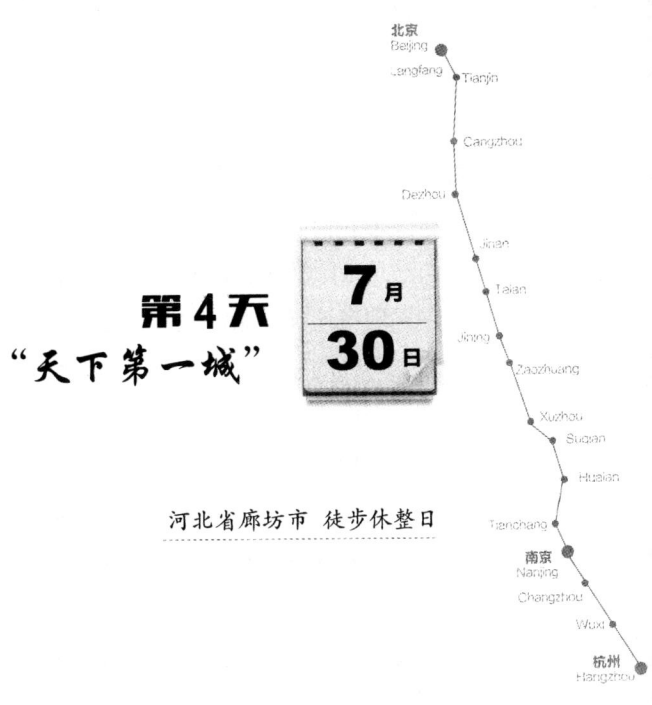

7月30日

河北省廊坊市 徒步休整日

　　今天是我们的第一个休息日，廊坊市红十字会的志愿者带我们参观"天下第一城"。当我被告知这是一组按照明清时期北京城1:1比例新落成的建筑群时，立刻幻想自己走进了超大号的乐高游乐园。（乐高游乐园是我的最爱！）到了之后，眼前的景致让我大吃一惊。这完全是一座再现当年情景的古城，宫殿楼阁，水榭花园，建筑工艺精细，让人印象深刻。当然用的也不是塑料玩具砖块，真是太神奇了！

　　导游丽丽为我们介绍了第一城的历史和规划。建造"天下第一城"是为了推动廊坊地区的旅游业，除了服务于河北地区的游客，还吸引北京人到这里度周末。城墙内有可以容纳5000人的五星级酒店，供游客居住，举办各种会议。酒店采用传统的建筑材料和工艺，而且仅用10个月就拔地而起。而在英国，光是拿到规划许可就至少要两年。当然，这并不是说基础设施建设不是英国人的长项，要是真不好，外国投资者也不会愿意去英国发展。这其实是土地所有权和使用权限的问题。在中国，土地归国家所有，并由国家授予使用许可。一旦国家决定要在哪里做什么的话，获批的过程是很快的。

而在英国，整个过程可能涉及上百个私人机构，你可能要硬着头皮和它们一一打交道；它们都有产权，先解决了这个问题你才能拿到许可。我想，在未来，一旦中国私企发展起来，政府决定建设大型基础设施的能力就会变弱，所以中国现在这样抓紧时机赶快建设实在是明智之举。

能工巧匠的精湛手艺让人赞叹，但大自然总是更胜一筹。雪琳和我来到了湖边，湖面上碧叶接天，荷花盛开，香气袭人。最后一站是参观城中的佛教寺庙，我相信宗教是生命中重要的一部分，就像爱情、友情和有意义的工作一样。庙宇角落处的两棵祈福树挂满了人们留下的心愿卡，其中有一条好像包含了所有人的愿望："保佑全家平安健康，保佑工作顺利，婚姻幸福，孩子懂事、努力学习。"

在大多数大教堂、清真寺、犹太教堂或者其他宗教场所，常常能看到人们留下相似的心愿。这使我想起自己担任保守党副主席时做的一些工作。那时我们没有采取旧有的民意测试方法，把人们按照学历、财富或家庭背景分成不同的社会群体，而是让人们自己选择相应的描述来自我定位。结果显示大多数人都将自己描述为"我是一个认真工作的普通人，正在努力为自己和家人创造更好的生活"。我想如果在中国问相同的问题，大多数人也会这样回答。这是大家共同的心愿，共同的梦想，更是所有政治领导人共同的责任。每个国家的领导人都应该尽全力帮助民众实现这些愿望。

第5天 冬奥会与个人佳绩

7月31日

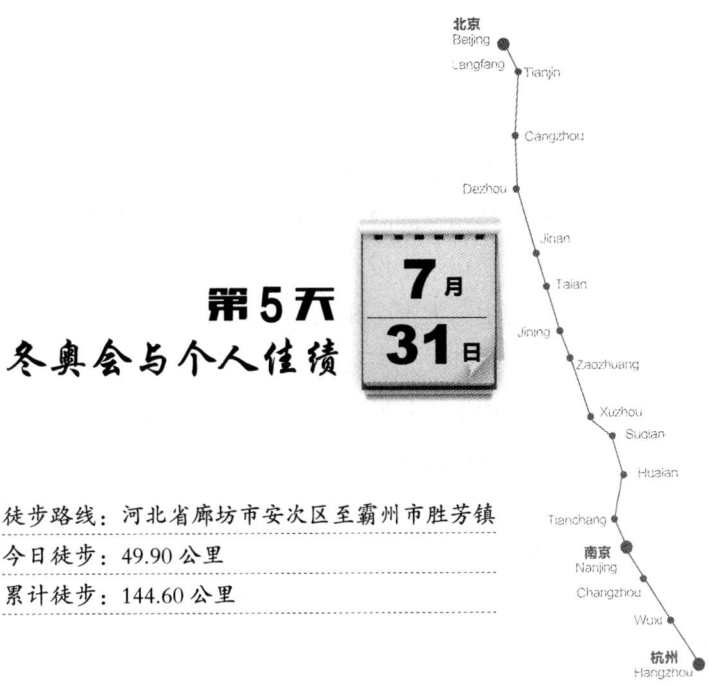

徒步路线：河北省廊坊市安次区至霸州市胜芳镇

今日徒步：49.90公里

累计徒步：144.60公里

    直到凌晨3点，雪琳还在忙着校正我博客的中文翻译。她时不时地把我叫起来解释一些术语和表达，我尽量表现得很耐心。那些术语可是我花了好大工夫想舞弄舞弄文字功底才用上的，但在雪琳这儿却造成了不解。英文中有很多谚语。诸如"to coin a phrase"（引申意思为"杜撰一个词语"）、"to pull your leg"（引申意思为"开你的玩笑"）类似的表达，常常会造成很大的误会和不解。所以翻译我的日记，对雪琳真是个苦差事。

    全程陪同我们的中国红十字会联络部部长张明女士，是我们这次徒步活动的总负责。每天早晨，她都会根据情况的变化带来一张最新的详细修改好的徒步计划表，上面写明前一天的结束地点和今天要完成的里程，而这些变化也会及时通知到下一站。她对细节的重视和协调能力让我非常佩服。

    我们从廊坊市区一路向南。天气似乎比昨日凉爽了一些，加上昨天的休整，脚步感觉轻快许多。我决定争取利用今天的好天气多完成一些里程。我们7点30分准时出发，中午时分已经走了接近20英里（32公里）。那时的我，感觉信心满满。

中国的基础设施建设得相当不错。不管是小道、大马路，还是立交桥，建得都和欧洲国家一样好，甚至可以说比除了德国之外的其他欧洲国家更好。尽管道路基础设施质量极高，交通状况我就不敢苟同了。放眼望去，同一条车道上，大卡车和成百上千的三轮车齐头并进，中间还夹杂着各种现代的小轿车，奔驰、宝马、路虎、大众，喇叭声此起彼伏，震得我好像整个身子都跟着产生了共鸣。一个高速发展、永不停歇的国家，大概也就是这番景象了。虽然交通状况有点混乱，但好在我没看到一起交通事故。

　　到达胜芳镇汉庭酒店的时候，我们得知北京再次赢得了2022年冬奥会举办权，宾馆的咖啡厅里的电视都在报道这一消息。大家目不转睛地一遍遍回看着新闻里国际奥委会主席打开信封宣布"北京"的那一幕，脸上洋溢着兴奋的表情。

　　取得冬奥会的主办权对中国来说意义非凡。2008年，北京奥林匹克运动会和残奥会获得了巨大的成功。成功申办冬奥会，意味着北京将成为第一个既举办过夏季奥运会又举办过冬季奥运会的城市。我喝着茶，也深深沉浸在这成功的喜悦中。

第6天 8月1日
来自陌生人的温暖

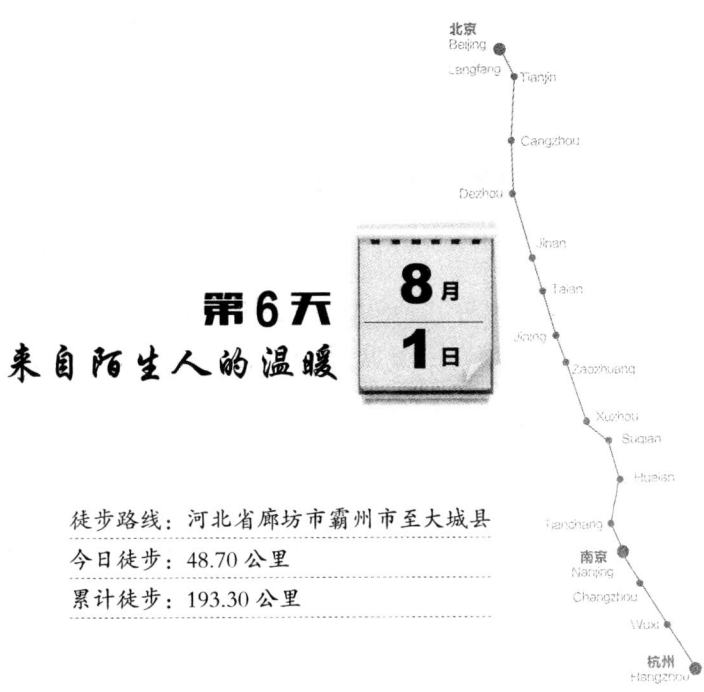

徒步路线：河北省廊坊市霸州市至大城县

今日徒步：48.70公里

累计徒步：193.30公里

由于一只微微起皱的短袜，我的右脚小拇趾上磨出了一个小水疱，着实让人疼痛难耐。鉴于我之前徒步的亲身经历，我意识到若听之任之，后果将不堪设想。我清楚地记得由于水疱感染我曾被困法国北部三天动弹不得的悲惨经历，所以我非常庆幸雪琳这次陪在我身边。她可以说是半个足部护理专家，她带来的足部护理修复霜还真有奇效，昨天用了，今天脚伤就痊愈了，又能继续踏上徒步征程。

雪琳的另一项任务是打理沿途的费用支出。我觉得自己十分幸运，因为沿途红十字会随行人员已经根据我们的预算情况帮我们一路预订到性价比非常高的经济适用型酒店。今天入住的汉庭酒店，价格只有100多元（约合20镑），无线网络、淋浴、大床都配置齐全，还包括我和雪琳的早餐，干净整洁、经济实惠，完全满足我们的需求。在我们的徒步中不时会住在连锁酒店，我感觉这些连锁酒店的体验度和欧洲的Premier Inn、Travelodge或是Ibis连锁经济型旅店一样棒，而价格只有这些旅店的一半，这对于要在中国待上70天的我们来说无疑是一个利好消息。尽管一到大城市，住宿的酒店价格会贵很多，但即便如此，50～70英镑的价位想要在北京住上一个不错的酒店也已足够。

据统计，中国赴英旅游人数近年来翻了一番，从15万人次增长至30万人次，但是英国赴中国的游客相比却少得多。相比充满阳光、沙滩且就在家门口的地中海，英国人一般不会选择到"跋山涉水"才能到达的遥远东方来度假。但对于那些喜欢新鲜食物，而且口味独特的旅游爱好者来说，我强烈建议你们试试"中国"这道美味佳肴。中国饮食中所讲究的新鲜时蔬、米饭与茶的搭配较之英国的啤酒、汉堡、面包的组合有着不同的风味。年长一些的游客在中国一定会发现这里尊敬老人与智者的儒家文化令人耳目一新，这是与西方崇尚年轻、活力的观念截然不同的。除此之外，我所体会到的最大的不同之一便是这里无论什么年龄段都相处得十分融洽，完全没有代际间的隔阂。我和雪琳在一些大型城镇的时候，经常会在晚上散步。所到之处常常看到人们成群结队地随着音乐扭动起舞。无论是青年人，还是奶奶爷爷辈的老年人，或是小孩子都置身其中享受音乐和舞蹈带来的快乐。我认为这是因为中国文化强调不酗酒的良好习惯，这使得各个年龄段的人都能和谐相处。

几天徒步下来，我还切实感到这里人们的淳朴友好。昨天一位先生看见我后，穿过马路将手中的一瓶未开封的冰茶送给了我；还有一位年轻的女士把车停在了我们前方，从后备厢里取出一箱矿泉水，分给我和同行的队员。我已经徒步行走了7年，但免费赠送我食物的事之前只遇到过两次。第一次是在阿尔巴尼亚，当时一位卖瓜的小贩在与我留下一张合影后欣然送给我一块西瓜。第二次是在德国的杜伊斯堡，一位星巴克的服务生在得知我是在徒步路程中写日志，坚持要为我的一杯咖啡买单。但这类事在中国短短的一周就已连续发生了两次。这些可爱人们的慷慨解囊又增进了我对中国，或是更确切一点说，对真实的中国人民的了解。

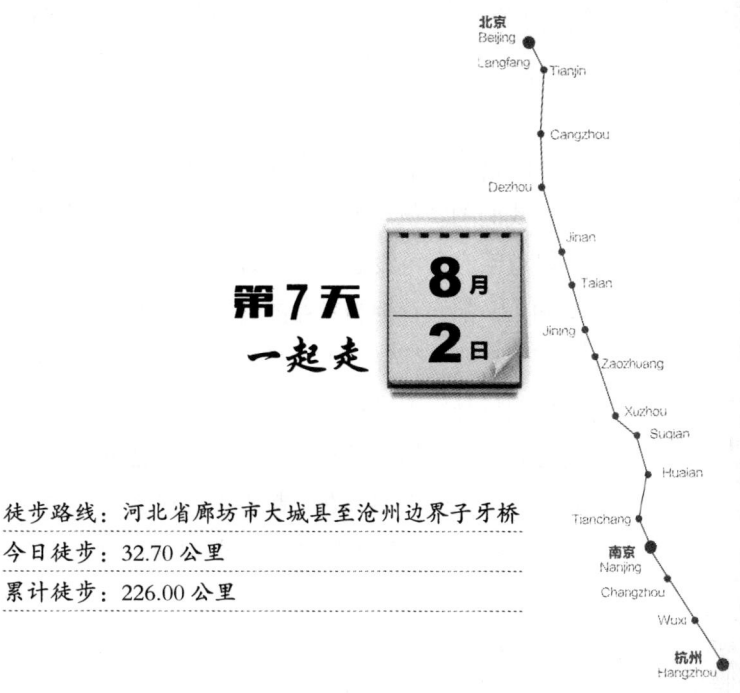

第7天 一起走
8月2日

徒步路线：河北省廊坊市大城县至沧州边界子牙桥
今日徒步：32.70公里
累计徒步：226.00公里

    之前我都是自己独自徒步。不得不承认我体重超标也上了年纪，如果和别人同行，彼此都可能会在对方不想停下来的时候喊停。大家走得节奏不同，有的稍快，有的稍慢，可这一小点变化对于一整天的长途徒步来说影响很大。行走的时候大家有时会想聊天，但像我这样岁数的人要在如此的高温天气中行走已属不易，更别谈聊天了。当然，如果是在森林或海滩上漫步个几英里，这时候要是有人能陪着聊天再好不过。但无论怎么看，在40摄氏度的高温中走30多公里并非那么美好，在这样的情况下讲话对我来说就成了一种负担。

    为了能多享受一会凉爽的清晨，一大早我们就出发了。我发现今天又多了几位红十字会的志愿者，他们穿着印有"为和平徒步"字样的T恤，看起来棒极了！我们一共大概8个人，在大家一起大喊一声"加油！"之后便上路了。为了不让我在徒步时消耗更多体力，大家很默契地跟在我的身后。我们徒步时集中精力，休息时开心聊天。这一路红十字会的志愿者付出了很多心血，确保我们适时停下来喝水休息，保证大家都有冷饮。

因为是周末，途中当地市政府副秘书长一家和他女儿的同学也加入了我们，我们的队伍达到 14 人。我本来以为副秘书长跟我们走个几英里就会坐车打道回府，可没想到他一直在我们的队伍里。下午我们又遇到几个骑自行车的人，都穿着相当专业的骑行服，若告诉别人他们是去参加环法自行车大赛都不会有人怀疑。可能是被我们这支烈日下生气勃勃的队伍所感染，刚开始他们只是停下来照相，后来问能否加入跟走一程。我当然同意啦。队伍变得越来越大，始终没一个人退出。走过小城镇和村落的时候，我们的动静可不小，毕竟这么多人在一起走呢。到达今天的目的地的时候，我们竟然走了 30 多公里！按照我们这几天的新习惯：每天晚上快结束的时候，张明女士会让大家一起庆祝到终点的最后几步，这个小小的仪式让我觉得自己好像刚跑完马拉松一样，胜利的喜悦油然而生！

算上一路不断加入的人，今天我们团队的人数最多，集体成就感此刻特别真实。这远比我一个人跨过终点、接受大家的欢呼庆祝有意义得多，我甚至感觉到自己精神上的升华：从一个独自行走的"我"变成一个庞大团队中的一员，更重要的是我对此感到非常高兴。美国著名的作家及天主教修道士托马斯·莫顿(Thomas Merton)是一位出色的心灵导师，他是这样描述这种感觉的："只有通过付出无私的爱才能获得真正的幸福。越与他人分享，这种无私的爱就越多，所得到的真正的幸福就越多。"而我也更加理解了中国那个著名的谚语："一个人走可以走得更快，可与人同行才能走得更远。"

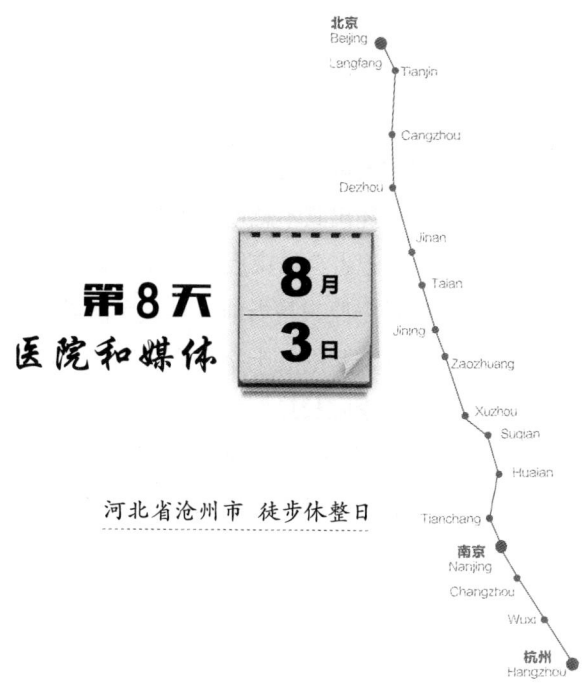

第8天　医院和媒体

8月3日

河北省沧州市　徒步休整日

今天是休整日，河北省沧州市为我组织了媒体见面会。我在英国出席过不少这样的场合，记者们的问题从来都不围绕主题本身，而总是试图寻找一个能获得独家新闻的角度。虽然在当今的英国，媒体自由不受任何政治因素控制，但其通常会受到发行量或阅读量等现实因素的影响，这种媒体市场导向给新闻界带来的影响是：媒体倾向于夸夸其谈、炒作或炮制爆炸性新闻，只关注图片形象而非实实在在的信息。而我想这也许不是媒体的过错，而是我们这些读者观众造成的。我们能集中注意力的时间越来越少，到了只有精力关注推特或微博上只言片语和图片的地步。大多数故事都远比只言片语和图片复杂，遗憾的是，在高速运转的当代社会，我们没有时间和意愿去了解一个故事，只是想要些娱乐和品头论足的谈资。

沧州的这场记者会却和我在英国参加的那些不大一样。记者们问的都是正事儿：为什么徒步、都走过了哪里、和谁同行、对河北的印象如何……我们甚至还交流了孔子的名句，比如"有朋自远方来，不亦乐乎"。雪琳在记者会上充当我的翻译，每当我有点离题或谈到敏感话题时，我都注意到她似乎需要翻译更久，仿佛是在补充："麦克的意思实际上是……"，后来这些记者还出其不意地来拍我徒步，他们也要证实一下我不仅是嘴上说说的吧！

记者会结束后我们几个就近散步。酒店旁有一栋气派的大楼，令我惊讶的是它原来是当地青县人民医院。出于职业习惯我很想进去看看，恰好和我们在一起的红十字会会长和这家医院的李院长是老同事，马上帮我们电话联系。李院长热情地引领我们参观。医院很新，几个月前刚开始接收病人，有1000个床位。除此之外，还有着自己的停车场和辅助病人休闲疗养的公园。我脑子里唯一能用来做比较的一家医院，是英国的纽卡斯尔市的维多利亚皇家医院，几个月前我刚去那儿探访过。那里有600~700个床位，却已经是全英最大的医院之一了。

走在医院宽敞的走廊里，一切秩序井然，安静祥和。我不禁感叹：这地方绝不是草率建成的。这些非常用心的设计都是为了能更好地帮助病人减少焦躁，为他们提供更多的活动空间。

对比中英的医院，我还发现了一处不同：中国医院会设置医疗保险窗口。我和院长聊起英国的国民健康保险制度，没想到他对此十分熟悉。我一直以来都认为英国的国民健康保险制度（简称NHS）是英国文明史上最伟大的发明之一，连中国的医师和管理者都把NHS看得很高很重，打算在中国也尝试运行这个体制。虽然中国比英国大20倍，不知道能否照搬，但这想尝试的念头就足以说明NHS的先进性了。虽然中国将来可能要实行类似NHS的体制，但目前还是采用原有的保障体系。中国的医疗保险可以报销就医费用的80%，剩下的20%，要么病人自己支付，要么当地政府报销。我问如果病人没有保险，也付不起剩下的20%的费用，怎么办？回答是病人会先接受治疗，之后再商量如何付费，这个时候红十字会也会介入帮忙。

之后，我们消毒，穿上卫生服，戴上手套，全副武装参观了手术室：一个县级医院，有16间手术室，每一间都配置了最新的医疗设备，大部分的仪器都是飞利浦的。

当我们回到医院前台的时候，我问李院长，门两侧悬挂的大字是什么意思。他说：这些话来自中国古代医圣孙思邈，意为"作为医生的第一条原则就是仁爱至上；第二条原则就是关爱患者，无论患者年龄、贫富、社会地位，一视同仁"。我赞叹这个从古至今的传承：一个医生不只要有高明的医术，更要具有高尚的医德。

我相信，医院、学校还有其他公共基础设施的质量，都是衡量一个社会是否健康发展的标志。今天的访问，证明了沧州在各方面都达到了标准，这是一个充满活力、健康发展的城市。

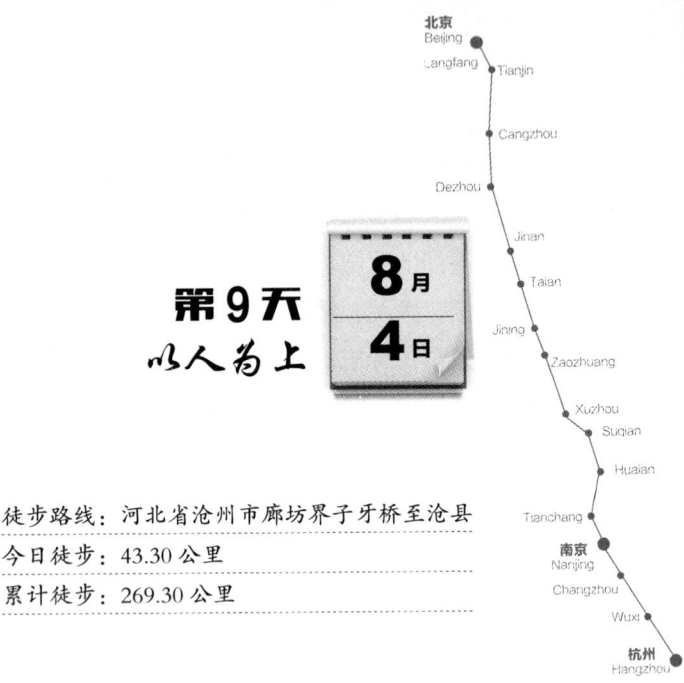

第9天 以人为上

8月4日

徒步路线：河北省沧州市廊坊界子牙桥至沧县
今日徒步：43.30 公里
累计徒步：269.30 公里

  出发前在网上看到红十字国际委员会发出的消息，70年前的今天，美国在日本广岛投下一枚原子弹，3天后在长崎又投下一枚。红十字国际委员会这条信息提醒我们：虽然已经过去70年了，如今仍有数千人遭受1945年这起事件的影响而饱受疾病困扰，仍需要长期医护治疗。

  1945年7月，欧洲大陆上的战事已经结束。7月26日，美国、中国和英国在德国波茨坦发表《中美英三国促令日本投降之波茨坦公告》，要求日本无条件投降，否则"以吾等之军力，加以吾人之坚决意志为后盾，若予以全部实施，必将使日本军队完全毁灭，无可逃避，而日本之本土亦必终归全部残毁"。但是日本没有同意。8月6日，一颗原子弹落在日本广岛，瞬间摧毁了整个城市，造成25万人伤亡，绝大多数为平民百姓。这其中近一半人当场丧生，另一半则在因烧伤和辐射而饱受数月煎熬后死去。全城超过90%的医护人员丧生，所有医院和诊所都被夷为平地，即使幸存下来的人也无法得到及时的治疗。水源受到辐射污染，食物短缺，疾病不断扩散。然而几天后，第二颗原子弹降落在长崎，3.9万~8万民众遭到同样无情的伤害。

8月15日日本投降。人类历史上，仅有这两次动用了原子弹。

在中国讲这样的事要格外谨慎，因为"二战"期间中国遭受了日本惨无人道的侵略，尤其是1938年至1943年长达五年的重庆大轰炸和1937年南京大屠杀。英国也一样，战争期间也有英国人被日军拘留当作俘虏。我们对自己同胞所遭受的残暴虐待感到十分愤慨，但这是否意味着我们要无视敌对方曾经遭受的苦难？人们根据国际法判定了两国谁对谁错，那么是否向敌对国的受害者表示同情就说明我与"正义"相悖？我们无法改变过去，但如果还想改变未来，我们就要换换想法，满怀双方共有的对人性的尊重，而非紧抱着历史的敌意。

我想用今天的徒步来纪念那些受害者，纪念那些因1945年的广岛惨剧曾经或至今仍在经历伤害的无辜的人们。这不是不爱国，这只是我作为一个"人"发自心底的对"人类"的感怀。

第11天
向劳动人民致敬

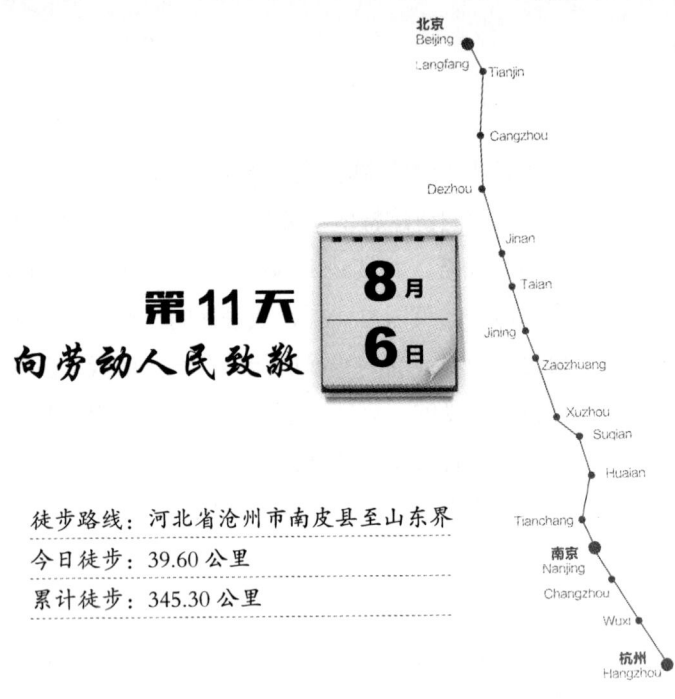

8月6日

徒步路线：河北省沧州市南皮县至山东界
今日徒步：39.60公里
累计徒步：345.30公里

> 人生真正的喜悦，莫过于找到一个自己认为是伟大的事业，并为之奋斗；做一个努力的人，让努力化作宇宙间的一股力量，而不做一块不切实际、自私自利、怨天尤人的行尸走肉。我的生命属于社会整体，在我有生之年，能为社会尽我绵薄之力，是我莫大的荣幸。我希望在我生命终了之前，能竭尽所能，因为工作越努力，生命越有价值。我为生命的本质而欢欣鼓舞。生命并非一支瞬息即逝的蜡烛，而是我紧握手中的冉冉火炬，在传给下一代前，我希望能将它熊熊燃烧，光芒四射。
>
> ——萧伯纳

我出生在一个商人之家，父母曾经营小型的家庭企业。也许正是因为如此，我一直对那些努力工作、喜欢挑战的人感到由衷的敬佩。对我来说，工作是一件非常崇高的事情。对于那些整天埋怨生活不公的人，它是一剂良药，专门治疗胡思乱想、自怨自艾。它提倡在为他人服务的过程中实现自己的价值，激励人们确立人生的目标并为之奋斗，享受收获的喜悦。所以对我来说，工作这个词是那么的高尚。我很难把它和那些碌碌无为、穷困潦倒的人联系在一起,和那些闲散的有钱人更是毫无干系。当然我知道,这样说太一概而论,两者中总有些例外。

在徒步的路上,我遇到过很多努力工作的人,有在田间挥汗如雨的农夫,有在市场上竭声叫卖的摊主。当我正午顶着烈日毅然前行的时候,我心里和他们有了莫名的感应;擦身而过时,他们也似乎对我示以敬佩和尊重。

我停下来和一对正在悉心修剪枣树的夫妇攀谈。他们眼神中略带焦急,盼望着他们的 11 亩地(约 0.73 公顷)能在 9 月大获丰收,因为中秋节前后正是一年中价格最好的时期。和世界各地的农民一样,他们也十分担心随时到来的狂风大雨会将他们的辛苦经营毁于一旦;而全面的大丰收也可能会压低价格,让他们的利润缩水。马路前方,一个养鹅养猪的养殖场主迎上前来,以为我是俄罗斯人。俄罗斯人是他养殖场的主要消费者之一,所以俄罗斯市场对他们很重要。他还要带我参观他的养猪场,告诉我因为猪肉出口需求的增长,他打算要把养殖场扩大规模。我们本来打算坐在路边简单吃点盒饭,但是污水处理厂的经理执意邀请我们去他办公室坐坐。他说好歹办公室里有个电风扇,可以让我们凉快凉快。参观时,我受到了工人朋友们的热烈欢迎,就像我是他们集体中的一员似的。

早晨出发的时候,我们遇见一些养路工人正在烈日下沿着我们的徒步路线清理路边沟渠,修剪草坪。我猜他们的平均年龄也有六七十岁了。傍晚时分我再次见到他们,他们快要收工了,我也即将到达终点。这是我一天中第三次与他们相遇,每一次我们都彼此招手致意。这一次,我停下来和他们交谈甚欢,他们甚至还让我操作了他们修路的工具。

今天的一切不禁让我陷入沉思。一路所见的劳动景象,让我感叹中国的经济发展取得今天的成就绝非偶然。西方社会,我们习惯于低估人的价值,这也是为什么人们很早就退休了。在我工作的英国上议院有许多有着世界上最聪明的大脑还毕生致力于自己事业的人。有些到了 90 岁还依然在工作。而我呢,今年是 55 岁,有些人私底下议论我可能快要退休了。殊不知,对我来说,没有什么事情比退休更糟糕了。我想我会一直工作下去,直到我不能做为止。

  如果我 85 岁那年，人们发现我正头顶烈日在山东的公路上手拿着长耙辛勤劳动，或者躺在路边的草地上惬意休息，到那时，我想我的人生的确做到了鞠躬尽瘁。那时，我可以无愧地宣布，生命的火炬在我手中时，我曾让它熊熊燃起。

第13天 优秀的管理者

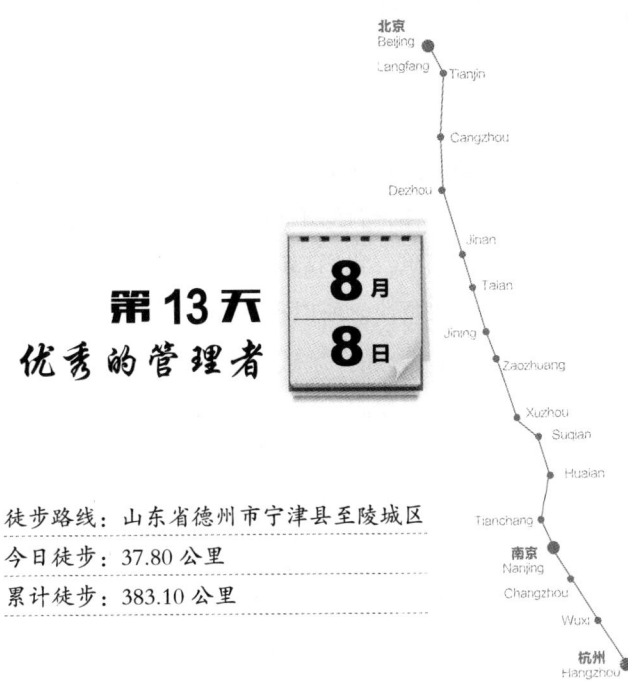

徒步路线：山东省德州市宁津县至陵城区
今日徒步：37.80 公里
累计徒步：383.10 公里

　　至今日我已经徒步 11 天之久，沿途高温潮湿的天气以及我一时间难以适应的空气质量使得我每天都倍感疲劳。要不是当地红十字会志愿者们的大力支持和帮助，我绝不可能在 10 天左右的时间就完成 320 公里的路程。志愿者们饱满的激情以及对工作的热忱每天都激励着我按时启程上路并坚持完成每天的目标里程数。这些来自各乡镇、市、省的志愿者之所以能够在顺利完成交接任务的基础上井然有序地开展工作还真是多亏了张明女士悉心的组织安排。而在今天，来自山东省的红十字志愿者队伍将会接过河北省递来的接力棒。

　　能够再次来到山东的感觉真的很棒，因为我 1997 年第一次访问中国时的第一站就是到山东。山东省经济实力雄厚且幅员辽阔，拥有 1.17 亿的人口，几乎是全英国和法国人口的总和。

　　好，让我们回到志愿者团队的主题。如果说我在心中已经有一张关于我认识的人的管理能力的排行榜，那么张明女士令人眼前一亮的表现则让她很快就跃到榜首。仔细分析考虑之后，我发现雪琳和我在管理方面都讲求高效与高产，我们习惯在尽可能短的时间内高标准地完成任务。由于我们十分热衷工作，有时不知怎的不太希望将工作分派给他人去做，其实我们的想法也很简单，我们都认为与其跟人讲解老半天如何做这件事，还不如自己亲手去做来得快。所以我们往往都是亲力亲为、披挂上阵，而这却恰恰忽略错失了团队管理的"乘数效应"。

和我们一样，张女士本身也是雷厉风行，工作效率极高，但不同的是，她能够很好地掌握团队这一个整体在完成集体项目时起到的重要作用。于是我们就一个领导者的管理方法展开了一系列讨论。这也如同以美国经典小说《第二十二条军规》为蓝本拍摄成的电影中的台词一样："倘若你觉得自己很笨的话，其实你并不愚蠢，因为只有当你意识不到自己笨的时候，你才是真的愚蠢。"所以我们将所观察到的一个优秀领导者应该具备的素质一一列出，供大家一起学习借鉴：

个人信心：如果一个领导者对自己不够自信，那么就会给人一种看不到任何希望的感觉。缺乏自信的管理者会不自觉地对批评变得十分敏感，认为旁人所有其实是对客观事情的批评都是在针对自己。这种人需要过多的溢美之词以维护其所谓的自信和安全感，这就导致了他们不善于夸奖他人。他们的不自信和安全感的缺乏不断怂恿他们去讨好迎合他们的老板，从而忽视了自身团队成员的感受。这种类型的人会把所有团队的功劳都往自己身上揽，但却拼了命地撇清与团队所承受批评的关系。

鼓励：在我所生活的英格兰东北部有一句众人皆知的俗语，即"轻轻地挠痒痒总比用力挠抓令人感到舒服"。这句话所表达的意思是通常当人们受到鼓励、赞美时会表现得更好，而当一个人反复受到责骂怪罪的时候，负面情绪不断积压，结果则可想而知。从精神或是肉体上击垮一个人很容易，但如果要重新将他扶正，让他有勇气继续前进，则是难上加难。

倾听：究竟在团队中领导者分别该花多少时间在传达指令和聆听反馈上呢？我认为：一个好的团队领导者必须拥有优秀的倾听能力，因为只有通过倾听那些一线工作人员的反馈才能不断了解到哪块工作环节需要提高与优化。倾听其实并没有想象中那么费事，被认为是最发人深省的管理类书籍之一的《一分钟经理人》（作者：肯·布兰佳）迄今已售出了1300万册，而此书所表达的基本观念就是高水平的管理并不会占用你大量时间，而在劣质的管理中，往往你投入了大把时间和精力，但效果却并不显著。

多表扬、少批评：关于这块内容我在"鼓励"中已有提及，我们每一个人其实内心深处最希望的是感受到自己被欣赏、被需要。想想你上一次为什么跳槽吧，其实并不是因为你讨厌这家公司或部门，真正的原因可能就在于你没有感受到自己被上司所赏识——无数商学院的调研已经论证了这一观点。欣赏的另一个意思就是尊敬。

抓重点：许多失败的管理者只会无止境地放大自己团队成员的缺点。与其正好相反，成功的管理者则会不断发掘他们的潜力。我爱看足球比赛，经常看到一些团队中许多天赋极高的运动员在球场上没有发挥出其应有的水平，但往往是在换了教练之后，那些球员的竞技状态一下子就得到了爆发，在绿茵场上所向披靡。其中很重要的一点就是教练给队员们所注入的信念从中发挥了作用。其实还有一个事例可以加以说明：一天，一个聪明的管理人员来到一个大型工地，问工地上一位正在劳动的工人在干什么，工人答道："我在砌砖。" 那位管理者说道："不，你正在造一座教堂！"所以，往大局看而不是局限在琐碎的小事上。

学会发现才能：打造一支好的团队就如同完成一幅拼图。根据盒子外面包装的提示，你知道最终自己想要的成品是什么样子，但在盒子里面你却只会发现1000块形状不一的拼图碎片。我认为一个好的管理者首先要能意识到的一点就是：每一片拼图形状大小不一，但他们在完成整个拼图的过程中扮演着同样重要的角色，因为只有当他们都在各自的位置上各司其职贡献自己的那分力时，整个拼图才能完美地呈现于世人眼前。

学会冷静：该出错的总是无法避免，这就是生活。当事情发展偏离了既定轨道时，明智的做法并不是刨根究底去追究哪个环节出了错，而是应该设身处地思考如何将损失降到最低，如何把事情扳回正轨。保持一个冷静的头脑和一颗热忱的心对我们来说可能就是最重要的了吧。

拉迪亚德·吉普林写过一首诗名叫《如果》，请原谅我无法将它翻译成中文，因为这首诗里有太多英国文化气息浓厚的词组搭配，但我认为这首诗很好地诠释了我们能在张女士身上所看到的一个优秀管理者应该具备的品质：

如果周围的人毫无理性地向你发难，你仍能镇定自若保持冷静；
如果众人对你心存猜忌，你仍能自信如常并认为他们的猜忌情有可原；
如果你肯耐心等待不急不躁，
或遭人诽谤却不以牙还牙，
或遭人憎恨却不以恶报恶，
既不装腔作势，亦不气盛趾高；
如果你有梦想，而又不为梦主宰；
如果你有神思，而又不走火入魔；
如果你坦然面对胜利和灾难，对虚渺的胜负荣辱胸怀旷荡；
如果你能忍受有这样的无赖，歪曲你的口吐真言蒙骗笨汉，
或看着心血铸就的事业崩溃，仍能忍辱负重脚踏实地重新攀登；
如果你敢把取得的一切胜利，为了更崇高的目标孤注一掷，
面临失去，决心从头再来而绝口不提自己的损失；
如果人们早已离你而去，你仍能坚守阵地奋力前驱，
身上已一无所有，唯存意志在高喊顶住；
如果你跟平民交谈而不露谄媚之颜；
抑或与王侯散步而不露谄媚之颜；
如果敌友都无法对你造成伤害；
如果众人对你信赖有加却不过分依赖；
如果你能惜时如金利用每一分钟不可追回的光阴；
那么，你的修为就会如天地般博大，并拥有了属于自己的世界，
更重要的是：孩子，你成了真正顶天立地之人！

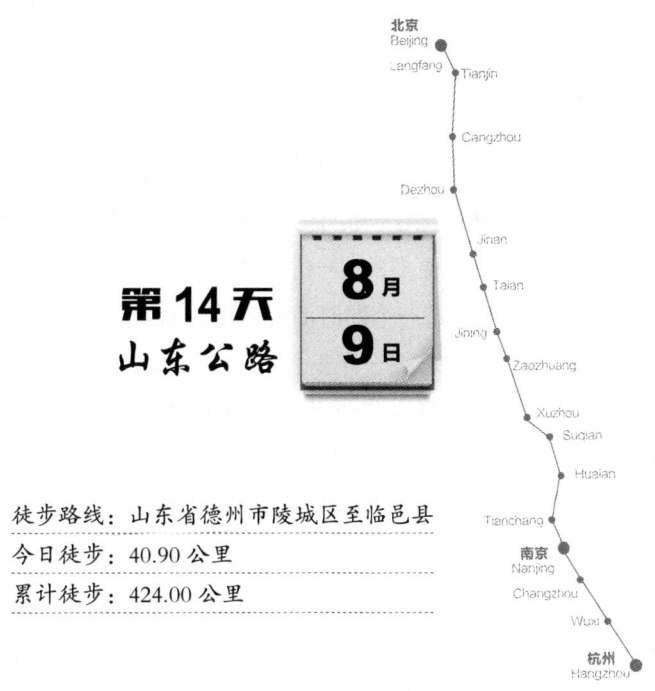

第14天 山东公路
8月9日

徒步路线：山东省德州市陵城区至临邑县

今日徒步：40.90公里

累计徒步：424.00公里

我和山东的公路在过去的几天中可以说是亲密无间。出了河北省后，我们一直沿着它向南进发。山东的路走起来相当舒服，不仅每公里会有提示牌，连每走100米都会标示出来。这对我调整、控制行走速度十分方便。这些路标和手机步行软件一起，让我能更轻松地做些计算，以便决定每天徒步的起点和终点。

沿路风景徐徐展开，中国经济发展的轨迹一览无余。牧羊人赶着羊群在马路和河边走走停停，仿佛置身另一个世界，无论是拥挤的交通还是零星的过客，对他都毫无影响。熙熙攘攘的村庄、小镇、集市、商店装点在路旁。相比于城里人，村民们会更加热情地向你招手，大声喊着"你好"或是"欢迎来到中国"，然后还会可爱地和你要张合影。

大部分的村庄都分布在公路的两旁。每个村庄都会有自己的大门，上面刻着中英双语的村名。我们路过的村子，常有村民请我们到村子里歇歇脚、坐一坐。偶尔也会有年轻人等在村路的尽头，给我们送水。我还意外地收到过他们送的冰棍儿。我设想，要是有时间研究研究中国农村的社交媒体一定非常有趣，因为我惊讶地发现，"老外徒步"这条消息通过微信、QQ、微博，正在一传十、十传百。微信就是中国版的What's app或者Twitter，微博则更多的是一个博客网站。微博和微信在中国都有着约5亿的国内用户。QQ是一个即时消息软件，有着超过8亿的国内用户，和What's app的全球用户总数一样多。

有人告诉我说，中国不敢放宽对美国几大社交媒体公司的限制，怕Facebook、What's app、Twitter会垄断中国市场。也许的确会这样，但是还有一种可能就是中国的QQ和微信会占领美国市场，借机发展成为世界品牌。

沿着公路，我们时不时会停下脚步和遇到的村民交流。我们会谈到越来越先进的农业设备和科技发展，一个家庭不需要夫妻两人同时看守田地。这样，妻子就可以在新开的服装工厂或者其他出口产品的工厂工作。当夫妻二人都有收入时，他们就可以实现许多愿望，比如买点新衣服，买辆三轮车，还有送孩子去读书。不久的将来，他们的村子也许要被推倒重建，原有的平房会被高楼取代，他们也会搬进水、电、煤气齐全的公寓，小区还会配有新的学校和医院。对于老人，他们在村子里生活了一辈子，习惯了简单的生活和那些熟悉的面孔，搬进全新的公寓对他们来说没什么吸引力。我不禁感叹，世界工业化的进程看来都是一个样，这是一个必经的时期。

当然，过不了多久，随着交通工具的不断发展和汽车的普及，人们便不会想住在那拥挤狭窄、千篇一律的公寓楼里。这时很多人又会考虑把家搬到郊区。我想说的是，从经济发展的角度上来说，中国现在经历的一些社会现象都很正常，是实现工业化的必经之路。这样说也许会让中国的领导者们稍稍安心。但是不久之后，随着教育的普及、城市化的加深以及中产阶级力量的壮大，他们也将遇到新老经济体制碰撞产生的新的挑战。

第15天
"美丽中国"手机摄影大赛

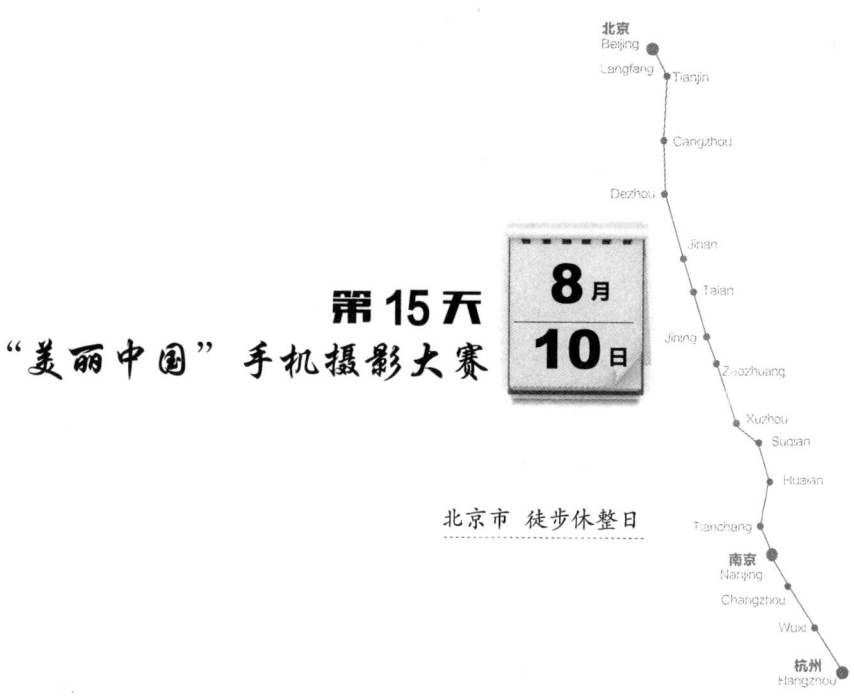

8月10日

北京市　徒步休整日

　　为了参加《中国日报》举办的"美丽中国"手机摄影大赛的启动仪式，我们返回北京两天，并因此得以领略传说中的中国高铁。

　　高铁的时速达到每小时300公里，从漂亮的德州东站乘坐高铁出发，只用了90分钟就驶过了我花了整整两个星期才走完的路程。在如此炎热的天气坐上有空调的高铁简直就是享受，而且无论是候车站还是车厢内，都非常干净整洁，舒适宜人。到达终点北京，正当我们准备离开车厢的时候，一位工作人员径直走了过来，利索地把所有座位转成了面向旅途的方向，我觉得这一小小的举动简直太有爱了，因为我个人非常不喜欢旅行时背对着火车前进的方向，而聪明的中国人想出了这个体贴又周到的解决办法，简直太妙了。

　　我很喜欢坐火车旅行，我觉得火车旅行有一种特殊的优雅，如果我在中国生活的话，我一定希望自己能够住在这些高大上的高铁站附近。这段火车旅行瞬间让我兴奋起来，精神一下子大受鼓舞。为了记住我当时的感觉，下车后，我们没有马上离开车站，我让雪琳为我录像，口述了当时的感觉，还让她在火车正好开过来的时候为我照相，将火车纳入照片背景。得知当前中国高铁已经通达绝大多数主要城市，我想今后在中国无论去哪，乘坐高铁都会是我的第一选择啦。

　　因为"为和平徒步"，我被提名为《中国日报》举办的"美丽中国"手机摄影大赛的国际荣誉摄影师。《中国日报》是一份全球发行的报纸，在伦敦地铁站出口处，你会发现《中国日报》非常显眼地和伦敦《都市地铁报》和伦敦《金融城早报》排列在一起，给进出地铁的各行各业的人们提供时下最新的资讯。在各大报刊出版量纷纷减少的今天，《中国日报》却依旧一路高歌猛进，印刷量不断攀升。作为中国了解世界、世界了解中国的重要窗口，《中国日报》有着非凡的前景与潜力。在接受了报刊、电视、网络记者的采访后，我们会见了《中国日报》副总编辑康兵先生。在和他的谈话中，我们交换了意见，也了解到他在国际媒体行业的真知灼见。如同来时的高铁之旅一样，这次愉快的交谈也令人神清气爽、非常愉快。我认为《中国日报》推广手机记录美丽中国是个好点子，手机拍照功能的进步使人人都可以成为摄影师，而能在徒步途中用我的手机随时随地捕捉沿途美好的景象也正是我此行的愿望，我希望自己也可以为推动手机拍照发挥一些作用。

　　当我们来到楼下会场，便看到许多年轻人聚集在那里，高举手机急切等待。伴随着尖叫声，被誉为中国的安吉丽娜·朱莉的著名女演员姚晨翩翩出场。姚晨的到来引爆了整个会场的氛围，也让我切实感受了一回什么是明星效应。连在场的许多媒体界、商业界"大佬"，似乎都心甘情愿地做一片"绿叶"。通常一个成功的项目往往需要选择大众心目中最有影响力的人作为其代言人，看来姚晨完美地符合这一条件。她的微博粉丝有 7000 多万，难怪她在《时代》周刊的"全球互联网最具影响力的 30 人"中榜上有名。了不起的中国！

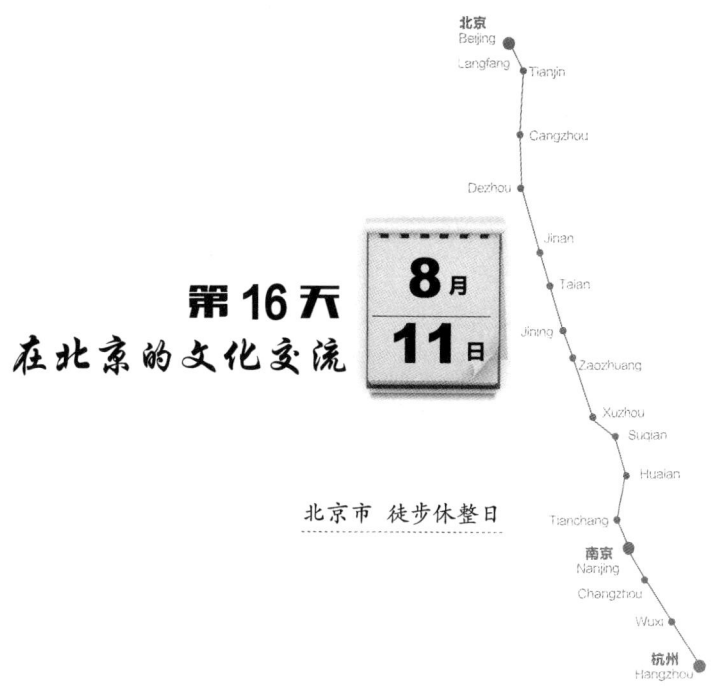

第16天
在北京的文化交流

北京市 徒步休整日

回到北京，我们荣幸地收到英国驻华大使吴百纳 (Barbara Woodward) 的邀请去她的官邸喝下午茶。因为担心堵车我们出来得很早，提前半个小时就到了大使官邸。尽管早到，我们还是被热情邀请提前进入，边品茶边等待。我们的吴百纳大使这段时间忙得不可开交：英国外交大臣菲利普·汉蒙德正在亚洲区域访问，中国是继日本和首尔后的又一站，他将于明天抵达北京，来讨论一系列非常复杂的问题。

吴大使热情地接待了我们，并对我的和平慈善徒步很感兴趣。她今年2月才刚上任，之前曾在中国当过老师。在这里生活和工作了这么多年之后的她不仅中文流利，还变成了"中国通"。在中国，了解文化比会说汉语更有用。语言不通的确会造成误解，而如果对中国文化缺乏足够的理解和尊重则会造成更多的误解。

英国的外交官员在中国面临的许多巨大挑战之一便是他无法从一个中国人的外表去判断他是否有权有势。在英国，一个人的外表就能直接反映出他是否有权。有权的人往往着装体面，口音标准，那职衔一看就让人肃然起敬。

他们能自信从容地提起大名鼎鼎的人物，滔滔不绝地讲述文化体验；不论是人民币对泰铢汇率的短期展望，还是纽约古根海姆博物馆里新添了俄国画家瓦西里·康定斯基的作品，他们都能信手拈来，侃侃而谈。尽管教育为更多的人创造了机会，社会流通性也有所增大，但英国阶级分层依然较为明显，精英阶级尤为稳固，一般人不易进入。而中国政府官员的构成机制却与此不同。雪琳是中国侨联的海外委员，我们中午受到中国侨联副主席乔卫先生的接见并共进午餐。他在北京可是一位颇具影响力的大人物，但却是我见过的最低调最谦和的部级官员。

　　这使我联想起前几年和雪琳去上海的另一次经历。那时候上海有个英国商务活动，雪琳以英国中华总商会常务副主席的身份参加。当时还有尊敬的约克公爵安德鲁王子殿下，他因一直致力于推进中英两国的贸易而深受人们的敬佩。那次活动上有位英国投资方的总裁因迟迟在中国拿不到申请的执照而十分着急，专程飞到上海试图解决问题。一位英国高级外交官按照来宾的着装和头衔忙于接待中国 VIP 贵宾。雪琳无意间发现一位没有按照酒会着正装要求而是穿着极普通的夹克衫的人坐在角落里，她很好奇，就过去与他聊了起来。一聊才发现他正是那位总裁要找的政府官员。在中国的文化当中，如果屋里有比自己职位高的官员，中国人一般是不会主动把自己推到人前面去的。于是雪琳就牵线搭桥介绍他们认识，后来那项投资申请就顺利通过了，中国欢迎您！

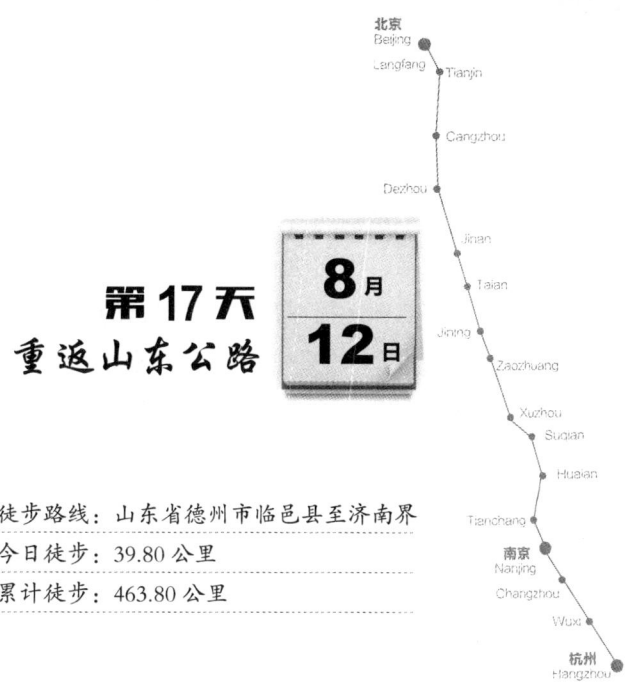

第17天 重返山东公路

8月12日

徒步路线：山东省德州市临邑县至济南界
今日徒步：39.80公里
累计徒步：463.80公里

  过去的两天，我在北京的行程满满当当，回到德州已经很晚了。昨晚和红十字会随行人员确认今天的徒步路线时得知，我们计划走的那条公路因为施工有7公里左右路段封闭了，这导致我们必须绕行很远才能回到上次徒步的终点。为了争取时间节省体力，我们决定设法从那条封闭的路线通过。感谢红十字会争取到公路管理部门的允许，我们得以不去绕路啦。

  因为施工，道路坑洼满是烟尘，走起来很累。但也正是如此，一路非常安静，没有了大卡车的呼啸而过，更幸运的是我们一直沿着一片景色宜人的森林公园行走。快到终点的时候，我们翻过一个小山丘，下山迎面竟是临邑县公安交通大队门口。交通大队的领导知道我徒步的消息，特意邀请我们来办公室吹吹空调，歇歇脚。休息之余，我们再次研究了地图，今天的徒步任务是到达德州与济南的界河大桥。在那里，济南和德州两个红十字会要做个简单的交接，这意味着德州的徒步告一段落，济南之旅即将展开。

  经过两天的休息，我神清气爽精神百倍，最快的时候每小时能走上6公里，就连午饭时都不打算休息，想尽快完成今天的任务。徒步以来我们看到的大多是郊区，偶有些地方会显露些城市化的迹象。不管走到哪儿，当地的人们都是既热情又好奇。真希望能有时间和他们多多交流，听他们谈谈自己的生活，也向他们解释我在做什么。接近济南边界的时候，一个满脸微笑的青年热情地招呼我们到他经营的摩托车维修店看看。店里堆满了各种零件和正在维修中的摩托车。我很喜欢他的车库，熟悉的景象和味道让我想起了祖父的车棚。我的祖父是个钢铁工人，闲暇的时候他总喜欢捣鼓修理一些家电，连他孙子的自行车都可以修好，这足够证明他在这方面的天赋。在我一个小孩子眼里，那简直不是车棚而是神奇的洞穴，什么坏了的东西在里面待上一会儿出来时就变好了。在西方社会，我们很早就过上了比较铺张浪费的生活，东西坏了，习惯直接买个新的。这种风气大大增加了个人消费债务。中国在这点上没有重蹈西方社会覆辙，这也是为什么像摩托车修理这样的店铺能在这里稳定地经营下去。

  我们终于到了那座桥。脑袋里有个声音弱弱问我，要不要再多走点？想想还是算了吧，今天已经很圆满了，留点体力明天还要继续。济南红十字会的志愿者们已经等候在那里，欢迎我们的到来。和往常一样，我很高兴见到新的志愿者，同时又难过于不得不和德州的朋友们道别，大家不停地照相，留下彼此的记忆，最后我用中文对他们说了一句"干得好"以表我深深的谢意。

第18天
紧急事件中的红十字会

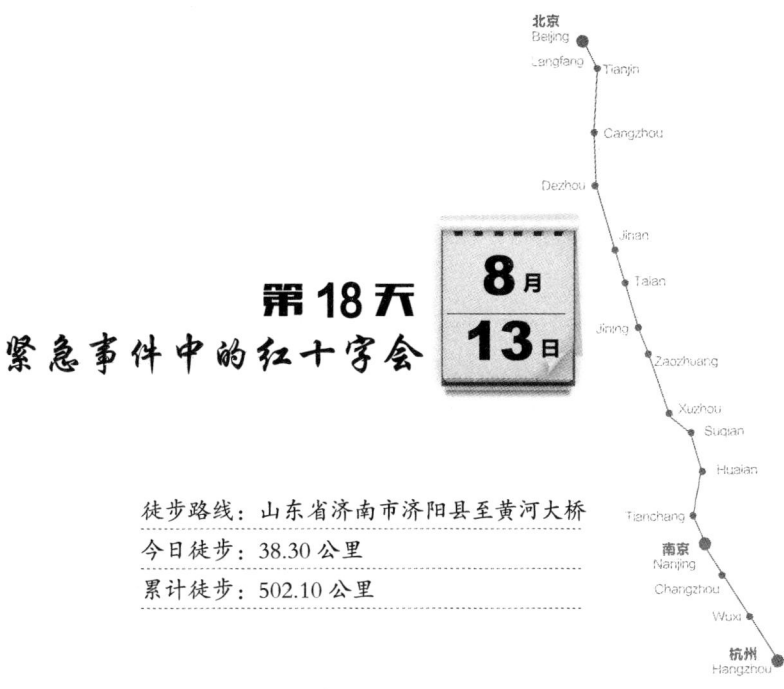

徒步路线：山东省济南市济阳县至黄河大桥
今日徒步：38.30 公里
累计徒步：502.10 公里

今天的徒步目标是跨过黄河大桥，到达济南市区。

清晨抵达昨日结束的界河桥边时发现，昨天空无一物的地方，一夜之间成了繁忙的早市，水灵灵的新鲜蔬果琳琅满目，让人目不暇接。在中国文化中，人们十分注重食材之新鲜，再加上不少地区还缺少保存食物的冰箱，每日采购的传统得以维持。我特意询问了一些菜品的价格，一个卖辣椒的摊主说过去一年里辣椒从每斤1.5元跌到了1元，而卖蒜的小贩则说蒜价在同时期几乎翻了一番。我喜欢这种小市场，因为没有人会暗中操控以刻意的低价或所谓的"促销"来倾销产品。这里决定价钱的就是简单的供求关系，而且还可以讨价还价。

大约在午饭时间，我觉察到红十字会的工作人员收到了坏消息——天津滨海新区的一个化工厂发生了爆炸。最初的报道估计事故已造成数百人伤亡。这对红十字会来说是件大事，因为他们是这类突发事件的第一救援方。我想起上周我们刚刚经过天津附近，当时那些与我们一同徒步的红十字会工作人员和志愿者们现在是不是正在爆炸现场展开紧急救援？是不是正在为伤者开设献血中心？想到这里，不禁觉得这次可怕的事故离我很近，也更加坚定了我们为中国红十字会筹集善款的决心，因为只有这样它们才能继续在危难时刻提供高质量的紧急救助服务。爆炸发生的时候，英国外交大臣菲利普·哈蒙德碰巧在天津访问，他也承诺英国的救灾专家团队会为这次的救援行动提供支持，这让我倍受鼓舞。

  我们一路都关注着灾情的进展，得知当地红十字会救援人员已经到达现场，位于北京的红十字会总会正在紧急就近调运救援物资。随着越来越多的坏消息从天津传来，我们整个下午的情绪都非常低落，加之极度高温，今天最后的15公里几乎是我走得最艰难的一段。更糟的是，几天来的腹痛似乎突然加重，完全没胃口吃东西，而这又引发了胃痉挛。最终我还是忍着疼痛坚持走过了黄河大桥，实现了今天的目标。而此时我已极度不适、筋疲力尽。回到酒店后我被立即安排就诊，按照医生的建议，明天暂停徒步，休息一天。

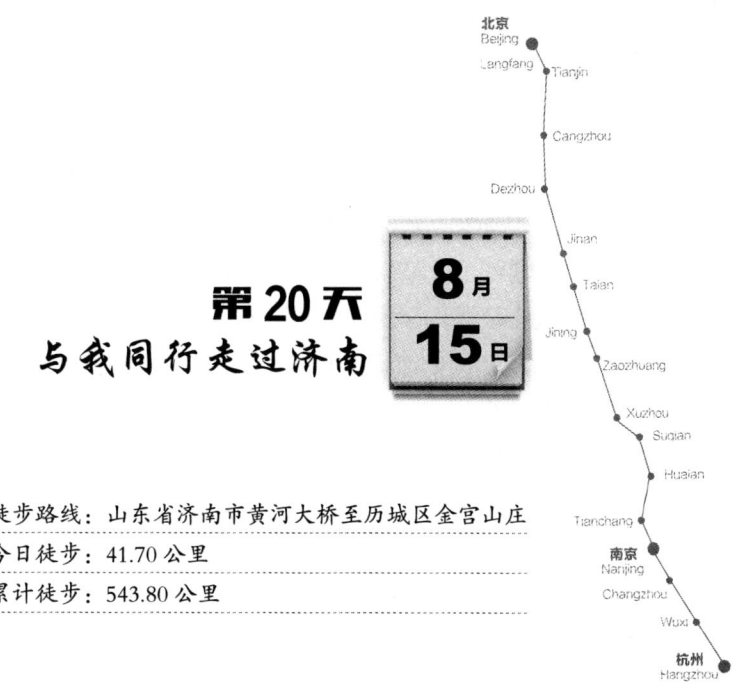

第20天
与我同行走过济南

8月15日

徒步路线：山东省济南市黄河大桥至历城区金宫山庄
今日徒步：41.70公里
累计徒步：543.80公里

    昨天几乎全天躺在床上水米未沾。今早还是很不舒服吃不下饭，但想着这额外休息的一天耽误的里程，便把身体不适扔到一边急着开始今天的徒步。我从昨天结束的地点走了不到1公里，就看见有人挥舞着"500公里"的大牌子为我加油。像这样的点点滴滴总会激励我，令我更加有力地迈出下一步。

    今天有许多人加入到我们的徒步队伍。一大早，有20多位山东浙大校友会校友在赵志强会长的带领下来到我们中间，陪我一起徒步了约10公里。中国红十字会副会长王汝鹏先生今天也加入到我们的队伍当中，还带上了自己正在放暑假的13岁女儿一起来陪我徒步。小姑娘很喜欢走路，而且以前也走过差不多远的距离。我回想起自己的第一次"长征"，那一年我14岁，要在围着英格兰诺森伯兰郡威南村的环形路上走25公里。我竭尽所能，走到15公里的时候实在走不动了，脚上还打起了血疱，于是我就跑到泰恩河边，把脚伸进河水里好好舒服了一会儿，最后不得不搭车到终点。因此我总是非常敬佩那些年轻的徒步者。王会长在红十字会是位德高望重的领导，推动了不少重要的改革。我对他印象最深刻的一件事是：他曾花了六个月时间成功参与组织了一次从香港到北京长达3000公里的义行活动,为希望工程筹集了200万英镑的善款。对此我深表敬佩!

通往下一站泰安的路有两条,一条是翻山而过,里程较远;捷径是穿越长约1公里的隧道。为了节省时间我们选择穿越隧道。当然了,有红十字志愿者在就意味着我不能像以前那样马虎随意,而是要做好防护:穿上荧光安全服,拿着手电,还务必要戴上口罩以阻隔隧道内的汽车尾气。

走出隧道完全是另一片景色。灰蒙蒙的城市被抛在隧道的另一头,雨水把空气洗刷得更加清新,眼前是济南著名的风景区千佛山,还有绿树鲜花簇拥的街道和一片片漂亮的新建住宅。这种体验我只有在穿过旧金山金门大桥到加州米尔谷的时候才有过,而米尔谷始终是我心中最佳的养老地点。

济南南部的近郊十分繁华。到处都是金融服务公司、IT公司,有很多穿着时尚、年轻的职场精英,开着德国汽车去购物中心逛奢侈品商店或看电影。中国不仅在地理地图上有鲜明的区域对比,经济地图上也是如此。

傍晚时分,我们在G104国道上和济南市巩宪群副市长会合了。我自己多年从政,算是了解政治家的想法,但今天加入徒步的中国领导们给我留下了十分深刻的印象。这里并没有媒体报道,王汝鹏副会长和巩宪群副市长加入徒步没有一点做秀的意思,纯粹是为了自己的信念,为了支持我,为了对和平和友情的珍视。我在内心感谢他们的陪伴。

第21天
会有"这样的日子"

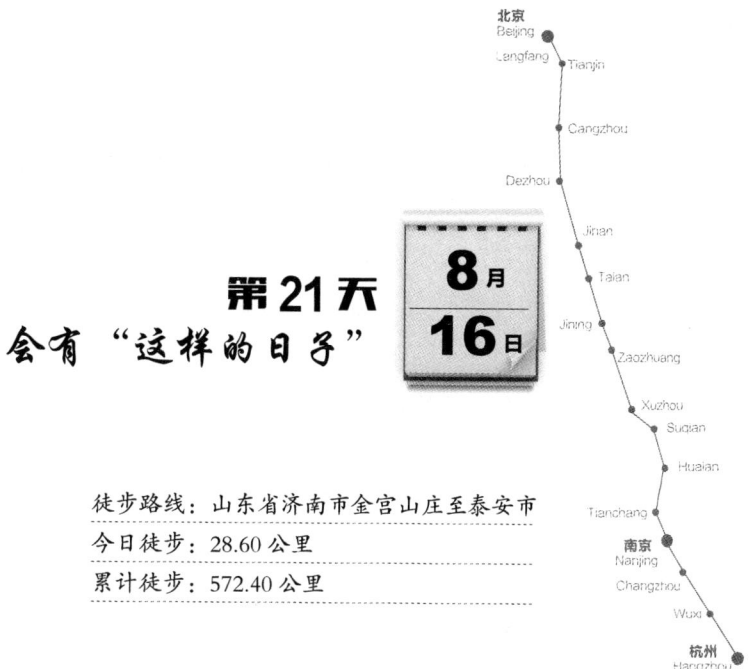

8月16日

> 徒步路线：山东省济南市金宫山庄至泰安市
> 今日徒步：28.60公里
> 累计徒步：572.40公里

英国歌手范·莫里森有一首好歌叫《这样的日子》。我手机里就有这首歌，徒步的时候经常听，特别是在好日子里。它开头的几句歌词是：

不常下雨时，
便有这样的日子；
无人抱怨时，
便有这样的日子
一切都简单安好时，
妈妈告诉我，
便就是这样的日子。

因为酷热和身体不适，几天来的徒步非常艰难。今天是星期天，当我在泰山脚下的住处醒来时，映入眼帘的是蓝天白云、葱葱绿树和潺潺流水，不禁赞叹这是徒步开始以来最美好的一天。此刻我真希望那些曾与我们在高温中走过繁忙的城市和公路的徒步者们也和我在一起，享受到这样的好天气。

一大早向泰安进发，我们选择了一条捷径，即翻山而过。住宿地前的那座山就是济南和泰安的分界线，我们将在山顶告别济南与泰安红十字会会合。全天里程并不长，但因要走山路还是有些挑战。

山路并不陡峭，沿途风景如画，就在我觉得有些累了的时候，看见济南红十字会的周蔚向我们招手，说发现了休息的好地方，于是我们随着她来到了邢家村。小小山村历史悠久民风朴实，大部分村民都姓邢。村主任热情邀我参观他们的"镇村之宝"：500岁高龄的古树和700年仍然清水充盈的老井。我饶有兴味地跟村民学着用老式的工具打水，往井里投下一个空桶，装得满满地提上来，那水的纯净与清凉真是世上最美妙的体验。我被当作尊贵的客人，村民们为我摆好桌椅，桌子上是茶水和用井水冰过的西瓜，我们一起坐在古树下。我问："来贵村访问的老外多吗？"村民们你看看我，我看看你，摇了摇头："没有，你是第一个。"我感到很惊讶，又问了一遍，但答案还是一样。之后他们请来村里年纪最大的老人，他肯定知道答案。这位老者个子很高，穿着一件像是军队制服的衬衫，他穿过广场坐在我旁边。我问他高寿，他说他也不确定，大约95岁上下。村民们接着问他记不记得任何来过邢家村的外国人。他思忖片刻，摇了摇头说没有。

我俩坐在树荫下，在张明女士的翻译帮助下相谈甚欢，村民们围成一圈观看。老者向我讲述了他1943年抗战时期从军与占领济南地区的日军作战的故事。我问他长寿的秘诀是什么，他说是劳动。他至今仍在劳动。我告诉他我的祖父刚过完100岁生日，他十分惊讶。我接着说道，在英国百岁老人都会收到一份非常特殊的礼物——女王亲自送的生日贺卡。他看起来更惊讶了。我于是开玩笑说，他100岁时也有可能收到习主席的贺卡。村民们都笑了起来，说这是个好主意。村主任说到时候他一定会送老人一张贺卡，但似乎跟习主席的比起来就没那么有吸引力了。

告别了村民后我继续往山里行进，想着这真是一个十分愉快的经历。我竟然是第一个来到邢家村的外国人，也许我会被他们载入邢家村的"村史"吧。

中午我们在一个可以尽览周围景色的农家乐休息，遇到一群夏令营的孩子也来到此地用餐。孩子们年龄8～16岁，来自全国各地，刚刚走完32公里，很乐意和我分享他们这一路上的趣事儿。最触动我的是这些孩子们在简单的徒步过程中收获了巨大的成就感，彼此间还建立起了亲密友谊。也许没有人比我更能理解他们，徒步给了我成就感，给了我友谊，还有许多其他宝贵的精神财富，尤其是在"这样的日子"里。

第24天
宁阳县的友谊盛宴

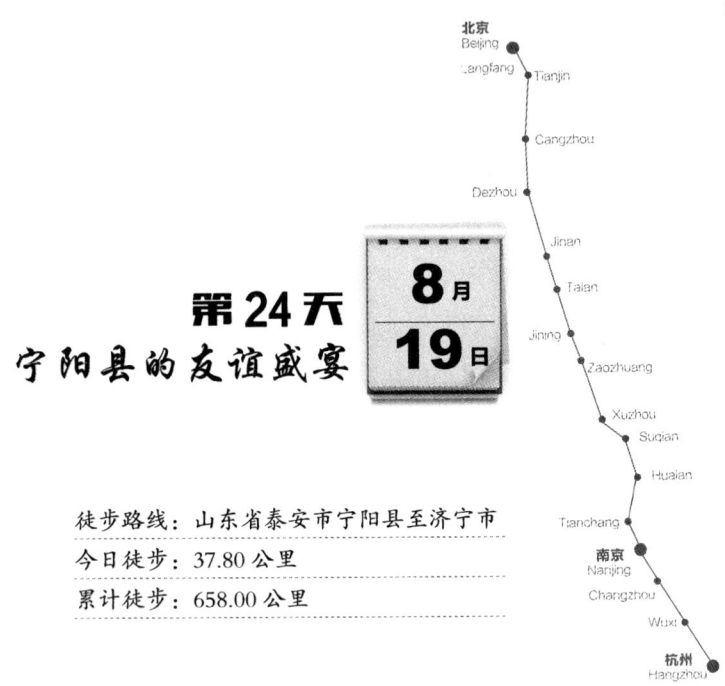

8月19日

徒步路线：山东省泰安市宁阳县至济宁市

今日徒步：37.80公里

累计徒步：658.00公里

    在整个徒步过程中，我感到饮食是中英两国文化差异最明显的地方。比如吃饭的时候，中国人习惯把各式各样的菜放在一个旋转的玻璃底盘上，大家一起吃，主人会不时给重要的客人夹菜，以表示对客人的关照和欢迎。如果你拒绝这番好意，对主人来说是非常不礼貌的。这样的做法会让西方人十分不解。对于西方人来说，大家一起吃饭一般是你想吃什么自己点，自己加调料。如果还想再多吃点，就自己夹。拿我来说，上一次有人给我夹菜的时候我只有4岁半，而且那人还是我母亲！

    我是一个饮食非常传统又简单的人，遇到自己不熟悉的食物常常拒绝，或者吃得很少。而在中国，让客人吃多吃好是非常重要的事情。一路上我能感受到，我的红十字陪同人员、每一个住宿的酒店，都千方百计琢磨什么食物更对我的胃口。有一天早晨，餐厅准备了煎鸡蛋。按理说早上吃鸡蛋再好不过，但我习惯于水波蛋，所以，我问有没有水波蛋？经过雪琳的解释，两个美味的水波蛋立刻端上桌来。我表示了感谢并告诉他们做得很好吃。结果，从第二天开始，每个住宿地的早餐都会有两个水波蛋放在我面前，我想，一定是有人把这个消息传递到了下一站。可自从有天我不怎么舒服，早饭时没碰这个水波蛋，水波蛋就自此从我的早餐桌上消失了。还有一天我实在是胃不舒服，早餐唯一能吃得下的就是清淡的果酱三明治，再配点绿茶。结果第二天吃早饭时，切好的白吐司、橘子果酱加上一杯绿茶就已经等着我了。那天我胃口不错，又吃了些橙子和哈密瓜。当然我们同样没有多说过什么。

今天路经宁阳县，张明女士告诉我说，当地领导希望邀请我在县政府午餐。我一听，心又沉了：我实在没有胃口，不想吃太多，而且下午还要走20公里呢。一想到要拒绝人家的好意，推掉夹到面前的菜，解释为什么我不能多吃，实在有点小烦恼。然而让我没想到的是，他们没有把我带到大桌子和旋转的玻璃底盘前，而是把我和雪琳让到一个小房间，桌子上摆好了适合我们口味的新鲜切片面包、橘子酱、绿茶，当然，还有水果。我顿时被他们的体贴和关怀所打动，也很为自己之前的想法惭愧。

一张餐桌，可以见证文化差异产生的趣事，也可以目睹文化差异产生的误解。但是，一旦我们明白了某些习惯背后主人的用意，餐桌就会变成一场友谊的盛宴。

第25天
追寻孔子的足迹

8月20日

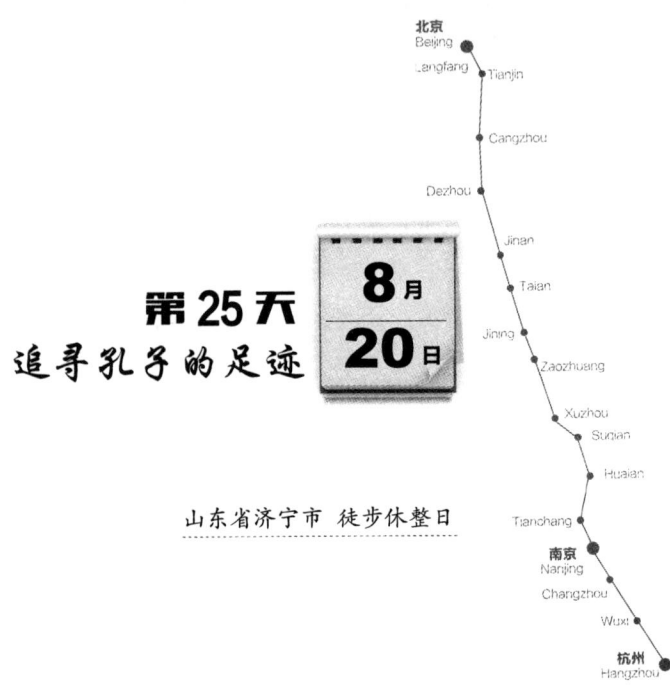

山东省济宁市 徒步休整日

"攻乎异端,斯害也已。"
"不忘久德,不思久怨。"
"听而易忘,见而易记,做而易懂。"
"譬如为山,未成一篑,止,吾止也。譬如平地,虽覆一篑,进,吾往也。"
"君子之过也,如日月之食焉:过也,人皆见之;更也,人皆仰之。"
"己所不欲,勿施于人。"

很多西方人都是听着孔子的名言长大的,只是我们一直不太了解它们的出处。今天来到了孔子的故乡,山东省曲阜市,我终于有机会感受这些智慧背后的切实意义,在圣贤诞生的地方思考如何把它们运用到实际生活中去。

孔子出生于公元前551年。他的父亲曾是鲁国军队的一名军官,孔子3岁时父亲去世。孔子所在的时代正好是中国封建社会的开端,而孔子却并非出身于封建贵族。在鲁国,权力和金钱主要集中在三大家族手中,每个家族都由一个卿大夫统领,在大夫之上,是鲁国的诸侯。

纵观孔子的政治生涯，他极其痛恨社会腐败与不公，尤其是那些以强凌弱的行为；他因宣扬高标准的社会道德规范，日后成为一名德高望重的老师；他没有蓄意挑战封建体制，而是努力营造一个高效而公正的社会，为将来的繁荣发展打下基础；他并不宣扬众生平等；他的官位也并不高，区区一个地方县官而已。当日后鲁国贵族变得整日观舞听乐、吃喝玩乐时，孔子很失望，便决定辞掉官位，周游列国，那年他54岁。

孔子侍奉鲁国公很多年，看到他变成这样，非常痛心。于是他的授课重点转向了宣扬他的政治主张，希望可以激发下一代人，帮助他们建立一个更好的政府。他游说了很多地方，但是很多观点并没有被接受。68岁那年，孔子回到了他的家乡曲阜，把他剩下的时间和精力都用于教书育人。

他教学的一个主要观点就是，要想成为一名好的领导者，首先要从在家培养好的行为习惯、孝敬父母开始。一个人在家里如果不是一个好儿子、好兄长、好父亲或者好丈夫，在公众面前也不可能成为一名好领导。道德高尚的领导自然会赢得下属的信任和尊敬，成为榜样。这和封建时代意大利的政治家马基雅弗利在他的《邦主鉴》中宣扬的思想完全相反。

天命观是孔子最伟大的思想之一。在徒步经过他家乡的时候，我对这一思想产生了强烈的共鸣。天命观认为，各国之间的纷争终将结束，一个基于道德、宣扬秩序、崇尚和谐的法制体系可以使各国和平共处；讲真理、守诚信应是人人尊敬的品德，而拥有这些品质的人，将会成为统治社会的中坚力量。

这是个多么伟大的思想，经过2500年思想长河的洗刷提炼，变得越发明亮。但是它的真正精华，还是体现在我们日常行为的点滴和生活中那些不经意的小事上。

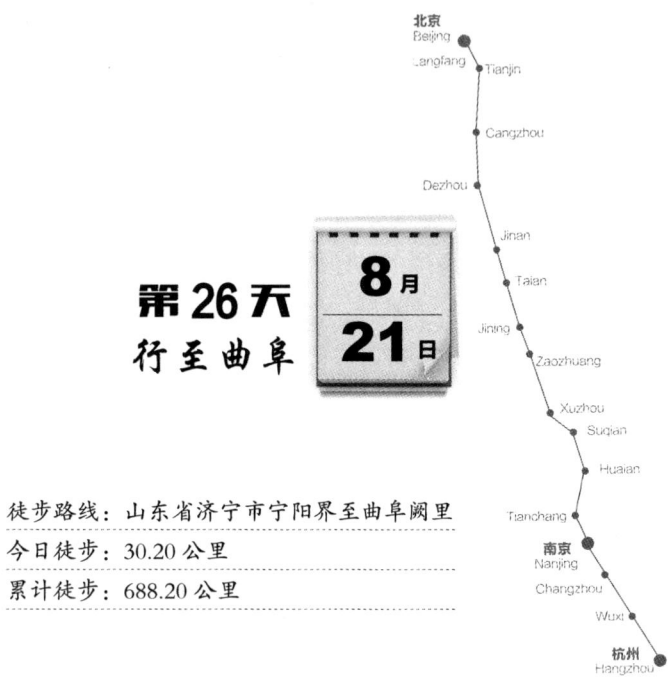

第26天 行至曲阜 8月21日

徒步路线：山东省济宁市宁阳界至曲阜阙里
今日徒步：30.20公里
累计徒步：688.20公里

毫无疑问，曲阜是我徒步中国至今最喜欢的一座城镇。

除了这里迷人的中国传统文化气息，今天早上与迄今为止两个年纪最小的红十字志愿者的相遇也让我很有感触。小陈和完颜来自曲阜第一中学，都是17岁，高中一年级。他们从微博上了解到"为和平徒步"并看到红十字会招募随行徒步志愿者的消息，就报名了。在徒步休息间隙，我们天南地北地聊天，能听他们谈谈对未来的希望和自己的梦想，感觉特别好。

完颜的理想是和爷爷一样成为一名医生，能够治病救人。年轻人经常会把家庭成员当成自己的榜样。榜样总能促使人自我激励，更上一层楼。我的个人经历就告诉我，一个人的成就大小并不在于先天赋予他的能力和才智，而取决于他如何充分利用和发挥自己的才能。

英国的伊顿公学是世界上最古老（建于1440年）也是最富名望的私立学校之一，被誉为"精英摇篮"，曾培育过不胜枚举的政界、科学界、商界、文化界领袖。有人曾告诉我，伊顿公学的前任校长在新生入学第一天的欢迎大会上说："伊顿曾造就过19位英国首相，而我希望你们将来做得更好。"

这位校长深谙成功人生的真谛，其关键在于拥有美好的愿景与规划，而不仅仅局限于是否有着出众的先天条件。换句话说，成功人生的真谛在于你要相信自己能通过努力实现目标，而非无止境地抱怨为何自己没有像他人一般的才智、美貌和背景。

世界级富豪、阿里巴巴CEO马云曾经在杭州当过导游，他高考三次落榜，且直到30多岁的时候才第一次接触到电脑。但在众人的怀疑之中，他始终没有灰心丧气，这点在他走向成功的道路上起到了极为关键的作用。请记住这句话："如果你觉得自己做得到，你很可能就真的做得到；如果你觉得自己做不到，那你很可能就真的做不到。"

以我为例，我身体已然发福，虽多年从政却也没为国家社稷立过大功。在我50岁之前我从来没有走过超过16公里的长距离，现在在我54岁时，我竟然敢于挑战北京到杭州1700公里的路程。每当我走完8公里时，我都感觉到我的整个身体快要散架了，真想找个椅子躺下算了，每次都是心中那份信念支撑着我走完接下来的30公里。20世纪30年代，一群法国科学家利用黄蜂来评估研究固定翼空气动力学定律，最后得出的结论是：黄蜂不可能飞起来，因为黄蜂翅翼的表面积和其自身的体重体型严重不成比例。但幸好黄蜂们不懂什么固定翼空气动力学，科学家的研究成果吓不倒它们。当试验器皿盖一打开，黄蜂嗖地一下就飞得无影无踪。想想，这多耐人寻味！

完颜已经在朝成为医生的道路上努力了，家中的长辈为他树立了榜样，更重要的是，他对自己充满信心。

在今天徒步即将结束的时候，我们路过了曲阜的一个酒桶厂。厂长非常好心地让我们在院子里的树荫下乘凉。休息间隙，我了解了酒桶的制作工序。他们是用纸做过滤，但这个纸不是我们日常所用的纸，他们使用的是"古法造纸"，就是用公元105年蔡伦在山东所发明的造纸术的工艺生产出来的纸。蔡伦造出世界上真正意义上的第一张纸，开启了交流的新时代。之前人们都是在丝绸或是竹简上书写，这些材料要么贵，要么重。造纸术从东方传到西方。在欧洲发掘出的最早的纸质文献已经是900年之后的事情了，而直到1490年，英国才正式出现造纸业。能看到1900多年前的造纸技术如今依然在曲阜熠熠生辉真的令我无比激动。当我要离开的时候，厂家友善地送给我几张通过古法生产的纸，我把它们小心收藏起来。

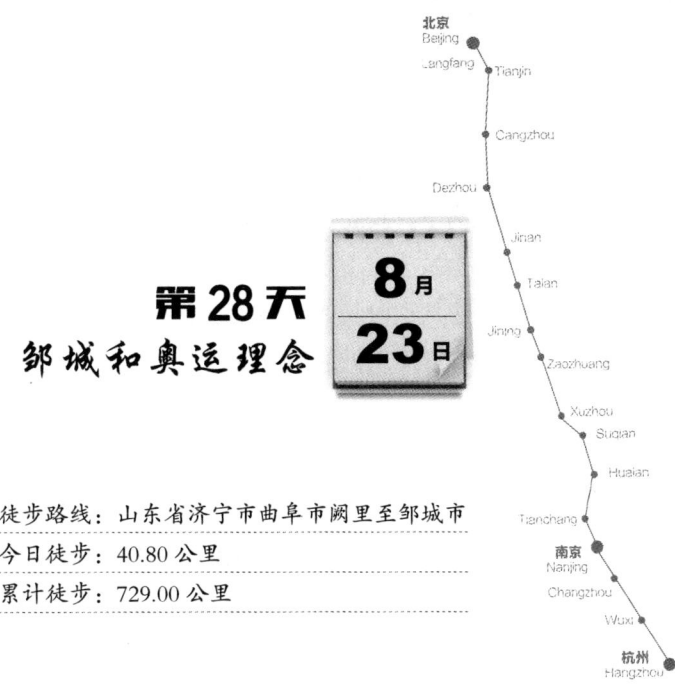

第28天
邹城和奥运理念

8月23日

徒步路线：山东省济宁市曲阜市阙里至邹城市

今日徒步：40.80公里

累计徒步：729.00公里

    今天我们于7点30分踏上征程。这是个天气晴朗的早晨，我们重新走上了国道G104，可以说自从在200公里前的济南踏上这条国道开始，它就成了我每天徒步形影不离的伙伴。

    行至曲阜和邹城的分界线时，我们不得不和来自曲阜中学的小陈和完颜道别。当我们分别时，小陈交给我一封信。他的英文手写体可比我的好看多了，语法也好，我忍不住诵读一遍。我在信中能感受到远超他这个年纪的深刻思想与成熟睿智。正因如此，这封信让我对未来充满信心。他写道："我认为和平并不是一国之事，而是与地球上的所有人息息相关。我们都是世界公民的一分子，所以我们必须为实现世界和平出一份力。" 我边读边祈祷每个人都真的能做到这点。小陈的信让我感到意外和感动，分手后他写的这些话一直回荡在我的脑海，觉得陈同学的观点和孔夫子的天命观中所倡导的和谐世界十分契合。我在心中祝愿他有美好的未来。

    这几天，北京正在举办世界田径锦标赛，我和雪琳会在晚上看转播。我热爱运动，如果我能任意改变自己的人生，我会尝试成为某个运动项目中的佼佼者，如此，我便有机会在全世界最盛大的奥运舞台上一展身手，与他人一较高下。我还记得之前看冬运会的冰壶比赛，在看到参赛队员们的主要职责是擦拭冰壶途经的道路时，我不禁对自己说："这个我也能做啊！"美好的梦想从那时起就扎根在了心中。我认为，全球性体育比赛的举办在减少国家冲突方面所做的贡献仅次于联合国。为荣誉而相互竞争、激发对手的斗志是人之天性。在过去，这些大多通过战争的方式得以体现。如今体育正以势不可挡的趋势将之取代。

当今的奥运会依旧没有完全实现公元前776年奥林匹克运动会创办之初所宣扬的和平理念。古时奥运会的举办之意并非在于庆祝竞技体育的成就，而在于庆贺五洲欢聚和共有的人道情怀。参赛的运动员不能携带任何代表其城邦的标志进入奥运会竞技场。在踏入比赛大门前，所有参赛选手都要暂时将自己所谓的政治身份搁置一旁，而在竞技场上，运动员们也只有一个目标，那就是为奥林匹克精神而奋斗。

如今我们离这个目标似乎仍有很长一段距离。我不禁暗想，有多少观众会打开电视收看两个不代表任何国家的运动员相互竞争的奥运会？有多少人会仔细倾听颁奖时所放送的奥运会会歌？又有多少运动员会在胜利时刻披上代表奥林匹克的会旗？我猜应该不会多吧。

第29天
雷德格雷夫与前赛艇运动员

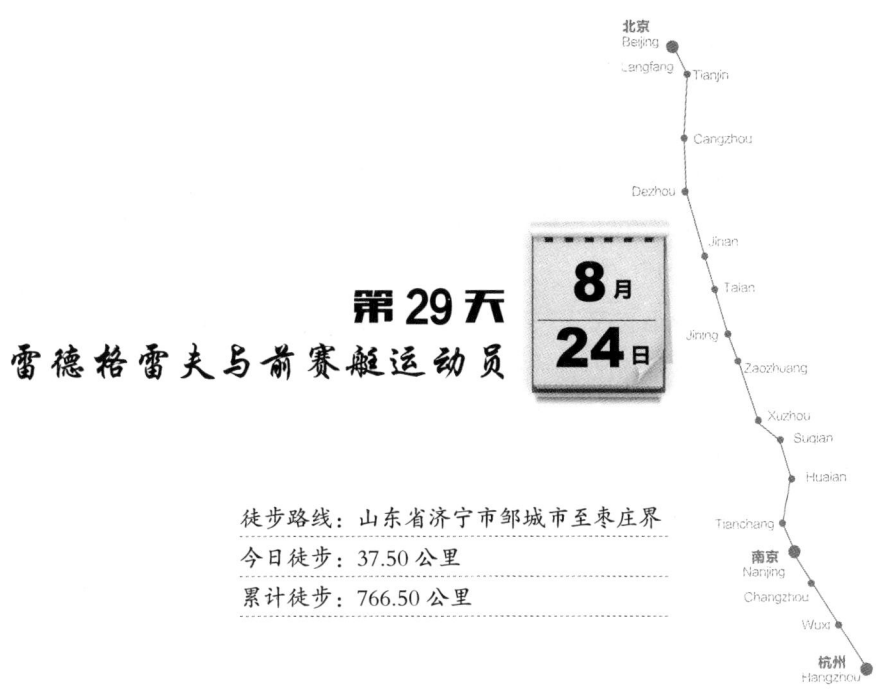

徒步路线：山东省济宁市邹城市至枣庄界
今日徒步：37.50公里
累计徒步：766.50公里

    今天加入的两位志愿者是退役运动员小王和小朱。小王现在是田径教练，小朱在体育局工作。小朱曾经是划艇运动员，亚运会金牌获得者。而鼓舞他坚持这项运动的便是他的偶像，英国赛艇运动员史蒂芬·雷德格雷夫。小朱向我展示了他手机里大量史蒂芬·雷德格雷夫爵士的照片。他是史上最伟大的赛艇选手，是世界上唯一一位从1984年到2000年连续参加5届奥运会并夺得5枚金牌的赛艇运动员，被女王授予爵士爵位。小朱告诉我们雷德格雷夫成为他的偶像不仅是因为他杰出的运动成绩，更因为他那坚韧不拔的伟大精神。他有糖尿病，每次比赛和训练前都要打针，但他从未放弃并成绩辉煌。这成为在那些艰苦训练中激励小朱的力量。

    一个远在英国的运动员居然对一个彼时还在山东上学的小伙子有如此深的影响，着实令我感慨。的确，有时我们根本不知道自己的言行给他人带来多少正能量或负能量。有人曾经问过一个问题，如果善言一次能得到10元钱，恶言一次能得到5元钱，你这一生究竟是会富有还是贫穷？

    我记得有次看英国广播公司（BBC）的节目，雷德格雷夫爵士又一次被授予了奖章,而他却把自己的奖章献给了来自英格兰马洛教区的弗兰西斯·史密斯先生。当被问及为何如此的时候,他说史密斯先生曾是自己上学时的英语老师。有一天这个英语老师对这个高个子男孩说:"你划过赛艇吗?我觉得你很有天分。"就是这寥寥数语的鼓励,成就了一位伟大的奥运健将,甚至间接激励了一名中国的年轻人从事赛艇运动。我很想知道这个小伙子为什么不再参加比赛了,他看起来还很年轻,遗憾的是我们没有时间长谈。

  语言有着惊人的力量。它能编织梦想,亦能摧毁梦想;能引人奋进,亦能令人绝望。据统计我们每天会说约三万个词,而其中微乎其微的十几个词便成就了一个伟大的奥运冠军,而十几个词也可能轻而易举地使一个梦想破灭。当我写下这些文字的时候,在朝鲜和韩国的非军事区,两国还在高声指责对方,这种言语交锋与导弹一样充满攻击力,使得这一地区处于恐惧和绝望的笼罩中。话语真的很重要,因为说过的话会被铭记。请谨言慎行。

第31天 孟子和理雅各

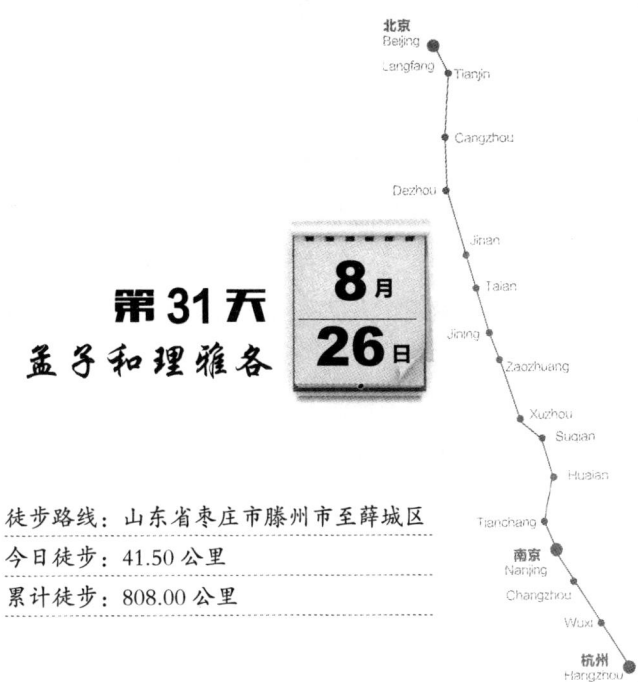

徒步路线：山东省枣庄市滕州市至薛城区
今日徒步：41.50 公里
累计徒步：808.00 公里

我们于昨天抵达徒步路上的重要一站也是山东的最后一站枣庄市，并将于今天走过 800 公里，这意味着我们就要完成整个行程的一半里程。昨天晚上的一场雷雨，使今天这里程碑式的一天空气格外清新，我们的徒步因此轻松了不少，上午的进度极佳。我们都想加紧步伐，一鼓作气，争取在下午 4 点以前到达目的地。事实证明我们做到了，在到达市中心广场后，我们结束了今天的行程。

昨晚枣庄市赵冠华副市长对这一地区的介绍，让我了解了不少这里的历史和经济情况。赵冠华副市长也是徒步爱好者，看上去年轻富有活力，还专程和我一起走了一程。我十分感激他对"为和平徒步"的兴趣和支持。想到迄今为止已经有十几位途经省、市的领导接待我，给我介绍当地情况，有的还参与到徒步中，我感到很荣幸。

思绪回到前天走过的邹城，这是中国历史上另一位伟大哲人孟子的诞生地。孟子是孔子儒学的传人，正是通过孟子我们才得以解读孔子《论语》中许多言论的真正含义。与孔子不同的是，孟子反对绝对服从权威，许多观点在某种程度上和西方先哲苏格拉底和柏拉图有异曲同工之妙。比如他有一句名言"尽信书，则不如无书"，反对盲目迷信书本知识。他还说过"民为贵，社稷次之，君为轻"，认为统治者必须倾听民众的声音，而对于人民来说，推翻罔顾人民的暴君甚至是一种义务。在公元前3世纪就有这样的言论，他是多么敢言的一位思想家啊。

孟子笃信"人之初，性本善"，且人性之善需要通过教育来引导。他还认为最终体现个人价值的是为社会付出了什么，而非从社会中得到了什么。这使我想起我的祖母最喜欢教导我们的一句话"施比受更精彩"，我一直在为做到这一点而努力。

我想起把孟子思想介绍到西方世界的先哲詹姆斯·理雅各。他曾是伦敦传道会的苏格兰代表，于1861年在香港居住期间主持翻译了《孟子》。事实上我在维基百科上发现，他于1873年曾和我走过同一条路线：从济南出发，南下经过曲阜和泰山，再经由枣庄转道大运河，抵达上海。

之所以提到这段历史，是因为我为自己的国家在鸦片贸易和洗劫焚毁圆明园事件中的所作所为感到羞愧。当时的西方人在传教热情和商业利益的驱动下盲目自大，对古老深邃的中华文明不屑一顾。理雅各是基督徒，然而当他拜访我此次徒步的起点北京天坛的时候，他觉得自己一定要脱鞋，以示敬意。他极力反对英国对华鸦片贸易政策，是禁止鸦片贸易协会的发起人之一。他于1876年起在牛津大学担任中国语言文学教授，毕生致力于中国经典名著、诗歌的翻译，译著收录在多达50卷的《东方圣书》中。

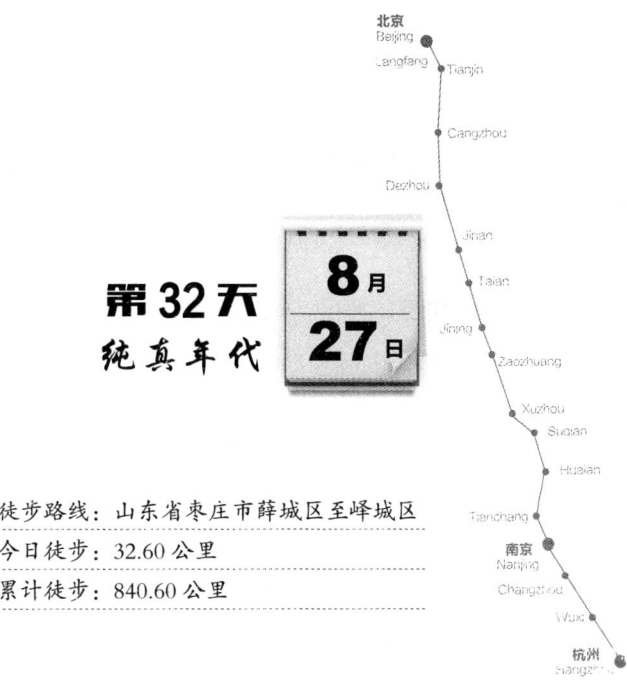

第32天
纯真年代

8月27日

徒步路线：山东省枣庄市薛城区至峄城区
今日徒步：32.60公里
累计徒步：840.60公里

　　昨晚的散步，让我再一次被这里的生活景象所震撼。相比英国，这里的市中心显得是多么热闹。街上人很多，街边的小摊靠着小电灯还继续做着生意，营造出游园会般的气氛。有家店铺门口的大屏幕上正在播放电影，几户人家围坐着看得津津有味。再走几步，则是一些人在跳广场舞。在我看来，这里的氛围之所以不同是因为没有人喝酒，而且男女老少都和谐共处。中国对酒的消费量很大，但人们通常是在家里或者在餐馆喝酒，街道是适合全家人出行休闲的地方，晚上10点后依旧如此。

　　广场上的舞者无论男女都衣着得体，我特别喜欢这种以家庭为单位男女老少聚在一起其乐融融的景象。中国人爱笑，而且是高兴起来大家一块儿笑，而在英国，我们很多时候是在"笑"别人，自己笑了，身边的人却不一定笑得出来。这跳舞的场景就像20世纪四五十年代在英国远郊的乡村舞会，轻松欢乐。在英国，老年人只和老年人来往，年轻人则只和年轻人玩，这种分隔让我们失去了老少共处的快乐。只有到了圣诞节和其他一些节日，长辈晚辈才会聚到一起——可能这就是传统节日的魅力所在吧！老年人都曾年轻过，年轻人也都将老去，所以老老少少应该学会多多共处，一同去发现生活中的快乐。

今天一路走来，我看到了迄今为止最美的风景之一。我们沿着当地新建的生态旅游区，或者说是沿着绿色的 G312 国道行进，沿途是延绵不断的石榴园，山上的寺庙漂亮气派，举目皆是美好的乡村风光。

途中我们在幸福农场停下来休息。我第一次见到葫芦，它们沿着葡萄藤生长，差不多有甜瓜那么大。葫芦象征着好运，人们常常将它晒干用来装酒。我们在农场主的葡萄藤下边休息边品绿茶，还借机好好欣赏四周的美景。我们的老朋友北京大学网络安全学院执行院长刘新元、武夷山慈心园茶博园开发有限公司董事长李少林女士和总裁薛建君女士特地从北京赶来支持我们，也陪着我走了一段。休息时薛女士给大家唱了首特别好听的中文歌。我问她唱的是什么，她说是首关于和平与和谐的歌。在手机伴奏下，她又唱了几首，歌声好似天籁般动人。之后我用手机播放了《我和你》——也就是2008年北京奥运会的主题曲。这首歌一直在我的"最常播放列表"里。我告诉雪琳，在认识她三年前，我就下载了这首歌，因为自打在北京奥运会开幕式上听过后，这旋律就在我的脑海中挥之不去了。

中国社会体现出一种纯真和教养，这些品质，在以年轻人为主流、充斥着性和酒精的西方文化中早已不复存在。希望中国不断对外开放、越来越现代化的同时不要失去这些美好品质——全家一起在晚上出门遛弯，大人们围着孩子转；希望这个东方国家能保持那份为她增添了威严与神秘感的含蓄谦逊。

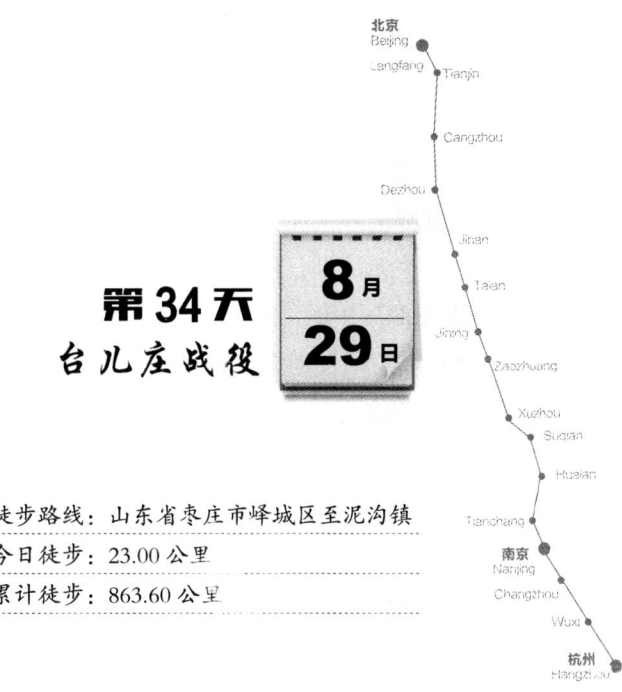

第34天 台儿庄战役 8月29日

徒步路线：山东省枣庄市峄城区至泥沟镇
今日徒步：23.00公里
累计徒步：863.60公里

    1938年在中国打响的台儿庄战役相当于1940年英国的不列颠之战，是一个重振精气的关键时刻。

    台儿庄是军事战略要地，地处津浦、陇海两大铁路干线交界处，不仅大运河穿城而过，而且还是江苏、山东两省边界。这是一座文化和历史地位很高的围城，这也就解释了为什么对于入侵中国的日军来说台儿庄那么重要。1937年抗日战争全面爆发，日军以优势装备迅速南下占领上海，首都南京陷落，日军意图通过占领台儿庄攻陷徐州交通枢纽，实现全面占领中国。在这样困难的局面下，一个大部分由农民组成的、装备落后的军队却在台儿庄战胜了当时强大的日军，使全军士气大振，坚定了全国军民抗战的决心。

    "二战"中的不列颠之战，也被视为"二战"欧洲战场的转折点，因为它阻止了德国入侵英国的计划，所以同样的，台儿庄大捷则是中国阻止日本入侵的转折点。一想到今年是反法西斯战争胜利70周年，这场战役的胜利就更具有重要性。

    我们乘船沿大运河到达台儿庄大战纪念馆，在这里后人深切缅怀、纪念那些为国家奉献出生命的勇士。所有国家都尊重战士们那种国家高于一切的勇气和牺牲精神，某种程度上没有他们的牺牲和奉献，就没有我们今天的国家，也无法享有和平与安全。在纪念馆我们听到了更详细的战争故事，也看到了战争中留存下来的文物、地图和艺术品。

参观的过程中有个记者来问我的感受。我首先表达了自己对中国军队的敬佩，他们为了战争的胜利牺牲了自己的宝贵生命。然后我表达了自己的痛惜，因为这些牺牲本不应该发生。这些战士被迫参与到战争之中，为了国家而战。我们应该来这里缅怀先烈，表达对他们的敬佩之情，并牢记历史，守护这得来不易的和平。

我用相机记录下了展馆里的中英文对照结语，因为它正好表达了我的想法："我们要学习他们坚韧不拔、宁死不屈、血战到底的英雄气概，为祖国的和平统一，为中华民族的振兴，为世界的和平与发展做出自己的贡献。"

第35天 前往台儿庄

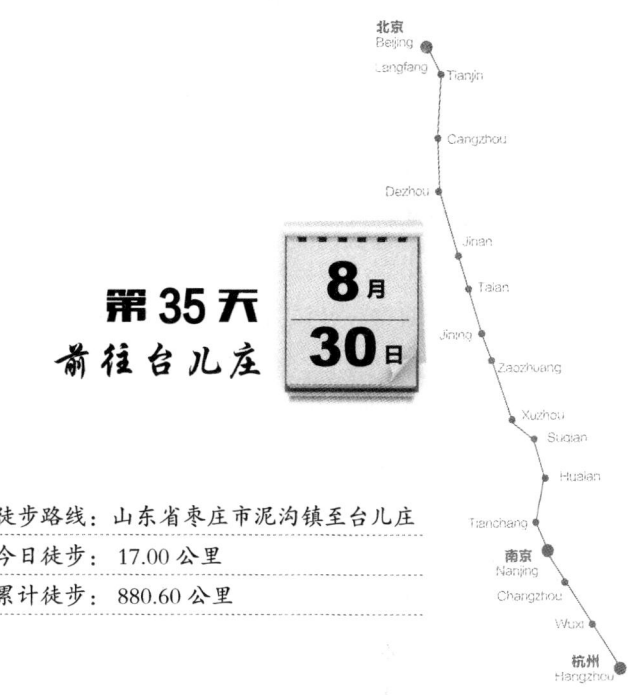

8月30日

徒步路线：山东省枣庄市泥沟镇至台儿庄
今日徒步：17.00公里
累计徒步：880.60公里

今天徒步距离较短，只安排了不到20公里，这是因为早晨、下午和晚上安排了好几个重要活动。

今天早晨，雪琳和我荣幸地受到全国人大常务委员会副委员长、中国红十字会会长陈竺以及中国红十字会常务副会长徐科女士的接见。他们于昨天晚上抵达，今天早晨就要赶回北京开会，我对他们在繁忙的日程下专程从北京赶来看望我表示感谢，也特别感谢了徒步以来中国红十字会给予我的帮助。我曾在英国议会与徐科女士有过一次愉快的会见，与陈竺会长则是第一次见面。他不仅是一位德高望重的国家领导人，还是一位造诣很深的医学博士，曾经留学法国，是一位典型的学者型领导人。他的儒雅风度与和善气质令人印象深刻。与陈竺会长的会谈令人鼓舞，我们谈到我即将到达的台儿庄以及那场著名的台儿庄战役，也谈到他的家乡江苏省，以及我徒步以来的感受，我想，在我的徒步进程中，这的确是一个难忘的经历。

明天就要离开山东进入江苏了，今晚山东省红十字会副会长为我们举办了一场简单的欢送晚宴。在山东省徒步持续了将近4周，我们和当地的团队已经相当熟悉。像李楠和刘师傅，我们之间已经超过了一般朋友的关系，就像亲人一般。

中国的餐桌礼仪，较西方来说，要复杂正式得多，而且因为幅员辽阔、民族众多，各地风俗不一样。比如在山东，与北京和其他地方又不一样。一般来说请客者，在这里称之为主陪，要坐在圆桌面向门或厨房的位置，这样方便和服务员交流，也可以及时迎接到来的宾客。最重要的客人是主宾，要坐在主陪的右侧。而副陪坐在主陪的对面，副主宾则坐在副陪的右侧。其他的座位也按照相应的礼仪分配，有时候客人之间可能会相互推让，让对方坐在更重要的位置。大家都就座后，按当地的风俗，主陪先讲话，然后是副陪，客人则是在最后讲话。

主陪招呼大家一同举杯。一餐晚宴，主陪要祝三次酒。每祝完一次，客人们要起身，轮番相互碰杯。就算在敬酒这个过程中，区分地位的礼节也十分重要：两人碰杯，相对年幼或是位分稍低的人的杯口，要比年长或地位较高的人的杯口低。这个礼节，常常会使得年纪位分相当的两个人相互谦让，尽量放低自己的杯子，来表示对对方的尊敬。中国的餐桌上通常都会放一个大玻璃转盘，食物就放在转盘上面。几轮祝酒之后，当需要再次敬酒的时候，客们人也可以不必起身，大家就简单用杯子碰一下玻璃转盘即可。

今晚，招待我们的主人敬完三轮酒之后，我尝试着想去回敬。可就在这时，我看到了雪琳示意我坐下。后来她解释说，按当地的风俗，要是我作为客人提议大家碰杯敬酒的话，那就代表晚宴就要结束了，而我们才刚刚开始，我敬酒是不合适的。之后，副陪又敬了三轮，然后等到果盘上了之后，雪琳微笑着端起了她的酒杯，我就知道，现在是时候我来回敬了。最后的环节是大家互相交换小礼物，一起合影留念。

在经历了中国上至早餐下至晚餐的餐桌礼仪之后，我觉得还是走在S344的省道上更省事儿，更"安全"。

第36天
你好，江苏

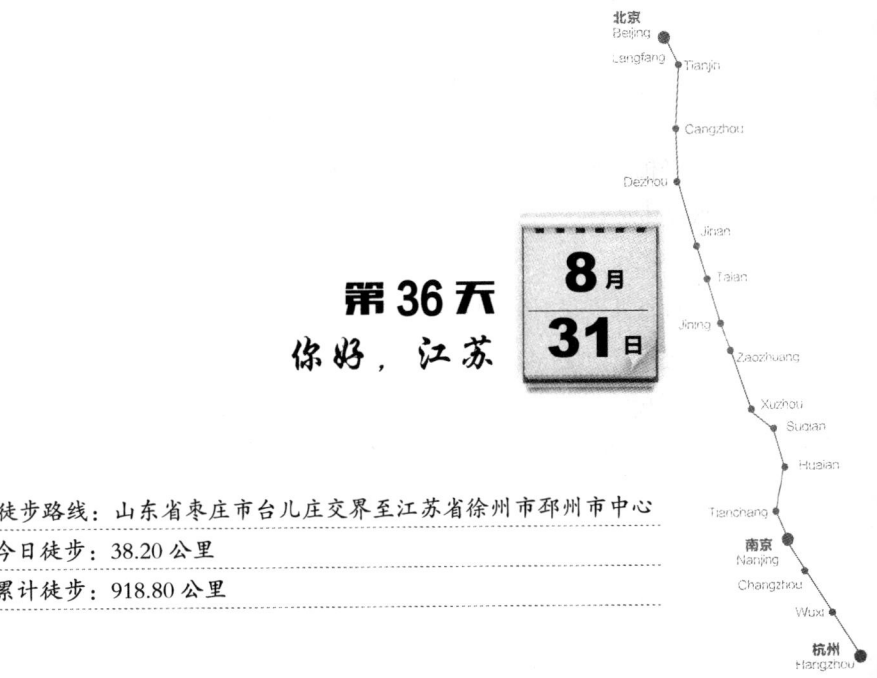

8月31日

徒步路线：山东省枣庄市台儿庄交界至江苏省徐州市邳州市中心

今日徒步：38.20公里

累计徒步：918.80公里

今天又是里程碑式的一天，我们从台儿庄跨过运河大桥，进入江苏省徐州市。今天也是令人感伤的离别日，我们告别了山东红十字会团队以及与我们在枣庄一同徒步的志愿者们。整整30分钟，大家都依依不舍地在桥边道别，合影留念。

我被大运河迷住了，禁不住在桥上停下脚步观赏。尤为吸引我的是桥下的造船厂，那里正在建造三只驳船。我的家乡在英国的泰恩河畔，那里的造船业名声响亮，焊工们在生锈的钢板上工作的画面深深印在我的脑海里。造船业是一项非常重要的战略性产业，所有发展中国家都设法通过有补贴的军事订单给养这一产业，刺激其发展。之后他们将造船业国有化，但最终这一产业会向造价成本更低的地区转移。就拿泰恩河畔来说，韩国造船业的兴起标志着该产业在这里的终结，但泰恩河畔地区很快转向了海上石油开发产业，因而许多原来造船业的技术被保留了下来。在此之后，我们又开始建设海上风电厂。谁知道下一步又会是什么呢？一组简单的数据告诉我们，世界上绝大部分新船是在东北亚制造的——41%在韩国，21%在日本，24%在中国，世界的其他地区加起来仅占到 6%。

邳州是中国著名的大蒜产区，沿途都是收获的大蒜和加工点。我停下来和一些农民聊了聊，得知这里的大蒜以质量好著称，不仅占有大部分国内市场，而且一直行销海外，包括英国，其最大的市场则是巴西。我们讨论了大蒜的种植，比如好蒜的标准是什么。他们告诉我质量好的大蒜，每瓣之间蒜皮完整而不开裂，且表面略有红紫色。这种颜色表明味道上乘，自然价格也高。我想起在伦敦常去的英国超市里，一头大蒜的价格约合人民币 5 元。我把这告诉那位蒜农后，他大笑着拿起 10 头质量最好的蒜，说 5 元能从他这里买这么多。这让我想起了一个关于全球化的有趣问题：一头蒜在邳州值 5 角，到了伦敦就变成了 5 元，4 元 5 角的差价去了哪里？我问蒜农，他说他也不知道，但我觉得他应该从蒜价中多获益些。

行程接近尾声时我又收获了一大惊喜。我们路过的一所学校的操场上正在进行传统民俗表演竹马戏的彩排，人们身上的传统服饰绚丽多彩，古老的民间乐器营造出热闹的气氛。学校的孩子和他们的家长围着操场，对表演如痴如醉。表演的情节是大家所熟悉的那类，角色有正有邪，经过艰苦较量，正义最终战胜了邪恶一方。多么完美的一场表演！

这不就是最原汁原味的文化交流吗？在当今英国，许多的文化活动已经专业化了，但我今天看到的表演，纯粹是当地蒜农自发的文化活动。它既没有当地政府的文化事业拨款，也没有任何企业提供赞助，只是当地人聚在一起，为自己的历史和文化欢庆。这场表演里所有的元素都是原创的：从缝制戏服，到制造、涂绘面具，到奏乐等，由各家各户各尽所长，手工完成。这种本土家庭元素，使传统文化更真实。表演的每分每秒都让我如痴如醉，这正是我想看到的真正的中国。

第37天　邳州的"希望之家"

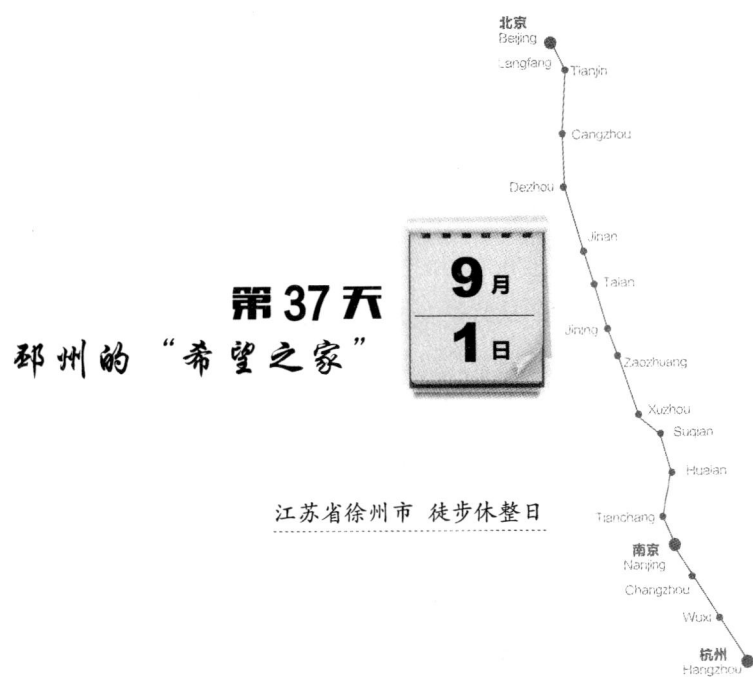

江苏省徐州市　徒步休整日

今天参观邳州红十字会"希望之家"康复中心对我和雪琳产生了强烈震撼。在这里，我们目睹了超凡的勇气、乐观、执着，以及对生命的渴望。这是一次永生难忘的经历。

在理疗室里，我们停在一个小女孩的床前。她大概两三岁的样子，因脚踝及膝盖骨畸形正在接受治疗。她仰起头，冲我们笑了一下，好像在说"我没事，没有看着那么难受的"，我被她的勇气深深打动。走到隔壁的屋子，里面放着一台机器，有个5岁左右的小男孩正在用那台机器练习踏步。他面对着墙，这有助于他集中注意力。当我们经过的时候，他抬起头，想要向我们展示他能迈出一大步，尽管很艰难。他努力迈上台阶，再迈下来，反复进行了好几次，每完成一次，我们都为他欢呼。他的理疗师礼貌地示意我们差不多可以离开了，否则小男孩会不停做下去。实际上每次疗程，他最多只应该做一两次。这般对生命的热忱多么让人感叹！我已经是做爷爷的人了，看到他们，心里很不是滋味。他们是孩子，可以是任何人的孩子。我这个年纪，在中国，小孩叫我"爷爷"，可是今天，当希望之家的孩子这么喊我时，我的眼睛湿润了。在他们稚嫩的脸庞上，我仿佛看到了我的孙子马修的样子。

希望之家建立于20世纪90年代。当时邳州遭遇了洪水灾害，水质污染导致小儿麻痹症疫情爆发。600多个1~3岁欢蹦乱跳的孩子感染了小儿麻痹症，从此失去了行走的能力，其中100多个孩子只能爬行。当时的邳州市红十字会会长也是防疫站站长张辅世先生自此将自己的命运和这些孩子的命运牵系到一起，把自己的一切都献给了孩子们的康复，他的夫人、子女也都投入到这项事业中。他白手起家建起"希望之家"，倾尽全力收治病残儿童，为他们筹款治疗。为了让孩子们有一技之长将来能自食其力，为了让他们活得更有尊严、更快乐、更健康、更自信，"希望之家"组织孩子学文化，用练乒乓球和其他体育锻炼的方法帮助孩子们进行康复训练。经过他们的努力，"希望之家"竟有100多个孩子考上了大学，获得一技之长、有了工作，建立了家庭。"希望之家"还成为"奥运冠军的摇篮"。就在这里，诞生了2012年伦敦残奥会12枚金牌得主和2枚银牌得主。2016年里约残奥会，他们蓄势待发，希望再获佳绩。

我们所生活的社会，通常会把遭遇不幸当作一种资本，习惯认为自己的不幸处境不是自己造成的，而是别人的错，亲人、社会应该竭尽全力来弥补自己的损失。但是，请看看这些孩子，他们的不幸简直难以言喻，但是他们的脸庞上依旧洋溢着欢乐与希望。他们的确是生活的受害者，但是他们没有自暴自弃，怨天尤人，他们通过自己的努力成为生活中的赢家。我在学校的留言簿上留下了整整三页让我动容的话语：尽管学校因为培养出了许多出色的运动冠军而闻名于世，但在我眼里，今天我在学校遇到的每一个人都是冠军，不论是那些坚强的孩子们，理疗师，他们的父母、祖父祖母，还是学校的管理者。对希望的执着，让他们成为生命的强者。这种信念激励着我们每一个人。

当年的孩子们现在已经30多岁，各自有了工作和家庭。"希望之家"的创办者张辅世老人已经辞世，他的儿子和儿媳妇继承了他的遗愿，希望之家转为继续救助脑部残疾的儿童，而年轻的一代也为"希望之家"带来新的理念。目前除了红十字会，还有很多组织在背后默默支持着它的运营，这其中还有来自挪威的国际合作开发署，不断有来自世界各地的一批又一批的志愿者到这里来志愿服务。

我们最后来到大教室，一个五岁左右的孩子，用熟练的英语欢迎我们，然后全体孩子演唱了中国传统歌曲《好一朵美丽的茉莉花》。我得知孩子们是特地为我和雪琳学习演唱这首歌曲时非常感动，大概是因为之前我徒步的时候无意间提到过，这是我和雪琳最爱的歌曲，在我们的婚礼上还唱过吧。演唱结束后，我被邀请讲几句话，我站在那里，却热泪盈眶说不出话。

我非常感谢能有机会亲身体会这一切，我知道，"希望之家"的精神能在未来的日子里一直激励着我勇敢向前。

第38天
体育与和平

9月2日

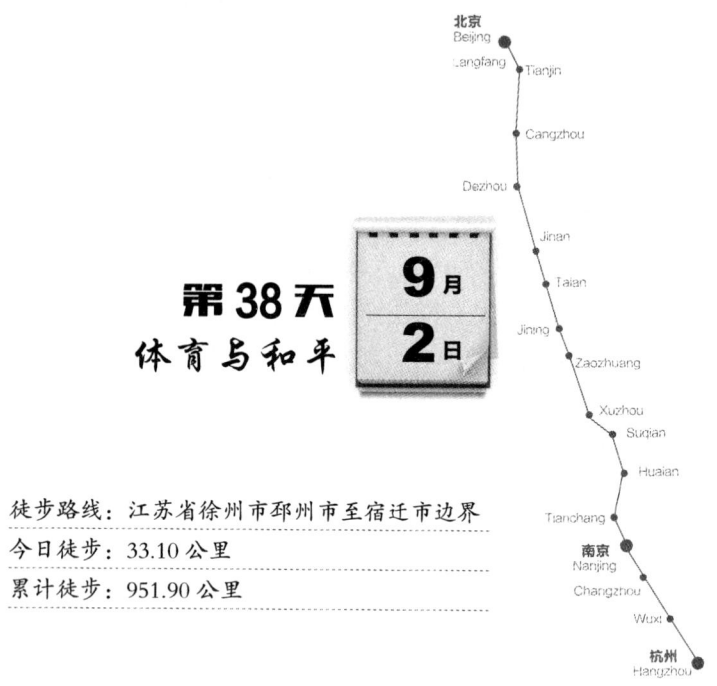

徒步路线：江苏省徐州市邳州市至宿迁市边界
今日徒步：33.10 公里
累计徒步：951.90 公里

今天是很安静的一天，雪琳和张明女士都回北京去参加反法西斯战争胜利 70 周年的大阅兵观礼了。截至下午 5 点，我们一共徒步了 33 公里。因为结束得早，我得以到沙沟湖水杉公园悠闲散步。从北京一路走来，我一直感叹中国的公园都特别棒。不仅公园维护得好，连路边的篱笆也修剪得整整齐齐，或许是因为这边的劳动力成本较低吧，但这种对公共场合的维护恰好体现了社会的价值。

漫步河边，我看到不远处的亭子旁边有一片篮球和羽毛球场地。所有场地都有人在使用。我很喜欢篮球。我的儿子马修在美国读大学时是个非常出色的篮球运动员，后来他成了一名篮球教练。我喜欢和他一起讨论各种赛事，看他打球或是看他训练球员。

看着公园场地里正在进行的篮球比赛，我不禁对人性还有体育有了些许感悟。体育和商业一样，在许多方面都对维护社会秩序有着非常重要的作用。原因很简单。

首先，我们必须承认人类天生就喜欢竞争和划分领地。竞争对手可能是一块儿打球的同事或同学。一个队伍里很快就会划分出等级,谁非常有潜质,谁资质平庸。比赛一开始,选手们可能有些摸不着头脑,但是用不了多久,大家就可以看出来谁最有天赋,然后便由他掌控局势。然后其他队员就可稍稍放松,接受自己在团队中的地位,享受同伴的陪伴。

其次,在一个团队里,队员之间的友谊在平时可能并不凸显,但在比赛中一个团队对抗另一个的情况下,队员之间的友谊与合作会增进许多。团队内部打比赛时,大家都是一个个散落的个体,而一旦面对竞争对手,队员之间的纽带便会加强,大家不再嬉笑打闹,而是牺牲小我,齐心协力为了团队的荣誉而奋斗。比赛前,大家还都是朋友,可一旦划分出两队,不同队伍的选手就像是来自两个国家似的,铆足劲儿要和对方一拼高下。

第三,在观看公园场地的篮球比赛时,我发现了两个非常有趣的现象。一开始旁边场地有两个漂亮的姑娘在打羽毛球,打完后,她们就到篮球场地来看比赛。这一来,场上的男球员立马变得不一样了。小伙子们甚至都不用看这两个女孩,光是知道她们在球场旁,两边队员的气势和能量就足以提升,他们的身体对抗变得更加激烈,叫喊争执也增多起来。这个现象再正常不过了,因为竞争和较量的背后就是男性想要显示自己的强大,从而赢取异性芳心。话是这么说,可男孩的这点心思似乎没起到太大的作用,因为两个姑娘没多久就离开了,篮球赛也随之恢复到了原来的节奏。

第四,我一下子就注意到,场边有一个两岁左右的中国小男孩,非常可爱。他和他的妈妈也在看比赛。每次男孩的妈妈让小男孩自己站在地上,他就会想去玩篮球,总是跟着球往场地中央跑。是什么使得这个两岁的男孩想要参加比赛?为什么你给小男孩一个棍子,他会立马用这个当作武器然后去戳别的孩子?为什么你把同样的棍子给个小姑娘,棍子就成了一个魔法手杖?这就是基因还有男性激素作用的结果,它们决定了男性天生就喜欢竞争,喜欢用武力来建立自己的权威和领地。

你可能会觉得这是胡说八道,好吧,也许。但是如果你看看现在世界范围内最热门的一些电脑游戏,像什么英雄联盟、反恐精英、魔兽世界、使命召唤、坦克世界,你会发现里面充斥着各种搏击和战斗。

那些当权的政客和军事精英，越能承认这种基因所决定的天性，人们也就越能清醒地认识到是什么让人们陷入战争、恐怖主义、暴力。这种好斗的本能和天性越多发泄到篮球场上，世界也就变得越安全。

第39天　9·3大阅兵

9月3日

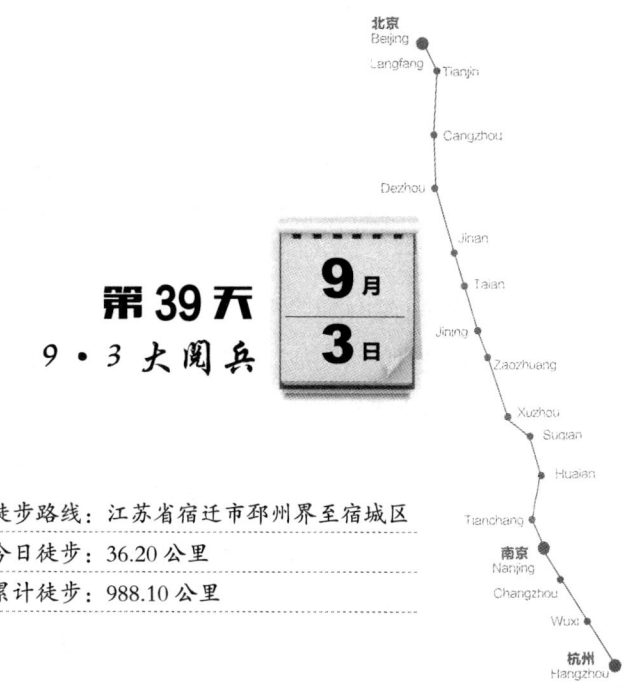

徒步路线：江苏省宿迁市邳州界至宿城区

今日徒步：36.20公里

累计徒步：988.10公里

今天，北京举行了中国人民抗日战争暨世界反法西斯战争胜利70周年大阅兵。雪琳作为英国华侨代表非常荣幸地受邀前往北京出席阅兵观礼。对于中国人来说，这是个重要的盛典，可谓举国瞩目。市民期待着这个时刻，等在电视机前观看阅兵直播。

今天的徒步计划是36公里。为了能省出时间观看典礼，我和红十字会随行人员商定早点出发，争取10点钟赶到蔡集镇，在镇上找个地方看直播。抵达蔡集镇的时间刚刚好，朱镇长把我们请到他的办公室。那里有一个漂亮的大电视，观看阅兵直播的效果特别好，还有无限量续杯的绿茶。

阳光明媚，蓝天下的天安门广场宏伟庄严，静静迎候着这一盛大仪式。据说参加阅兵的部队官兵多达1.2万人，另外参与展示的还有500多件重型武器和200多架飞机，我看数量远不止这些。典礼以简短的部队行军和军演开场。被检阅的士兵们看起来几乎就像机器人一般，每一步都整齐划一。训练有素的部队离不开每个个体的努力；牺牲个人的想法、身份，甚至是生命来实现集体的利益，这种品质使人类变得无比强大。

多年从政的我对习近平主席在典礼上的讲话感触颇深，他讲道："正义必胜！和平必胜！人民必胜！"我相信这几句话一定会传遍四海。

阅兵典礼有条不紊地进行，没有半点差池。首先出场的是"二战"老兵，这样的安排很妥当，因为战争能够胜利，老兵们功不可没。这和几周前在伦敦进行的"二战"胜利纪念日仪式差不多。伦敦这个纪念庆典在英国女王的主持下进行，整个国家向"二战"中7.1万名死去的英国士兵表达感激，并向生还者予以荣誉表彰。在仁安羌战役中，如果没有中国远征军前去营救被困住的英缅一师，英方的死伤数量还会更多。

每个国家都有一段不能忘怀的历史。英国的白厅纪念碑前，常年放着花圈；教堂里，总有一隅是为纪念牺牲者、宣扬和平而设置的。伦敦纪念日典礼的最后是骑兵展示，同时皇家飞行队在天空呼啸而过。看起来伦敦纪念典礼和北京阅兵表达感谢的方式不一样，我认为这种不同源于两国的不同经历——英国历史上没有遭受过任何国家长达8年的残酷侵略。伯明翰或曼彻斯特那样的大城市，也从来没有像南京那样目睹包括男人、女人还有孩童在内的30万公民被屠杀。

阅兵典礼的最后，7万多只和平鸽与上万个气球，寄托着中国人民对和平的祈求和对未来的憧憬，一齐飞向天空。时代在改变，过去的一切终将是历史。现在的日本拥有民主市场经济，而不是"二战"时的天皇专制，正如现今的德国也不再是"二战"时的纳粹集团，而英国，也早已不是鸦片战争时期侵略中国的那个英国。每个国家在历史前进的过程中，都会经历不堪回首的黑暗时期，中国也概莫能外。

阅兵结束了，是时候继续我的徒步啦，向宿迁进发！

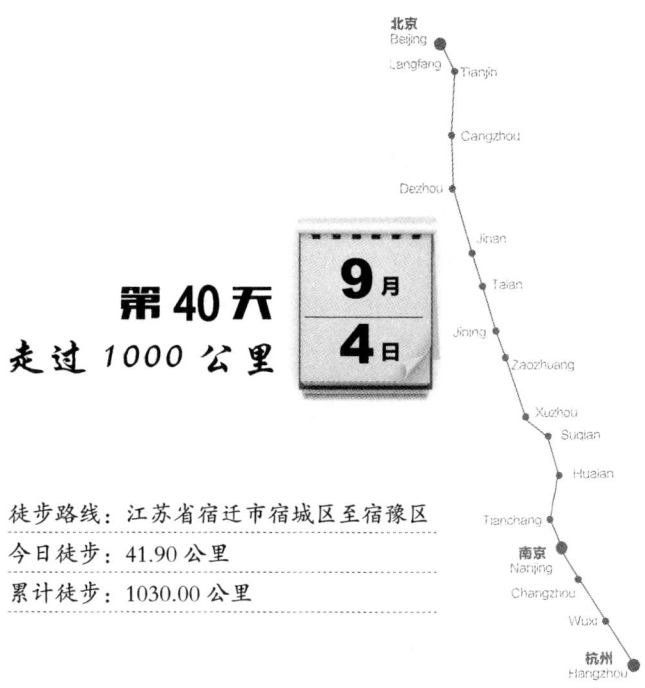

第40天
走过 1000 公里

9月4日

徒步路线：江苏省宿迁市宿城区至宿豫区

今日徒步：41.90 公里

累计徒步：1030.00 公里

旅途中我发现了许多趣事。以前在国外每次雪琳和我入住酒店时，她都会打电话给前台索要牙刷和牙膏。对于此事，我一直觉得挺怪的。现在在中国，我发现无论宾馆多简单多朴素，牙刷与牙膏外加一把梳子和浴帽一定是房间的标配。

另外一件趣事是，我走了5个星期完成了900多公里，可旅程中只见过一个"老外"。在中国那么久才看到一个"老外"让我没想到。再想想中国在全球经济中的重要作用，这就更让人惊讶了。

在路途中我的两个儿子为了能和我保持联系都注册了微信，这是中国的一个社交通讯软件，功能类似 What's app 以及 Facetime。如果要让我说说当前什么最让人惊喜，那就是我坐在中国乡村宾馆的前厅还能与身处美国得克萨斯州的儿子进行30分钟的视频通话。我可以通过视频和孙子马修聊聊开学这几天的近况，而他也能在屏幕里向我展示他的家庭作业。我还可以和正在巴西的儿子艾利克斯侃侃那些英超球员的转会续约新闻。视频通话的画质同样一流，并且这一切全都是免费的！这究竟是怎么做到的？

经过一天的长途跋涉我到达了宿迁市中心。这是一座美丽的现代化都市，坐落在骆马湖畔。宿迁有着丰富独特的地域文化，同时也是中国古代英雄项羽（公元前232年—公元前202年）的家乡。项羽的生平经历和亚历山大大帝十分类似，不过比亚历山大还要早上100年。亚历山大大帝在20岁时成为马其顿帝国（现在的马其顿共和国）的君主。他在位期间，马其顿帝国的疆域一度扩张到非洲，到了公元前320年，其领土几乎触及目前中国的西部。然而，亚历山大大帝在32岁那年去世。项羽在27岁那年成为西楚霸王并征服了强大的秦朝，死时年仅30岁。

有句古话叫"好人不长命"，纵观历史，许多了不起的人物都不幸英年早逝，比如：戴安娜王妃、肯尼迪、圣女贞德、安妮·弗兰克、马丁·路德·金、巴迪·霍利、李小龙、莫扎特和凡·高等等不胜枚举。公元前442年，希腊哲人希罗多德首先提出了这一观点，后来借威廉·华兹华斯长诗《远游》中"英才易早逝，皆因尘埃填心渴欲饮，烛烧成灰泪方尽"的诗句而广为人知。不过威廉·华兹华斯本人倒是活了80岁。从某种角度来说，对于这些人物，大家所记住的都是他们的年轻活力以及那戛然而止的生命留给大众的惋惜。但我却发现，随着年龄增长，我越来越不赞同这一观点了……

噢，对了，雪琳和张明女士参加阅兵观礼后也及时从北京赶了回来。我们在通往淮安的S325省道上相遇，大家在路边一家蘑菇厂门口搞了个简单的仪式，庆祝我已徒步1000公里。

第41天
国际生态四项精英赛

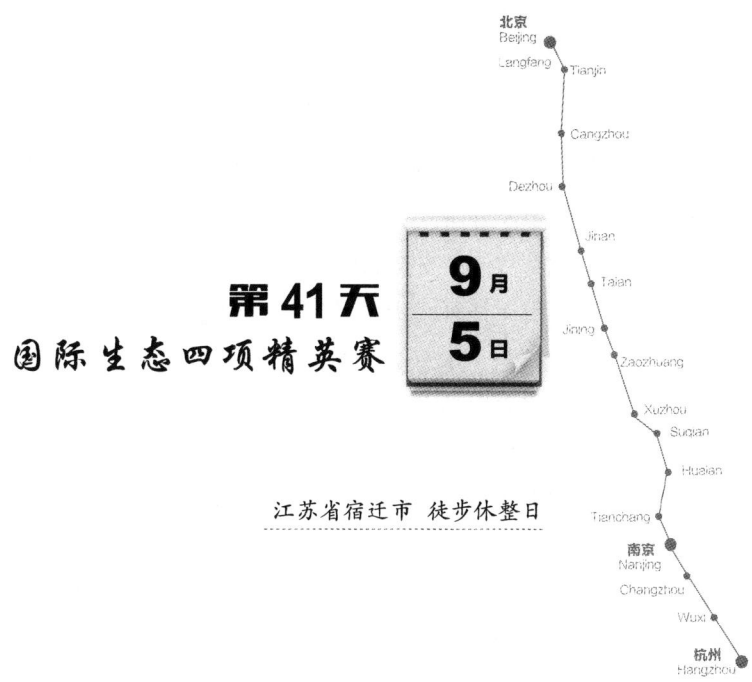

9月5日

江苏省宿迁市 徒步休整日

今天是休息日，我们荣幸地受邀参加"2015年宿迁骆马湖国际生态四项精英赛"开幕式，我还受邀在开幕式上讲话。昨晚赛事T恤送达了我住的房间，虽然T恤尺码有点小，但由于徒步稍稍瘦了几磅，我居然成功穿进去了，还是挺开心的。

到骆马湖的时候，我们惊讶地发现成百上千名运动员还有赛事工作人员早已聚集在了湖边。这是一个国际赛事，还有不少外国运动代表队。四项精英赛事包括跑步、自行车、游泳和皮划艇，比赛总距离超过58公里。"生态四项精英赛"中的"生态"就是指将激烈的体育竞争和自然环境融合到一起。策划者希望通过这个赛事，让人们更好地意识到体育可以为人们提供更多探索自然的机会。

我们总说，这个世界太过拥挤，然而如果地球上所有的人肩并肩站在一起，一个洛杉矶大小的地方(500平方英里／1295平方公里)就足以容纳所有。实际上，我们拥有足够多的空间，但是因为经济发展的原因，人们的目光都集中在了城市。随着全球化的扩张，我们需要改变目前的工业化趋势，加之先进的 IT 技术和快速发展的网络技术，我们没理由都挤在昂贵、污染严重的城市。开幕式上，我们得以与宿迁市委书记魏国强和市长王天琦相识，我非常赞赏他们支持这样一个关注生态环境的赛事。

我在开幕式上的致辞以"生态（Eco）"一词为主题。Eco 这个词来自于希腊语，本意为"家园"。所以生态学（Ecology）的字面意思就是关于家的研究和学习。生态精英赛实际上是为了加强人们对共同家园的关注，加深大家对这个家园的了解。很多时候我们喜欢从政治角度去审视这个世界。地图上条条线线将地球划分为 200 多个国家和地区，其中还有许多区域存在领土纷争。

然而，国家之间的边界是出于法律秩序考虑而人为划分的。曾经有人告诉我，如果你有机会从太空站向下俯视我们的蓝色星球，在白天你根本就看不见人类的痕迹，除了苏伊士和巴拿马运河，还有中国的长城。在晚上，你也许会看见人类聚居的地方灯光闪烁，然而却并不能看出任何迹象告诉你哪块是英国，哪块是美国，从哪儿到哪儿是中国的地盘，瓦努阿图的领土又在哪儿。所有的国家、城市、山川、沙漠、河流和海洋全部交织融汇，共同构成了这个美丽的星球，构成了我们共同的家园。

有些事情一个国家靠自己的力量就能够解决，然而关爱我们的星球、我们的家园，却需要所有国家一起努力；对于环境的保护，每一个国家都应该参与进来，为之努力；维系我们的家园，不是一个人或者一个机构的责任，而是全人类共同的义务。所以"生态（Eco）"不只是你我的事，而是我们大家的事。生态或许无法改写历史，但我们现在的行为却注定影响未来。我希望宿迁对保护生态所做的努力不只局限于此，而是将它继续下去，将生态环保的理念传播得更广更远。

第42天
笃信人性本善

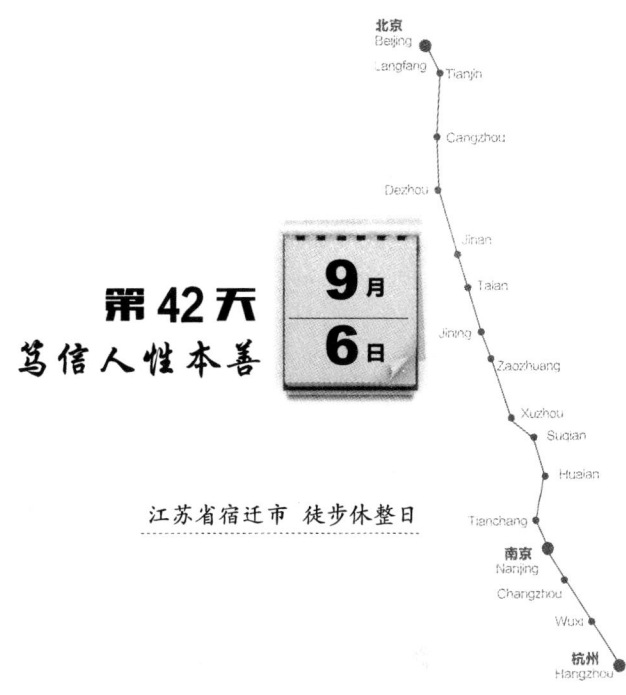

9月6日

江苏省宿迁市 徒步休整日

此次徒步能和红十字会一起工作，我和雪琳一直心怀感激。这让我们有机会遇到很多鼓舞人心的人，了解他们从事的伟大事业。邳州"希望之家"的参观还历历在目，我们一到宿迁，就又受邀参观了宿迁市儿童福利院。和邳州的"希望之家"一样，宿迁市儿童福利院从这些残障孩童一出生就开始照顾他们。但不同的是，宿迁市儿童福利院还是一个孤儿院。

刚出生的孩子毫无过错，却带着残疾来到人世，这样的事情总让我们痛心。难道仅仅因为残疾，这些孩子就被父母抛弃？孩子是父母爱的结晶，这种爱本应呵护他们的一生，可他们却……我几乎不忍心想下去。当然，我说这些并不是要指责这些父母，因为我无从知晓他们在做出抛弃孩子的决定前都经历了什么，想了什么。我在福利院只停留了一个小时，如果需要长期不分日夜地照顾这些孩子，我对这些父母的看法会不会有所改变？

和在"希望之家"的经历一样，这些年轻生命最震撼我的，是他们身上满满的爱与快乐。为了补偿他们在身体和智力上的缺陷，上帝似乎赋予了他们更为强大的内心和灵魂，而这种巨大的内在力量感染着他们身边的所有人。

我和福利院的员工及护理人员交谈，他们说这种感染力是支撑他们工作的重要力量，但他们也还有别的任务。

原来除了提供最及时的医疗护理，福利院还要为孤儿们安排收养家庭。孤儿院有一片区域被称为"荣誉厅"，骄傲地展示着这里曾照顾的孤儿和他们来自世界各地的收养家庭的合影。我心中溢满了对这些收养家庭的崇敬，顿时想起了《圣经·马太福音》中的格言："不论你为了谁，所行何善，即使行之甚微，天道酬善。"

我一直都愿意相信人性本善，虽然有的人并不认同。他们说，自身利益是人类行动的唯一理性根源。我却坚信孟子的性善论，我们前几周才走过这位伟大先哲的家乡邹城。他曾用一个故事阐释人性本善：若陌生小孩落井，众人都会焦急紧张，为孩子担心。这种心理，非欲讨好孩子有钱的父母，非欲取盛名于乡里，非忧虑不施援手招来指斥，而是因为动了不忍之心、恻隐之心。孟子认为，这种"恻隐之心"是人类所独有之本善的起点。

我们的电视和手机屏幕常常被关于世界各地人类种种恶行的新闻所覆盖，这有时会让人忘记人性本善。事实上，人们缺乏的并不是"恻隐之心"本身，而是激发"恻隐之心"的机会和经历。我和雪琳今天有幸得到了这样的机会，我想我们的生活将因之改变。

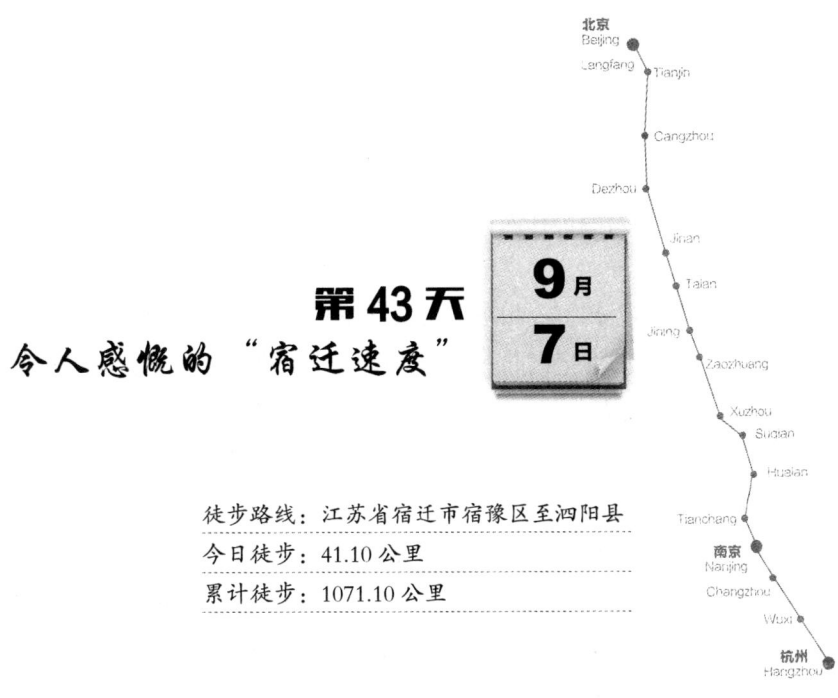

第43天
令人感慨的"宿迁速度"

徒步路线：江苏省宿迁市宿豫区至泗阳县
今日徒步：41.10 公里
累计徒步：1071.10 公里

　　昨晚与魏国强书记和王天琦市长再次相会。二位也都是实打实的徒步爱好者，他们都十分希望将宿迁打造成一个"更适宜徒步的"城市，希望听听我这个远道而来的英国人的意见。我受国际生态四项精英赛的启发，不失时机地提出了建议，宿迁可以创世界之先，每年举办"为和平行走"活动。国际生态四项精英赛的成功之处就是做到了运动与生态环境的有机结合，那么"为和平行走"也可以借助这个理念，将和平与生态环境的因素融合起来。我的建议得到了他们的热情回应，当即就想到了三台山森林公园，认为那儿会是一个不错的活动举办地。当得知我还没有机会到访三台山森林公园时，几位领导和雪琳把我"晾"在一旁用中文热烈交谈了好一会儿。交谈的结果令我喜出望外，第二天一大早 7:30 徒步前往淮安之前我们先去参观三台山森林公园，并在那里的国际友好交流纪念林种一棵树。我的疑问是去公园简单，但现在已经晚上 8 点，还是星期天，工作人员又如何在如此短时间内组织好这次植树活动呢？"放心，这里是宿迁"，是他们给我的回答。

　　回到房间已是晚上 10 点，雪琳收到一条短信希望确认明日（星期一）植树纪念牌上的中英文字。早上我们从宾馆出发来到了令人心旷神怡的三台山森林公园，在入口处等待我们的是一位导游以及几辆小型高尔夫球车。这位英文导游言简意赅地在五分钟内介绍了三台山森林公园并将我们带至了纪念林前。魏书记和王市长以及许多志愿者已经在那儿等着我们了。

魏书记指向一边的两棵树，告诉我说这就是我们一会儿要种的两棵桂花树。桂花树是宿迁的市树，也是雪琳家乡、我们此行的最终目的地杭州的市树。我们手持铁铲，走向种植地点，一块写有中英文的纪念种植仪式的牌碑已经立好了。

那么短的时间是怎么筹备好这一切的？我还没缓过神来呢，一旁有人端着相机咔嚓咔嚓记录下了我们植树的过程，转眼间魏书记和王市长和我们道了别。从开始到结束似乎只有五分钟！

他们走后我一个人静下来开始思考，如果在英国组织这样一场活动需要多久。除去星期天这个客观事实不说，我估摸着还得有规划审批、树木健康检查、纪念碑内容审批，此外，根据欧盟采购条例，树木以及铁铲的采购还需要公开招标，在场出席人员也得接受检查确保他们具备足够的卫生安全经验来监管植树过程。当然全面的风险评估以及法律责任豁免也必不可少。种植过程中须有急救受训人员在场，参与植树者还须穿戴高能见度反光夹克、保护手套、保护鞋具、保护帽以及护目镜。最后，专门针对下雨的应急预案也要有所准备。

而在宿迁，他们就是"放手去做"……这也许就是欧盟经济增速1%被称为"复苏"而中国经济增速7%却被称之为"走缓"的缘由吧。

第45天
小小淮安，大大世界

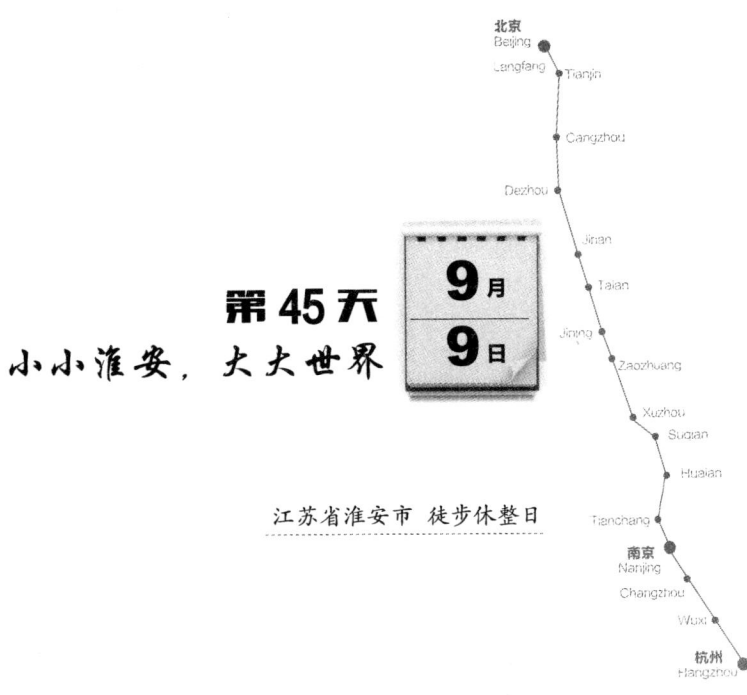

江苏省淮安市　徒步休整日

　　淮安在中国知名度甚高，不仅因为它是京杭大运河上的一颗明珠，还因为它是中国国务院前总理周恩来的出生地，淮安人为此深感骄傲。我承认到淮安前我并不是很了解周总理，但下午在周恩来纪念馆的参观，使我对他肃然起敬。周恩来相貌堂堂，曾到西方留学，从1949年到1976年，担任国家总理长达27年。他是中国的思想革命先锋，相当于西方的共产主义革命英雄切·格瓦拉。周总理一直对毛主席忠心耿耿，对人民鞠躬尽瘁，被称作"人民的好总理"，在中国深得爱戴。周恩来纪念馆展示了周的生平，其中事迹十分感人。有机会到淮安，建议去看看。

　　现在是快速抢答时间：中国的周恩来总理与美国著名的基督教福音布道家、自杜鲁门以来11位美国总统的属灵顾问葛培理牧师（Billy Graham）有什么关系？答案是这样的：淮安是周恩来总理的出生地，也是葛培理的妻子路得（Ruth Bell Graham）的出生地。路得的父亲在淮安是位医生，也是位医学传教士。后来路得一家人搬去朝鲜平壤，路得在那里的一所基督教学校上学，和朝鲜开国国家主席金日成成为校友。有趣的是周总理也是一位外交家，他曾在日内瓦会议和朝鲜战争后的万隆会议上缓解了冷战对峙的紧张态势，并组织了1972年尼克松总统的访华，带动中国走向世界。而葛培理牧师最大的外交成就是促进了20世纪90年代早期朝鲜半岛南北双方的关系。

真可谓小小淮安，大大世界。

第46天
市委书记在和平村

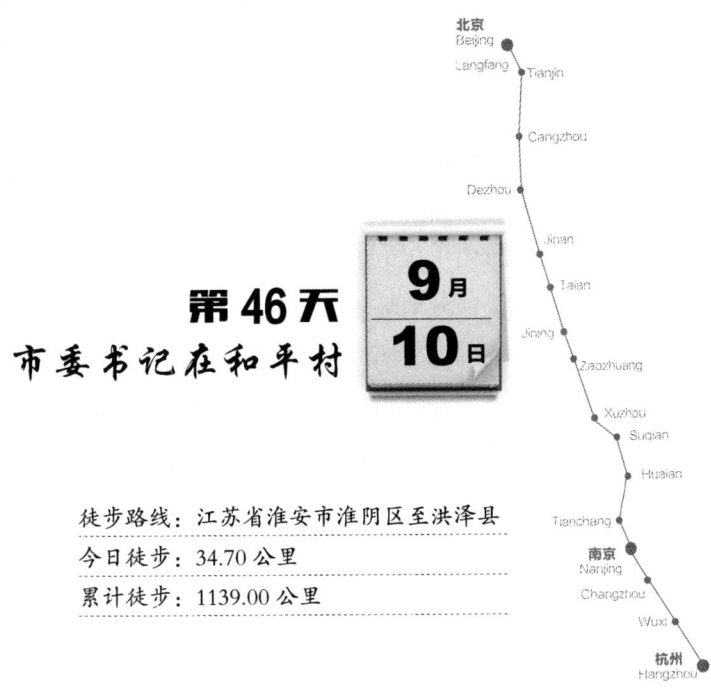

9月10日

徒步路线：江苏省淮安市淮阴区至洪泽县
今日徒步：34.70 公里
累计徒步：1139.00 公里

徒步第46天，沿着S205省道顺路而下，公路上已经可以看到"南京——215 km"的路标牌，这令我士气大增。

午休时间，我们停在S205省道旁的一个小镇。"贝茨勋爵，欢迎您光临淮安，您这次可真是选对了休息的地方，这里是和平村！"一位身材高大、气质优雅的男子面带微笑操一口流利的英语来到我的面前。这位迎接我的英俊男士正是姚晓东博士，现任中共江苏省淮安市市委书记。要向西方人解释清楚市委书记在中国的重要性可不简单。但倘若打个形象的比方，将伦敦市市长、伦敦警察局局长和伦敦红衣主教的权力相叠加起来，那就几乎八九不离十，相当于市委书记职位的权力了。淮安是一个有着500多万人口的地级城市。

正因如此，当看到市委书记姚晓东身着蓝色的"为和平徒步"T恤衫，刚刚结束北京的会议回到淮安就赶来这里，当地的志愿者们简直忍不住要揉揉自己的眼睛看看是不是真的。作为一名政治家，所有"套路"我早已熟知，我的意思是当我早晨被告知有一位特殊来宾要前来与我一同徒步时，我脑子里想象的便是象征性地一起走几步路，拍大量照片。但是，这位姚晓东书记却和我一同走完了今天下午的全部 12 公里。

我们边徒步边聊。从他口中我得知，他不仅多次造访过伦敦，还和我们共同的朋友韦鸣恩勋爵一道在英国国会的上议院餐厅共进过午餐。这段对话使得昨天提到的已经够"小"的淮安变得更"小"了。我了解到，姚晓东书记的学术背景和早期职业侧重点和新闻有关，这对于市委书记来说算是很少见的，以前见过的一些书记大多是做管理出身的。

我们就淮安当下所遇到的如何确保在经济增长的同时不污染环境这一挑战进行了一番详谈。淮安整体地势平坦低洼，各种水域交织，有着潜在的洪涝风险。对于淮安人来说，拥有关于水位上涨以及气候变化模式的知识储备并不是为了进行科学探究，而是"生存需要"。我们还谈到了医疗保健等话题，姚书记十分希望能够从英国国民医疗服务体系中汲取经验。我很高兴，我们的国民医疗服务体系不仅在英国国内获得好评，还得到来自中国的认同和赞许。

徒步结束后，姚书记邀请我共进晚餐。我们品尝了当地特产小龙虾，书记还介绍了小龙虾的奇迹，它是如何带动了一个贫困地区的发展，这让我对这里再次刮目相看。

姚书记和我一样都是哈佛大学肯尼迪政府学院前院长奈伊教授的忠实"粉丝"。奈伊教授关于美国要增强"软实力"以推进其战略目标的言论非常著名。软实力是指相对于军事、贸易圈等硬实力而言的文化、教育、旅游、体育、商业、艺术，等等。我们就中国的软实力储备以及如何在未来运用这些软实力又谈了很多。其实，正是"软实力"将来自中国共产党和英国保守党的两个政治人物联系在一起。通过这次坦诚的交流，我们更加尊重彼此的文化。

说来也真是奇怪，人们对于某些地方的记忆很多时候并不来自当地看到的景物，而是在于所遇见的人。在淮安城与和平村遇到的这些可爱的人们，将永久留存在我美好的记忆中。

第47天
准备在南京金陵中学的演讲稿

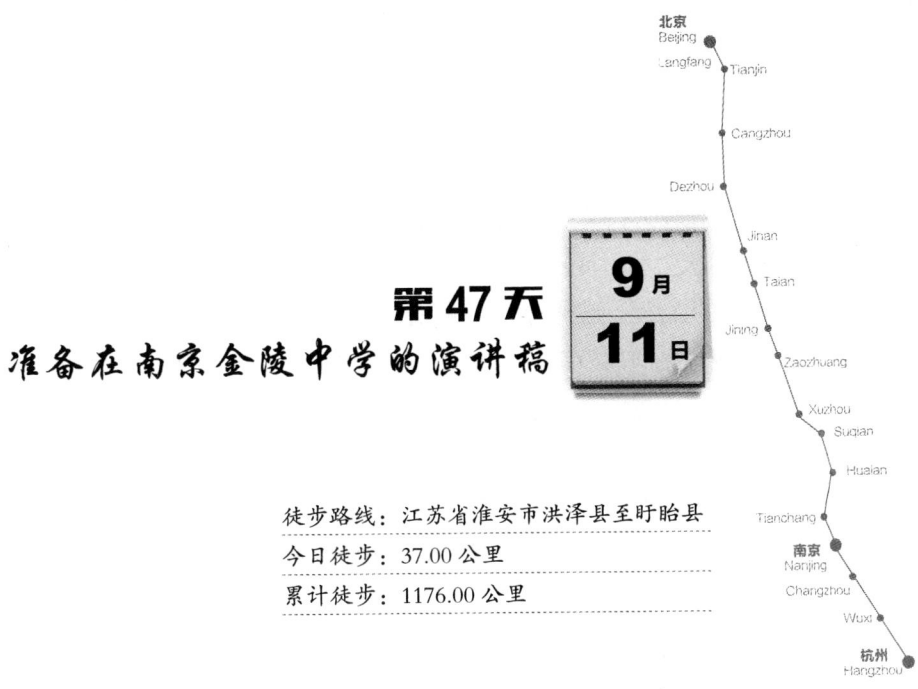

9月11日

徒步路线：江苏省淮安市洪泽县至盱眙县
今日徒步：37.00公里
累计徒步：1176.00公里

    我们此行最重要的一站南京就在前方，按计划我将在南京金陵中学就文化在构建和平中的作用做一个演讲，该演讲已被列入中英文化年的系列活动。路上我一直在构思演讲内容，先在这里和大家分享我的底稿。

    我坚信：文化能够连接你和我。若想深入探讨这个话题，我们首先必须弄清什么是文化。文化（culture）这个词，在英语（更准确地说是拉丁语）中和农业（agriculture）有些相似，这给予了我们一些启示。"文化"一词的意义与"耕作"（cultivate）紧密相关，字面上讲就是"栖息、耕作和养护"思想和灵魂。文化被认为是人类有别于其他物种的决定性因素，正是培养思想和塑造灵魂的能力，将我们与其他动物区分开来。

    将文化描述为耕作，这种说法根植于这样一种设想：文化的土壤要足够肥沃。在数千年甚至是百万年里，我们缺乏这"肥沃"的土壤。然而似乎又是在很短的时间内，文化的土壤又变得沃野千里，盛满了诸如壁画、音乐、图腾崇拜、宗教仪式和神话传说等千变万化的内容形式。当毫不相干的原始部族结束采摘渔猎的流浪生活，定居下来从事耕作的时候，人类文化开始突飞猛进地发展。

在今天，文化已经深入到世界的每个角落和生活的方方面面。我已在18个国家为和平徒步，走过7000多公里，还从未见过哪个国家没有自己强烈的文化特征，这种特征体现在食物、语言、音乐、服饰、艺术、戏剧、宗教、传统、民间故事等各个方面。随着电影、电视和互联网的出现，我们的世界似乎正在走向文化全球化，许多国家正在努力守卫其传统文化，因为文化对于一个地区、种族乃至国家的自我认知至关重要。

这是为什么呢？这是因为文化是我们的根，是自我归属感的来源，是"我们从何处来"这个问题的答案。每个家庭都有自己的文化——母亲做的饭、父亲坐的椅子、最心爱的歌、纪念照、最喜欢的服饰、独一无二的传统……这些"家庭文化"塑造了我们，是我们身份的来源。我们当然不能指望每家的文化都完全一样，但我们不该惧怕差异，如果我们能包容不同文化，社会就得以繁荣发展，众人也都将从中获益。

然而现实并非如此理想。我们的新闻中充斥着战争与冲突，就在当前，全世界还有40多场战争正在进行中。问题出在哪儿？我认为争端皆因文化而起，皆因一部分人认为自己国家的文化应当支配世界，别的文化都不重要。在徒步路上我与各个国家的人交流，我惊讶地发现他们都认为自己国家的人民最友好，食物最美味，音乐最动听，战士最骁勇，景色最美丽，历史上的领袖最伟大，宗教最饱含真理……

如我所言，文化是我们人类认知的核心，所以当有的人试图贬低某种文化或用自己的文化取而代之时，他们其实是在贬低乃至摧毁我们作为人类的特征，这当然会挑起敌意，造成严重后果。举个最简单的例子：你试试批评你最好朋友的妈妈做的菜，看看你们还能做多久的好朋友？

请允许我用另一种方式解释这个问题：刚来到人世时，我们的"硬件"和"操作系统"都是一样的。随后不同的家庭、文化和教育不断给我们装上不同的软件。我这台电脑上的文件、照片、邮件、应用等等和另一台的不同，但它们能够互相连接，因为最根本的"操作系统"允许甚至鼓励我们连接，因为文化恰恰需要交流。我们越是尊重彼此的文化，我们的交流也就越多；

交流越多，猜疑和不信任就越少，尊重和理解就越多。人类关系中的理解与互信越多，冲突的可能性就越小。所以，文化能连接你我。我们只有勤于"耕作"，才能收获和平的果实。希望我能为大家带来些许启发。

第48天
"为和平徒步"的十万个为什么

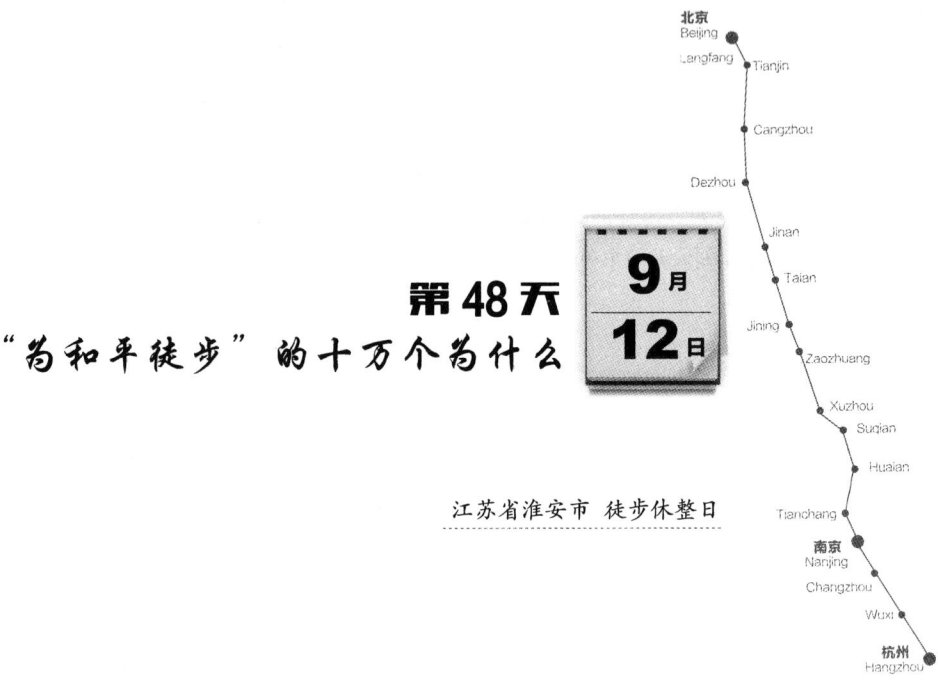

9月12日

江苏省淮安市 徒步休整日

在我一路从北京往杭州的徒步旅途中，人们问得最多的就是"为什么"。请允许我在这里一一作答：

为什么要徒步？

当我还是个孩子的时候，我卧室的墙上挂有一幅地图，我从那时起就常常幻想自己能够有一天走遍全世界。这只是我年少时的一个梦想，却一直没有机会去实现它，直到2009年，有一次我鼓励一群年轻人去放手追梦，他们却反问为什么我没有去追寻自己的梦想，那时我便下定决心，开始踏上徒步征途。很快地我就意识到作为一个年近半百的准爷爷级人物，我要给自己的徒步一个清晰明了且富有意义的定位。随着年龄的增长，我们的体力不如从前，但是心力却随着时间的历练而更加坚定。于是我决定为"和平"而徒步。此外，我还发现我可以通过徒步为慈善事业筹集善款。自2011年起，我在夫人雪琳的支持和陪伴下每年都会进行一次长距离徒步，如今我已走过18个国家，行走路程加起来超过了8000公里，已筹得超过12万英镑的慈善善款。

为什么是为和平徒步？

进行长距离的徒步需要有一个足够强大的理由和信念支撑，对于我来说，这个理由和信念就是和平。人们因试图通过战争与暴力而非和平对话的方式来解决分歧而造成灾难性后果的例子在电视新闻以及历史书白纸黑字的记录中比比皆是。我记得曾经看过许多军人行军备战的黑白历史照片，我经常会想，需要做些什么才能让他们不必走上战场，要做些什么他们才能欢庆和平？我至今仍旧没有找到答案，但是我发现，宣扬和平可以避免这些无谓的损失。

为什么在中国徒步？

今年是特殊的一年，全世界人们都在纪念人类史上最惨烈的第二次世界大战结束70周年。中国在"二战"中伤亡惨重，我原本的徒步路线（北京至南京）就是为了向中国为"二战"做出的贡献致敬。此外，今年也是首届英中文化交流年，通过举办各种不同的文化活动，我们能更好地认识到体现在体育、教育、时尚或茶饮等各方面的文化如何拉近两国间的距离。最后，之所以最终决定本次徒步起于北京止于杭州是因为北京是中国的首都，而杭州是雪琳的家乡。有人曾对我说："麦克为宣传和平从北京走到南京，而为爱情从南京走到杭州。"我想这话概括得不错！

今年徒步为哪家慈善机构筹款？

雪琳和我十分高兴能与中国红十字会在此次徒步中密切合作。中国红十字会是世界范围内最大的志愿者组织之一，每年约有超过200万的志愿者定期参与到慈善工作中。他们的工作包括教授急救培训、组织捐血、资助贫困家庭、灾害应急等等。在中国红十字会的帮助下，我们在江苏省选定了两个项目作为这次徒步所筹善款的资助对象：一个是位于邳州的专门关爱治疗残障儿童的"希望之家"；另一个是专为残障孤儿提供帮助的宿迁福利院。我们在徒步间隙访问了上述慈善项目所在地，在那里，我们被红十字会工作人员专注认真的工作态度以及工作成果所深深感动。至今我们已经接受了超过500位社会热心人士的慷慨捐助，已筹得17万元人民币。我非常希望在10月5号我们抵达杭州时，该数额能够突破50万。

徒步中最深刻的印象是什么？

要说给我留下深刻印象的事物，首先是中国人民的热情与友好。这些可爱的人们来自各行各业：赶羊群的牧羊人、卖石榴的小贩、坐着小木船在湖面上采菱角的阿姨、维修道路的工人、加油站的服务员，面店外玩棋牌的老者们，以及前来与我一同徒步并且给我引路、确保我安全的红十字会志愿者们。这一路上似乎我遇到的人都兢兢业业、努力工作，我真心钦佩他们。紧接着给我留下深刻印象的是城市外随处可见的自然美景、运河水道两侧成荫的树林、荡漾着莲花的小湖、巍峨壮丽的泰山等等。第三件令我印象深刻的事是我徒步经过的那些路面的质量。从北京出发徒步至今，我所走过的道路已经不胜枚举，而中国公路的路面质量完全可以和欧洲道路媲美，有些路段甚至还优于欧洲。

在中国徒步所遇到的最大挑战是什么？

经过了近50天的徒步，我已经走过了1200公里并到达了江苏省淮安市。最大的挑战毋庸置疑来自天气。身为英国人，我不怕雨，但有点受不了酷暑。在这儿，气温高湿度也高，又闷又热，在这种天行走真的是极具挑战性，有那么个别几天我们不得不在正午12点至下午3点时段停止徒步，在树荫下休息片刻。我已经54岁了，体力也不是很好，在如此天气下徒步真的是让我有点举步维艰。

徒步至今最难忘的经历是什么？

途经泰山的时候我路过了一个小村庄叫邢家村，记得那里的人们围坐在一棵参天古树四周，见到我后，他们热情地邀我加入。我们就一同围坐在500岁的古树下，喝着从700岁的古井里打上来的清凉的井水。他们谈了当地的风土人情，我也分享了伦敦的生活点滴，大伙好不快乐。其中一位村里最年长者还告诉我，我是迄今为止他们村里的首位外国客人，这位老人2015年已经95岁且还是一位经历过"二战"的老战士。大家看着照片，聊家庭，聊食物，十分投缘，这一幕仿佛让人一下子回到了20世纪50年代。接着大家一起合影留念，随后，就如同这里汲水于井一般自然，村民们纷纷掏出了智能手机开始扫描我们的二维码，这样一来便可以通过微信交流共享所拍的照片。我不禁感叹，这真的就是个地球村，大家之所以有幸成为其中一分子，不是因为我们来自不同国家，而在于人类彼此间的共性。

第49天 时尚盱眙

9月13日

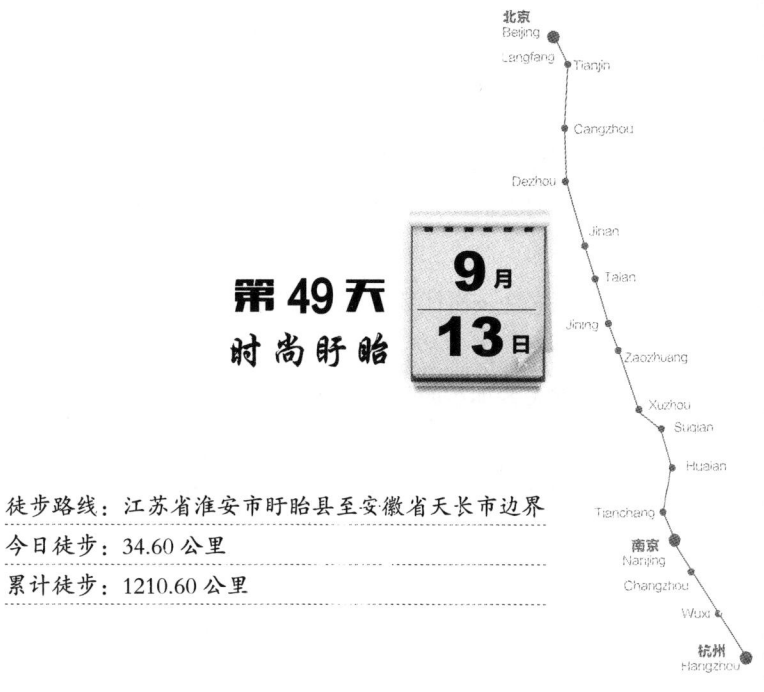

徒步路线：江苏省淮安市盱眙县至安徽省天长市边界
今日徒步：34.60 公里
累计徒步：1210.60 公里

"Vogue"在法语里是时尚的意思，也是世界最著名的流行时尚杂志的名字。Vogue 杂志于 1892 年诞生于美国，现在在全球 20 多个国家发行，其中也包括中文版。这个词甚至衍生出一个英文习语：如果说某人"in Vogue"就表示这个人很时尚。为什么我要讲这些呢？因为今天我们下榻在洪泽湖南部盱眙县的沃阁（Vogue）酒店，所以我觉得自己是真真正正的"in Vogue"——特别"时尚"。

酒店员工对我们的照顾真的是好极了，对我的"为和平徒步"非常钦佩，提出不收我们的房费以表示对我们的支持。雪琳耐心地解释说，我们坚持要全程自己承担所有住宿费用，但如果他们愿意，可以把钱捐给我们支持的红十字会邳州"希望之家"和宿迁福利院项目。没有想到的是，酒店连夜发动全体员工为我们筹集善款。当晚，酒店就转给我们一张两万人民币的大支票，这一善举让我们非常感动。

让客人满意是中国文化的一部分，甚至可以追溯到孔子的理念。比方说沃阁酒店的厨师想要让自己做的菜品符合英国客人的口味，于是早餐的时候我们竟然吃到了苏格兰国菜肉馅羊肚。这道菜由羊杂和燕麦做成，吃的时候要用刀叉而不是筷子。我绝对没想到能在这里吃到肉馅羊肚，而且它的味道非常棒，简直和我在苏格兰吃到的一个味儿。

这又一次让我看到文化的差异。我很难想象英国的酒店会为一个中国的徒步者提供面条、饺子，并附上筷子。英国人对待客人最热情的方式就是告诉客人各种东西都放在哪里，让他们像待在自己家一样，然后跟他们说还有别的需要的可一定要告知。在英国的酒店里，我想如果一个中国客人入住酒店问是否有饺子和筷子，酒店员工也一定会尽可能满足客人的需求，但英国绝不可能一开始就主动去这样做。因为他们担心没有给客人足够的自由选择空间，或者最糟糕的是让客人觉得他们擅自替客人做了决定。

雪琳和我讨论了今早的"肉馅羊肚事件"。她说，中国人之所以这么做是因为觉得多考虑别人的需求也会给自己带来快乐。这使得我想起我的母亲，她是位优秀的女主人，总觉得自己为客人做得还不够好。我们很少看见她坐在桌边吃饭，因为她总是在厨房忙着，不是在准备下一道菜就是在洗刷碗碟。我们总是劝她快坐下跟大家一起吃饭，享受家庭时光，洗碗做饭这些事就交给我们来做，可她总是说能给我们和客人做饭端菜让她自己也觉得非常高兴。

这么看来其实不同文化间的差别并不那么大。为别人付出或服务能给自己带来幸福和满足，只考虑自己却不行。如果我们都意识到这一点，也许为别人着想就会成为一种"新时尚"，世界就会变得更有"人情味"。

第50天
中石化、1200公里和简·奥斯汀

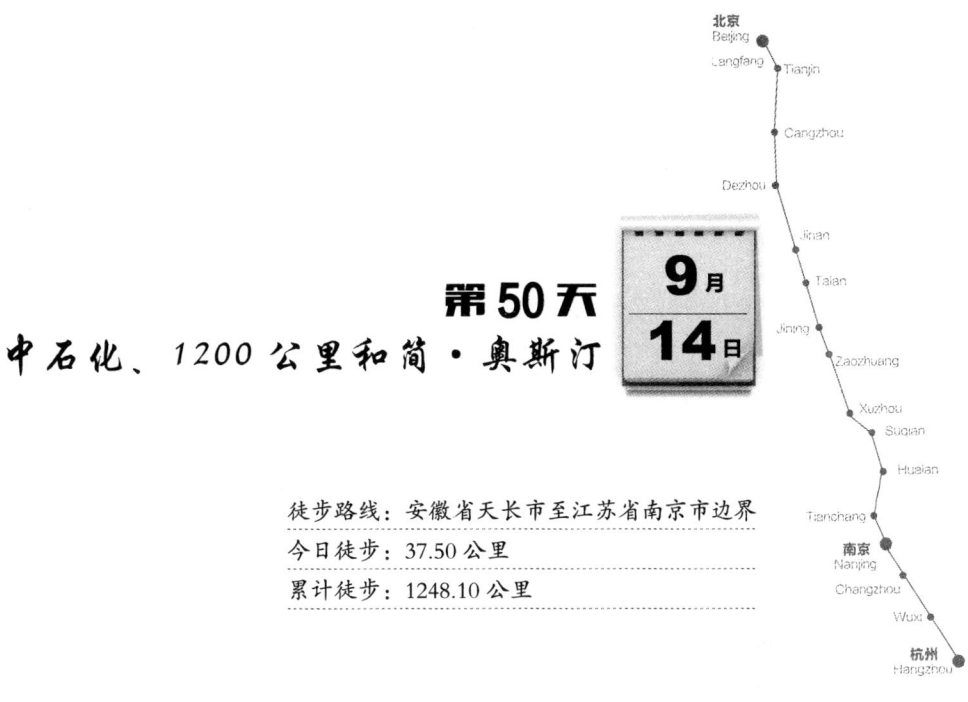

9月14日

徒步路线：安徽省天长市至江苏省南京市边界
今日徒步：37.50 公里
累计徒步：1248.10 公里

  沿着漫长的 S205 省道行走，一路上遇到了不少中石化加油站的员工。他们是一群欢乐的穿着蓝色工作服的年轻人，站在加油站前边，和沿途经过的我们一起拍照。他们构成了一个强大的信息网，在我们徒步的同时，消息很快从一个加油站传到下一个加油站。

  今天是特殊的一天：第一，在我昨天越过了 1200 公里之后，今天我不得不和陪同我走了一周的淮安志愿者们分别；第二，今天是徒步的第 50 天；第三，我们仅用了一天的时间就走过了徒步中的第四个省——安徽省；第四，今天徒步结束时，我们在 S205 省道上第一次看到了终点"杭州——335 km"的标志，真的激动人心；第五，我们走进了南京地区，也遇到了在接下来几周和我一起徒步的南京市红十字会的志愿者们。

  从北京出发至今已有将近两个月了，这几天我明显感觉到了季节的变化。地里的庄稼不再翠绿而泛起了暗黄，树叶也从枝头飘落，一切都在变化中。这是个富有诗意的季节：回顾夏天绽放过的机遇，展望即将结束的一年，但却心怀微小的希望，期待它们经过严冬的考验，在来年的春天花满枝头。我爱诗歌，爱文学，我曾希望自己能成为一名诗人或作家，但我深知这需要极大的天赋。

简·奥斯丁（1775—1817）就是这样一位得到上天眷恋、被赋予文学天赋的宠儿。她是英国著名的小说家之一，她的著作包括描述爱情故事的《傲慢与偏见》和《理智与情感》。在知名度略逊于这两部作品的《劝导》中，她用以下句子描写秋天。

"她乐于散步，一定是她想在明媚的天气里四处走走，看看枯黄的树叶和篱笆，欣赏这一年时光的最后一抹明亮，回味那充满诗意的、描绘秋色的绝美佳篇。秋天，这季节总是给多愁善感的人带去无尽的感想，这季节活跃在诗人的笔下，勾勒出一幅幅美景，或耐人寻味，或动人心弦。"

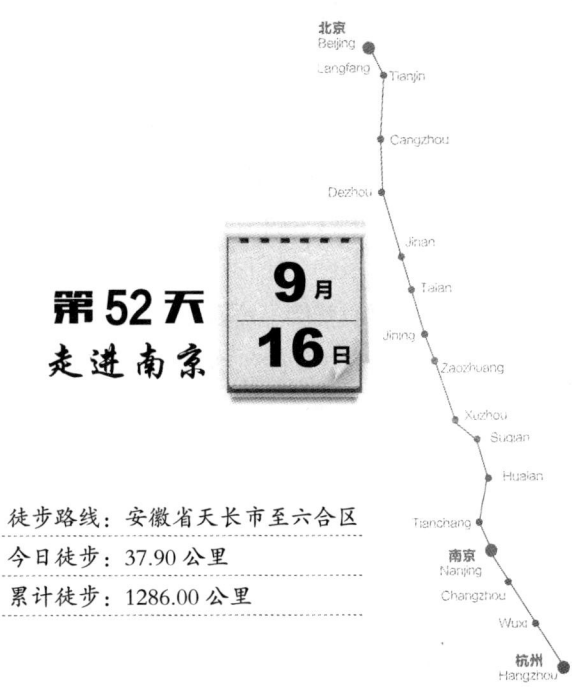

第52天 走进南京

9月16日

徒步路线：安徽省天长市至六合区
今日徒步：37.90公里
累计徒步：1286.00公里

  由于S205省道在修整，我们今天取道县道X203公路，从前天的结束地点天长市边界进入南京。我很高兴选择了这条路，比起笔直的省道，它很美，有意想不到的曲折变化，能看到变化的风景，经过数个小城镇和可爱的小村庄。明显觉得这里的人更富裕一些，不时会看到高级住宅区，如果能有钱在这里买套房的话，我猜住户们在家就能欣赏连绵的山峰、静谧的湖面、碧蓝的天空，远离都市的喧嚣。

  两个月，我们已经告别了酷暑，从盛夏走到初秋。田里是正在收割的庄稼，似乎沿路所有的空地都被铺满了麦子，麦子堆成一堆，晒干后装进大口袋送往集市。我喜欢农村生活尤其是耕作劳动这种质朴的美，人们日出而起、日落而休，晴天耕作，雨天休养。种下种子，浇水施肥，阳光洒下来，大自然自行运转，最终获得丰收。

  而现实早已不是田园生活的节奏。在繁忙的城市生活中，现代通信昼夜不停，装有空调的办公大楼全年无歇，我们常常意识不到自己在做什么或为了什么，我们无法立竿见影地看到自己辛勤劳动所得的明显丰收。

今天沿途的风景堪比不久前走过的万亩石榴园。

走过一路美景回到酒店，一打开邮箱就是铺天盖地的邮件。每一封都是紧急事件，要我几个小时内做出决定。我一直回复邮件到天亮，回完最后一封时我就倒下睡着了，电脑却还一直亮着。想起 X203 县道沿途遇到的农民简单而快乐的生活真是心生羡慕。

第53天 南京长江大桥

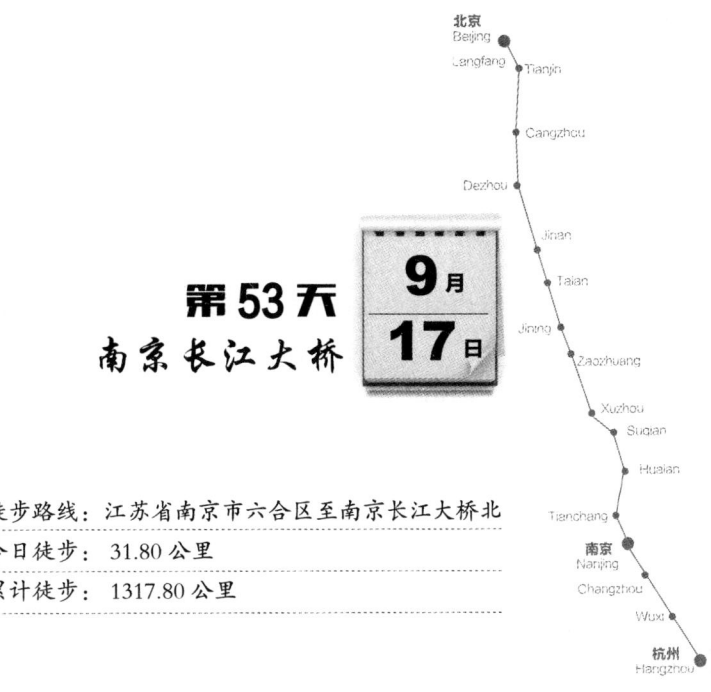

9月17日

徒步路线：江苏省南京市六合区至南京长江大桥北
今日徒步：31.80公里
累计徒步：1317.80公里

今天的徒步路线是从六合区出发，前往南京长江大桥，但今天还不会越过长江——这让我有点儿失望。每次即将到达一个大城市时，我都士气满满。这样一座横跨长江的大桥，总是有足够的理由让我们停下脚步流连。

南京长江大桥对于中国有着特殊的历史意义，走过南京长江大桥将是本次徒步的一个重要里程碑，我们这次徒步重要的朋友和支持者，中国红十字会副会长郝林娜女士将加入到明天的徒步队伍中。与郝会长一起来的还有王纪言先生，凤凰卫视的创办人之一、凤凰卫视执行董事，也是一位成功的商界名人，张明女士透露给我们：他可能会给我们的筹款工作带来好消息。我们准备在明天上午10点钟登桥，不可以提前，具体的原因我先留个悬念，明天揭晓。

吃早餐的时候雪琳提醒我，不要忘记徒步背后更深层次的使命：为"希望之家"等红会推荐的项目筹款；在纪念"二战"结束70周年之际，传递和平与和解的信息；让更多人了解首届中英文化交流年。

这一使命意味着我们不能在徒步中只是行走，我们需要抽出时间，向潜在的捐赠者解释我们此行的目的，以争取他们的支持；需要不时更新我的博客和社交媒体网站；要抽时间做一些宣传；还要在我经过每个市／县／区时和当地加入徒步的红会志愿者交流……

坦白说，长距离徒步本身对于54岁的我来说，已是一个很大的挑战，但我还是很感激雪琳的提醒。徒步本身并不是此行的目的，我们肩上的使命才是，徒步只是实现目标的方式。她说："不要在徒步中迷失，忘记使命。"这让我思考良多，边走边忆起了大卫·里恩导演的史诗电影《桂河大桥》中的场景。

"二战"期间，日军占领了缅甸边境的一个战俘营。出于战略需要，日军将在缅甸与泰国交界修建一座大桥，同时希望战俘营里的战俘出力修桥。英军战俘在这里受到非人般的待遇，很多人因疾病和营养不良死亡。为了给同僚争取好些的待遇和生存条件，英军战俘代表尼科森上校（亚利克·基尼斯饰）不得不同意参与建桥。英军战俘在建桥时的工程水平奇高，令俘虏他们的日军肃然起敬。大桥竣工的场景就是：尼科森上校充满自豪地望着他领导的英军建起的这件神作。远处的火车鸣起了笛，第一辆载满日军的火车即将穿越大桥。突然尼科森发现了一条引线，这条引线连着英美特种兵埋伏好的炸药，准备炸毁新建成的大桥和火车。尼科森并没有配合和自己同仇敌忾的特种兵，掩护他们的炸桥计划。相反地，他向日军报告了这件事，试图阻止炸桥行动。对于尼科森来说，桂河大桥是保护他的士兵免受非人虐待的筹码，是维持英军战俘仅剩士气的唯一源泉，大桥是他们在被俘的黑暗岁月里的一种动力，一丝光明。然而此时的尼科森已经忘记了作为英军的上校，自己身上肩负的使命是打败日本侵略者。导演大卫·里恩在这部影片中很好地诠释了人生经常面临的两难处境。电影的最后一幕，似是尼科森终于觉醒：他中弹倒下，压到炸药引爆装置，炸毁了大桥。

当然，《桂河大桥》中的情节肯定不能解释我们推迟跨越长江大桥的理由。但这对我确实是一个及时的提醒：做一件事时，一定要时刻问自己，为什么要做这件事。

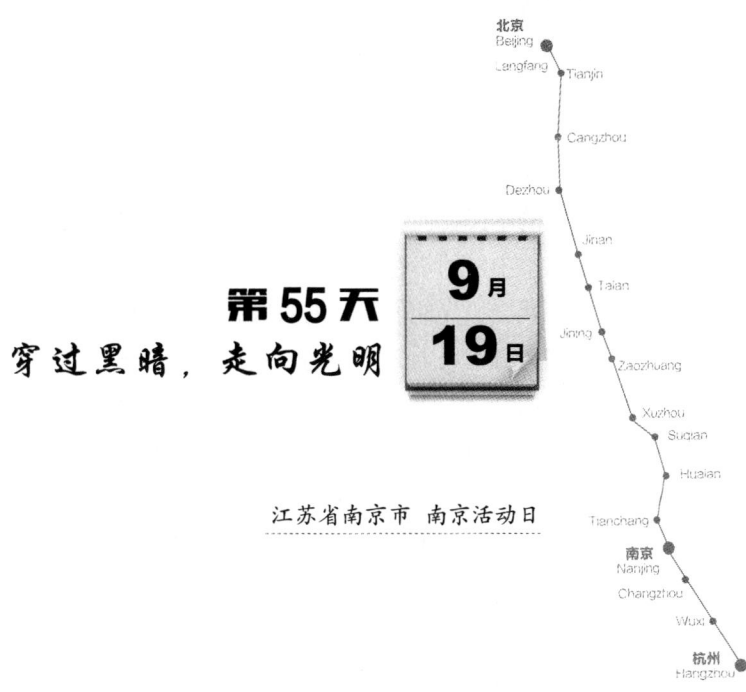

第55天
穿过黑暗，走向光明

9月19日

江苏省南京市　南京活动日

　　南京是"为和平徒步"的重要一站，我们将在这里做三天停留，开展一系列活动。南京对于世人来说并不陌生，因为这里曾经上演过南京大屠杀的惨剧。日本军队于1937年12月13日占领南京之后展开了野蛮残暴的屠杀平民行动，在短短6周时间之内，用斩首、扫射、集体活埋等极端方式残杀了30万手无寸铁的无辜平民，男人女人孩童无一幸免，此外，还有至少2万的妇女惨遭强奸。这一暴行不仅是南京，也是人类文明史上黑暗的一页。这一个个触目惊心的数据都被记录保存于侵华日军南京大屠杀遇难同胞纪念馆中。我们把参观侵华日军南京大屠杀遇难同胞纪念馆放在第一天，如果我们不首先彻底审视这段历史，又怎能正确向世人传达和平的重要性呢？

　　和世界上许多与战争有关的其他纪念馆一样，如位于耶路撒冷的以色列犹太大屠杀纪念馆，侵华日军南京大屠杀遇难同胞纪念馆建于当时埋葬遇难者的遗址之上。大部分展厅置于深色的地下空间，使前来参观的人身临其境地感受到战争所昭示出的人性之阴暗。纪念馆大厅巨大的墙壁上印刻着大屠杀受害者的名字。看着墙上一个个钢铁镌刻出的名字，我的脑海中浮现出他们身为他人子女和父母时的一张张鲜活面孔。

这就是战争，它使人丧失正常人基本的人性。当不再视对方为人类之时，无辜的平民在他们眼中也就无异于屠宰场中待宰的鸡鸭畜禽。作为亲历奥斯维辛集中营的幸存者，维克多·弗朗克曾说道，面对新押送来的犹太人，德国士兵会扒光他们所有的衣服，剃光他们的头发，拿走他们的身份证明而在他们的身上纹上一个号码。从那时起，那些犹太人不再有名有姓，他们只有一个代号。如此，邪恶罪行也更容易产生。

我不想在此详述纪念馆中所记录的种种暴行，因为这一幕幕让人感到深深的不安，对于想要深入了解南京大屠杀的人可以自行上网查阅了解相关资料或是亲自前来纪念馆参观。我的感受是，人类怎么可以对自己的同类做出这种丧尽天良之事？当我们变得冷血的那一刻起，当我们变得不再对自己于受害者身上所做的暴行感到丝毫同情的那一刻起，邪恶就萌发了。

我在德国人约翰·拉贝的展区久久驻足，他的事迹在令人压抑的纪念馆中闪现出人性的光芒。约翰·拉贝，时任德国西门子公司中国南京分公司经理，西门子公司1937年设址于中国当时的首都南京。他在目睹了当时种种泯灭人性的暴行与屠杀后，不顾危险、奋不顾身地抗议并尽其所能阻止侵华日军对中国人民施暴，毅然打开私宅收留中国难民，拉贝的家成为600位难民的安置点与临时居所。接着他和十几位外国传教士、教授、医生、商人等共同发起建立面积达4平方公里的安全区，并担任安全区国际委员会主席，为大约25万中国平民提供暂时栖身避难的场所。当时的红十字会在安全区开展了大量人道救助工作。

第二次世界大战结束后，拉贝回到德国。因曾是纳粹党员，他先后被苏联和英国逮捕，1946年6月被同盟国去纳粹化后释放，失去工作，生活拮据。但南京人没有忘记他，他们筹钱帮助他的生活，中国的国民政府也每月为他提供金钱和粮食接济。1950年拉贝于西柏林逝世，日记资料由他的孙子保存，为战后审判日军暴行提供了重要证据。1997年，他的墓碑由柏林搬到南京。

走出纪念馆的时候我思绪万千，展览中的画面不停在我脑海中浮现。我应邀在博物馆准备的敞开的红色本子上留言，我的身边围满了人想要知道我会写些什么。思忖片刻后，我提笔写道："为和平徒步，为了当今的和平，我们首先要和过去言和。纪念馆的展览不只展现了人性的邪恶，还展示了人性的美好,美好如约翰·拉贝以及他和别人共同建立的南京安全区。过去的南京总让人想起那些无法言语的凶残,我希望,并且祈祷,未来的南京将因和平与和解誉满全球,穿过纪念馆中黑暗的长廊,必将走向光明的未来,和平之旅漫漫,我与你们同行。麦克·贝茨,写于2015年9月19日。"

第56天 捐款大突破

9月20日

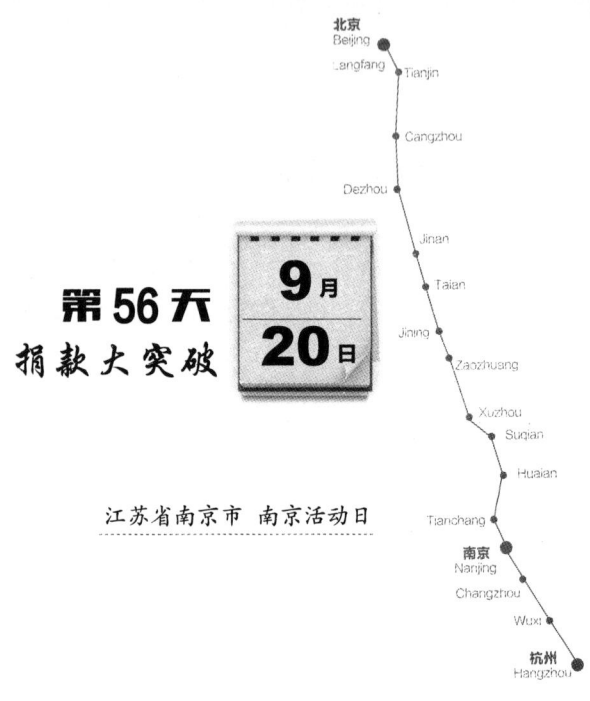

江苏省南京市　南京活动日

我总说本次徒步我们有三个目标：首先是完成徒步。现在我们已经比原计划提前到了南京，离终点只剩300多公里。第二是宣传"为和平徒步"，证明我们同是人类大家庭的一员，只要努力就能带来和平。我们一路直接或间接通过博客、微信等社交媒体同数百位青年分享了这个想法，这个目标也已经实现。但接下来的两周还要为最后一个目标努力，就是在中英两国为我们在红十字会的项目筹集善款。雪琳定的目标非常高：50万人民币，前几周我们筹得的善款差不多只有10万人民币。

雪琳是个商界才女，她只要定了目标无论如何最后都要实现。这也是为什么我们是徒步的最佳搭档。我是个很糟糕的筹款人，因为我不好意思向别人要钱。但是我能走路，我能在徒步里程上给自己定好目标，不管沿途有多少困难我也总能达到甚至是超过目标。

我想筹款是有秘诀的，就和徒步一样，要有明确的目的。徒步伊始，当我们为慈善项目筹款的时候，人们决定捐款前总想先弄清楚他们辛苦挣得的钱最后会用到哪里。这就是为什么我们后来选定为邳州"希望之家"和宿迁儿童福利院筹款时，人们的捐款热情开始高涨。

今天江苏浙大校友会的负责人顾秋组织了120多人前来支持"为和平徒步"，陪我们在南京的古城墙上走一段。校友会的朋友帮助制作了微信捐款二维码，这样校友会成员就能通过微信用手机捐款。有600多人通过这样的方式捐款，小到一元多则几千，我们一下子收到了12万元人民币的捐款。

雪琳在英国的朋友王俊设计了一项很成功的活动，在南京邀请中学生参与一个"慈善学徒"活动，为这次徒步募集善款。这个活动吸引了200多名学生踊跃报名，最终30名优秀学生入选。这些同学被分为6组，每组得到500元作为启动资金，他们要在一周的时间设法用这些钱来策划筹集到更多的钱。这个项目非常成功。一周活动结束后，我们在侵华日军南京大屠杀遇难同胞纪念馆见到了这些年轻人，并举行了一个捐款仪式。他们的活动竟带动了700多人参与捐赠，共筹款30109.40元！我们深深被他们的投入与执着所鼓舞，并为之感动。

中国红十字会郝林娜副会长不仅自己捐款，还通过自己的好朋友凤凰卫视王纪言先生推荐了三个捐款企业，慷慨地给了我们一张大大的15万元人民币的支票。到目前为止，已有超过1000人奉献爱心，给予捐款，这个数字非常重要。如果有更多的人关注我的博客或加入徒步陪走，那么就会有更多的人了解我徒步的目的，或多或少也会给我们捐款。

与此同时，英国有个网站通过减税的方式让纳税人向英国红十字会捐款，目前这个网站已经筹集了4116.95英镑，约4万元人民币。

刚开始的时候筹款并不顺利，但是通过雪琳、中国红十字会的努力以及上千人的支持，现在我们已经筹到46万元人民币了。加上在英国收到的约4万元人民币，我们已经完成了此次徒步筹款的目标数。这太神奇了！这些善款能改善许多需要帮助的孩子的生活。当然，雪琳可不是那种提前达到目标就罢休的人，她觉得在10月5日我们到达终点杭州之前，很有希望还能做得更多更好。

请让我代表我自己、雪琳、中国红十字会和英国红十字会，向帮助我们的人们真诚地说一句："谢谢！"

第57天 我的"南京宣言"

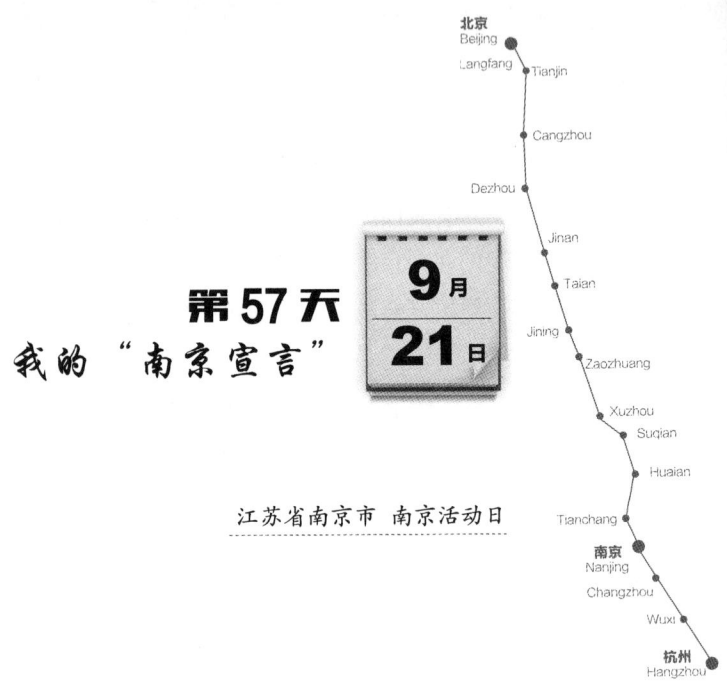

江苏省南京市 南京活动日

今天是9月21日,联合国国际和平日。连续几天来,我被南京大屠杀的历史所震撼,更被这里热爱和平、支持参与我的徒步行动,热心为我们的慈善项目捐款的故事深深感动着,并感慨于"为和平徒步"所产生的积极影响。当有人建议我在徒步行程结束后建立一个相应的组织,继续为倡导世界和平贡献力量的时候,我被打动了,觉得这确实是一件值得仔细考虑的事。

在此之前我从未想过要建立一个组织。我和雪琳的想法本来是结束这次徒步以后,就着手准备2016年里约奥运会期间的"为奥林匹克休战徒步"。我以前一直都是单人徒步,雪琳和我对于徒步前的筹备、徒步以及募集善款已经掌握了一套有效执行模式。说实话我有点害怕组织,成立一个组织就会遇到各种协议承诺、官僚风气、虚荣和无尽争端。我之所以徒步,就是想要挣脱这种政界特有的束缚,做些真正有意义的实事。但是话说回来,若是没有组织,那些和我有同样想法的人该去找谁呢?难道我们不该尽力帮助他们吗?

我被那些热血青年的理想激励着,草拟了一个提案。不知道这个提案能否引起大家的共鸣，也希望听到大家的意见，让它更加完善。我的提案如下：

宗旨：创立一个青年组织，为年轻人提供一个探索文化差异的平台，使他们能够从本土、本国和世界三个层面思考和平与相互理解，并为此付出行动。

目标：搭建一个国际间交流沟通、联结不同文化、丰富大众知识与经历的网络平台组织，以此促进和平。

设想：设立一个名为 PAX 的组织（PAX 在拉丁语中是和平的意思），涵义是"文化交流促进和平"，就从南京开始。

基本原则：快乐，教育，尊重，服务，收获，成就。

定义：

文化交流的平台。涵盖的领域包括教育、体育、艺术、音乐、戏剧、宗教、舞蹈、哲学、文学、餐饮、历史、影视、时尚和语言等。

文化（culture）这个词和农业（agriculture）的词根在英语中有些相似，"文化"一词的意义与农耕过程紧密相关，字面意义就是"栖息、耕作和养护"思想和灵魂。这给予了我们一些启示，文化被认为是使人类区别于其他物种的决定性因素，正是培养思想和塑造灵魂的能力将我们与其他动物区分开来。

将文化描述为耕作，这种说法根植于这样一种设想：这个世界是一块培育文化的沃土，经过了千百万年后，收获了诸如壁画、音乐、图腾崇拜、宗教仪式和神话传说等千变万化的内容形式。当毫不相干的原始部族结束采摘渔猎的流浪生活，定居下来从事耕作的时候，人类文化开始突飞猛进地发展。

组织架构：PAX 是由为和平徒步基金会牵头建立的非政府组织。某国/地/区可向基金会提出申请，经审查符合标准，可以在当地设立 PAX。申请标准如下：对年满 16 周岁申请者开放申请。PAX 不允许任何理由、任何形式的歧视。我们鼓励会员多举办残障人士也能参与的活动。每个地区的 PAX 分支机构会被命名为"代表处"。每个地/区设立一个代表处，在特大城市可能会设立次一级的办公室，专门负责某些特定职能或区域。

PAX 旨在促进国际文化交流，可以看作是个民间外交组织。代表处的人事结构将会仿照使领馆进行设置：每个代表处由一名 PAX 大使领导，下设有公使、参赞、各级秘书及随员。

PAX会设置四个活动部门（艺术、教育、哲学和体育），每部都有负责人。每个代表处都要从中选出一个部门作为"主项"或"特长项目"重点发展。PAX还要避免涉及官方政治领域。PAX的宗旨是尊重和理解不同的文化，绝非改变它们。所有代表处必须尊重当地文化、政治氛围。为避免官僚风气，所有的交流都在社交网络上进行。

PAX成立的目的是促进不同文化间的平等交流。这从根本上讲是因为所有人首先都同为人类，有着共同的人性。我们的"文化身份"由我们的家庭环境、教育和人生经历反映出来，对我们来说是独一无二的。因此PAX欢迎大家提出意见建议甚至质疑，但必须要以促进相互理解为原则和共同目的，不能是刻意的挑衅。

活动：所有PAX代表处会在下述重要日期组织活动，并在网上发布报告，介绍活动细节。

4月6日——联合国国际体育促进发展与和平日

9月21日——联合国国际和平日

每届夏季、冬季奥运会的奥林匹克休战期开始

PAX年度大会，也是为各代表处总结反馈、颁发奖项、举行任命仪式的时刻

每年一度的"为和平徒步"

补充说明：可以看出PAX代表处的工作是基于实实在在的活动，而非官僚主义。也就是说，代表处的工作是通过文化交流活动促进和平。可以展开的工作形式包括：

- 会员们以讨论的形式，分享自己独特的文化身份；
- 在PAX内部及同其他组织举办体育比赛；
- 召开经验分享会，从有海外经历的留学生、在中国的外国教师和学生身上学习经验；
- 组织参观有助于了解新文化的场所，如博物馆和历史景点；
- 组织风格多样化的舞会和音乐会；

- 开展以不同哲学思想为主题的讲座；
- 邀请来自不同国家和地区的政要、商业人士及外交人员演讲并交流心得；
- 庆祝重要的宗教节庆，探访重要的宗教场所；
- 在"电影之夜"观看并讨论世界各地的电影……

奖励机制：

PAX 鼓励会员在工作中终身学习，长期服务。为和平徒步基金会将拟订方案并监督评奖活动的参与和评选。

在当今世界，商界、政界和教育界都需要有文化交流意识和敏锐洞察力的年轻人。PAX 向世界承诺：我们能够让年轻人更好地了解并探索文化的真谛。

最后，如何让 PAX 更好地丰富人们的文化意识，以促进各群体间的和平友好呢？欢迎听到大家的意见。

第59天 9月23日
中国少年之声

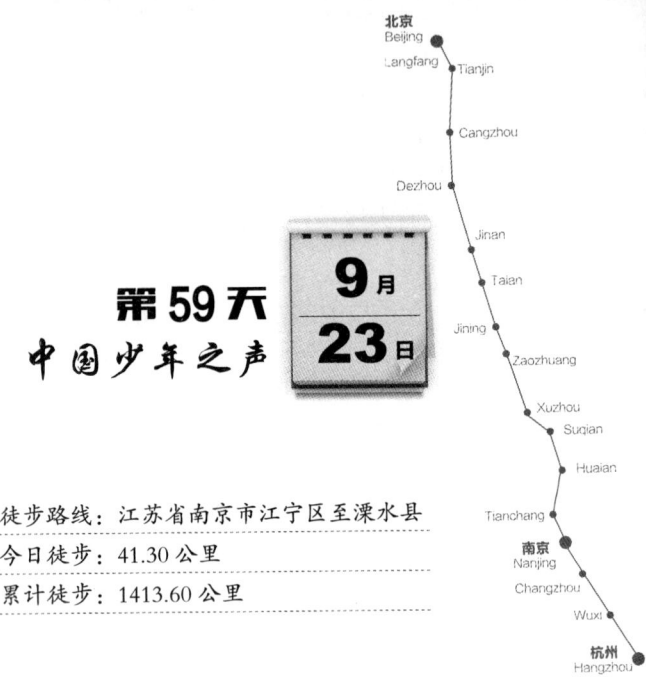

徒步路线：江苏省南京市江宁区至溧水县
今日徒步：41.30 公里
累计徒步：1413.60 公里

今天已经是离开南京市区的第二天了，我的思绪又回到了在南京时的种种经历，尤其是在侵华日军南京大屠杀遇难同胞纪念馆见到的那些年轻人，他们不辞辛苦地为红十字会的项目筹款。其中一名学生代表全体年轻人的致辞令我印象深刻，雪琳还把中英双语的演讲稿照了下来。平时总是有很多人告诉我们年轻人脑子里都在想什么，但我们却很少有机会从他们口中听到这个问题的答案。今天我就把这个中国年轻人说的话分享在这里：

亲爱的麦克·贝茨勋爵，亲爱的青年朋友们：

今年是中国人民抗日战争暨世界反法西斯战争胜利70周年，今天是麦克·贝茨勋爵与我们年轻人一起在侵华日军南京大屠杀遇难同胞纪念馆举行纪念活动的重要日子。当麦克·贝茨勋爵与夫人不远万里、不辞辛劳地传播和平思想时，我们更不能忘记这一段历史背后隐藏的血泪与屈辱。回望那段峥嵘岁月：我们不能忘怀民族英雄们浴血奋战、驰骋疆场的英姿，我们不能忘怀56个民族同仇敌忾、众志成城的精神，我们更不能忘记在我们的家园有30多万同胞惨遭杀戮。这历历在目的数目、这触目惊心的往昔每时每刻都在提醒我们勿忘国耻，警钟长鸣！而今70年日月已逝。我中华少年时刻也未敢忘记先辈英烈们捐躯赴国难、视死如归的伟大奉献，时刻也未敢忘记为了牢记历史，珍爱和平。值此，向青年朋友们发出倡议如下：

一、铭记历史，勿忘国耻

让我们一起去学习、了解那段历史，让我们一起记住那段沧桑岁月教给我们的宝贵经验。一起为了更好地建设伟大祖国、早日实现中华民族伟大复兴的梦想而奋斗！

二、珍爱和平，牢记责任

和平与发展是时代的主题，是世界人民的共同愿望。我们当代中学生所处的和平时代来之不易，为历史不再重演，为扶助弱势群体，为正义得到伸张，我们要牢记身负的责任，勇敢地肩负起社会与国家的责任，让和平的橄榄枝永不凋谢。

三、艰苦朴素，敏而好学

昨日之艰苦，今日之繁荣。作为一名中华儿女，我们不应在物质条件丰富、社会稳定安康的时期背弃我们的传统：勤俭与好学；杜绝奢侈安逸的享乐主义；培养艰苦朴素、敏而好学的良好习惯。

四、坚定理想，励志笃行

少年当立志，笃行乃成才！我们不惧少年立志，壮而拼搏，老年才能得偿所愿。我们不惧千磨万击，山高水远，路遥马亡方可抵达成功。在当今充满权力和金钱诱惑的社会中，我们不能被其所奴役，我们要为梦想不断奋进，为未来踏实奠基。愿君能坚定理想，一展抱负，得偿所愿。

最后，让我们一起铭记历史，珍爱和平。将这份热情落实到行动中，为中华民族的发展、为世界和平、为建设人类美好家园而努力奋斗。

这个年轻人说的这些话，应该被全世界听到，这样我们成年人，包括来自不同国家和文化背景的成年人就可能会去尝试理解这些话语背后真挚的想法和希望。

第60天 9月24日
北京活动日

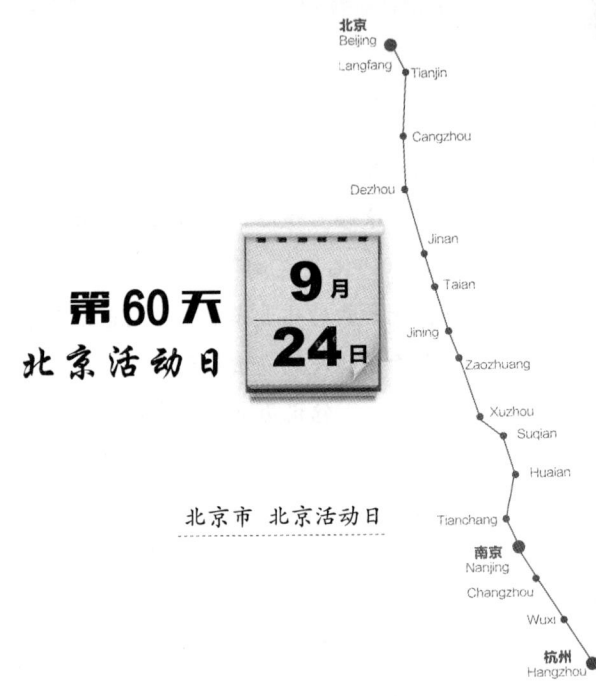

北京市　北京活动日

　　感谢江苏省红十字会将我们的徒步路线从原计划沿高邮经扬州到南京，调整为从淮安经安徽天长市直抵南京，这让我们比原计划少走70公里，不仅节省了体力，还提前了2天时间，使得我们有可能接受有关方面的邀请拿出两天时间回北京参加各种活动。

　　一下火车我们便去中国侨联拜会林军主席。林军主席是个大忙人，他负责处理5000多万海外华人的相关事务。他大约60岁出头，饱读诗书，很有思想，擅长书法，因为经常出差旅行，睿智又开放。见过我们，当晚他就要动身飞去印度尼西亚参加世界华商大会。林军主席很关心我们的这次为和平徒步以及徒步的目的。聊天的时候他说"你应该考虑选择短一点的路程徒步，这样就不会走得太累，也就有多点时间和精力去看看了解所在的地方"。

　　海外华人所处位置列表读起来蛮有意思的。有不少华人在隔壁的泰国（932万）、马来西亚（696万）、印度尼西亚（280万）和缅甸（160万）。也有不少华人分布在新加坡、菲律宾、柬埔寨和越南。当年内战失利后，国民党军大规模地迁徙到了新加坡、马来西亚、印度尼西亚、菲律宾还有台湾地区。在所有国家中美国的华裔种族人数位列第三，达到了370万。其中许多人在19世纪到达美国，以修筑铁路或帮助开采金矿为生。加拿大有150万华裔，大多数是香港回归时受邀搬去那儿的。秘鲁有130万，至于当时为什么要移民、又是怎么移过去的还有待研究。欧洲国家中，在法国的华裔人数最多，有70万，英国排名第二，60万。非洲和俄罗斯东部的海外华人数量增长最快，港口城市海参崴尤其如此。日本（67.7万华裔）和印度（无数字记录）居然排在列表很靠后的位置，还真挺让人惊讶的。

和漂泊在海外的人保持联络提醒着我们大规模人口迁徙早就不是什么新鲜事儿了。几个世纪以来，迁徙都是因为战争或者饥荒导致的，这点在之后也不会变，因为人的本能就是如此，哪儿能吃得饱，过得安全，能使自己和家人拥有更好的未来，就去哪儿。数百万英国人也因此在过去的几个世纪中迁去了美国、加拿大、澳大利亚、新西兰和南非。澳大利亚的英国移民数量比其他国家都多，达到了20.7万，美国和西班牙分别有7.2万和5.2万。

在北京期间我们还受邀参加英国商贸部和英中贸易协会举行的晚宴，与正在访华的8位英国国会议员见面。这周中国媒体对英国的关注度极高，为了推动英中贸易，英国财政大臣乔治·奥斯本正带领政府高层部长代表来到中国。财长设定目标要将英国打造为仅次于美国的中国第二大贸易伙伴，还提到了两国贸易关系的黄金十年。这确实是激动人心！国家之间若联手促进贸易而不是控诉对方，全世界都会受益。

晚宴上主办方热情邀请我说几句，和在座的各位商界精英分享我一路的经历。我的观众或许更关注上海证交所内的形势，要和他们谈和平、希望、为了慈善事业徒步1700公里我有些没把握，于是我遵守我父亲关于讲话的建议："如果五分钟还没有把气氛搞起来，那就熄火坐下得了。"我觉得我大概说了两分钟就坐下了，但随后雪琳和我与那些商界宾客聊得很开心。看来确实要牢记——"切勿主观臆断他人！"

第61天
交流的重要性

9月 25日

北京市　北京活动日

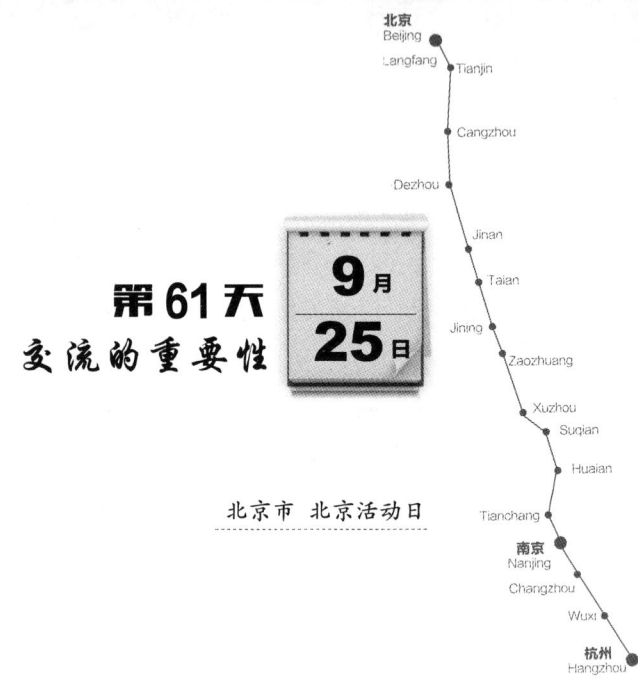

今天下午我们前往凤凰卫视参加一个访谈节目。凤凰卫视北京总部大楼在朝阳公园附近，建筑非常壮观，外观看起来像一个巨大的甜甜圈，但设计的背后却寓意颇深。建筑的光滑玻璃幕墙和外表的钢铁斜肋能够收集雨水，回收的雨水用于整个建筑的供水系统。双重表皮结构很好地增加了空气流动并能保持舒适的室内温度。

雪琳是建筑师出身，看到这个建筑的她如获珍宝，一下子有许多问题要问个清楚。建筑是基于"不禁城"这个概念设计而成的，这就不得不提北京的紫禁城。紫禁城非凡人能入，而这所建筑的结构却向人们还有世界展现出截然相反的理念：它不是当年的紫禁城，它欢迎所有人的到来。建筑往往能反映出支撑一国经济的哲思和自信。

在过去，中国的许多建筑杰作都出自知名建筑公司的外国设计师之手，像赫尔佐格和德梅隆设计了"鸟巢"，北京的国际机场则是诺曼·福斯特的作品。这个新建造的凤凰卫视的媒体中心好像在向世界宣告："我们中国人自己也做得到！"（而且开销还少得多）。整个建筑让人叹为观止，穿梭其中，其乐无穷。但我们并不是为了参观这个建筑才来到这里的，凤凰卫视对我们的这次徒步中国一直十分关注，而它在伦敦的欧洲分公司，对我之前在其他国家进行的徒步也十分感兴趣。凤凰卫视有个节目，每周一期，叫作"公益中国"，他们想以这次为和平徒步活动为主题邀请我们以及我们的合作方中国红十字会做一期访谈节目。

在现代社会的慈善活动中，媒体发挥着重要的作用。媒体不仅能促进筹款，更重要的是某个慈善项目一旦经媒体宣传推广，其目的和目标就好像得到了某种程度的认可。雪琳早就意识到这点，由此组建了微信和微博平台，它们对捐款量的增加起到了重要作用。能吸引到媒体的注意力很不容易，毕竟很多慈善事业都值得推广，而媒体的数量却是很有限的。

这也是为什么慈善组织越发倾向于找明星来代言。在组织募捐上，安吉丽娜·朱莉在英国或者姚晨在中国若能出场走一步路，其所能筹集的善款，就会远远超过一个默默无名的政治家走1700公里筹到的款项。凤凰卫视、中央电视台、中国日报、北京晚报、新京报等对这次徒步十分关注，这对我们来说是个巨大鼓舞，媒体的宣传报道每天都能为红十字会带来切实的捐赠与帮助。

英语中"交流"一词的拉丁词根并没有涉及"说"或者"写"的意思，而是与"分享"一词有关。这就意味着如果交流足够顺畅，观众、采访者和被采访者都会从交流中有所收获。

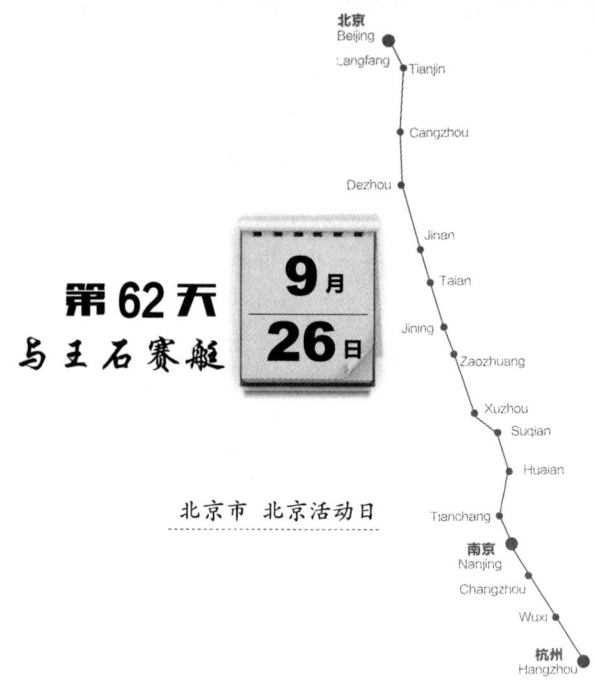

第62天 与王石赛艇

9月26日

北京市　北京活动日

在京的另一个活动是出席亚洲赛艇活动新址的开幕仪式并参加"为和平摇滚"（Rock and Row for Peace）的慈善典礼。我们一大早5:30就从酒店出发来到位于北京西北部海淀区的稻香湖。这里广阔的河流水域以及周围壮丽巍峨的群山，为赛艇运动提供了适宜的河道与优良环境，再加之湖区本身位于赛艇运动精英培育摇篮北大和清华这两所中国顶尖名校之间，有着一定的赛艇运动基础，稻香湖自然成为亚洲赛艇运动的交流推广中心。而亚洲赛艇运动也在中国著名企业家王石的大力推广和支持下稳步向前发展。

从某种程度上来说，王石称得上是不折不扣的中国传奇。作为中国最大的房地产开发商万科集团的董事长，王石被公认为中国改革开放以来最具代表性的人物之一。此外，他也提出了诸如"绝不行贿"以及"高于25%的利润就不能做"的企业道德理念。尽管本着超过25%的利润不做的取舍之道，王石依旧成功地铸造起庞大的商业帝国。王石说起话来温文尔雅，且非常勤勉好学，按他的话来说，实际行动总是胜过满口空话。他曾两次攀顶珠穆朗玛峰，并在2010年59岁时打破纪录成为中国登顶珠峰中年龄最大的人。王石还曾徒步探险南、北极，更值得赞叹的是，他竟然能够在公司董事长与学生角色之间切换自如（王石曾分别在剑桥和哈佛大学游学深造）。

王石认识雪琳且对她敬佩有加。他通过雪琳朋友圈的微信分享，读到了我每天的博客日志，并且决定要支持我们这一慈善活动。

我们一起出席了"为和平摇滚"的慈善典礼，王石董事长介绍了我的"为和平徒步"。然后我被邀请与王石各领一队，进入赛艇比赛环节。大家在大屏幕上关注着赛程进度条，气氛相当热烈。在之前雪琳与王石团队微信交流期间，雪琳曾问我："你之前有没有划过船？"我回道："当然啊！"支撑我这一果断回答的是我脑海里闪现的儿时在盐井公园湖（Saltwell Park Lake）泛舟的景象以及我在牛津大学和杜伦大学读研攻博时所参与的几次划船经历。和队友们见面，气氛非常愉快，他们刚刚结束在剑桥的高强度训练，似乎个个年龄、体重都只是我的一半，体质却胜我十倍。所有参赛选手都换上了专业的紧身赛艇行头，就好比自行车手运动服一样能够很好地展示出身体的每组肌肉群。此时我才发现我的着装是多么不专业。我让雪琳向主办方解释一下我的着装有些问题，但她却只是在一旁微笑着从车上的行李箱内拿出一双旅馆的简易拖鞋给我。

见到赛艇的那一刻，我的心一下子凉了半截，我没指望自己的屁股能够装进这艇里面。接着又有人问我是想划桨还是坐艇首。他们都说着一口标准流利的英语，但此刻对于我这个"赛艇门外汉"来说简直就像是听天书一样毫无头绪。

我上了赛艇，更准确来说应该是"勉强挤进艇内"。我们所在的赛艇造型光滑流畅，内部空间狭长，坐在上面就感觉像直接坐在湖面上一般，哪怕是一个非常小的动静似乎都会将水带到船舷上。我的脚码很大，脚放不进船内所固定的鞋套，所以缺乏一个很好的发力点。比赛开始，我捣鼓了几下船桨，试图出一份力，但我的举动立即招来了一声"把艇稳住"的指令。接着，队员们发现如果我和我后面的队友都不划桨的话，船体能够更平稳地前进。很快队友们发现虽然只有六个人在划，但比起先前八个人不协调地使劲，船反而前行得更快。从这件事我意识到划艇中保持平衡的重要性。

终于我们回到了出发的岸边平台，我从来没有对陆地有如此殷切的渴望。能够顺利回到岸边而没有半路翻艇很是为我挽回了些颜面，让我暂时卸下了心理包袱。直到回到赛艇俱乐部静静享用早餐时，我才重新想起自己是多么对不住我的队友们。我猜也许很多人在琢磨：一个身材走形、不会划桨甚至无法进入艇内的人怎么能够完成1700公里的徒步呢？嗯，我想，关于这方面，我仍然会写进日志向大家解释的……

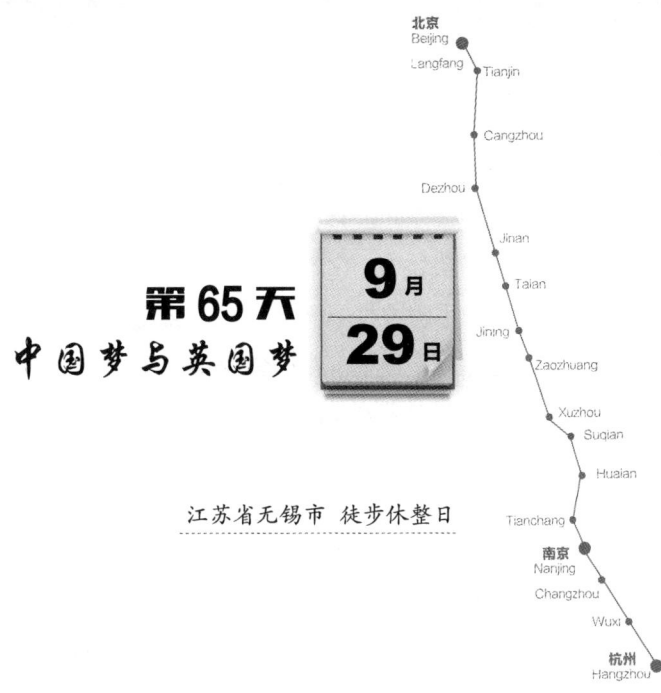

第65天 中国梦与英国梦
9月29日

江苏省无锡市　徒步休整日

"中国梦"一词开始流行，始自2013年中国国家主席习近平做的一系列有关中国特色社会主义构想的演讲。它听起来有点像西方人最熟悉的美国梦：所有人生而平等，且有追求自由与快乐的权利。

习主席提出，中国梦是关于"中华民族的伟大复兴，具体表现是国家富强、民族振兴、人民幸福、社会安康、军队强健"。他还说，"广大的青少年要志存高远，增长知识，锤炼意志，为中华民族的伟大复兴做贡献"。

说到这里我想起了一个很深刻的问题，曾有一名记者问我："您如何比较中国梦和英国梦呢？"

我是这样回答的：如果你在英国问年轻人他们的梦想是什么，男孩可能会说成为知名球星，女孩可能说是歌星。问题就在这里：我不相信球星歌星是他们的梦想，那是别人的梦想。我坚信每个人都有深刻而独特的人生梦想，但由于怕同伴们嘲笑，人们通常只分享那些可为大众接受的、早已千篇一律的梦想。这无疑是对他们不为人知的天赋和真正梦想的一种浪费，这些天赋和梦想原本有着鼓舞和照亮整个世界的力量。若要说"英国梦"乃至"西方梦"

的缺陷，大概就是过于个人主义，过分关注梦想的一些"实际利益"，比如名望、金钱或是权力。好的社会应当鼓励人们探索并发展自身独特的天赋、才能和梦想，这不仅是为了自己，更是为了社会全体。

中国青少年比起西方同龄人更具集体意识，这是由历史及哲学思想等文化差异造成的。中国青少年不仅仅思考个人梦想对自身有何意义，还思考个人梦想对家庭和国家有何意义。习主席在他的中国梦演讲中巧妙地抓住了这一思维。

中国梦和英国梦之间另一个关键的区别是，失败在中国文化中被视作巨大的耻辱，因而人们常常不愿冒险。然而在英美文化中，最大的失败或许就是根本不曾尝试。

我继而想到，或许纠结于中国梦和英国梦的区别并没有太大意义，反而思考它们的共性更有益。如果两种梦想的构成相似，导致它们失败的原因或许也有相近之处。

第一，很多人过早地确定了自己的梦想。想要发掘自身的禀赋，你必须有足够多的经历。有了经历，才能找到自己的特长。就像金字塔原理，基底建得越宽，塔身才可能越高。我对年轻人的一个建议就是丰富经历：不要只尝试一项运动，去尝试尽可能多的运动，这样你才会知道你真正擅长哪一项。不要只埋头于一个科目，尽可能多地去探索，这样你才会发现真正的强项。多旅行，多探索；尝试广交朋友，分享他们不同的兴趣与热情；多读书，多交际。

第二，培养逆向思维，从结果出发想问题。想象自己在终老时回望人生，问问自己：成功是什么？若我的梦想实现，生活又会是什么模样？

第三，时刻监测自己的动机。动机即一切。不光要知道自己的梦想是什么，还要知道为何为之奋斗。

第四，结交益友，那些追求梦想而非扼杀梦想的益友。我已经54岁了，身边有四个十分信赖的朋友，我们已经相识至少25年了，到现在我们还是定期聚会，为彼此提提建议，打气加油。你需要能真诚直言、了解且关心你的朋友，这非常重要。

第五，不要因为别人泼了你冷水，或告诉你梦想难以实现就轻言放弃。这些人应该专注于实现自己的梦想，所以别让他们影响你的步伐。通常人们不看好别人的梦想，这不是因为他们认为你会失败，而是他们嫉妒你会成功！

第六，专注自身长处，而非不足。人们总习惯纠结于自己的短处，为缺乏某些技能唉声叹气，却忘了好好发挥自己的特长。我们拿自己的不足和别人的长处比，觉得自己一无是处。弥补自身不足的最好办法就是集中精力，培养自己的特长。

最后，梦想永不过期。只要我们还在呼吸，梦想就与我们同在。实现梦想，永远不晚。

第66天
越来越强大而有深度的中国

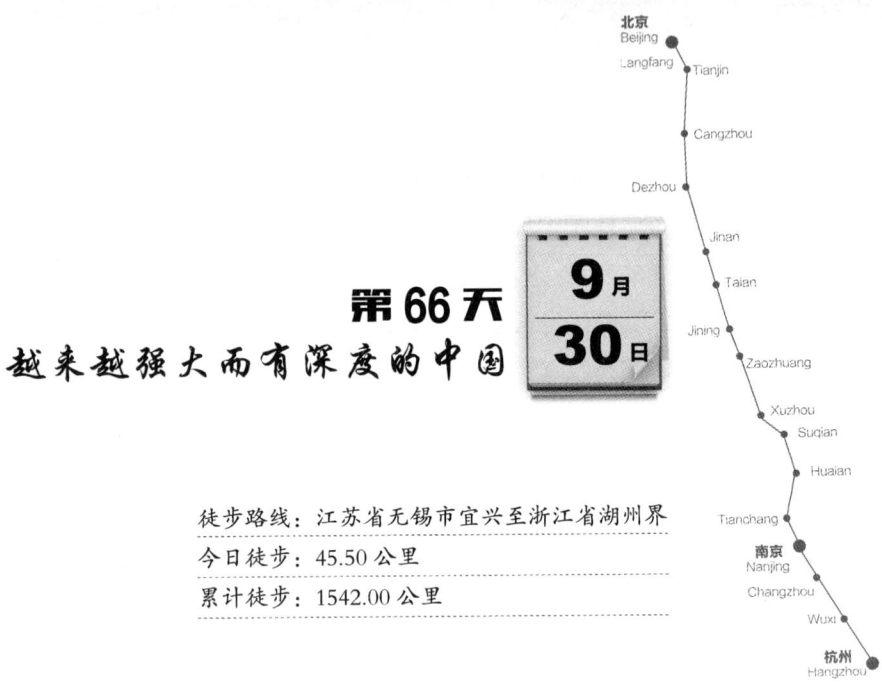

9月30日

徒步路线：江苏省无锡市宜兴至浙江省湖州界

今日徒步：45.50 公里

累计徒步：1542.00 公里

又回到了 G104 国道，今天也是我们在江苏省的最后一天。

一直以来我对各种事态发展的趋势都很有兴趣，也颇有研究。人们都说社会无时无刻不在慢慢发展，而媒体却只关注"爆炸性新闻"，不关注日常点滴的进步。一两件事看不出真相，而一连串的事件在一起才可以看出趋势。从北京出发徒步以来，我见到不少寺庙，其中不少是新建的。从这种趋势或许可以看出，中国人想要更深入地去挖掘和探索这个古老国度的哲学史和思想史。

自 1984 年起，中国在经济上实施了改革开放，但是全面深化改革却很少为人们谈起。我认为全面深化改革对中国的影响非常深远，应该给予它更多的讨论和关注。我对中国的全面深化改革，和对改革开放一样，都持积极态度。宗教还有哲学的发展源于人们对自我意义的寻找和探索，它们使得我们成为一个真正意义上的人而不是动物，因为作为人类，我们有欲望把物质世界上升为精神世界。世界范围内的每个文明都曾建立起宗教或哲学体系。这些体系赋予我们道德准则、习俗仪式，解答了我们从哪里来，为何而来的困惑，还告诉我们最终将要往哪里去。

中国历史悠久，而现代人总能从中找到灵感获得启发，儒家、道家、法家、墨家，以及外来的禅宗佛教等，不一而足。忽略这有着五千年历史的智慧、文学、建筑，是对国家文化根基的毁灭性的摧残。对人类历史和文化的否认是缺乏安全感的表现，而拥抱它们则体现了自身的强大。如今，这些历史珍宝再次为现代中国社会所重视并赢得了其应有的地位，中国社会也将会越来越稳定。经过这千百年历史的滋养，中国的文明定将枝繁叶茂，结出更灿烂的果实。

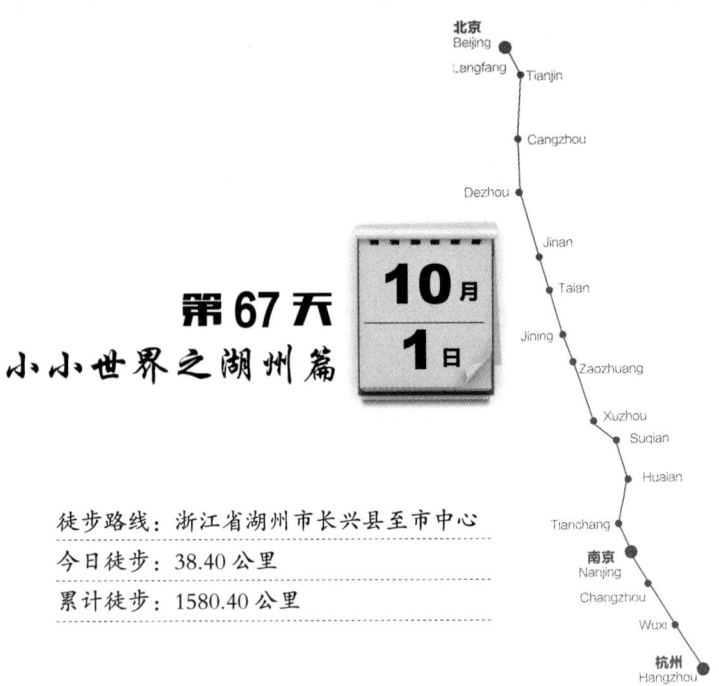

第67天
小小世界之湖州篇

徒步路线：浙江省湖州市长兴县至市中心
今日徒步：38.40公里
累计徒步：1580.40公里

  当沿着G104国道一路南下跨过江苏省至浙江省界线时，太湖便以她那动人的美景向我们的到来表示亲切的欢迎。太湖是中国第三大淡水湖。眼前的景色让人不禁再次感叹自然资源在人类文明发展过程中起到的至关重要的作用。我想这就是中国早期文明多发源并兴起于长江三角洲地区而非戈壁大沙漠的原因吧。长江三角洲地区有着丰富的淡水资源以及广袤肥沃的平原耕地，再加上其汇聚了众多湖泊河流的天然河网与大海相连，这为航海业与贸易业的发展提供了有利的自然条件，这也是为什么土地管控在当地十分重要了。

  沿太湖行走，天空飘着些许小雨，风也很大，但这并不影响在壮丽太湖背景下我们的好心情。我们终于不是走在大马路上，既要迎着大风费劲前行，还时不时会被沿途经过的卡车溅一身泥水。相反，我们沿着湖边大道边看美景边徒步，这真是一件令人心旷神怡的乐事。根据我一路徒步下来的观察，中国公路边用于保护植被的树篱和栅栏都做了很用心的设计和布置。从太湖边举目望去，这些树篱和栅栏，包括公交车站的设计都具有浓厚的艺术气息，非常好看。从太湖到湖州市区之间 20 公里的路程作自行车骑行赛道再合适不过了，并且我相信它一定会成为世界上顶级的赛道。当然，对于徒步爱好者来说，这段路程也可以是一个很好的运动场地。

途中，由于突然一阵骤雨来袭，我不得不在一个公交车站暂时避雨。正当我坐着休息喝着水时，一位身着印有英国国旗 T 恤的女士拿着手机朝我走来。我当时脑子里的第一反应就是她也许想和我这个"长相奇怪"的外国人来一张合影，但是她的意思却是想让我看她手机里的内容。我朝她微笑了一下看了看她的手机，只见手机里面显示的是一张我和一位年轻人在英国国会上议院露天平台上的合影。原来眼前这位女士名叫李卉子，也是位红十字会的志愿者，看到湖州红十字会招募陪同我徒步的志愿者就马上报名了。照片里的小伙子名叫马理唯奇，是她的儿子，目前正在伦敦攻读硕士，并且也是为和平徒步援助团队里的一员，负责把我徒步的英文博客翻译成中文。天呐！这么一看，世界简直是太小了！

李卉子女士是位画家，她为我的"为和平徒步"创作了一幅惟妙惟肖的卡通漫画。我很喜欢这幅特意为我创作的作品，前几天中秋节时我就用这幅漫画作为我们向朋友问候节日的祝贺卡。除了这些，李卉子女士还交给我一笔数额慷慨的捐款，来支持此次徒步的慈善项目。

这一天，李卉子女士坚持和我一道走完全程。能够遇见和自己志同道合的人，看到他们为共有的理念而执着付出，对我而言真是备受鼓舞。

第69天
关于"人身安全"

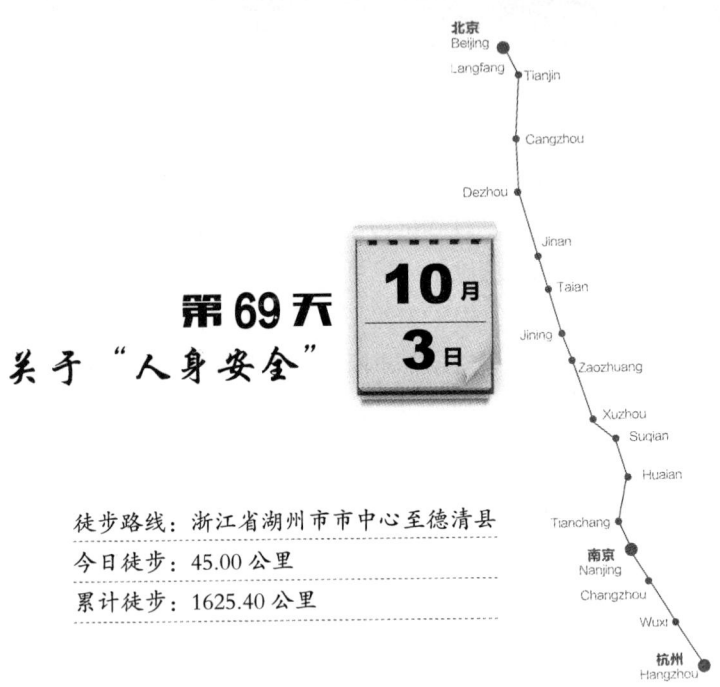

徒步路线：浙江省湖州市市中心至德清县

今日徒步：45.00公里

累计徒步：1625.40公里

今天的事儿都怪我。看见酒店马路对面有家星巴克，一激动就开始过马路。我以为当时车都在等红灯，然而并没有。我没看见卡车另一侧的摩托车，导致我和雪琳都差点被撞出去。

算是有惊无险吧。我就在想：在中国这一路我都走得很安全，这样的事几乎没发生过。又想起2014年我和一个从青岛一路骑车到北京的小伙子讨论行程，他当时说骑车就够危险的了，要在这么繁忙的路上徒步简直是"九死一生"。

当然了，我并不想拿命开玩笑，可目前看来他大错特错了。实际上我白天沿着马路走，晚上沿着村庄或小镇走，始终觉得非常安全。中国是一个井然有序的社会，尽管有时候表面看起来闹哄哄的，但背后有强有力的道德规范在约束。

之前我都是独自徒步，所以从安全角度讲你可能觉得我一人走并不安全，尤其是我还背着所有家当：现金、银行卡、手机、相机、护照还有电脑。我记得有一次在萨拉热窝，一位来自英国大使馆的安全顾问对我进行了严厉的

"批评教育",说我现金和随身带的东西加起来至少1000欧元,简直是吸毒人士朝思暮想的目标!

涉及人身安全的时候我可没左耳进右耳出。我不喜欢在黄昏、夜间或者大雨天里走,我习惯徒步的方向和身边车辆行驶的方向相反,这样我能悄悄地观察司机经过的时候到底注意到我没有。但是在中国,我必须顺着车流方向徒步,而且大多时候我是和别人一起走,所以我们这一路也是挺引人注目的。

以往的徒步,当晚上走在小镇或者城市里时,我总是走有灯光的地方。如果有可疑人士出没,就尽量避免眼神接触。眼神接触是挑起纷争的重要原因,无论是盯着人还是动物,都会被认为是在挑衅。而且人们往往通过眼神交流来衡量潜在攻击对象的缺陷和优势,动物也大多如此。避免眼神交流的话,对方在判断你的能力上就多少有些困惑。

目前为止我走过18个国家,中国和其他国家一样甚至比其他国家更安全。我想知道这方面的具体数据,于是我去查了这些国家谋杀和自杀率的国际排名,查询结果似乎印证了我的想法。中国的谋杀率仅为1/100000,排在218个国家中的第188位,是全球谋杀率最低的几个国家之一。英国、法国分别排第190位和191位。

仅这样做比较还是不够的。印度谋杀率为3.5/100000,美国排在第111位,谋杀率为4.7,菲律宾8.8,俄罗斯9.2,南非31,牙买加39.3,委内瑞拉53.7,洪都拉斯90.4,伊拉克8.8,阿富汗6.5。这样一比,就可以看出洪都拉斯、委内瑞拉、牙买加和南非这些国家的谋杀率有多高。

大多暴力犯罪率高的国家在毒品交易、其他形式的组织犯罪或酗酒上都有严重问题。瘾君子们沉溺于毒品,为了下次犯瘾时能有毒可吸不顾一切。毒品或酒精摄入过度后,人就没了自制力。还有受帮派文化影响的人会用尽一切办法来维持自己在组织里的地位。

中国暴力犯罪率还是较低的,这可能与政府在控制那些导致犯罪的因素方面做得较好有关。这当然不容易,中国在2014年处决了550名罪犯,是全球处决罪犯人数最高的国家,是伊朗的两倍,而美国仅为35人。当然我还要加上另一组数据表达我的观点：当按每百万人口计算处决率的时候，中国的处决率就下降到了第 10 位。

中国人可能会提出每 10 万人里有一个杀人犯的话，就意味着将有 13410 名无辜民众遭到伤害，而相比之下每年处决罪犯人数其实只有 550 名。但我始终反对死刑，因为首先我相信生命是神圣的，没人有权决定别人的生死。第二，法庭有时也会出错，我们常收到报告说某个案子有了新证据，之前判定的谋杀犯是无辜的。坐 10 年 15 年牢不得自由当然难熬，但最终会刑满释放，而被处决就不同了。第三，我相信自我救赎。我知道那些本身不是恶人的人在生气的时候会失去理智，做出不好的事情，但我相信他们能正视自己的所作所为，试图用自己余下的时间来弥补所犯的错误，哪怕大多时间他们都只能在监狱中度过。

肯定有人对此不敢赞同，我建议大家去读雨果的《悲惨世界》，或是看看其改编的影视作品，回味一下主角冉阿让和主教米里哀的相遇。我之所以推荐这部作品是因为雨果在中国是位很有声望的作家。那个年代西方只有少数思想家认为英法联军火烧圆明园是"野蛮人"的行为，而雨果就是其中之一。

第70天
雪琳母亲的问题——徒步的意义

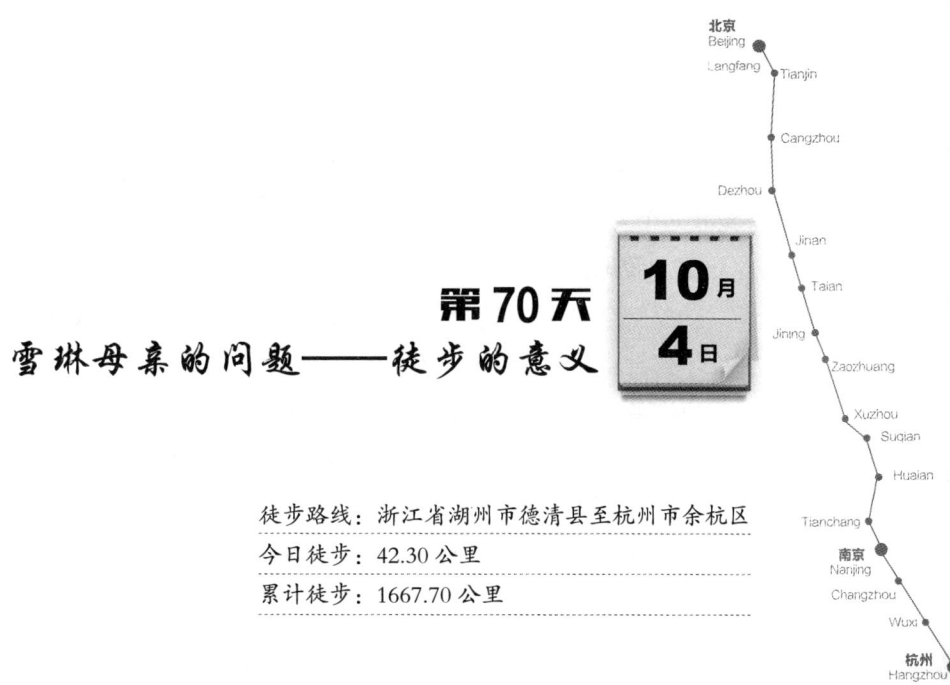

10月4日

徒步路线：浙江省湖州市德清县至杭州市余杭区
今日徒步：42.30公里
累计徒步：1667.70公里

  今天雨下得很大，我们从东林镇出发，沿着河岸走。岸边的小路因为下雨十分泥泞，为这次徒步新买的运动鞋鞋底已经基本被磨平了，这让我走起来像在跳芭蕾舞，更准确地说是像大象穿着溜冰鞋。还有一天徒步就结束了，下雨影响了我们的进度，到午歇时我们只走了原计划18公里中的12公里。

  雪琳希望我今天能走到第70天的目的地——余杭的仁和镇。这不光是因为我们想明天最后一天少走一点路，更是因为她希望我们今晚能留出点时间回杭州的家，和她妈妈一起晚餐。我们拿着被雨水浸湿的地图，讨论哪条路是通往杭州的捷径——是沿着河边还是国道？最后我们选了国道，事实证明这是个明智的决定，我们下午5点终于赶到了仁和镇。

  踏进雪琳母亲家漂亮屋子的那一瞬间太美好了，那儿简直是这个世界上我最心爱的地方之一：它是一片水泥森林里的一抹绿洲，花园里排布精致的花草树木引来了远方的鸟儿。在这里你每天都会在清晨鸟叫声中醒来。我觉得鸟鸣是世界上最美妙的音乐，因为它动听的旋律，也因为它是生灵间的对话与交谈。

我很骄傲能成为一个杭州女婿,有吴妈妈这样的丈母娘。她见到我眉开眼笑,给我一个大大的拥抱,然后拍拍我的大肚子,问我的中文学得怎么样了。还好这一路上我记住了大概50个中文词,我把这些词随机排列组合,混搭在一起,一股脑全说了出来,想让她对我刮目相看。然而事与愿违,我说出来的中文不仅没让她刮目相看,还让她笑得前仰后合。

吴妈妈准备了可口的晚餐,我们都大快朵颐。吃完饭以后,吴妈妈突然满含哀伤地看着我,说了很多话。我问雪琳她说了什么,她的答案让我有点吃惊:"妈妈说,为什么你拿生命作赌注,走这一趟徒步?你的健康最重要,为什么要拿它冒险?为什么要在最该享受人生的时候,偏给自己寻找这种挑战?" 我向来知道雪琳和她妈妈说话都非常直接,但还是冷不丁有些不知所措。

我今天在倾盆大雨中艰难跋涉了42.3公里,说实话我根本不享受其中的任何一秒钟,我只想早点结束。我的T恤和短裤都被雨水湿透了,跟皮肤敏感处一直摩擦,腿上有多次擦伤,吃饭时只能半坐在椅子上。我知道不该这么说,但是我实在是好累好累,已经受不了了。吴妈妈可能察觉了我的情绪,忍不住问了这个显而易见的问题。那究竟为什么呢?

我身处政界,有幸成为英国国会议员,在内政部担任国务大臣。我将这些工作,将为我的国家和保守党服务,视为至高无上的荣誉,而这同时也是非常艰巨的重任。我在工作上倾尽全力,但在政界有时会觉得工作举步维艰——当然这可能跟英国的政治体制和我的能力有关。徒步对我来说是一种直接而实实在在的行动。每天结束的时候,我能在地图上看到今天走了多远,在网上看到为慈善组织募捐了多少钱,且有机会通过对话、博客等方式了解并分享别人的想法。

除此之外,一个从政的人在政界专攻的领域并不一定是他最热爱的。我最热衷的是和平。

我在牛津数据分析公司做了七年顾问及研究主管,得以认识冲突的根源。那之后我还在杜伦大学读了两年伦理学和外交政策博士,虽然由于进入上议院工作后,只能放弃攻博,使我并没有能完成全部学业,但我至今还一直在广泛阅读和研究这一领域的课题。我认为我们正处于和平的边缘——人类崇尚暴力的雄性荷尔蒙和好战倾向可能随时被激发。而这实际上是个人类学问题——它们植根于人类的部落性动物本能而非政治原因。解决这个问题，我们需要从竞技体育、教育、文化交流和国际司法制度几个方面着手。

我的核心观点是，我们所有人都拥有共同的人性。世界上有正有邪，但正邪其实都在我们一念之间。世界各地的文化、语言和宗教各有差别，但决定这些的并不是所谓神的旨意，而是我们出生的族群，这完全是偶然的。我们应该把彼此共同的人性放在首位，不同的文化次之。这样我们才会少些猜疑，少些因彼此间的不同而施加威胁，少些优越或自卑；我们才会更多地寻求合理解决争端的方式，即通过一致同意的司法制度，这种司法制度应基于平等、权利、责任等基本原则。

一个没有战争的世界？这听起来太不现实是吗？然而我感觉自己就像15世纪大航海时代前夕的探险家，内心深处坚信在大西洋和太平洋之间一定有一条航道，只是还缺乏确凿的证据。在一瞬间探险家有强烈的冲动，不再满足于地图前的分析论证，直接踏上一条船，去寻找那条航道。对我来说，徒步就是踏上那条船。我徒步已走过了18个国家，最震撼我的并不是国与国之间细微的不同，那都只是些文化上的差异，并且常常被过分夸大；真正让我震撼的是国与国之间巨大的共性，那种共性令人敬畏、鼓舞人心，并仍然有待我们去探索。

我仍需进一步证实这个理念，为我的核心观点提供有力的论据。要用这个理念说服中学生都不易，更何况是我的政界同僚。我并不聪明，也不擅雄辩，要提出观点已经不易，更何况是给出有力的论据。所以我立足脚下，好好徒步，希望能以此实现和平愿景。

第71天 跨越终点线

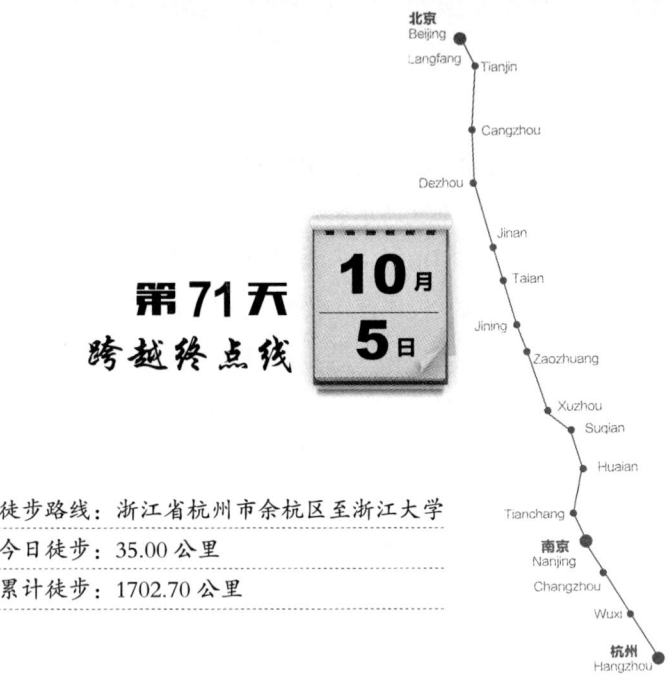

徒步路线：浙江省杭州市余杭区至浙江大学

今日徒步：35.00 公里

累计徒步：1702.70 公里

    今日是"为和平徒步"的最后一天，我们把雪琳的母校浙江大学作为我在中国"为和平徒步"的终点。2011 年我在进行第一次为和平徒步时遇到了雪琳，我们对和平与慈善怀有同样的激情。徒步中国，感谢雪琳一直以来给予我的支持和陪伴，而今天，我就要到达终点！

    我们出发的位置在杭州的余杭区，距浙江大学校园 35 公里，预计下午即可抵达。我知道，这最后的 35 公里将会为我整个中国徒步之行画下浓墨重彩的一笔，留下一个完美的句点！

    雪琳和张明女士与浙江红十字会以及浙江大学一起都在忙徒步结束典礼，会场布置、来宾接待、媒体签到……中国红十字会总会郝林娜副会长也专程来到杭州。除了在为和平徒步 T 恤上签字，写感言以及预先想一些到时候拍照可能要用到的造型外，唯一让我担心的就是前头等着我的 35 公里。

    经过上午几小时的徒步，我走下了 G2501 绕城高速开始往杭州城进发。杭州是中国最漂亮也是最发达的城市之一，有人间天堂之美誉，目前人口超过 2100 万。杭州城四周群山环绕，盛产龙井等名贵茶叶。此外，杭州还是久负盛名的丝绸贸易中心。风景如画的西湖每年吸引无数海内外游客前来参观，也正是因为西湖，才使得杭州成为马可·波罗笔下的"东方威尼斯"，而马可·波罗似乎对这个描述还不够满意，所以还特别增注道"杭州是世界上最优美且最富丽堂皇的城市"。坐落于长江三角洲与京杭大运河的最南端，杭州得天独厚的地理位置使之成为商业集散中心，贸易往来络绎不绝。

时至今日，杭州依然在商业贸易领域发光发热，扮演着十分重要的角色。坐拥众多优秀大学以及世界上最大的高科技公司之一阿里巴巴，再加上良好的自然环境条件，杭州正逐渐朝着科技中心的目标迈进。走进杭州城，映入眼帘的是各式豪车，琳琅满目的高级时装以及古驰、LV专卖店，高端的河景公寓（房价甚至比伦敦和纽约的还要昂贵），好一派繁华景象。

整个上午一直在下雨，我们沿着京杭大运河向杭州行进，这满足了我希望能够真切体验一把沿着运河行走的感觉。运河沿路景色醉人，只不过下雨湿滑的路面以及落叶使得徒步稍有困难。一口气走10公里我们进入了西湖商业区。胜利在望，此刻的我可以说是已经火力全开，徒步速度达到每小时6公里。雪琳建议我走慢点，因为我们有充足的时间在4:30到达浙大校区。听了雪琳的话，我顺势找了家星巴克稍事休息。入座后，我查看了下计步器上显示的英里数。我随身携带了装有Moves软件的两部苹果手机，这样我能更精确地核准每日徒步里程数。根据软件上显示的数据来看，我已经走了16.98公里，即将走到终点，所以我们当下决定，与其直接走过曙光路到达终点，不如沿着西湖进军，这样一来可以更好地领略西湖美景，二来可以突破1700公里大关。

走过玉古路，穿过著名的杭州植物园，雪琳和张明部长加入到我的行列中。和这两位对我本次徒步最重要的人一同走到终点，这正合我意！与我同行的队伍大概有30~40人，队伍长到我无法一眼望到头，这其中包括红十字会志愿者、浙江大学校友、亲朋好友以及活动支持者们。

越来越接近学校大门时，遥遥望见一大群人举着雨伞在雨中等待欢迎我的到来。我在高声欢呼中和大家一起共同朝着终点线走去，稍稍停顿调整心态后，我跨过了这根象征着这次历时两个多月的徒步圆满完成的红色丝带。

一旁的学生们手捧鲜花向我走来，中国红十字会总会副会长郝林娜、浙江省政协副主席吴晶、浙江大学党委副书记任少波和省红十字会领导也向我表示了诚挚的祝贺。在场的每一个人都希望能与我来一张合照以记录当时的情景，对于如此具有历史纪念意义的一刻，我当然是恭敬不如从命。

这真的是一次令人难忘的返校之旅，能够作为浙大以及杭州女婿我倍感自豪，当然，我也为我的妻子感到骄傲！

正式的欢迎和结束仪式在学校图书馆举行。浙大校友会还在校门口酒店给我预定了钟点客房，这样我能在结束仪式前沐浴更衣，打理一番。走进客房，我坐在椅子上，和雪琳相视而笑，此情此景和一级方程式比赛结束后获胜者回到休息室脱掉比赛头盔换上普通帽子称重简直一个样，而此时此刻，任何语言描述似乎都是苍白的，我们的征程终于完成了！

我们回到校园并被引入图书馆大厅。一眼看去，大厅已经有几百号人就坐，巨大的"为和平徒步"背景板也格外显眼。红十字会联络部部长也是我本次中国徒步的亲密伙伴张明女士，担任本次结束典礼的主持。浙江省政协副主席吴晶女士及中国红十字会副会长郝林娜女士在典礼上做了致辞。郝女士在整个徒步过程中给予了我很大的支持帮助，我们在北京徒步开始时就见过两次，她还专程在我抵达南京时来看望我并陪我走过南京长江大桥，而现在在结束典礼上又再次会面。此外，浙江大学罗建红副校长以及党委副书记任少波也向我表示了祝贺与欢迎。

整个徒步活动共募得9万英镑的善款（折合约90万元人民币）。此外，我们还通过英国的Just Giving网站为英国红十字会筹得了5706英镑的善款。在典礼上我们亲手递上了5张价值共5万英镑的支票（折合约50万元人民币）以示对江苏邳州红十字希望之家项目、宿迁孤儿福利院项目、浙江和山东的关爱抗战老兵项目以及河北助学项目的资助。这些项目的负责人亲手接过善款，让整个典礼更具意义。

我在典礼致辞中特地表达了对中国红十字会张明女士的感谢，感谢她在整个徒步活动中作为团队领导所做出的卓越贡献。能够认识张明部长并在一路上得到她的帮助真的是我们莫大的荣幸。此外，我还要感谢陪伴着我一起徒步过的人们（700多人）以及为了慈善事业伸出援手的社会各界热心人士（1000多人）；感谢沿途省市区20多支红十字会志愿者团队的向导；感谢浙江大学校友会、伦敦的后援支持团队，正是因为你们出色的翻译才使得更多人了解到我这一路每日的行程、经历和随行感悟见闻，感谢中央电视台纪录片摄制团队从北京到杭州全程辛劳跟踪拍摄。

在座的观众有的可能曾通过各种渠道听到过对我的褒奖。我非常担心这些赞扬会因突出我个人的"功绩"而模糊我此行的目的和重点。实际上我们每个人都是伟大的，都有能力完成了不起的事情。这和年龄、教育程度、社会和职业地位、健康、财富都无关。如果能跟从内心，着手当下而不是好高骛远，并且心存勇气，敢于尝试并踏出第一步，那么任何一个人都能成就了不起的大事。如果你觉得我说的话有所夸张，那不妨亲自去邳州"希望之家"看看，在那里你会见到许多孩子，他们尽管身患残疾只能依靠轮椅活动，却依旧怀有梦想，希望能在2016年里约热内卢奥运会上实现残奥会金牌梦。如果你想让自己的人生更有目标，更有理由去为之奋斗，就去看看那些鲜活的例子，然后从当下做起，从自己做起。

回家、回顾

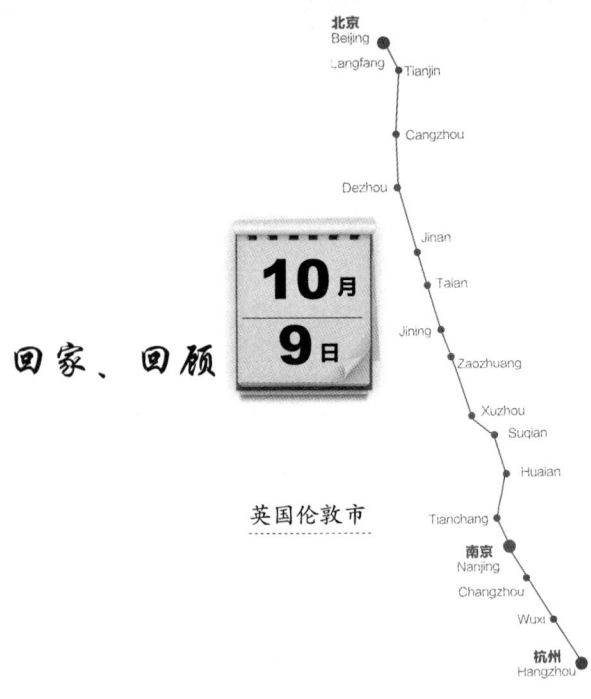

英国伦敦市

原本以为今天到场的朋友不会太多,可是当我和雪琳到达位于伦敦唐人街的中国城大酒楼时,70多位朋友早就迎候在那里了,房间里装饰着欢迎回家的横幅,大屏幕上滚动播放着我们徒步的照片,让人不禁哽咽。雪琳开心地笑了,她虽然参与策划了这场惊喜的庆功会,但就像大家欢迎我徒步归来一样,这同时也是对她所取得成果的一个肯定。

这次的欢迎宴会是由英国浙江联谊会、我们的老朋友黄萍会长还有其他朋友们一起筹办的。对于中国人这种能在短时间内迅速筹办起复杂而专业活动的能力,我早已经深深领教。

雪琳和我入座后惊喜地发现今晚到场的有许多来自中英各界的重要人物:大英帝国皇家官佐勋衔、伦敦华埠商会主席、中国城大酒楼集团主席邓柱廷,他是"为和平徒步"的第一个捐款者;中国驻英国大使馆费明星总领事和李辉参赞;全英华人华侨中国统一促进会总会会长单声博士及夫人中华传统文化研究院院长桂秋林女士;英国华人参政计划负责人李贞驹律师;英国华人金融家协会主席王昌南博士;英国中华总商会执行主席朱善明先生;

还有特地从纽卡索赶过来的英国中文教育促进会会长伍善雄 MBE。

黄萍女士告诉我们其实还有更多的人想来参加，但欢迎晚会席位在几天内就一抢而空。这次的为和平徒步中国行之所以牵动华侨华人的心，不仅是因为我是踏在中国的大地上。他们常说会感到自己被英国主流社会所忽视。在英国，大约有 60 万的华人，占了英国 1% 的人口。在 19 世纪伦敦和利物浦的海上贸易时期，华人就渐渐移民英国，可以算是最早来到英国的外来移民群体了。

英国华人对英国社会有着很大的贡献。他们既以自己的中国血统自豪，也因自己的英国身份骄傲。在英国，很少看见中国人参与犯罪或者扰乱社会秩序的活动，他们的孩子在教育上都是超越各国的佼佼者。老一代华人给 NHS 医疗资源造成的负担极少，因为他们有着非常健康的生活方式以及与生俱来的企业家精神，总是活力百倍。我知道，他们感觉被忽视是因为他们总是低调谦逊（除了中国的新年），也因为他们从没有在媒体面前流露过悲伤。所以像我这么个"疯狂的英国人"花时间去了解他们的国家和文化，这让他们倍感欣慰。

一般来说，我的演讲不超过 3 分钟，观众眼里就会流露出那种切切实实的无聊。然而今天我讲了足足有 20 分钟了，在座的来宾依旧兴趣盎然，这对于一个政治家来说，简直是莫大的鼓舞！回望徒步，到底是什么才最让我难以忘怀？

- 中国基础设施的质量
- 城市与城市间广袤无垠的大地
- 平凡人的欢笑与善良
- 中国人的办事效率
- 野外山河湖泊动人的美丽
- 进行中的对中国文化与哲学的再探索
- 中国人民对英国的真切友谊
- 中国社会以孩子为中心的文化和对教育的重视

- 中国社会几代人间的力量
- 中国社会的纯真、重感情,而非愤世嫉俗
- 第二次世界大战带给中国人民的伤与痛
- 中国人民的慷慨大方——超过 99% 的红十字会捐款都来自中国人

在演讲的最后,我表达了对雪琳的感激——没有她我不可能开始这样一次远征。记得中国之行的最后一晚,浙江大学为我们举办了一场结束晚会,120 多位校友和师生参加。在晚会快要结束之际,浙大党委副书记送给雪琳一份特别的礼物,那是一份她在浙大学习 8 年期间每年的成绩单和学业总结。从记录来看,雪琳在校 8 年学习中,只有一次成绩低于 90 分,报告上写着:她是一位"极其优异的学生,前程似锦,必将大有作为"。我希望学校的老师们能为她已经取得的成果而感到高兴,但是我认为,她的能力远不止这些,她可以实现更多,就像如今的中国。

英文篇

为和平徒步

WALK
FOR
PEACE

Preparations
Red Cross Society of China & HM Government of the UK

    Preparations for the walk have been quietly underway for months in both China and the UK:

    First there was the uncertainty of the General Election. Clearly, the outcome of the election on May 7 would indicate whether I might have more or less time to walk. If the Conservatives won, then I would need to support their legislation as it went through the House of Lords. Also, If we won, then there was a possibility that David Cameron as Prime Minister might ask me to continue to be a minister in the government, or he might have decided to promote someone new into the role—if that had happened then clearly the demands on my time would not have been as great, so the walk could be longer.

    I have been a member of the Conservative Party since I was 18, in 1979. I owe it so much for the opportunities that the successive leaders of the Party, from Margaret Thatcher to David Cameron, have offered me. When it came to this election, I wanted the Party to win not just for the Party but for the country. I believed passionately that we had turned the country round since 2010.

    I worked incredibly hard for the election. As hard as I ever worked when I was the candidate in the election in 1987, 1991, 1992 and 1997, and my wife, Xuelin, and I were sitting on the phones in Campaign HQ urging voters to go out to vote when the Exit Poll came out predicting we had won. The euphoria I felt at that moment was as great as I have ever felt in any election.

If we had lost and Labour had won, then I would have probably set off trying to realise my childhood dream of walking around the world for the next five years, but they didn't and I was honoured and humbled when David Cameron called me and asked me to stay on at the Home Office as he promoted me to Minister of State. As soon as the election was out of the way, I began the gentle process of seeking permission to undertake another walk for charity, this time in China.

In the UK parliamentary system we get very long summer breaks—normally two and a half months—this is so that members of the House of Commons who are elected can spend a long period of time in their constituencies listening to the concerns of the people they represent. In the House of Lords we are not elected but appointed by the Queen on advice from the Prime Minister, so for us the summer recess is literally a long holiday or for the many members of the House of Lords who have very demanding jobs, it is an opportunity to focus on that rather than having to come to the House of Lords to vote each day. For me I don't have an outside job. Politics is my job. So since 2009 I have used my summer to undertake a walk for a charity or cause I believed in.

After two months I finally got word that the Home Secretary (my direct boss), the Foreign Office and Number 10 (on behalf of the prime minister—my ultimate boss) had all agreed to my undertaking the walk providing arrangements could be put in place to allow important decisions and actions to be taken by colleagues in my absence. This was very generous of them to agree, and the fact that it was the first UK-China Year of Cultural Exchange with the Chinese premier due to make a state visit to the UK in October I know were important considerations in the approval process.

Xuelin and I work as a team on all walks. My job was to get approval from London. Xuelin's job was to get permission from Beijing. I am not sure whose was the most difficult. Initially, we made the approach to Ambassador Liu

Xiaoming in the Chinese Embassy in London. It can sometimes take a bit of time to understand why a politician from one country would want to walk in and raise funds for a charity in another. It sounds crazy. Yet China would not be the first but the 18th country I had walked through in the cause of peace. There was a further sensitivity about walking in China different from any of the European countries I had walked through ....

We were pleased that the Chinese Embassy in London and the Ministry of Foreign Affairs of China are very supportive to our walk in China from the start. To make the logistics of my walk go smoothly, they recommended the Red Cross society of China to assist us.

The Red Cross movement has 150 years history since it was founded on the battlefields of war-torn Europe. Their aim is to save human life and human dignity irrespective of nationality and to promote a peaceful and harmonious world. It was a perfect fit with the ethos of our 'Walk for Peace'. The Red Cross has been in China since 1904 and has a long and respected reputation, as it does the world over. It is probably the largest volunteer network anywhere in the world, with over 2 million volunteers regularly giving their time to delivery of their projects in China.

Xuelin and I were very happy to work with the Chinese Red Cross. Xuelin built a great relationship with the Red Cross. By the time we depart from London, we had not only the permission from China, but also a detailed plan, including the route, daily mileage arrangements, accommodation and other visits along the way that would help me understand the real Chinese history and culture. They wrote a three-page report on guildance on foot, weather, traffic and local customs, etc. This was our fourth long distance walk and we had never been so prepared. It makes me think, having a good plan is halfway to a success.

The final but essential part of the preparations was to build a project team who might work with Xuelin and I in the UK whilst we were in China. There are a huge number of communications and technology challenges and we felt the need for a larger team of volunteers than on previous walks so that the work did not become too onerous so as to interfere with their studies. We were overwhelmed by the responses of outstanding young people who wanted to work with us on translations and social media; they are: Jessie Huang, Jessica Liu, Xiao Xiao, Emily Hu, Liweiqi Ma, Katy Xiao, Violet Ma and Yong Xuan Li. We met for the first time as a team to have tea in Parliament just before we left and expressed our gratitude for their willingness to help the cause.

So, the permissions were agreed in London and Beijing. Support was in place in London and Beijing. We were ready to walk.

July 27 Day 1
Departure

Route: The Temple of Heaven – Daxing District (South Sixth Ring Road), Beijing
Today walked: 11.50 miles / 18.40 km
Total walked: 11.50 miles / 18.40 km

Every journey has its beginning and its ending. The traveler will take great care to ensure that both locations speak to the purpose of endeavour. My first walk began on Holy Island; my second from the Temple of Hera, Olympia, Greece; my third from 10 Downing Street; my fourth from the Tomb of the Unknown Warrior in Westminster Abbey. I had in my mind that as Monday 27 July was the exact third anniversary of the Opening Ceremony of the London 2012 Games, that I wanted to start from the Olympic 'Birds Nest' (National Stadium).

The only problem was that the Official Start Ceremony had been set by the Red Cross for 2 p.m. from the Temple of Heaven. I suggested that I could make a personal start from the Olympic stadium at 8 a.m. and walk the 10 miles/16 km south to the Temple of Heaven where we could have the Official Start.

My partners in the Red Cross didn't think this was a good idea because they didn't want me walking across Beijing by myself when they had been tasked with keeping me safe. More importantly, Xuelin didn't think this was a good idea. I confess to feeling a little stubborn. I didn't want to lose control. I was then reminded by Xuelin of an old Chinese saying, 'If you want to go fast, go alone; if you want to go far, go together.' I wasn't the only one investing time and energy in this walk—Xuelin was and the Red Cross was. They were all stakeholders in the collective venture. I/we decided to start from the Temple of Heaven as planned.

It proved to be exactly the right choice not least because the temperatures were well into forty degrees and humidity and air quality in the city unusually high and low, respectively. We arrived at the Temple of Heaven at the same time as a senior official from Hangzhou, Zhejiang (our destination point). I was amazed that a few senior officials from the Zhejiang Government, including its Foreign Affairs Office Director, Jin Yonghui, would make the equivalent of a flight from Rome to London just to see me off on a walk. Of course, I shouldn't get too carried away, as the honour was as much for Xuelin as a respected community leader from that city and province as it was for me, but it was a thought appreciated by me for both reasons.

There must have been about 150 people attending the ceremony, and we heard excellent speeches from officials talking about what this meant to them. Part of the meaning was hidden in the history of the Temple. I had not appreciated that this sacred site had been used to house British and French forces as they fought the Second Opium War in 1865 and again when they invaded with Germany to put down the Boxer Rebellion in 1900. I guess that we in Britain may have had similar hesitant feelings if the Chinese troops had invaded Britain twice and used St. Paul's Cathedral as their military base. Well, the Chinese people were gracious in allowing such a nationally sacred site to be used to send good wishes to a Brit who had come on a different type of mission than some of his predecessors—a mission of peace and friendship.

Two things went through my mind as I stood in front of the distinguished audience of well-wishers:

The first was a real fear that I could barely stand up in this heat, never mind walk twenty miles. Could I actually do this? Was I just too unfit? I was worried that the praise for my endeavour may be a bit too soon. I could imagine myself collapsing under the heat and humidity at the gate to the

Temple of Heaven. My confidence was reduced a bit further when two young and athletic walkers from chinawalking.net joined me to say they were going to walk part of the way with me.

I was getting that feeling of the tightrope walker who shows up at Niagara Falls to walk across. He takes one look down to the pounding waters of the falls and certain death if he falls and then another behind him to the cheering crowds urging him on. Which is more important to him, his fears or the cheers? Ultimately, if he is to safely cross the falls, it is because he closes his mind to the fears and the cheers and concentrates only on getting the first step right.

My second thought was an appreciation for the generosity of the Chinese people. I walked in the Temple to the ceremony and was given flowers; a renowned Chinese calligrapher turned up with a scroll on which he had written in Chinese, 'The journey of a thousand miles begins with a single step.' Another attached some Buddhist prayer bells to my rucksack to keep me safe along the journey. Minister Qiu Yuanping from the State Council Chinese Overseas Affairs Office walked with me as far as the river, a courtesy which was extended to honoured guests although perhaps being a Brit it might be as much to ensure I was on the right road as to ensure that I wasn't thinking of coming back.

Gradually, the crowd of well-wishers reduced, but Madam Linna Hao, Vice President of the Red Cross, stayed with me to the fifth ring road. Madame Linna Hao had studied in Cardiff and spoke excellent English, and we spoke about a range of themes particularly social mobility and wealth and the growing number of *fu'erdai*, literally rich in the second generation. Here was a Conservative and a Communist agreeing on a central aspect of economic and social policy, namely that 'wealth without work' is a social problem because it stifles creativity and risk-taking and creates a culture of entitlement.

Beijing is configured by a series of ring roads in much the same way that London is defined by the M25 and the North and South Circular roads. The difference is that Beijing used to have two but now it has six, and there are even plans for a seventh and eighth—such is the unrelenting growth of infrastructure to support the growing population.

By 6 p.m. I had been reduced to a pool of sweat by the heat, and after 11.5 miles I see signs for what I referred to as the 'Ring of the Sixth Happiness' after one of my favourite movies of all time, *The Inn of the Sixth Happiness,* with Ingrid Bergman. I began to explain the plot of the movie, but felt my head going faint and the eyes beginning to roll. I decided to leave that story for another day and counted my many blessings for a good start.

July 28 Day 2
In the Suburbs of Beijing

Route: Daxing District, Beijing
Today walked: 26.30 miles / 42.30 km
Total walked: 38.60 miles / 60.70 km

I have long admired great travel writers—Paul Theroux, Colin Thubron, Rory Stewart, Patrick Leigh Fermor and Marco Polo to mention but a few. They have an extraordinary gift which makes them great travel writers—the ability to transport the reader to the place they are writing about. It is a gift, but not one I possess.

I have been writing about my travels on foot since 2009. I guess I must have written about 500 blog entries totalling around 350,000 words—enough to fill three or four books—but I have been unable to reach the heights of my literary heroes. But the purpose of life and writing is not to copy someone else's style but develop your own.

I might wish to play the piano like Lang Lang. Sing like Michael Buble. Kick a football like David Beckham. Run like Usain Bolt. I can't, but I can walk. I can communicate some random thoughts I have when I am walking. I can take a decent picture with an iPhone. If we choose to waste our lives being disappointed about what we can't do, then we will never have the joy of discovering and sharing what we can.

Good days walking are often followed by bad days. Each day of walking has a unique set of challenges which are presented for us to try and overcome. I hadn't managed to reach our designated hotel at the end of

Day 1, so we had to drive back to the place we stopped. I was dropped with Wang, my guide, at a junction which looked like the place we had stopped but wasn't. I thought it was a few hundred metres back up the road, but it was nearer 2.5 kilometres. We arrived back at the starting point and my heart sank as I realised we now needed to walk back all that way for no gain.

Just then Zhang Ming, Head of Communications for the Red Cross turned up in our support vehicle. Ming has a wonderful 'no nonsense' style, being a highly efficient lady who had played a key role in the Beijing Olympic Organising Committee. She had seen what had happened and said, 'Jump in! You don't need to waste time walking that stretch twice.' And with that, like Dorothy in the Yellow Brick Road, we were whisked back through time to the point at which we had been dropped.

My legs were suffering from cramps on account of the loss of fluid on Day 1 and insufficient salt, and as Day 2 went on they didn't go, they intensified. I took some ibuprofen, which helped or made me think it helped.

At this point we were still in the suburbs of Beijing and walking along the roadside. There is a smell in the air in heavily populated and polluted cities and it is like the smell of a room which has had some building work done on it. It is really the taste of dust in the air. You can get used to it as you do on particularly hot and humid days in London but it is not comfortable. In fact, the experience of walking in 40 degree temperatures and high humidity along roadsides is a bit like walking on a treadmill for ten hours in a sauna. But what was the place like?

Sorry, failing to describe the place again. In many ways Beijing's outer suburbs are no different to any other major city I have been through. There was perhaps a less sharp distinction between poverty and prosperity. For example, we passed dozens of huge new apartment blocks on the outskirts of the city where a two-bed apartment costs around £100,000—in other words, comparable with the suburbs of many English cities such as Leeds, Birmingham, Manchester and Newcastle. The difference is, of course, is that

China has a per-capita GDP of around $7,500, whereas the figure of the UK is around $45,000 (sorry to mix currencies). The point being that there are large parts of China which are at least as affluent as the UK, in other words (First World), and correspondingly very large parts which are still (Second and Third World).

This could make for a highly volatile social mix but that is less evident here. There seems to be no embarrassment or tension on either side that at the gates to the apartment blocks there spring up instant markets selling all types of foods and the well dressed young professionals will wander round among the bare-topped male farmers sitting displaying their produce on the back of rusty tricycles.

Another thing I noticed was that I walked for an entire day and never saw another Westerner—or any other racial group for that matter. I realised that I was deeply privileged to be able to wander down these roads. Then, suddenly, as I had stepped into a different world, the tall buildings were reduced to trees and the people replaced by sheep and the smells were the fragrance of the lotus flowers in full blossom. Men line the riverbanks tending flocks of sheep and fishing. It was a universal image of peace and tranquility. Was this the real China I had hoped to discover?

July 29 Day 3
Misunderstandings

Route: Daxing, Beijing – Anci District, Langfang, Hebei Province
Today walked: 21.10 miles / 59.70 km
Total walked: 34.00 miles / 94.70 km

Police officers have a universal effect on our behaviours. In China, as in the UK when passing a police car, motorists slow down to a crawl, keep their eyes straight ahead and never toot their horn. I suppose I had a pre-conditioned response when one young police officer (they all look young at my age, even judges look young at my age) starting shouting at me—pointing at my stick. I kept moving. He followed, still talking. I was trying to think what I could have 'possibly done wrong' with my stick. Is it against the law to carry a stick in China? Or was it that golf swing I used when we last stopped to whack a peach stone into the hedge? All sorts of things were going through my mind, but only one thing was going through his. The problem was I didn't know what it was.

Never far behind, my guide, who spoke a bit of English, caught up with me to explain that the police officer felt that I shouldn't be using a stick. 'Why?' I asked, expecting some obscure clause in highway law to be quoted. His response surprised me. He said, 'The police officer said your walking technique is wrong—you shouldn't walk with just one stick—it was better for you to swing your arms, or if you must, use two sticks.' Never in one million years would I have guessed that the police officer was speaking about my walking style.

I thanked the police officer in my basic Chinese and he smiled. He started to walk along the road with me, throwing out random English phrases. I responded with random Mandarin phrases. We both laughed. Just as we were getting along well, a Black VW Passat (used by senior police officers) pulled alongside and the tinted glass window was lowered. There was a tirade directed at the young police officer, and I am guessing that he wasn't offering him advice on his walking technique, for he ran off like an Olympic sprinter to the next junction.

Later in the morning we took a rest break, and as we sat at the roadside drinking iced tea the same young policeman appeared again, looking nervous. I could see him checking out to see that there weren't any VW Passats in the neighbourhood. Then he jogged towards me and handed me a folded piece of white paper. I was a bit confused. When a police officer hands you a piece of white paper in the UK, that means you are in serious trouble. He left and I opened it. It was beautifully handwritten. I put it in my bag and showed it to Xuelin that night. When she read it, I was so touched, he had written:

'I really admire your spirit and determination to walk. The problem is that because of your age, size and fitness, I really worry you won't be able to complete your journey. If you don't mind, I would like to offer some advice.' He then went on to advise me to stop every three hours and rest for 30 minutes. When you rest, raise your legs 30 degrees and massage your knees, etc., to stop using my walking stick ….

I reflected that this was more than a lesson in walking, it was a lesson in life. Virtually all arguments, rows and even wars begin with misunderstandings. One person simply misunderstood what the other person intended. Sadly, in many cases those misunderstandings are never resolved until it is too late and more damage is done. Had I not had my guide, then I might have gone away thinking the police officer was trying to be rude and bossy instead of being caring and helpful. Our instinct is always to interpret things we don't understand as hostile rather than helpful. A great teacher, St. Francis of Assisi, had a daily prayer: 'O Divine Master, grant that we may not so much seek to be understood as to understand.' We might remember that next time someone does something we don't quite understand at first.

July 30 Day 4
Tourist (Human) Potential

Langfang, Hebei Province
A Day Off

Those clever Chinese people, they think of everything: At breakfast I was served a slice of bread with the jam already swirled into it. This not only saved time, it avoided a mess of jam pots, messy knives and sticky fingers. Brilliant! Why didn't we think of that?

It was a good start to a day off, in which the local Red Cross volunteers were taking me to see Grand Epoch City, a replica of the the centre of Beijing, including temples, Tian'anmen Square and the Forbidden City. I had visions of LegoLand Windsor on a slightly bigger scale (and I love LegoLand!). When we arrived, I was amazed that they had rebuilt the centre of the city on a 1:1 scale. Not with plastic bricks but with clay bricks—just like the original. Amazing!

The idea for the Epoch City was to develop tourism in Langfang, as visitors would be able to experience all the wonder of the ancient centre of Beijing without having to pay enormous hotel bills and fight their way through the traffic to get there. They had actually built hotel rooms into the inside of the city walls (how cool, literally, is that), and the quality of the craftsmanship was impressive.

As impressive as man's creations are, I have to say that nature beats them every time and the highlight of the visit was when Xuelin and I were taken to the lakes, which were overflowing with lotus plants in full bloom—and there is nothing quite as radiant and fragrant as a lotus.

Lily, our guide for the visit, took us round, explaining the history and dimensions of the Epoch City. They had built a huge five star Fu'an'gong Hotel with over one thousand rooms using traditional materials in ten months. In Britain it would take at least two years just to get the outline planning consents. This is not to say Britain is not good at development, it is, which is why so many foreign investors want to come there. It is simply a question of land ownership and permissions. In China the state owns the land and grants the permissions, then when it decides what it wants in a particular place it will happen very quickly. In Britain you might be dealing with a hundred small private owners who might be affected by the development. They all have property rights which must be addressed before permissions are granted. As private ownership expands in China, the ability of the state to make big infrastructure decisions will be reduced, which is why they are so very smart to do them now.

The final part of our tour was a visit to the Buddhist Temple with grand statues and incense burning. I am a spiritual person in the sense that I believe that religion is as much a necessary part of our human lives as love, family and meaningful work. But it wasn't the grand statues which caught my attention but a prayer tree in the corner of the temple on which thousands of visitors had hung messages and prayers. Xuelin and I spent ten minutes just reading through the messages. One seemed to capture them all:

'Wish the whole family peace and good and health. Pray for good work. Pray that that they have a happy marriage. Pray that their child will study hard and be well behaved.'

You could have found a similar prayer card in most cathedrals, mosques, synagogues or other places of worship and spiritual significance in the world. It reminded me of some work which we undertook when I was Deputy Chairman of the Conservative Party in which instead of the usual opinion poll technique of trying to categorise people into certain social groups by education, wealth or family background, we simply asked people to self-describe themselves from a list of statements. The statement which, by a very long way, was how most people identified themselves was 'Ordinary hardworking people just trying to build a better life for themselves and their families.' My guess is that if we asked the same question in China, the people would probably top the poll again. It is a universal prayer, a universal dream and a universal duty on all political leaders to do their very best to help them achieve.

Sorry, I have wandered off the point of tourism but I still have 60 days to go, so I have plenty of time to return to it later.

July 31 Day 5
Winter Olympics & Personal Best

Route: Anci District – Bazhou, Langfang
Today walked: 31.00 miles / 49.90 km
Total walked: 90.70 miles / 144.60 km

Xuelin had been up until 3 a.m. in the morning supervising the translation of my blogs into Chinese and waking me occasionally to explain phrases and terms in the early hours, which I tried to do with good grace. The problem for the Chinese, and indeed most languages, is that in English we tend to use a lot of idioms: 'to coin a phrase', 'to pull your leg', etc., which cause deep confusion and frustration. The Chinese are also frustrated by the English habit of 'beating around the bush'—sorry, not being direct. In English we use a lot of conjunctive adverbs, euphemisms and 'padding' around what we want to say. In Chinese, where each word has a character of its own, the language is much more direct, as demonstrated by the Chinese Restaurant sign which read:

'All you can eat buffet. Not mean all day buffet. You no come stay 4 hour. You eat. You go home.'

That makes English people smile but the prefacing of a request with, 'Sorry to trouble you. Is there any chance you might happen to know how one might find a shop that might sell various types of bread?' Instead of 'Where is the bakery?' leaves Chinese smiling too.

Madam Zhang Ming, who is Director of Communications for the Red Cross and our project manager for the walk, is like Xuelin in her incredible capacity for work. Each day Madam Zhang Ming would bring down a new set of detailed revised plans for the walk, which reflected where we got to the previous night and the ripple effect of the changes will have been communicated down the line. The attention to detail was incredible. They even marked out where the public WCs are on the route, which kind of had me thinking, 'What are hedgerows for?' Only joking. On one such visit I discovered an important bit of information in this regard. Most WCs in China do not supply toilet paper. You are expected to carry your own. Not sure why. There are just some things you don't want to ask your host. Anyway, it is a fact which I now know. I am also taking a little adjustment to the absence of a seat—sorry, let's change the subject ….

We set out from Langfang City heading south for Dacheng. The temperature unexpectedly cooled to around 30 degrees and there was a gentle breeze. In addition I was refreshed by my rest day. This has all the makings of a very good walking day and I was determined that we should make the most of it. We set off at 7:30 a.m. sharp and by lunch time we had already done nearly twenty miles. What was more, I felt good about it.

Most of the time I am not on the new highways, as pedestrians would not be allowed, so we take a less direct route on our travels. The quality of the infrastructure in China is extraordinarily good. The walking paths, roads and cycle paths are as good as anything I have experienced in Europe and better than all except Germany. The roads are tree-lined to provide some shelter from the sun. Whilst the quality of the infrastructure is world-class, the same cannot be said for the vehicles using them. You have vast numbers of heavy trucks and busses sharing the space with hundreds of small motorised tricycles, and weaving in between them at speed are the modern executive cars—Mercedes, BMW, Range Rover and VW being the most popular. This is a nation, it seems, constantly on the move. Travellers by foot are extremely rare. Communication therefore is vital and this is done by horns, especially the trucks and busses that have horns that seem to reverberate through your entire body. Still, in what seems like chaos on the roads I have not witnessed any accidents.

I press on and reach our hotel in Shengfang having completed 31 miles. When I arrive, Madame Zhang is in a celebratory mood, and I think that it might be for me completing over 30 miles but it was because it had just been announced that Beijing had won the 2022 Winter Olympic Games. It was fantastic news, and as we sat in the cafeteria of the hotel all attention was of those wonderful scenes when the president of the International Olympic Committee opened the envelope and declared 'Beijing.' This meant a great deal to China. They had done a fantastic job of hosting the Olympics and Paralympics in 2008 and Madame Zhang was part of that team. This meant that Beijing would be the first city in history to host both the Summer and Winter Games. I was caught up in the celebration as the iced tea flowed. Our only concern about the announcement was that Madame Zhang may be brought back to Beijing to start work on the Games and without her we might still be navigating our way around the outskirts of Nanjing in 2022.

A good day all round.

August 1 Day 6

The Kindness of Strangers

Route: Bazhou – Dachengxian, Langfang
Today walked: 30.20 miles / 48.70 km
Total walked: 120.90 miles / 193.30 km

Due to a slightly wrinkled sock, I had developed a painful blister on the little toe of my right foot. It seems nothing, but I know from painful experience that small problems become big problems if they are not treated. I spent three days in northern France unable to walk because a small blister became infected. I am blessed to have a Xuelin with me on this walk. This is the fourth major walk we have done together and most of the problems health or logistics we have encountered before, and like all good teams we work well together. Xuelin has the tough end of the deal because she has become a specialist in foot care. This time she produced some foot-repair cream from the Dead Sea, which my nephew Daniel had brought back from a visit to Israel over a year ago—Xuelin had kept it and added it to her tool kit. It worked a treat and the next morning I was fully repaired and ready to go.

Another part of Xuelin's role is that she deals with the bills: We have been very fortunate because the Red Cross team has managed to identify great budget hotels with wi-fi, shower and a bed, which is all you need. There have been some great chains that we have been able to stay in for 200–300 yuan per night (₤20–₤30), including breakfast for both of us. The hotels are just as good as any Premier Inn, Travelodge or Ibis that you would find in Europe, and yet at least half the price, which makes a very big difference for us when we will be here for seventy nights. Once you reach the big cities, then the prices rise, as you would expect, but even in Beijing you would be able to get a good standard hotel for £50–£70 per night.

This does beg the question: Why has foreign tourism to China not taken off in recent years in the same way that foreign tourism from China has? The number of Chinese tourists coming to the UK has doubled in recent years from 150,000 to over 300,000 and yet UK tourist visits to China number in the low tens of thousands. It could be that what Brits are looking for is sun, sea and booze, and those three things aren't as easy associated with China as the Mediterranean resorts. Still, for those seeking an experience, different from the norm, and at the price of a package holiday to the Med, they really should consider China more seriously.

Older tourists will find the Confucian culture of respect for age and wisdom refreshingly different from the youth-obsessed Western culture. I have also found the food with its emphasis on fresh vegetables, rice and tea a good change from beer, a burger and a bun at home. One of the biggest differences I find is the inter-generational nature of society here. Xuelin and I will often go out for a walk at night when we are in a larger town and city. You will invariably hear music coming from a park, and it will be from the dance groups who come out to perform group dance activities in the evening. All ages will be there—teenagers, grandparents and grandkids all just enjoying the fun of doing dance moves together. It is the absence of alcohol which changes the culture and allows people, children and the old, to feel un-threatened by the young men. I have seen this before in some Muslim countries which are coffee and tobacco countries, but their societies are segregated by male and female so you don't get the same whole community feel.

It is something that every nationality says about themselves but few who say it have had much experience of anything to compare it with: 'The people are so friendly here.' Having walked through eighteen countries, I have to say that with the exception of the Republic of Ireland, there is very little difference between the friendliness of any particular nationality. You smile—people smile back—but most of the time we simply don't connect unless we are buying or selling. I am not quite sure why but China is currently proving to be closer to the exception of Ireland than the norm of everywhere else.

It could be that I have been walking for four days and I have never seen another foreigner, never mind another Westerner, so therefore you stand out as a novelty and people want to take pictures of you and with you because of your round eyes, big nose, white skin and the fact that you are walking (with a stick) in the middle of the day! They ask in such a friendly way that you cannot say no even when you are 25 miles into a challenging walk.

One test, which is not scientific but is interesting, is spontaneous generosity. What I mean is that I have walked thousands of miles and only twice have people offered me food for free (many, many have come along the roadside to try and sell). The first was in Albania, where a melon seller asked for a photo with me and gave me a large slice of melon. The second was in Duisburg, Germany, when a Starbucks' Barista asked me about what I was writing and insisted on buying me a latte coffee, and the third and fourth were yesterday when a young man ran across the road with an ice cold bottle of water, which he gave me and then a few hours later a young lady pulled ahead of us in a car and opened up a boot to show a tray of bottled water which she offered to me and members of our team. So, I have been walking for seven years and there have been four occasions of this spontaneous generosity and two happened yesterday on Day 6 of the walk in China. I hesitate to mention these thoughtful acts because we don't want to encourage them—we want people to be generous to the Red Cross, whom we are here to support, and not to us, but it is just meant as an interesting observation about the real China or more precisely the real Chinese people.

August 2 Day 7
Travelling Together

Route: Dachengxian, Langfang – Qingxian, Cangzhou
Today walked: 20.70 miles / 32.70 km
Total walked: 141.60 miles / 226.00 km

There is a Chinese saying, 'If you want to go fast, travel alone. If you want to go far, travel together.' On all my walks up until now I have walked alone. I am not fit. I am old. If you walk with other people they might want to stop when you don't and vice versa. They will always walk at a very slightly different pace, which over the course of a long day can make a huge difference as you have either had to slow down or speed up from your original pace. Also, people want to talk—fair enough, but in this heat and at my age I barely have enough energy to walk, never mind talk. Sure, if you have going for a five mile wander through a forest or along the coast, it is great to have conversation and company but not when you have to do 30 miles in 40 degree temperatures. So, taking people with me seems like carrying unnecessary baggage—why would you do it? Today would provide an answer.

We made an early start on the walk to try and get the cool of the day. I noticed that there were more Red Cross volunteers than the previous day, all looking wonderful in their 'Walk for Peace' T-shirts. About eight walking in all. We gathered for the ancient Chinese custom of taking smart phone pictures, first the group shots, then one brave soul (normally female) would step forward and ask for an individual picture, then everyone else would want an individual one. Everyone is laughing. It's fun. All of a sudden I, being old, forget those aches and pains from yesterday and start to look forward to the day ahead. Then with our collective loud *Jia You!* (Come on!) We set off.

One of the few instincts that I have developed to a high level through walking is a sense of direction. I sense this through the sun and even my shadow on the road. I sensed that rather than travelling south, we were actually travelling west. I thought it might be a short distance but it must have been for an hour. Eventually, I mentioned this to Madame Zhang and she explained that the local volunteers were trying to avoid some of the busier roads and second that the provincial border with Tianjin and Hebei was at this point and the local volunteers wanted to keep within their province. Fair enough.

Just then another family group arrived—I thought to take a picture. It was the Deputy Secretary General of Langfang City, who had shown us very kind hospitality with the Deputy Mayor when we had visited the Epoch City a couple of days before. I was without a translator and so the Secretary General's daughter stepped forward and said, 'This is my father. He met you yesterday. We are his family. He would like to walk with you.' I replied 'Yes, of course' and mentioned a few rules for safety about walking alongside the busy roads in what was now a group of around 14.

I was walking out in front, struggling as usual with the humidity, but from the outset I heard numerous conversations going on in the group behind. They were sometimes laughing and joking. Sometimes you could hear in deep debate. The Red Cross volunteers went to great efforts to make sure that when we stopped for a water break there were enough cool drinks to go around. I thought that perhaps the Secretary General might stay for a few miles and then be whisked away in a black limo, but he was still with us at lunch and we had a good talk.

After lunch we passed some cyclists in full cycling gear, they wouldn't have looked out of place on the Tour de France. Initially they paused for pictures. They then said that they had heard of my walk through a social media group for outdoor pursuits and wanted to know if they could join us. Of course, I said and so they followed on. The group was now growing and people were not leaving. As we walked through the small towns and villages, we were creating quite an impact because there were so many of us walking. This in turn meant many more stops for photos but it was fun.

As we arrived at our stopping point for that evening, we had done almost thirty miles. It has become a bit of a tradition that when we finish the day Madam Zhang Ming gets everyone together to cheer the final few steps, and I always feel as if I have just completed a marathon (which in distance terms I often have). This time the crowd was a lot larger than usual on account of the people we picked up along the way. But that sense of collective achievement was very real. It also meant more that it was not just me being cheered across the line but it was us. Experiences are diminished in value when they are exclusive and multiplied as they are shared.

I reflected on my son Matt's favourite saying when he was a young basketball coach, 'There is no "I" in team.' I felt that almost spiritual transformation from being a selfish individual to becoming a selfless part of something much bigger. What is more, I was happy about it. Thomas Merton, the great spiritual teacher, talked about just this feeling when he wrote: 'True happiness is found in unselfish love, a love which increases in portion as it is shared ....'

We then ended the day with that ancient Chinese custom of taking smart phone photos, first of the team and then one person (usually a female) would step forward to ask for an individual picture, but this time I said, *Meiyou* (no), for this wasn't a day for the individual, it was a day for the team and that made all the difference.

August 3 Day 8
Hospitals & the Press

Cangzhou, Hebei Province
A Day Off

Today was a day off. Well, let me qualify that: It was a day off walking but not a day off working. There were the blogs to be written. Xuelin is a brilliant manager. She always starts with the bar very low—'just one blog … even just a few lines would be great' and by the time the day is done we have four blogs and 2,500 words. Not that the work stops there. The blog is then sent back to the ever-patient team in London who carefully translate it into Mandarin Chinese.

In between the second and third blog we had a press conference from the press and media of Hebei Province and Cangzhou City. I have done a few press conferences in my time back in the UK and the questions are invariably not about the story, but in search of an angle that might give the journalist a unique take. Now of course the media in the UK are freed from any political constraint, but they operate under the often greater control of the need to sell papers or get viewers. In the UK media market place that can lead to a journalism that sensationalises, shocks and trivialises, focusing on images rather than messages. This is not their fault. It is ours, the reader and the viewer whose attention span has been reduced to 140 characters plus pictures. Sadly, most stories are way more complex than this, but in our superfast world we don't have the time or inclination to understand, only a demand to be entertained and to judge.

Sorry, off the soapbox now, but let's just say that the press conference in Cangzhou was a little different to those at home. The questions were on the facts: Why was I walking, where was I walking, who was I walking with, what did I think of Hebei? We even had time to exchange Confucius quotes on welcoming strangers and walking. Xuelin was my translator for the press conference, and if I tried to go a bit off message or controversial I noticed that her translations seemed to take longer as if to translate, 'What Michael meant to say …' Still I was very happy with this because communication is such a critical part of culture and it is not just what you say but the way you say it that counts. To give credit to the journalists, the next day they did unexpectedly arrive to film and photograph me on the walk and doubtless to do their duty to check that I was doing what I said I was doing.

After the press conference a few of us went out for a walk but it quickly came on to rain heavily. I pointed to an amazing building that looked as if it were either a luxury shopping mall or the HQ of Google or Goldman Sachs. To my astonishment it turned out to be a hospital: Qing Xian People's Hospital. I was with the President of the local Red Cross, who was a doctor, and he said that he knew the Dean and he was sure he would be happy to show me round. I was intrigued. I said yes.

Normally in China visits are planned long in advance and permissions need to be secured, but this was spontaneous. We went into the marble-lined entrance hall to the hospital and within a few minutes the Dean, Li Shuyan, was with us. I thought, wow, in the UK it can sometimes take a couple days to get to see a doctor and here I was with the Dean of the Hospital in 3.5 minutes. The hospital was new, only opened a few months ago and it had 1,000 beds. The only comparison I had in mind was the Royal Victoria Infirmary in Newcastle, which I had visited just a few months ago, and it had around 600–700 beds and was one of the largest in the country. This hospital had free car parking and even its own park to aid the process of recovery. I have always viewed the National Health Service as being one of the greatest components of our civilisation, and it was very clear from outset that Chinese doctors and administrators held the British NHS in very high esteem and it was the model which they were aiming to replicate, albeit for a country 20 x the size. Walking along the wide corridors there was an order and calm about the place which was not accidental but built into the design to reduce anxiety and give people space.

One difference I picked up on was the banks of cashiers at the back of the hospital because China may be moving towards a NHS model but at the moment it is still insurance-based. The state insurance covers 80% of the costs of treatment and the remaining 20% is either a patient contribution or can be claimed back from the local government. What I asked was the situation if someone had no insurance and could not afford the 20%. They would be treated first and then they would discuss how to pay the bill—at this point the local Red Cross Society would also step in to help.

We then went up to the operating theatres and needed to be scrubbed and gowned and wear a mask just to look around. There were sixteen operating theatres and each was equipped with the very latest in medical technology; most of the machines were made by Philips. As we made our way out back to the reception, I asked the Dean what the words over the entrance meant. He said, 'The first qualification for a doctor is that they should be kind-hearted. The second qualification is that they should give all patients—young, old, rich, poor, powerful or weak—the same level of attention and care.'

Our hosts were rightly proud of their hospital. I believe that the quality of our hospitals, schools and infrastructure—'public goods' if you will—are the hallmark of a healthy society. On the basis of this quick checkup Cangzhou certainly passed the test.

August 4 Day 9
Human First

Route: Qingxian – Cangxian, Cangzhou
Today walked: 26.90 miles / 43.30 km
Total walked: 168.50 miles / 269.30 km

As I prepared to leave the hotel, I received a social media notification from the International Federation of Red Cross Societies reminding us that August 6 marked the 70th anniversary of the dropping of the atomic bomb on the Japanese city of Hiroshima, followed by a second bomb on Nagasaki three days later, on August 9. The social media post from the Red Cross reminded us that 70 years on thousands of people still require long-term medical care because of illnesses that had their beginnings on those fateful days in 1945.

The war having ended in Europe the allies of United States, China and the UK, met at Potsdam and on July 26 issued a demand for Japanese unconditional surrender, warning of 'prompt and utter destruction' if they did not comply. They didn't comply. So, on August 6 a plutonium atomic bomb was dropped on Hiroshima, destroying in an instant five square miles of the city. Between 90,000 and 166,000 mostly civilians died—half incinerated at the point of implosion and half dying agonising deaths through burns and radiation over the following few months. Over 90% of the doctors and nurses in the city had been killed and all hospitals and clinics were flattened, so there was no medical care available for survivors. Water supplies were poisoned with radiation. There was no food. Disease set in. A few days later a second bomb was dropped on Nagasaki, where between 39,000 and 80,000 were killed in the same way. On August 15 Japan surrendered. These remain the only two occasions when atomic weapons have been used.

These are very sensitive issues to write about, especially in China, which was the subject of an unprovoked attack and brutal treatment by Japanese occupying forces in World War II, especially the bombing of Chongqing and the 'Rape of Nanking'. In Britain too we retain a deep resentment for the sadistic treatment of British prisoners of war by their Japanese captors. Does this mean that we should be immune to the sufferings on the other side? I don't think so. Does showing empathy for the sufferings of enemies undermine a clear moral view backed by international law as to who was right and who was wrong? I don't think so. We can't change the past but if we are to change the future, we must do so from a perspective of our shared humanity rather than enmity.

On this day on my Walk for Peace I chose to remember the innocent fellow human beings who suffered and are suffering because of the horrific events of this day in 1945 in Hiroshima. That is not being unpatriotic or undiplomatic, it is just remembering we are all human first.

August 5 Day 10
Milestones

Route: Cangxian – Nanpixian, Cangzhou
Today walked: 21.90 miles / 36.40 km
Total walked: 190.40 miles / 305.70 km

Milestones were invented by the Romans to allow their armies to know how far they were from the next garrison. The Roman Mile was 1,000 paces comprised of two steps to a pace. Being a good Roman colony the British kept the system for over a thousand years but updated in the sixteenth century. The kilometre (1,000 metres) is a much more recent 1790 invention of the French, which explains why the British didn't adopt the kilometre and the French said 'non' to the mile. A kilometre is equivalent to 0.621 miles. A Chinese mile is 500 metres but road distances are always given in kilometres.

All of this is perhaps of passing interest because without doubt the greatest benefit the mile-marker gives is to improve travellers' morale through letting them know how far they have travelled and confirm that they are on the right road, heading in the right direction. So, when I was greeted early in the day with a great fanfare of supporters proclaiming 300 km, I found myself forgetting my loyalty to the British Mile and embraced this 'milestone' (of course 'Kilometres tone' would never catch on).

We took a break with the local Red Cross volunteers for pictures next to a field of date trees—dates are a local speciality of this area. They are smaller and sweeter than their rivals. We took pleasure in making it this far and managed to set aside that we might have another 1,300 km to go before we arrive in Hangzhou.

The skies had cleared that day and the sun was very strong. I only realised how strong when I reached the hotel that evening and discovered the extent of my sunburn to the back of my neck and the calf muscles at the back of my legs. Most of the time on the walk so far there has been heavy cloud added to by dust, so seeing and feeling the sun accurately has not been possible. That is a problem for confirming a rough sense of direction. I know that if it is in the morning and I feel the sun on the left hand side of my face, then I am heading south and if it is the afternoon, then I will be travelling south if I feel the sun on the right hand side of my face. Shadow length will give you a good indication as to time of day—the shorter your shadow the nearer you are to midday. Why is this important?

Well, on this day I began to feel the sun on the front of my face in the morning so I knew that I was travelling east. The problem was that I wanted to be heading south. I mentioned this to Madam Zhang, who was able to provide an instant explanation in the shape of the map drawn for my route by local officials. The overriding concern of the local volunteers was to keep me safe, and so they had sacrificed this goal for the goal of directness. We had taken a route which had gone south, then east, at one stage north east in order to keep on the best roads. Had it not been for the sun and blue skies I would probably never have realised, but this also explained why my iPhone map was showing 130 miles direct to Beijing and yet I had walked close to 190 miles. We talked that evening about routes, and I said that I was very happy to take my chances on some of the less good roads in order to make progress.

It is in the Chinese nature to do everything in their power to make the guest welcome and meet their wishes, so they went away and came back with a more direct route which we embarked on the next day. I felt a little guilty because they were only trying to care for me and they worked so incredibly hard to make sure every detail was correct. That said, they are friends and I think they understood the reasons, namely that I am on such a tight schedule to make it to Hangzhou before the beginning of October. They did explain an interesting challenge though, and that was that the network of what we might call country roads is not as great in China as if a road is to be built between two villages, both the villages need to agree. If they can't agree, then the road simply goes around both, and it was along many of these roads we had travelled.

August 6 Day 11
'Up the Workers'

Route: Nanpixian, Cangzhou, Hebei Province – Ningjinxian, Dezhou, Shandong Province
Today walked: 24.60 miles / 39.60 km
Total walked: 215.00 miles / 345.30 km

This is the true joy in life, the being used for a purpose recognized by yourself as a mighty one; the being a force of nature instead of a feverish, selfish little clod of ailments and grievances complaining that the world will not devote itself to making you happy.

I am of the opinion that my life belongs to the whole community, and as long as I live it is my privilege to do for it whatever I can. I want to be thoroughly used up when I die, for the harder I work the more I live. I rejoice in life for its own sake.

Life is no "brief candle" for me. It is a sort of splendid torch which I have got hold of for the moment, and I want to make it burn as brightly as possible before handing it on to future generations.

George Bernard Shaw

It can only have been as a result of my small-family business upbringing that I have always had a huge respect for those who work hard and take risks. There is nobility about work. It is the antidote to the idle musings on why life hasn't served up all that you think you deserved. It is about doing something worthwhile. Have a purpose in life. Have the satisfaction of a job well done. It is about doing something for others and through that gaining benefit for yourself. For this reason I find it personally difficult to relate to the idle poor and even less to the idle rich—though I realise that there are very broad generalisations and there will be exceptional individuals in both categories.

The success of the Chinese economy is not accidental. Education is the most important thing you can give to a child, and this is every parent's passion for his or her child. Children are affirmed and instilled with self-belief. On that solid foundation is built an almost religious belief in hard work. There is then the savings culture—Chinese people are always saving for something and distrust the easy option of borrowing from a bank. They respect wisdom, especially from the elderly. The final layer is an entrepreneurial spirit—all/vast majority of Chinese people one day want to be their own boss. Put those six: affirmation, education, hard work, saving, wisdom and enterprise together in any country or culture and it will produce a world beater.

As I walk along I meet many people who are doing just that. Sweating away in the fields or selling produce in a market. I connect with them in a particular way, as I too am sweating away in the middle of the day and they seem to somehow respect that.

I meet a date farmer and his wife gently pruning the date bushes waiting nervously for the harvest of their eleven acres in September in time for the Moon Festival, when the best prices achieved. They express concerns familiar to farmers the world over—if there heavy rains and storms are going to come and damage their crops. Will there is a too big harvest of dates, which will reduce the prices?

Further down the road—a farmer of livestock, geese, all free range, comes out to meet me, thinking I am a Russian. Russians are very important because they buy a great deal of Chinese meat. He then took me to his pig farm next door, which he was planning to expand further because of export demand.

Later we had planned a packed lunch by the roadside but the manager of a water treatment works invited us into his fan-cooled office to shelter from the sun. It was as if I was adopted into an honorary fellowship of workers.

After lunch as we walked alongside the road, there was a road maintenance crew of about ten men clearing the gutters and cutting back the grass. We passed each other three times on different sections and would each time wave. This time I passed late in the afternoon and they seemed keen to talk and Xuelin translated. They even allowed me to try my hand at using some of their equipment. My guess is that the average age of the workers would be sixty or seventy.

This leads me to my final reflection, which was confirmed by the noble image of an elderly man I met on a bridge at the end of the day. He must have been 85 years old at least but he still had a rake in his hand and was clearing a roadside bank. In the West we have undermined a great deal of human value because people retire too early. I work in the House of Lords, where some of the most dedicated members and sharpest brains are in their nineties. I am fifty four years old. In some professions they would be starting to mutter that I might start thinking of early retirement. I simply cannot think of anything worse. I want to work till I drop, and if at 85 I am found on a grassy bank in Shandong Province in the heat of the day with a rake in my hand, then I would consider my life to have been a one of noble endeavour and reward.

August 7 Day 12
Healthy Living

Dezhou, Shandong Province
A Day Off

The Red Cross volunteers are carers and first responders. I have been particularly well looked after from a health point of view. I guess they took one look at me at the Temple of Heaven and thought, 'This guy won't be able to make 1,000 steps, never mind a 1,000 miles.' They even prepared an oxygen pillow and insisted on taking my pulse and blood pressure at the end of the day. My pulse was 82 and the blood pressure was around 100 because my arms are so fat they couldn't get the vessel to fully stick when the band was inflated, so we were never quite sure.

I confess that I have never taken my health terribly seriously on my walks—if I am still standing at the end of the day, then I must be okay according to my standards, but for Chinese people healthy living is the most important thing, apart from breathing. Food is not consumed for enjoyment but as a medicine for nutrition.

I remember when we were first married, Xuelin wanted me to drink turtle soup and stand on my head for 10 minutes each day. I can barely stand on my feet. I told her, and as for 'turtle soup', my kids were brought up on the *Teenage Mutant Ninja Turtle* TV series, and if I were to actually eat or even be rude to one of Leonardo or Donetello's brothers or sisters, I am sure they would never speak to me again.

I came in one day from work and saw Xuelin grimacing as she ate some grey thin meaty type food. I asked, what is that? She replied Donkey Skin! Why? I asked. It is supposed to be good for blood circulation! I began to worry. Had I married Hanibal Lecter's little sister? If someone told me I could live to 250 if I ate donkey skin, I would still probably push it to the side of the plate and carry on eating the fish and chips.

Yesterday when the temperatures were very high and even I was feeling a bit unsteady on my feet, Madam Zhang appeared with a 'wonder cure for heat exhaustion'. They were little plastic brown bottles of medicine. I didn't look keen. I was even less sure when I was given the name of the medicine, 'Huoxiangzhengqishui'. What's the matter with asprin or lemsip? These are short names you can trust? I feel a good rule is I should never take anything I can't pronounce the name of less than three syllables.

Madam Zhang thought I was being childish refusing to take something that was good for me, so she took the top off one of the bottles and drank the whole thing in one gulp ... she then burst out coughing; I feared she was going to choke to death, which would have been an extreme way of reducing the risks of heat exhaustion. I took another cool bottle of Diet Coke from the ice box and felt much better.

August 8 Day 13
The Good Manager

Route: Ningjinxian – Lingcheng, Dezhou
Today walked: 23.50 miles / 37.80 km
Total walked: 238.50 miles / 383.10 km

The first 11 days have been punishing because of the heat, humidity and all due respect to our wonderful hosts, air quality. I don't think there is any way I could have done over 200 miles in 10 days without the incredible support of the local Red Cross volunteers. It is their enthusiasm that I feed off in the morning and their sense of achievement which inspires me at the end of the day.

The fact that these teams of volunteers come together at county, town and provincial level and then perform to such high levels, instantly picking up the baton from the previous team, is thanks to their leader, Madam Zhang. We had a major change of team today with the sore team from Hebei handing over the Shandong team.

It was great to be back in Shandong Province, which was the first place I ever visited in China back in 1997. It is a vast province with huge economic power, and having a population of 117 million—that is almost the population of the UK and France combined (not a happy thought).

Back to the teams—if I am the worst manager of people that I know (and I probably am), then Madam Zhang is fast becoming the best in my opinion. Xuelin and I reflect on how we both have similar faults when it comes to managing: We are both productive and efficient individuals. We like things done to a high standard and in the quickest time possible. We both love work and somehow resent having to share it, so we don't delegate. We instinctively think 'It would take longer to explain what I want than it would take to do it ourselves.' So we carry on, on our own, missing out on the multiplier effect of that comes from successful management of teams.

Madam Zhang, like us, is highly efficient and productive. Unlike us, she realises that teams are a critical part of delivering major projects successfully. It was not by accident that someone with those qualities should play such a key role in the Beijing 2008 Games. Xuelin and I are keen to learn and we discuss Madam Zhang's approach.

So what are the key Ingredients of good team leadership that we have observed in Madam Zhang and we would recommend to others?

Personal security: People who are insecure in their roles and knowledge of themselves are hopeless leaders of people because people feel that insecurity. Insecure leaders personalises criticism as they take it as criticism of themselves rather than of the task. The insecure needs too much praise so tends not to give praise to others. They are insecure and so manage upwards constantly, trying to please their boss and neglecting their team. Such people will instinctively take every bit of credit meant for the team for themselves and pass on every bit of criticism meant for themselves.

Encouragement: There was a phrase popular in my native northeast area of England and it was 'You get more by tickling than scratching.' The point is people respond better to being told they are doing a good job, but you have a few ideas as to how they might be able to do a great job other than being given a dressing down. It is the easiest thing in the world to knock someone down, it requires great skill to pick someone up and enable them to make a contribution.

Listening: How long do you spend transmitting instructions to your team and how long do you spend listening to feedback? I would suggest that the good team leaders are good listeners. They are eager to hear suggestions as to how performance could be improved and the best source of that is from the people who are doing the job. This needn't take a long time:

One of the most transformative management books of all time is the *One Minute Manager* by Ken Blanchard—it has sold 13 million copies so far. The basic premise of the book is that good management need only take a few minutes but bad management can cost you months or even years in lost production.

Be quick to praise and slow to criticise: For the reasons already stated but most of all because a basic human need is for people to feel they are appreciated. Think of the last job you left; the chances are that it wasn't that you didn't like the firm or the department, it was because you felt underappreciated by your line-manager—that is what endless business school surveys tell us. Appreciation is spelt R-E-S-P-E-C-T.

Big picture: Most failing managers will look at a team and see only its inadequacies. Most successful managers look at the same team and see only its potentials. I love football and so often you see a team with some gifted players failing to deliver the performances on the pitch that they should. Then there is a change in manager, not the players, and all of a sudden the same players are world-beaters. Part of the reason for that is the vision which is instilled in them by their manager. One day a wise manager visited a major construction site, and he asked one of the workers what was he doing, he responded, 'I am just baking bricks.' The wise manager responded, 'No. You are building a great cathedral.' Focus the team on the big picture, not the small task.

Talent spotting: Building a good team is like putting together a jigsaw puzzle. You know what you want it to look like because you have a picture on the cover of the box, but inside all you just have are a 1,000 odd-shaped pieces. I think the best managers are the ones who recognise first that every piece is different but is of equal value, that they all have a place and their task is find a space where they fit in and contribute to the overall beauty of the picture.

Be calm. Things will go wrong. That is life. The question is not why did it go wrong but what is the wise thing to do in the situation now to try and put it right or minimise the damage? The qualities of a cool head and a warm heart are perhaps the most important of all.

There is a poem called *If* by Rudyard Kipling, which I won't translate into Chinese because much of it is word-play in English, but to me it captures the essence of the good manager and the qualities we have observed in Madam Zhang:

> If you can keep your head when all about you
> Are losing theirs and blaming it on you;
> If you can trust yourself when all men doubt you,
> But make allowance for their doubting too;
> If you can wait and not be tired by waiting,
> Or, being lied about, don't deal in lies,
> Or being hated don't give way to hating,
> And yet don't look too good, nor talk too wise;
>
> If you can dream—and not make dreams your master;
> If you can think—and not make thoughts your aim,
> If you can meet with Triumph and Disaster
> And treat those two impostors just the same;
> If you can bear to hear the truth you've spoken
> Twisted by knaves to make a trap for fools,
> Or watch the things you gave your life to, broken,
> And stoop and build'em up with worn-out tools;
>
> If you can make one heap of all your winnings
> And risk it on one turn of pitch-and-toss,
> And lose, and start again at your beginnings,
> And never breathe a word about your loss;
> If you can force your heart and nerve and sinew
> To serve your turn long after they are gone,
> And so hold on when there is nothing in you
> Except the Will which says to them: "Hold on!"

If you can talk with crowds and keep your virtue,
Or walk with Kings—nor lose the common touch,
If neither foes nor loving friends can hurt you,
If all men count with you, but none too much;
If you can fill the unforgiving minute
With sixty seconds' worth of distance run,
Yours is the Earth and everything that's in it,
And—which is more—you'll be a Man, my son!

August 9 Day 14
Shandong Highway

Route: Lingcheng – Linyi, Dezhou
Today walked: 25.40 miles / 40.90 km
Total walked: 263.90 miles / 424.00 km

The Shandong Highway and I have grown very close over the past few days. I have travelled its length since crossing over from Hebei Province. It has the great comfort of not only providing kilometre markers but breaking it down into 100 metre intervals. This is a huge help in pacing myself.

The landscape is a picture of China's economic progress: Shepherds with their flocks travel along the road and riverside impervious to the heavy traffic and the occasional walker. Then there are the bustling villages and towns, all with roadside markets as well as shops. It is in the villages and towns that people have the greater confidence to wave, shout 'Hello' or 'Welcome to China' and then ask for a photo. It adds to the time of the walk and breaks the stride but this is the purpose of the walk, to connect with the real China.

Villages are mostly located off the Shandong Highway and will have ornamental gates and the village name, often in English as well as Chinese. The villages are normally about 500 metres or so from the highway. At the junction of the village lane and the highway there is normally a traffic police officer standing smartly to attention. Often we are invited to come to the village to take shelter from the heat of the sun or for some food. Other times young people will wait at the end of their village lane and offer water or even on one occasion today, an ice cream.

It is an interesting study in communications in rural China because news of the 'foreigner walking' is sent through social media WeChat, QQ or Weibo. WeChat is the Chinese WhatsApp or Twitter and Weibo is more a micro blogging site. They both have about 500 million users. QQ is an instant messenger for China and has over 800 million users, the same number as WhatsApp globally. To place those numbers in some sort of context: Twitter would have 330 million active accounts but Facebook remains way out in front with 1.4 billion. We witness the power of social media in China every day as pictures taken from one village trigger some member of the next village to join in.

Some suggest that China is worried that currently blocked US social media firms Facebook, What's App and Twitter in China will dominate the market when the block is removed. This may be so but there is an equal possibility that Chinese social media giants QQ and WeChat will take a chunk out of the US market share when they become global brands and platforms.

We stop to talk to people along the Shandong Highway—mostly when Xuelin arrives and we can engage in conversation. We hear time and again how advances in farm machinery and technology mean that they don't need to have two people looking after the land, so normally the female, will go and work in the new factory making clothing or some other produce normally for export markets. With the two incomes they are able to get clothes, a motorised tricycle and send their child to school. Soon the villages are embraced by the cities and so the villagers are trading their traditional village homes for modern high rise blocks of flats with electricity, gas, water schools and hospitals. For some of the older villagers the offer of a brand new flat for their final years lacks the appeal of the village and home they have known their whole lives and previous generations. It is exactly the same pattern of industrialisation which has gone on through time the world over.

Of course, they will soon reach the level of prosperity that with cars they don't want to be cramped into blocks of flats and will start to build new homes back in the countryside. My point is there is nothing that I have yet seen in China which from an economic point of view has not happened in every other industrialising economy. It is classical industrialisation. This may give some comfort to the Chinese leadership but soon they will see new social challenges taking over from the old economic ones as a growing highly educated, entrepreneurial and confident middle class.

August 10 Day 15
Back in Beijing & Yao Chen

Beijing
A Day Off

Day 14 turned out to be one of the toughest days of walking I have ever undertaken due to the heat and humidity. I felt the symptoms of heat exhaustion coming down to cover me like a heavy cloud. The Red Cross team and Xuelin, ever mindful of my health, managed to arrange for a local council office which was open on a Sunday to allow me to lie down in a cool room during the heat of the day. Otherwise, things could have been a whole lot worse. We set off walking again at 4 p.m. and finished at 7:30 p.m., when it was getting dark and the busy roads offered a different type of challenge.

The two-day trip back to Beijing which Xuelin had arranged could not have come at a better time to aid my recovery. We left from the high speed rail terminal at Dezhou East and were in Beijing just in 90 minutes. Travelling at speeds of over 300 km, it made quick work of what had taken me two weeks to walk. I love rail travel. I grew up close to the main East Coast line and my earliest memories are of rushing down the bank to the bridge over the railway line to catch a sight of trains like the Flying Scotsman. I have always tried to live close to railway stations: Durham and now Victoria. There is an elegance about train travel. If I lived in China, I would love to live beside any of these spectacular high speed rail stations.

So, the experience of the rail journey lifted my spirits. Just as we left the train a staff worker came along and changed all the seats around to face the forward direction—I thought this was brilliant. I hate travelling with my back to the direction of travel, and yet again Chinese people had come up with an elegant solution.

Xuelin and I arrived in Beijing and we were met by representatives of *China Daily*. We were in town to help launch a smart phone photo competition called 'Amazing China' at its headquarters. *China Daily* is a true global publication—it is readily available alongside *Metro* and *City AM* on the London Underground. What is more, as many print publications are in decline, *China Daily* is increasing its reach. It is clearly positioning itself in the *FT* and *International Herald Tribune* space and such is the thirst for insights on China from within China, it has a very strong future.

From the moment we arrived at HQ we were shuttled from interview to interview by *China Daily*'s London Bureau Chief, who had flown in for the launch event. Given that this is a business publication, there was great interest in Xuelin's views and it was good to participate together. After the interviews by print, TV and online journalists, it was off to meet Kang Bing, who is Vice President of the China Daily Media Group. It was fascinating to get his insights on the global media industry. After the high speed rail journey this was high speed business.

At precisely 1:55 p.m. we were ushered to the lift and taken down to the large auditorium which had been set up for the launch. We arrived out of the lift and there must have been a hundred young people with smart phones raised waiting with anticipation. When I walked out of the lift, there was an almost audible sigh of collective disappointment—it is something you get used to as a British politician. But just then there were screams as they rushed across to the next elevator and this time they weren't disappointed. The reason? The actress Yao Chen, China's Angelina Jollie!

What is it about celebrity? Yao Chen just lit the auditorium up with her presence. I wanted to grab my iPhone and go across to film her arrival too, Xuelin held me back. Here were a collection of some of the most powerful figures in media and business and politics in China, but we were all willingly made spectators at the Yao Chen show. As so often, behind a very successful image a hugely intelligent person knows how to present her brand. their brand. Her micro blog has 78 million followers, mine has about 78, on a good day—well, on a day when I am mentioning Yao Chen in it. No wonder *Time* magazine named her in its list of the top 30 global figures on the Internet. Amazing China!

August 11 Day 16
Cultural Exchanges in Beijing

Beijing
A Day Off

We were very grateful for the invitation whilst in Beijing to meet with our (British) new ambassador, Barbara Woodward. In the Beijing traffic you can either be half-an hour early or half an hour late. We prefer to be either an hour early or on time. We arrived at the Ambassador's Residence half an hour early and were kindly allowed in and served a cup of tea. It was a hugely busy time for the ambassador, as the British Foreign Secretary arrived the next day on a regional tour from Tokyo and Seoul with very complex issues on the agenda.

Barabara Woodward was a gracious host and was very interested in the walk. She had just been appointed to the role of ambassador in February this year and had begun her working life in China as a teacher and therefore was fluent in Mandarin. What is more, she understood the culture very well having lived and worked here. In China culture is even more useful than language. More misunderstandings happen through lack of respect and understanding for the culture than misinterpretation of the language.

One of the greatest challenges facing British diplomats in China is that power does not always come conveniently dressed up in a way in which is easy to spot—namely a fine-cut suit, fine-cut accent, impressive title, confidently dropping the right names and the right cultural experiences.

Whilst weakening through education and social mobility, Britain still retains many of the characteristics of a class-based social system, especially at elite metropolitan levels. China is a bureaucracy.

We had just had lunch with one of the most unassuming and humble Chinese officials you could ever meet—Qiao Wei, a friend of Xuelin who is Deputy Chairman of the Chinese All Federation of Returned Chinese, but as Vice Minister is a highly influential figure in Beijing. This reminded me of one of the first visits I had made to China with Xuelin when there was a British Business Reception in Shanghai and Xuelin was present as a board member of the UK-China Business Association. The guest of honour was HRH Prince Andrew, who was hugely respected for the work he had personally done in promoting UK-China trade.

One of the problems was that a major UK investor was being frustrated by delays to his application. The CEO had flown in to try and unblock the delays. A senior British diplomat navigated the VIPs around the reception room in search of titles and fine suits, etc., brushing aside anyone who didn't 'look the part'. Xuelin happened to spot a casually dressed guy in the corner of the room. She was intrigued as to why he would be here and started talking to him in Mandarin. She was able to establish that he was in fact the local official who had the investment application on his desk but had some legitimate questions about the detail of the proposal, which he was hoping to have a chance to discuss with the CEO but in Chinese culture didn't want to push himself forward when there were other more senior figures in the room. Xuelin put the two of them together helped with translation, and within a few days the investment was agreed. Welcome to China.

August 12 Day 17
Back on the Road in Shandong

Route: Linyi, Dezhou – Jinan
Today walked: 24.70 miles / 39.80 km
Total walked: 288.60 miles / 463.80 km

It had been a packed two days in Beijing. We concluded with a visit to CCTV's studios to record an edition of *Dialogue,* which happens to be one of my favourite programmes formats on the English-version CCTV Channel—as to whether it will remain that after our appearance I don't know. Questions ranged vary widely from British education to WWII, sport and how Xuelin and I met. Xuelin was keen to extract every possible opportunity from the visit, this even included an interview with the Xinhua News Agency in the Beijing Station whilst waiting for the train back. We arrived back in Dezhou East late and we had an early start the next day.

The seven-km section of the Shandong Highway we were travelling along was blocked undergoing major road works, so it required some detour to get to the starting place. We had good guides from the local Red Cross, who at one point took me over a huge mound of earth and through a narrow gap in a fence to make it onto the road where the resurfacing was taking place. Following the direct original route rather than the detour because of the road works would save a day in walking, and that meant that as far as I was concerned it was a risk worth taking.

It was a hard walk and the dust was thick in the air from the road repairs, but just as we ended I was guided over another mound and into a police station in Linyi. I thought I must be in trouble again, but the local police chief had heard of the walk and wanted to show his hospitality. It was a welcome stop in a cool air-conditioned office and an opportunity to look at maps of the next section of the walk. The target for the end of the day was to reach a river crossing which was the boundary between Dezhou and Jinan, so there was to be a small ceremony to mark another handover. That was a good clear aim.

After two days off I felt fantastic: I was pushing a near 6-km per-hour pace. I felt so good I didn't want to rest for lunch but wanted to keep going to complete the day's walk as early as possible and then to get to the hotel and rest. I was walking mostly through rural communities with occasional appearances of urbanisation. As usual people were very friendly and curious. I wish that I had more time to talk to them and find out more about their lives and to explain what I am doing and why.

Some I did have the chance to speak to were a hospital dean, who invited me in for some tea and to cool down and of course to have my blood pressure taken. One of the advantages and disadvantages of walking with the Red Cross volunteers is that they take such a concern over my health. I seem only to have to sneeze and a packet of some medicine is produced and politely declined, but such attentiveness on their part would come into its own the next day.

In one of the final communities we passed through a man with the most wonderful smile came out to greet us. He ran a motorcycle repair shop. He was very busy but had time to show me around his garage, which was piled with spare parts and motorcycles in various states of repair. He had the instinctive look of the type of man whom I would trust with my motorcycle repairs if I had one. I enjoyed being in his garage because it reminded me of the sight and smell of my grandfather's shed. He was a steel worker but had a part-time fascination and talent for repairing all sorts of machines, even his grandson's bicycle. As a child it was less of a shed, it was more of a magical cave where broken things went in and came out fully restored. In the West we have become a throwaway society and moved from a 'make do and mend' to a 'buy new and spend' culture—this has left a legacy of consumer debt which China would do well to avoid our mistakes and keep the motorcycle repair man in business.

We arrive at the bridge—there is half a suggestion we might want to go further, but no, we had put in a good shift and we would keep the energy for tomorrow. As usual it was great to meet the new Red Cross volunteers from Jinan and sad to say *Gan de hao* (great job) to the team from Dezhou.

August 13 Day 18
Thoughts with Tianjin

Route: Jiyangxian – Huanghe Bridge, Jinan
Today walked: 23.80 miles / 38.30 km
Total walked: 312.40 miles / 502.10 km

It was a familiar start: We returned to the bridge where we had finished the night before to take a start. Our aim for the day this time was the bridge over the Yellow River and into Jinan City. Back at the bridge a bustling roadside market had sprung up. By the time we got there at 8 a.m. the market had already been going for three hours. There was such an incredible selection of fresh fruit and vegetables bursting with colour. In Chinese culture there is a great value placed on fresh food, and in many areas there is no refrigeration to stock up, so the tradition of daily shopping is alive and well. I asked how the prices were at the market—the chilli seller said that his price had fallen over the past year from 1.5 yuan to 1 yuan whereas the garlic seller had seen the value of garlic almost double over the same period. I love small markets because there is no manipulation with cross subsidies and promotional offerings, pricing is straightforward supply and demand (and open to negotiation).

Around lunchtime I could see that Madam Zhang and some of the Red Cross team were getting bad news. There had been an explosion at a chemical plant in the port area at Tianjin. Early reports indicated that there may have been over a hundred casualties. This was a major incident for the Red Cross because they are first responders in emergencies like this.

It made the awful events all the more real to think that we had walked around the edge of Tianjin the week before. To know that many of the Red Cross teams who walked with us would now be engaged in conducting search and rescue operations amidst the rubble of the former factory and operating blood donation centres for the victims personalised the tragedy for us. It also strengthened our determination to raise funds for the Red Cross Society in China so that it could continue to provide this incredible emergency service at times of crisis and disaster. I was also encouraged that British Foreign Secretary Philip Hammond, who had been in Tianjin that morning, had responded to the disaster with a pledge to support the rescue efforts with specialist teams from the UK.

Perhaps it was because of the general low mood which perpetuated during the afternoon as more reports came in from Tianjin and the very high temperatures that made the last 15 km some of the hardest I had ever walked. To complicate matters I had had an upset stomach (sounds pathetic even to mention it on such a day) which had meant that I had lost my appetite for food. This then led to stomach cramps. I made it across the Yellow River bridge but only just and then needed to get back to the hotel to rest. I began to worry whether I would be able to walk at all the next day even though that would knock us off schedule, having already taken two days out to go to Beijing. That said, not taking a day off might knock us off schedule later for longer. The decision was taken not to walk the next day, and I think the Red Cross team accepted that as their thoughts remained with their colleagues in Tianjin.

August 14 Day 19

Rest Day in Jinan City

Jinan, Shandong Province
A Day Off

I slept for almost twelve hours, waking at 7 a.m. I felt very weak. It seemed as if it took all my energy to brush my teeth, never mind walk 40 km. I was grateful we had taken the decision to cancel the day's walking. I went down for breakfast but couldn't face the prospect of eating anything again. This was now a second day without proper food. Not a good sign. Henry Kissinger, I am told, would respond to any piece of bad news with the phrase, 'What can I do now that I couldn't do before?' It is a very good tool for turning negative events into positive action. In answer to the same rhetorical question, I thought I could get up to date with my blog entries and find out more about the history and culture of Jinan, one of the major cities of ancient and modern China.

The population of Jinan is around 7 million (about the size of London). Because of its proximity to the Yellow River and its abundant natural resources, including lakes and 72 fresh water springs. It is sometimes easy to forget that the boundary of ancient China ran across Shandong and Jinan. In fact, remnants of the Great Wall of Qi built in 500 BC remain. It is a predecessor of the Great Wall of China built in 250 BC. Today Jinan is a typical global city much the same as many others with its high rise buildings and high speed rail, but its long history is what sets it apart.

I was honoured to be visited at the hotel by the Deputy Governor of Shandong Province before breakfast. Shandong Province has a population roughly twice that of the UK, so her kindness in visiting this traveller was particularly appreciated. As we walked in to the hastily set-out meeting room with marked seats for all those attending and UK and China flags, I was greeted at the entrance by the Deputy Governor. Normally, introductions with officials and visiting guests have a certain predictability but when the translator enquired, 'How is your diarrhea this morning?' I was a little wrong-footed. Not wishing to protest that it was a stomach ache not diarrhea that had resulted in my forced day off, I simply replied, 'Much better, thank you.'

The Deputy Mayor had been well briefed, noting that my first visit to China in 1998 had indeed been to Shandong Province. She explained the long history and natural beauty of Shandong Province and how it suffered under Japanese occupation. Then conversation turned to life in the UK, which she seemed to be particularly knowledgeable about. She later explained that her daughter is currently studying at university at Loughborough. It reminded me that of all the possible aspects of cultural diplomacy possible, education is the greatest. Shandong retains as a special memory for me because I undertook my business degree research project here in 1998. The UK was a special place to the Deputy Governor because her daughter was being educated there now.

Education links were the theme of the day, as Xuelin had arranged a meeting with members of the Zhejiang alumni association in Jinan. Zhejiang University is one of the top universities in China, and it had two major points of significance for this walk: First, Xuelin attended the university and is now President of the Zhejiang alumni branch in the UK. Second, my plan is to walk through the Zhejiang University campus in Hangzhou on the final few kilometres of the walk. They were very supportive though I was particularly interested in one of the alumni because he had been a classmate with Xuelin, and I wanted to try and get him to share some stories about Xuelin from her student days. I was surprised that after a long and funny set of comments in Chinese, his remarks were translated simply as 'Xuelin was a hard-working student.' The translator, of course, was Xuelin!

By the end of the day I was almost up to date with my blog entries and e-mails and had some very interesting meetings but the loss of appetite and stomach problems persisted ... though the diarrhea was now fine!!

August 15 Day 20
Across Jinan and Fellow Walkers

Route: Huanghe Bridge – Licheng District, Jinan
Today walked: 25.90 miles / 41.70 km
Total walked: 338.30 miles / 543.80 km

I couldn't face breakfast but I was keen to get back on the road. This was going to be a special day—I would reach the 500 km marker. It was also a Saturday, so the number of those joining the walk increased. Xuelin and I have been deeply touched by the number of people who have come along to walk with us. There is a large number of followers of the walk on WeChat, which Xuelin and the team back in London ensure is regularly updated, so for those in the area it is not too difficult to estimate where we will be and when, and if not then WeChat messenger can get a direct response.

It is one of my regrets that I don't get more time to speak with those who come along to join in. I apologise that I am so old and unfit that it takes all my energy to walk 40 km and every breath of conversation is one less I have to make a step. Early on in the walk I see that wonderful sign '500 km' in the distance being waved. It always puts a spring in my step.

Among those joining the walk today was Vice President Wang Rupeng of the Red Cross Society in Beijing. Wang is a very senior and respected figure in the Red Cross, having steered through a number of important reforms. That said, for me the greatest thing was that he had organised a walk from Hong Kong to Beijing (3,000 km), which took six months and raised £2 million for the Red Cross—respect!

He had also brought his 13-year-old daughter with him, who was very keen to walk, having walking similar distances in the past. I always reflect on my first 'big walk' was when I was 14. It was a 25-km circular route centred on Wylam in Northumberland. I could only manage 15 km before I stopped to bathe my blistered feet in the cool River Tyne and needed to get a car ride to the finish point. I am therefore full of admiration for younger walkers who come along and keep the pace.

As we passed through the centre of Jinan, there was a major road and public transport junction beneath flyovers towering over head. Beneath where we walked were hundreds/thousands of men seeking work. They would normally be from the country districts and come here each day, waiting to be picked up for occasional work normally on construction sites. It was an unusual scene in China as normally people are not waiting for work, they are doing work, any work.

We took an unusual route out of the city on account of the very large hills/mountains that surround the city. The reason was understood when we came to a large road tunnel under the mountain. I am always more than happy to take the risk of walking through the tunnel than walking over the mountain. Of course, being supported by the Red Cross volunteers meant that we approached the task in a far less relaxed way than I had done before with high visibility jackets, torches and even face masks to protect us from the fumes.

The tunnel must have been about 3 km long but we emerged into a completely different landscape. The dusty city was left behind and the place was covered with lush green hills and parks. I had only experienced this once before when I had crossed the Golden Gate Bridge in San Francisco and went through the tunnel into Mill Valley (still my No.1 place in the world to retire to). The green hills had an added purpose as they were deeply spiritual places with names like 'Thousand Buddha Mountain'. You could imagine pilgrims from the city of Jinan travelling across the mountains we had just come under to reflect and pray.

This prosperous southern suburb of Jinan City, high up among the mountains, was populated with financial services and IT firms. Smartly dressed young professionals drove German cars to the huge shopping malls with luxury shops and movie theatres. China is a nation of contrasts in landscape but most profoundly in its economic landscapes.

For the last stretch on the G104 we were joined by the Deputy Mayor of Jinan City and welcomed rain clouds to clear the air. I am a politician and I think I understand the political mindset fairly well, and I have been so impressed by the political leaders who have joined me on my walk. The reason is that there is no press coverage of the walk, so when President Wang or the Deputy Mayor of Jinan walk, it is purely out of a personal belief in the values of peace and friendship which underlie its purpose that makes their company all the more special as their motive is the same as mine.

August 16 Day 21
There Will Be Days Like This

Route: Jingong Villa, Jinan – Tai'an
Today walked: 17.50 miles / 28.60 km
Total walked: 355.80 miles / 572.40 km

There is a wonderful song by Van Morrison called *Days Like This*. I have it on my iPhone and play it often when I walk, especially on good days. The opening lines are:

> When it's not always raining, there'll be days like this
> When there's no one complaining, there'll be days like this
> When everything falls into place like the flick of a switch
> Well, my mama told me, "There'll be days like this"

After some very tough days on the walk due to the weather and my illness I rose from our accommodation on the edge of the Taishan Mountains. It was Sunday, with a clear blue sky above and green trees and running rivers all around. This was the best day I had experienced so far. I wished more of those who had struggled with us alongside the busy highways and cities could have been with us for this day as we began a steady climb into the mountain foothills, passing through small villages along the way. As the town gave way to the country so the friendliness of people who had time for each other and for strangers returned too.

One village in particular was to leave a deep impression on me because of the warmth of their welcome—Xingjiatun. The leader of the village came to meet me off the road with Madam Zhang and invited me to come and see the centrepiece of the town, which was a 500-year-old tree. I was not ready for a break but in the mood for learning more about the area I was walking through. I sat in the shade of the tree along with twenty or thirty villagers in a scene that would not have changed for 5,000, never mind 500 years.

Next to the tree was a 700 year old well. I have never used a working well before, but sending down an empty bucket and drawing up a bucket of pure clear cool water must be one of the greatest experiences there is. You could almost taste the purity of the water and the experience as the villagers hastily prepared some seats and a table under the shade of the tree to serve tea while the village speciality, watermelon, which had been cooled in the well overnight, is prepared as a delicacy for special occasions and visitors.

They seemed keen for me to talk to them so I talked about the tree: When that tree had just been planted in Europe Christopher Columbus was setting sail to discover America (I then hesitated because it is very likely that the Han Chinese people crossed the Bering Strait to the Alaska a thousand years before and were the forebears of what are now called Native Americans). When this tree was planted, the people of Europe still believed that the sun and the stars orbited the Earth until Galileo put us right.

I began to run out of examples, so being a good politician, I changed the topic. 'Do you have many Westerners visiting this village?' The villagers started looking at each other and then shaking their heads, 'No. You are the first.' I was surprised by the answer and checked again. The answer came back the same. Then they said they would go and get the oldest man in the village who would be able to tell. A tall, distinguished looking man in what looked like a military shirt came across the square and sat down next to me. I asked how old he was. He replied he wasn't very sure but about 95. The villagers then asked if he could remember any foreigner ever visiting Xingjiatun before. He thought, then shook his head and said, 'No.'

We sat together under the shade of the tree and engaged in conversation through Madam Zhang as the villagers stood all around and watched. The old man told how he had joined the army in 1943 to go to attack the Japanese, who had occupied nearby Jinan City. I asked him what he thought was the secret of his long life and he replied, 'Work.' He said he still worked and that was what kept him healthy. I told him that my grandfather had just turned 100. He was impressed. I then said that the highlight of reaching 100 in England is to get a personal birthday card from the Queen. He seemed even more impressed. I then suggested that when he reached 100, he might get a card from President Xi Jinping. 'Good idea.' They all laughed. The leader of the village said he would send him a card but it didn't seem to quite match the high expectations I had built up.

I carried on walking up the mountain and reflecting that I may go down in Xingjiatun history as the first foreigner to visit the village. We stopped for lunch at a fantastic cafe with wonderful views. Soon we were joined by about 30 to 40 young people from all across China, aged 12–16. They had just completed a 32 km walk as part of a summer camp activity. They were keen to talk and share experiences from the road. Most of all I was struck by the immense sense of personal achievement which the simple act of walking had given these young people and the closeness of the friendships which they had made along the way. I shouldn't have been surprised because it has given me all of that and so much more, especially on 'Days Like This'.

August 17 Day 22
Charity Appeal

Tai'an, Shandong Province
A Day Off

After the exertions in the Taishan Mountains the day before, it was good to relax in Tai'an for a day and take stock of the walk to date:

The walk was going well—355 miles was slightly ahead of schedule to finish in Hangzhou in early October. The illness I experienced in Jinan is gradually working its way through the system (no more detail necessary, I think!).

Through the walk we had managed to communicate the message Walk for Peace that 'We are all human first' and that should unite us. Our nationality, culture, language and religion are all 'add-ons', 'apps', if you like, downloaded onto the basic human system, and most are tribal and a complete accident of birth. If we choose to focus on that 95% we share with our fellow humans rather than the 5% of 'add-ones' that are different, then we can create a more peaceful and harmonious world. During the three weeks of the walk Xuelin and I have been able to share that idea with hundreds of people who have either joined us on the walk or come along to support it.

There is, however, a third purpose to the walk, and it is sometimes the most difficult to talk about because it involves money. We set out with the aim of raising £50,000 or 500,000 yuan to support the work of the Red

Cross Society in the UK but especially here in China. Xuelin and I have seen personally the incredible work which the Red Cross does, whether it is being a first responder to disasters such as that at the recent Tianjin chemical plant, caring for the young and the elderly, collecting blood donations, training millions in first aid or providing hardship loans to those who are ill and in need of medical care.

So far we have raised ₤3,500 through our Just Giving web site in the UK and ₤2,000 in direct donations to the Red Cross here in China. That is a total of ₤5,500, which is only around 10% of the target. (Xuelin and I are, of course, paying all our own travel and accommodation, so all donations go to the cause for which they are intended). This is not the first charity walk which Xuelin and I have undertaken, it is fifth. Xuelin is an amazing fundraiser and we are blessed with some very generous friends. Previously at this stage of the walk we might have hoped to have raised about half of the target funds (₤25,000), so we are well short of that.

Xuelin and I have a long discussion about why this might be different this time round. We identify that, of course, this walk is taking place in China, and many people who previously supported us back in the UK might not even yet be aware of it. We also talk about a culture difference between the UK and China in attitudes to charity and Xuelin thinks this might be something worth exploring in a blog.

The history of charitable giving in the UK stretches back the beginnings of our Judeo-Christian roots. The Bible proposes a tithe (10%) of income to be given to the church or charitable causes. With the establishment of Christianity as the official religion of Britain in the ninth century AD came an official tithe which was paid to the local church for the upkeep and building of places of worship and monasteries.

So, the concept of giving a proportion of your earnings away to the church was well established but it really wasn't until the British industrial revolution that charitable giving began to expand. The reason was that there was a large new wealthy middle class who had made great fortunes from very humble beginnings. They were from poor communities so knew the problems that they faced and felt an obligation to put something back. So it became normal for the wealthy middle class to put money into establishing schools, hospitals and homes for those who could not otherwise afford it them.

As more and more people became wealthy by their standards, they sought to follow the example of the wealthy industrialists of Victorian England and voluntarily support local charities caring for the poor, animals, the elderly or those with specific diseases such as cancer. It became to be seen as part of being a good society that it was not, and should not be, just left to the state to do everything—everyone has a contribution to make.

In the Bible Jesus is quoted as saying, 'It is more blessed to give than to receive.' This is not to suggest for a minute that Christianity has a monopoly on charity. All major world religions encourage followers to give a proportion of what they earn to the poor (and, of course, to the religious organisations that encourage them to give it). The point is that when we give, we implicitly acknowledge that we have been blessed with so much, more than we deserve and there are others, through no fault of their own, for whom fortune has been far less kind. This is our opportunity to balance the scales in their favour, not because the law demands us to but because our hearts inspire us to. That can make us feel good about doing good. Charity is 'twice blessed', as Shakespeare would put it, for its benefits fall both on the giver and the receiver alike.

August 18 Day 23
Through Tai'an

Route: Daiyue District – Ningyangxian, Tai'an
Today walked: 29.70 miles / 47.80 km
Total walked: 385.50 miles / 620.20 km

It was an early start as we made our way back up the S243 mountain road to the point where we had stopped two days before. The day was warm, even at 7:30 a.m., and so the coolness of the mountain breeze and the occasional shade of the trees were much appreciated. We were joined by a new group of Red Cross volunteers with wonderful bright orange jackets. I wrote yesterday about the benefits of giving money to charity but giving time is an even greater commitment, in the case of the Red Cross in China, just over 2 million people do that regularly.

The road from the mountain was mostly downhill, but it would have turns normally as it sloped down to cross a river and then there was a tough pull to make it up the other side. This variation of pace is interesting but physically challenging. The previous day we had visited Dai Temple, which I found to be a deeply spiritual experience. It had almost persuaded me to make the journey up the 5,000 foot Taishan Mountains. There is a strong part of spirituality associated with struggle, and the ideas of pilgrimage are key parts of most faiths. We assume that our spiritual enlightenment will be stronger having climbed for four hours to the mountain top than if we had just paid 5 yuan to light a candle in the temple. It is probably true, but as usual the experience owes less to the place and more to the motivation it evokes in us to want to seek it.

Back down on the ground it was hot, very hot. Conveniently, our route, took us past our hotel, so we were able to delay check out for a little longer and stop for the last few bits of food from the buffet breakfast. Then back out into the heat and what seemed like an endless detour around the top end of Tai'an before cutting through the western edge of the city. This route offered an additional benefit in that we were able to call in to the city department of health, in which the local Red Cross team is also located, and enjoy some free hospitality and good conversation. I wasn't rushing to leave, as it was hot outside, so after the usual round of photos I passed my camera across to the team and asked them to take some extra—another five minutes in the cool was worth it.

We followed the route of the G104 out of Tai'an and into the southern suburbs, which were full of partially completed blocks of flats. Judging distances was proving a challenge on the day. We were all very tired on account of the sun. The map was giving us one reading to the junction with the G3 expressway, but the Sat Nav and support car were giving us different readings. It was a bit like walking over huge sand dunes in the desert and at the top of each one you were expecting to to see an oasis and fresh spring water below, only to be disappointed—well, so we found it with each turn of the G104 searching for the G3. As it got dark and even the bright orange jackets of the volunteers were growing dim, we decided to stop after 47 km, only to find once we were in the car that the junction was just 500 metres away around the next bend. Such is life on the road. The 500 metres would be still there in the morning, but after a long hard day I was not sure I would be, so it was the right decision.

August 19 Day 24
Feast of Friendship in Ningyang County

Route: Ningyang, Tai'an – Jining
Today walked: 23.50 miles / 37.80 km
Total walked: 409.00 miles / 658.00 km

We arrived late into the hotel the previous night and the only place open was a Western style fast-food bar about to close, so Xuelin and I quickly shared a bowl of chips, ice cream and orange squash. If our hosts from the Red Cross were to hear of this, then they would be shocked. It is a huge part of Chinese culture to be welcoming and hospitable to guests from afar—as no less than Confucius stated in the opening of his *Analects* over two and a half thousand years ago.

On this walk it is food which has often proved to be the trickiest area of cultural difference. For instance, at mealtimes the Chinese tradition is to have up to a dozen different dishes on a revolving glass plate. Each guest takes what he or she wants, but the host will often show how honoured he is to welcome the chief guest by serving food onto the guest's plate. This comes as a shock for Westerners—the last person to serve food onto my plate was my mum when I was about four and a half! To refuse is to refuse the act of thoughtfulness and insult the host. I confess I have made this mistake sometimes.

For the Westerner eating is a formal and solitary occasion. You ask for what you want. You add your own seasoning. You take more if you want it. I won't get started on the toasting with drinks, as that is worthy of a blog on its own and my point is to show sometimes how cultural misunderstandings arise.

To take another example, at breakfast one day they were serving eggs. Eggs are a great food for starting the day but less so when fried, so I asked if they could do poached. After Xuelin explained a little what this meant, they came out with two great poached eggs. I told them how wonderful they were. Without saying another word the next day at a different hotel I came down for the breakfast buffet and there were two poached eggs, and each day thereafter at different hotels for a week—until I was unwell and unable to eat them, then they disappeared as quickly as they had come.

When I was unwell, I came down for breakfast and the only thing I could face was a plain white jam sandwich and some green tea. Again no comment was made, but the next day I came down and there was white sliced bread and jam/marmalade and a cup of green tea, but this time I was feeling a bit better so had some fruit—orange and melon. Again nothing further was said.

We then undertook our day's walk and we arrived in Ningyang County, where Madam Zhang informed me that we had been invited to join local officials for lunch. My heart sank as I really couldn't face a big meal, as I had a long way to walk and everything I ate at lunch would need to be carried for the next 20 km in my stomach.

We arrived at the offices of the county and were shown upstairs where a buffet had been prepared. I confess I felt just a little irritated at the thought of having to resist well-meaning attempts to fill my plate and questions as to why I wasn't eating enough. However, rather than sitting me at the large table they showed me into a small side room, and on the table set for Xuelin and me was a fresh loaf of sliced bread, marmalade, green tea and some fruit. I was so touched by this thoughtfulness of our hosts and ashamed of my own thoughts that preceded it.

The dining table can indeed be a place of cultural mystery and misunderstanding, but once we fully understand the motivations of those who host and prepare it, it becomes transformed into a feast of friendship.

August 20 Day 25

In the Footsteps of Confucius—Part I

Jining, Shandong Province
A Day Off

- Before you embark on a journey of revenge, dig two graves.
- Forget injuries, never forget kindnesses.
- I hear and I forget. I see and I remember. I do and I understand.
- It does not matter how slowly you go so long as you do not stop.
- Our greatest glory is not in never falling, but in getting up every time we do.
- What you do not wish for yourself, do not do to others.

Many of us in the West have grown up on Confucian wisdom quotes, often not appreciating their origin. Arriving in Qufu, the home of Confucius, has brought these quotes to life in a special way and placed them in a physical context to which I can relate.

Let me acknowledge firstly that I have just arrived in the town and hundreds of books and thousands of lives have been devoted to explaining the life and times of Confucius, so this is a very basic attempt to place the life in some kind of context for those, like me, who may know very little but be open to learning a little more.

Confucius was born here in 551 BC. His father was in the military in Lu State and died when Confucius was only three. He was not from a noble family and these were feudal times in China. Power and wealth rested in the hands of three aristocratic families, and each family was headed by a viscount and over them was the Duke of Lu.

During his political career he became respected as a teacher of high ethical standards who abhorred corruption and injustice, especially by the powerful against the powerless. He did not seek to challenge the feudal system but rather to make it work more efficiently and justly so it would survive and flourish. He did not advocate that everyone was equal. He served in relatively lowly positions, a governor of a small town being one, but when the Duke of Lu fell short of the standards Confucius expected, he resigned and set off on a journey around the small kingdoms of northeast and central China at the age of 54.

Disillusioned by the conduct of the Duke of Lu, whom he had faithfully served for so many years, Confucius began to practice less and teach more about good government, hoping to inspire the next generation. He toured many courts but few of his ideas took hold. He returned home to Qufu at the age of 68 and devoted himself to study and teaching.

His central teaching being that good political leadership begins with the leader developing good habits and practices starting in the home (filial)—you can't hope to become a great leader in public if you are not first a great son, brother, father or husband in private. Virtuous leaders will earn respect and inspire example amongst those they lead. It is the complete antithesis to that advocated by Niccolo Machiavelli in feudal Italy and written down in the *The Prince* and is refreshing for that.

One of his great themes which resonated with me on my Walk for Peace through his hometown was the idea of the Mandate of Heaven: A belief that there could be an end to the chaos and warring between states and they could peacefully co-exist under an ordered, harmonious, moral-based legal system where truth and honesty were the most revered virtues and those who embodied those virtues most would rise to the ruling class. It is a big idea that has been distilled by great minds for 2,500 years, but its beginnings are in our personal conduct and small unseen daily acts. What I have read and experienced so far makes me want to enquire more. The day after tomorrow I will visit his home, temple and tomb, which will be a good opportunity to reflect more on this.

August 21 Day 26
Walk to Qufu

Route: Ningyang, Tai'an – Qufu, Jining
Today walked: 18.70 miles / 30.20 km
Total walked: 427.70 miles / 688.20 km

We had the luxury of being based at the same hotel for two nights, but this meant a long journey back up the G104 to the border with Tai'an, where we had finished two days before. It normally takes the edge off the satisfaction to have to drive to a hotel at the end of a day's walking rather than finishing at the place we are staying, but I was very grateful for extra time in Qufu. Qufu is undoubtedly my favourite town visited on the walk so far—I stress town—as Xingjiatun will always be my favourite village. In both cases I stress also 'so far'.

On the map it didn't look like the most thrilling day of walking—30 km down the same busy road, but when we arrived at the start point, we were joined by some young students from Qufu First School who had been following the walk on the Weibo group, which is managed by Xuelin. It was great to have some time between stops to talk to Chen Bodong and Wanyan Junjie, who are both Red Cross volunteers about the walk and to find out about their hopes and dreams.

Wanyan wanted to be a doctor. His grandfather was a doctor. I think for most young people they get inspired by role models, especially from their family. Role models are also vital for raising expectations. My experience of life is that very little of what we achieve is down to natural ability and intelligence; it is more often down to our expectations of what we can do with what we have got.

Eton College, England, is one of the oldest (1440 AD) and most respected private schools in the world. Political, scientific, business and cultural leaders roll off a seemingly endless production line. I was told that one former head teacher used to say to all new students—'This school has produced 18 British prime ministers (now 19) —we expect you to do better.' This headmaster knew life is about great expectations, not just great talent. It is about what you believe you are capable of achieving, not an endless round of wondering why you haven't been blessed with the same brains, beauty or background as someone else.

Jack Ma of Alibaba, one of China's and the world's richest men, used to be a tour guide in Hangzhou and failed his entrance exam to university three times and didn't encounter a computer for the first time until he was 31, but he believed in himself when others doubted and that was the key factor that brought him success. It is said, 'Whether you think you can or whether you think you can't, you are probably right.'

I guess on a much, much smaller scale, an overweight and unfit minor politician from the UK who hadn't walked more than ten miles in his life before he was fifty can manage to walk 1,000 miles from Beijing to Hangzhou at the age of 54. When my body is creaking and wanting to collapse in an armchair after 5 miles, it is belief that gets me through the next 20.

In the 1930s a group of French scientists assessed the bumble bee against the laws of fixed wing aerodynamics and concluded that a bumble bee could not possibly fly because of the surface area of its wings was out of proportion to the size and weight of its body. Fortunately, the bumble bee didn't understand the laws of fixed wing aerodynamics and ignored the doubts of the scientists so when the jar was opened, he flew straight out of the laboratory window. Hmmm.

Well, the point is that Wanyan is halfway to being a doctor because he has someone who has shown it is possible and even more importantly, he believes he can.

Towards the end of the walk we passed the Wine Container Factory of Qufu. The owners very kindly let us shelter from the heat under the trees in their courtyard. Whilst we were there they told us how they lined the wine vats. They used paper. Not just any paper but the original paper preparation method invented by Cai Lun in 200 AD in Shandong. This was the first paper in the world and revolutionised communication because previously writing had been done on silk, which was expensive, or bamboo, which was very heavy. The technique moved slowly from East to West, for it was nearly 900 years later before the earliest paper documents were found in Europe and not until 1490 AD did we see paper production in the UK. It was an inspiring end to the day to see an invention and process of almost 2,000 years ago still alive and well in Qufu today. As I left they kindly presented me with some of these sheets of paper. Perhaps they hadn't appreciated that albeit 1,200 years after Qufu, paper production had now caught on back home.

August 22 Day 27

Confucius—Part II

Jining, Shandong Province
A Day Off

It was a day off, so my normal objective is to minimise the number of steps I have to take. Sadly, no one had informed Eva. Eva was our tour guide for the Confucius temple, home and tomb and was waiting for us at 8:30 a.m. to begin what turned out to be a very long walk around the historic sites of the city. Eva was very knowledgeable and enthusiastic about her subject. Before we arrived at the first site, I had already felt as if I had read the great man's biography.

Our first visit was the Confucius Temple. It was very grand with nine courtyards each with their own gate drawing you into the temple itself. Numbers are very important to the Chinese people—8 is the lucky number and 4 is the number you want to avoid—often a hotel will not have a '4th' floor but might have 8a and 8b. 9 was a number reserved for the Emperor. To have nine courtyards, nine pillars or nine steps was to confirm the highest status rarely seen outside the Forbidden City in Beijing.

I must confess I felt more at ease in the Confucius family home, which was on a more modest scale and focused around family living, reading and teaching. It revealed a tension, probably as a result of my lack of knowledge and understanding (despite Eva's best efforts) between Confucius the man and Confucianism the religion. There had been a broad symmetry in human development around the world from primitive religions based on tribal practices worshiping unknown gods such as the sun and moon, to sophisticated religions based upon more complex early civilisations worshiping known human gods/kings in temples/pyramids. Then after centuries of scholarly religious study and civilisation, there appear at almost the same time Socrates in Athens (470 BC) and Confucius in Qufu (551 BC), who were to create the first human philosophies of life and meaning. Neither wrote a book themselves; that was left to their disciples. Yet 2,500 years later their philosophies, though different remain at the cornerstone of Western and Eastern civilisations, respectively.

So why the tension? Well it was just that here was undoubtedly a great man, Confucius, who led a good life and sought to raise the standards of ethics in government and officialdom when it was not fashionable to do so. Rather than leave it at that and learn from that, after his death there emerged a range of claims made about his birth and life by his disciples, and these are recorded in the Temple and are the basis of the religion. For example, Confucius' mother, Madam Yan, visited a holy mountain before she conceived. Prior to his birth a unicorn appeared at his home with a book on his horn making prophetic claims about the new child's life. At his birth music floated down from the heavens saying, 'The Heaven senses a child-sage coming into the world so it plays music to accompany him.' There was then the visit from wise immortals after his birth who came down to pay tribute and so on.

We need religion as we need love. It cannot be rationally explained but we have a heart and we also have a soul. The point I was left reflecting on at the end of the day was that we have a heart and soul, and they have their wonderful place, but we also have a mind capable of incredible thoughts and insights. It was that great mind of Confucius that I wanted to discover more of in Qufu, but his teaching I had found obscured by their temple.

August 23 Day 28
Zoucheng and Mo Farah

Route: Qufu – Zoucheng, Jining
Today walked: 25.30 miles / 40.80 km
Total walked: 453.00 miles / 729.00 km

Because our walk had finished at the hotel in Qufu, we were able to set out from there at 7:30 a.m. on a beautiful morning. We rejoined the G104 Shandong Highway, which has become a trusted friend since joining the road 200 km back in Jinan. I had no explanation for it but I made very hard going of the morning session. In fact I might not have made an afternoon session had Madam Zhang not insisted that we break between noon and 3 p.m. from the heat of the sun at our hotel, which was on the way. It was an excellent bit of team management and meant that we were able to finish the day on schedule, which is good for health.

As we crossed the city borderline between Qufu and Zaozhuang, we had to say goodbye to two young students (both 17) from Qufu middle school. I wrote about Wanyan a couple of days ago, but as we parted it was Chen who was to surprise and encourage me. Chen had written a letter—his English handwriting and grammar were better than mine—so it was easy to read the text but the thoughts behind it showed a maturity beyond his years and gave me hope for a better future. In one section he wrote, 'I think peace is not the kind of affair of one country but also of everyone on earth. All of us are citizens of earth and should make our contribution to world peace.' 'Amen,' I exclaimed when I read it. I pondered this concept during the rest of the day, as it fitted with Confucius' view that there was a 'Mandate of Heaven' for a peaceful and harmonious world.

Over the past few days Xuelin and I had been enjoying the World Athletics Championships in Beijing. They brought back great memories of the 2008 Olympic & Paralympic Games. The highlight of this evening was the 10,000 metre race, in which Mo Farah was running for Britain. We wanted to see every step of Mo's preparations, but, of course, we were watching CCTV (the Chinese BBC), so the directors were paying more attention to the ladies shot put final, in which Gong Lijiao was looking for gold, but ended up with good silver. Coverage was uninterrupted from the third or fourth lap as a fascinating tactical struggle took place between the three Kenyan runners and 'our' Mo. I thought at one stage that the American with his long stride might be in with a good chance but in the final laps Mo showed his class. There was one heart-stopping 'Mo'-ment when he appeared to stumble on the final lap but he came home a comfortable winner.

I love sport. I think if I could have changed anything about my life it would have been to try and excel at any sporting discipline that might get me in with a chance of competing in the Olympics—surely the greatest honour on earth. I recall watching the curling competition at the Winter Olympics and seeing the team members whose job is to brush the way for the stone on the ice and thinking 'I could do that.' I couldn't, of course, but the dream lives on. The rise of global sporting competition has, in my view, done more than anything apart from the United Nations to reduce war and conflict between nations. It is a human instinct to compete for glory and to challenge rival tribes—this used to be done through warriors and violence, but it is increasingly being achieved through sport. In every human society in history the most revered members of society are its warriors. Through sport we have managed to create a new 'warrior class' who are also honoured with national pride.

Of course, we are still not at the levels of peace and civilisation as in 776 BC when the Olympics were founded. The ancient Olympics were not a celebration of their divided nationality but of their shared humanity. No athlete could carry any emblem or reference of his City State into the arena at Olympia. The athlete left his political identity at the gates of Olympia, and inside that arena and temple he and all his fellow athletes were Olympians only. We are still a very long way from that ideal. I wonder how many spectators would tune in to see one Olympian take on another? How many would shed a tear if it was the Olympic anthem played for every podium finish. How many athletes would drape themselves in the Olympic flag on their victory lap. Not many, my guess. No criticism, of course, but if I love sport, as I say I do, then I should be more than happy to watch the women's shot put final instead of the men's 10,000 metres—just don't test me too far, CCTV!

August 24 Day 29
Zaozhuang

Route: Zoucheng, Jining – Tengzhou, Zaozhuang
Today walked: 23.30 miles / 37.50 km
Total walked: 476.00 miles / 766.50 km

Back on the Shandong Highway for another long day, I notice that I am seldom taking out my iPhone to take pictures whereas in the early weeks I seemed to stop for a 'must take' shot every mile. Is this because there is nothing remarkable along the G104? Is it because I have become used to the sights and sounds of Chinese daily life—I hope not. I still have not reached half way. Sometimes it can be that we don't see the amazing because we have stopped looking for it. It is still there but we just wake up thinking it is just another day along the Shandong Highway of life and miss the rich colour and diversity of culture and nature. How can you walk 23 miles in a country like China and not be inspired and challenged by what you see?

On the road through Zoucheng I had been joined by two Red Cross volunteers who were both sports enthusiasts working, I think, in the local city sports bureau. Our communication was limited because they spoke little English and I, of course, spoke little Chinese. We did have one stop when Madam Zhang was able to translate a little for us because one of the volunteers produced his mobile phone on which he had scores of photos of Sir Stephen Redgrave. Redgrave is Britain's greatest ever Olympian, having won gold medals at five successive Olympic Games between 1984 and

2000. What was the connection?

Well my fellow walker today, Zhu Benguo, had been a rower inspired to take up the sport by Stephen Redgrave, who was his sporting hero. The young rower had competed in the Asian games. I thought it was amazing that a rower from Britain could have had such an impact on a young student in Shandong, China. Sometimes we will never know who we inspired and, sadly, those who we discouraged. Someone once said that if you received a pound (10 yuan) for every kind word you said and 50p (5 yuan) for every unkind word you said, at the end of your life would you be rich or poor?

I recalled one event on the BBC when Steve Redgrave was receiving yet another award, and he dedicated it to Francis Smith of Marlow, England. When asked later as to why he had done this, he explained that Mr. Smith was his English teacher at school and had said to the tall young Redgrave, 'Have you ever tried rowing? I think you would be good at it.' And with those few words of encouragement the career of a great Olympian and through him to inspire a young man in China to take up rowing too. I wanted to know why he wasn't competing; he looked at the peak of physical condition and couldn't have been more that 30, but time didn't allow.

Words are amazing. They have an ability to build and destroy, to inspire dreams and an ability to crush dreams. It is estimated that we speak 30,000 words per day, but it took only 13 to launch the career of a great Olympic champion and probably the same number to crush the hopes of others. As I write, words are being hurled back and forth across the DMZ between North and South Korea, like missiles spreading fear and despair in the region. Words matter. They matter because we remember them. Choose them wisely.

August 25 Day 30
Reflections on 500 Miles (800 km)

Zaozhuang, Shandong Province
A Day Off

This was not the day I was to hit the halfway milestone of 500 miles but it was a rest day in Tengzhou and so provided an opportunity for space to reflect on the journey so far:

This has been undoubtedly the toughest walking I have done in the 5,000 miles I have walked so far. The reason is the combination of weather and structure.

I have walked in higher temperatures before. Coming up through Albania in June/July 2011 it regularly got to 40 degrees and more, but there were two essential differences—on that occasion I had been walking for three months and so was very fit, and second, it was a dry heat, not a heavy humid heat, which is compounded with the poor air quality of the city areas in China.

The second reason why it is tough (and then I will turn to the many, many positives) is that it is a highly structured walk where even short breaks have been planned in advance out of great kindness and care by the local Red Cross volunteers. The challenge is that it is often the unknown and the spontaneous moments that have created an excitement in previous walks, such as to avoid the heat I would sometimes start at 3 a.m. and reach my new destination by lunchtime. Or, I might just not feel like walking at all and want to explore a place of particular historic or natural significance. Or, I might change the route at the last minute on the suggestion of a local person. These acts make the walk seem less like a treadmill session at the gym and more like an unfolding adventure.

I feel guilty in mentioning the negative aspects first: This is, after all, not something which Xuelin and I are undertaking just for adventure. If we wanted fun, we might choose to spend our summer two-month break on a beach or on a cruise. There is a serious purpose to this walk with its messages of peace and cultural exchange and the objective to raise funds for humanitarian projects through the Red Cross. I think Xuelin and I can certainly say that were it not for this purpose and objectives and the efforts of Madam Zhang, then we probably wouldn't have made it beyond the sixth ring road of Beijing.

Now let me turn to some of the many more positives:

First would be the privilege of getting to know and walk with so many wonderful Red Cross volunteers. We have been amazed that so many busy people have freely given of their time to come along and walk with us or support us. I haven't kept a count, but I would guess there have been a couple of hundred involved so far. They display the finest human qualities of care and commitment, which inspire me to keep going even when the going gets very tough. It is also through their involvement that the message of Walk for Peace is being spread through their own networks.

Second would be the number of people who have gone to extraordinary efforts to come and join the walk for even a few hours. There are too many to mention all but a few would be: James Chen, the famous artist who flew from Hunan to walk with us and encourage us; Shelly Hu, who travelled 8.5 hours by train from Xiamen; Wenjun Zhang, who has never done any walking before, came up from Hangzhou; Dean Liu, Siu Lam Li and her colleague Mrs. Xue Jianjun, who travelled down from Beijing to Tengzhou. Zhejiang University Alumni at various locations who have come out to meet and walk. All of these people have encouraged us with their willingness to identify with the cause.

Third would be the chance encounters with ordinary Chinese people along the way. The shepherds tend their flocks by the roadside. The market traders with the stalls stocked in the coolness of the early morning. The young people who shout 'Hello!' or 'How are you?' and capture a picture on their smart phone of this 'crazy foreigner' walking in the heat of the day through their town. The old people gathered under trees around a chess board or a card table. The local traffic police try to get us across busy roads safely in urban areas. All ages of people synchronised dance during the evening in the parks or market squares. The workers sweeping the roadside or working in the fields with whom we exchange a smile and a *Nihao* (hello) as we walk by.

Fourth would be the spectacular beauty of China: I think of the lakes and rivers covered in Lotus flowers as we came through Hebei; the majestic splendor of the Taishan Mountains; the fields of fruit-laden trees in Shandong; the Pomegranate Road of Yichang; the history and culture of Qufu; the temples of Tai'an; and the industry, architecture and energy of Beijing and Jinan.

Finally, it would be the over 100 people who have generously given funds to the Red Cross in support of our walk.

Thank you to all. *Jia You*!

August 26 Day 31
Mencius and Legge

Route: Tengzhou – Xuecheng District, Zaozhuang
Today walked: 25.80 miles / 41.50 km
Total walked: 501.80 miles / 808.00 km

There had been a spectacular thunderstorm the night before, so as we set out for this landmark day there was a freshness in the air that made the going easier than usual. As a result we made good progress before lunch and the added incentive of reaching 500 miles meant that we all felt we could press on with only a short break and try and finish by 4 p.m. We did and finished at a hugely impressive plaza and lake in the centre of the city.

I had had an excellent introduction to the area of Zaozhuang from the Deputy Mayor the evening before, so I knew a reasonable amount about its history and economy. It is a very impressive city and the layout and buildings are of a grand scale. The Deputy Mayor also came out to join me on the walk a couple of days before. I was very grateful for him for taking such an interest in the walk. I have had the honour to be received by about a dozen deputy mayors, or deputy governors on my walk so far. In China these visits are very important to build official blessing for the walk and the work of the Red Cross in supporting it.

Diplomacy in China is that China is more Confucian than Communist in some respects. It has a very strong 'pecking order' or social hierarchy. Hence, it would be an insult to the guest of a certain rank to have him/her received by someone of a lower rank and an insult to the host to receive a guest of lower rank. Prior to my arrival the Ministry of Foreign Affairs in Beijing had been asked to assess my 'rank'. They had concluded it was 'Vice/Deputy-Minister' on account of being 'the No. 5 ranked minister at the Home Office' (to be honest I had no idea that I ranked that high but Xuelin thought it best not to let on), so it was communicated that I should meet only those officials of similar rank on my journey.

The most revered person in history from Zaozhuang was Mencius—a disciple of Confucius. It is to Mencius that we look to discover the true meaning of much of Confucius' teaching, although he differed to the unquestioning reverence with authority and stated facts in a way that would have perhaps made him more at home with Socrates and Plato in the West. He stated, for instance: 'One who believes all of a book would be better off without books,' challenging the blind acceptance of knowledge and even arguing that it was almost the duty of the people to overthrow a leader who ignores the needs of the people and rules harshly, for the king must govern by example to and consent from the people—brave stuff for any philosopher, especially one in the third century BC.

Mencius argued that people had innate goodness and that this sense is sharpened through education. He also stated that ultimately we are only significant for what one gives to society, not for what one takes. This reminded me of one of the favourite sayings of my grandmother, who would urge us to be 'givers and not takers' in life. That is a high ideal that I struggle to live up to.

Of interest I am sure to my grandmother, who was a devout Christian, might also be that the teaching of Mencius came to the wider attention of the West because of a Scottish representative of the London Missionary Society called James Legge. It was Legge who prepared a translation of *The Works of Mencius* in 1861 whilst he was based in Hong Kong. In fact I noticed from a Wikipedia page that he had visited this same area in 1873 on a journey down from Jinan, through Qufu and Taishan Mountains and then on through Zaozhuang to the Grand Canal to Shanghai.

I mention this also because I have been ashamed to learn of my country's involvement in the Opium Trade and the destruction of the Old Summer Palace and to learn how arrogant Westerners with commercial or religious ambitions showed little respect for the ancient culture and sophistication of China. James Legge was someone who showed that there was indeed a different view and approach at the time and one which was in the spirit of Mencius.

Legge was a Christian and yet when he visited the Temple of Heaven, where I began my walk, he felt compelled to remove his shoes in holy respect. He was an ardent opponent of the British Opium Trade with China and was a founding member of the Society for the Suppression of the Opium Trade. He became professor of Chinese Language and Literature at Oxford University in 1876 and devoted his life to the translation of the great works of Chinese literature and poetry contained in the fifty volumes *Sacred Books of the East*.

I think in this First Year of UK-China Cultural Exchange we might understand more about each other if we were to examine the lives and example of Mencius and Legge, who though separated by 2,000 years of history, were united by their shared love of humanity.

August 27 Day 32
Age of Innocence

Route: Xuecheng District – Yicheng District, Zaozhuang
Today walked: 20.20 miles / 32.60 km
Total walked: 522.00 miles / 840.60 km

Xuelin and I took a bus ride into the city centre last night in search of a cashpoint machine and some food. I was struck again by how civilised and orderly the city centre was compared to the UK. There were large numbers of people out and about shopping at the roadside stalls that continue to trade by electric light, creating a carnival-style atmosphere. Families sat outside one shop that had placed a large screen to show a movie. Further along and there was one of several groups of formation dancers. The difference in the atmosphere is, in my view, because of the absence of alcohol and the presence of multiple generations and genders. Alcohol is clearly consumed in Chinese society in large amounts but this is either in a bar or at home. The streets, meanwhile, are left for families even until after 10 p.m.

The dancers form in lines of between five and ten. The best dancers are placed at the front so people can follow their moves. The novices start at the back. Small children are at the very front beside the sound speakers so they can be kept an eye on and also because in Chinese society children are the centre of the universe. I need to be very careful as a man how I describe the next point but the dress and moves of the dancers, male and female, are invariably graceful and modest and not at all sexually suggestive. The focus is on fun and exercise for all the family.

There is laughter but it seems always to be laughter with people than often in the UK, laughter at people. It is like a picture of a village dance hall in rural England in the forties or fifties. It reminds me that we all lose something in the UK when we section off generations. It is why Christmas and other formal occasions retain their appeal because they allow all generations of the family to intermingle as they were intended to. The old were all young once. The young will all be old. It is good to learn to live and laugh together.

The walk this day was one of the most beautiful that we have yet done. It was along a newly created garden or green route G312 through the mountains—it is known as the Pomegranate Way and leads into Yichang. As the name would suggest the road is lined with pomegranate trees and all kinds of other fruits and flowers. On the mountains there are some spectacular temples. It is idyllic.

We stop for lunch at Happiness Farm, where there are hulu fruit—I am not sure what its name is in English. In fact I haven't seen it before. It grows alongside grape vines and reaches almost melon size. The hulu fruit is considered to bring good luck. It is often allowed to dry out and used as a casket for wine. The owner of the farm invited us to take shelter from the sun under the vines of grapes and hulu and alongside the pomegranate trees—I don't think I had seen a pomegranate tree before.

Mr. Liu Xinyuan, the executive dean of Beijing University, Cyber Security College, Mrs. Li Shaolin, Chairman of Wuyishan Hearty Tea Expo Garden Tourism Development Co. Ltd. and Mrs. Xue Jianjun, President of Wuyishan Hearty Tea Expo Garden Tourism Development Co. Ltd. had joined us for a day from Beijing. As we sat resting from the walk, drinking green tea and soaking up the beauty of the surroundings, Madam Xue began to sing the most beautiful Chinese song. I asked what it was called and she said it was *The United Song* and it was about peace and harmony. She sang more accompanied by music from her iPhone. It was just so blissful and heavenly. I then played the tune *You & Me*, which was the theme from the 2008

Beijing Olympic Games—it is in my 'Most Played' list, and I reminded Xuelin that I had downloaded the song three years before we first met because I was so captivated by the performance at the Opening Ceremony for the Beijing Games.

I couldn't help but smile as I thought back to July 20, 2012, when friends and family came back to our home after the service and wedding meal in the Houses of Parliament. There must have been about 80 of our closest family and friends finishing off a very special day with us and the Champagne corks had been popping for some time. Some of Xuelin's friends asked if they could sing a traditional Chinese song in her honour called *What a Beautiful Jasmine Flower* it was wonderful and it was followed by a couple of others. It was then suggested that the English friends and family might offer a song to the groom—they struggled to respond with any song they knew the words to so in the end *I got God Save our Gracious Queen* followed by Rule Britannia and the first lines of *Three Lions on My Shirt* (a popular football chorus).

There is an innocence and refinement in Chinese society that we have lost, especially in the popular youth, sex and alcohol cultures of the West. I hope as China opens up and grows up in the modern world it will not lose this spirit: that the families will still lay first claim to the streets at night; that the children will continue to be the centre of the universe and that all ages on the planet will be welcome to orbit around them; that modesty can be allowed to retain its majesty and mystery and that the melody of the *What a Beautiful Jasmine Flower* may still be heard above *Three Lions on My Shirt*.

August 28 Day 33

Somewhere in Zaozhuang?

Zaozhuang, Shandong Province
A Day Off

'I have no idea where I am' might seem an unusual statement for a walker but it is true. Today was like navigating across the Gobi Desert. I ask if this is Zaozhuang and I am told that is the county, but this is Yicheng—no, says another, that is the district. I turn to my 'Moves app' on my iPhone, which logs every step I take and calculates distance and plots it all on a map and it says I am in Liuyuanzhen—everyone looks blank. After a few minutes I did not want to waste time by debating where I was, I just wanted to get moving—the maps are all in Chinese, so let me just say we spent most of the day walking along the S352 and the S344 crossing the S38 on the way and finishing at a Sinopec Petrol Station next to a small canal.

Map reading is one of the great joys of walking: sitting on a wall or even better in a cafe or a bar trying to work out where you are and how you might get to where you want to go. Map reading forces you to be observant of your environment, looking for hills, rivers, railways, and crossroads. When asking for directions, often people will say 'Oh I wouldn't start from here?' to which you want to respond, 'Where else I am supposed to start from?'

This is very much like life itself: Often we will feel we have lost direction over our career, our education and our family:

The first question to answer is, 'Where do you want to go?' For me that is Hangzhou on this walk but for many people who say their lives lack direction it is not because they do know where they are, it is because they don't know where they want to go. It was once said 'If you don't know where you are going any road will take you there.' This is so true. So first rule of navigation in walking and in life is 'be very clear about your destination'.

The second question then comes more into focus: 'Where are you now?' Where you are now is not where you want to be because if it was then you wouldn't be thinking of going on a journey to get there. As I stated earlier, you can only start from where you are. Often people will say, 'If only I had that qualification. If only I had this or that.' We focus on what we haven't got but don't focus on what we have. The truth is you can only start from where you are with what you have got—it may have been easier if you had started from somewhere else or were someone else: But you didn't and you aren't, so get over it and get on with it.

This should be it? You know where you want to be and you know where you are. Well, almost, but there is one more golden question which I would argue will determine more than any other the success of your journey. Why? What is it that you are seeking to achieve and how sure are you that it can be found in your destination and can't be found where you are? Who will benefit from you reaching your destination? Just you or will others benefit as well? Life is at its most revealing not when we say what we want or where we want to go but when we say honestly why we want it and why we want to go there.

August 29 Day 34
The Battle of Tai'erzhuang

Route: Yicheng District – Nigouzhen, Zaozhuang
Today walked: 14.30 miles / 23.00 km
Total walked: 536.30 miles / 863.60 km

The Battle of Tai'erzhuang (1938) was to the Chinese people what the Battle of Britain (1940) was to the British—a defining moment of national resilience and courage.

I think my hosts were a little apprehensive as to how a 'Walk for Peace' may respond to the famous military victory site. They needn't have been. I have visited many on my walks; in fact, I often design my route to visit them. I find that they are places for deep reverence at the sacrifice recording lives devoted to their country. All nations honour the courage and sacrifice of its armed forces above all else. There is a sense that without their sacrifice and service we would not have our security and identity.

Tai'erzhuang is a place of immense strategic importance being at the junction of the Jinpu and Longhai railways, the Grand Canal and the border of Jiangsu and Shandong provinces. It was a walled city of immense historic and cultural importance. It was not difficult to see the significance of such a prize to the invading Imperial Japanese forces. The Japanese forces were much better equipped and trained than the Chinese army and had made swift progress in occupying the country. The Chinese people's morale was low. The victory of a largely peasant army against the formidable Japanese forces at Tai'erzhuang brought a nation on its knees proudly to its feet.

Just as the Battle of Britain was seen as the turning point in the

European WWII, as it resulted in the German forces calling off their planned invasion of Britain, so Tai'erzhuang was to China in its efforts to defeat the invading Japanese forces. The significance of this famous victory was all the more so as this was the 70th Anniversary of the end of World War II. Our first visit via barge on the Grand Canal was to the museum which commemorated the Battle of Tai'erzhuang and contained detailed stories, relics, maps and art from the conflict.

As we emerged from the exhibition I was asked by journalists for my reaction. I first expressed my respect and honour for those courageous Chinese armed forces whose lives were lost in pursuit of this strategic victory. Next I expressed sadness that such a war should have been necessary, as China had not been the aggressor, it had been occupied and in places brutally, so the people of Tai'erzhuang and China should not have suffered in this way.

I then said that as we celebrate 'victory' in a military context, we needed to be careful that we presented the full picture of the human cost of battle and war, for there were 40,000 sons, husbands and fathers whose lives were cut short here and tens of thousands more who were maimed and suffered horrific injuries.

I then said that the finest way in which we honour the sacrifice of our fallen war heroes is to work tirelessly to ensure we do not add to their number. This sentiment I felt was best expressed in the closing message of the exhibition which was written in Chinese and English. It reads, 'We should learn from the martyrs' spirit of sacrifice and contribution to unity. We should learn from their heroic mettle and make our own contributions for the unification of peace and the development of the world.' How true those words! If only we could invest a small fraction of the heroism, struggle and resource into peace as we summon as nations in times of war.

The curators of the exhibition had it absolutely right. We should come and honour the example and courage of those who were forced to fight to regain and protect their country. We should leave stirred to play our active part in ensuring that peace so hard won is not lost.

August 30 Day 35

The Road to Tai'erzhuang

Route: Nigouzhen – Tai'erzhuang, Zaozhuang
Today walked: 10.60 miles / 17.00 km
Total walked: 546.90 miles / 880.60 km

Today was a short walk—a little over 10 miles. The shortness of the walk was because of a few important meetings at the beginning and the end of the day. Xuelin and I were honoured to meet the Vice Chairman of the Standing Committee of the National People's Congress, the President of Chinese Red Cross Chen Zhu and the Executive Vice President of Chinese Red Cross Ms. Xu Ke in the early morning. They came down from Beijing late last night and would have to leave immediately after the breakfast meeting to go back for important meetings in the capital. We were humbled that such senior leaders would come down to meet us on Sunday rather than inviting us to travel to the capital to meet them. Such is Chinese hospitality. We had met Ms. Xu Ke in London in the past but it is the first time we met with the President Chen Zhu. He was not only a highly respected national leader, but also a very accomplished medical doctor. He had studied in France and he is a typical scholarly leader and fluent in several languages including fortunately for me, English. He had a gracious and generous temperament. The talk with President Chen Zhu was very encouraging. We talked about my upcoming visit to Tai'erzhuang and it's significance in Chinese history. We also talked about his hometown of Jiangsu which we had walked through on our journey. It was a warm and memorable meeting and Xuelin and I left feeling immensely grateful for the privilege.

Talking of protocol, we almost caused a minor diplomatic incident, as after breakfast Xuelin went to pay the bill as usual for our food and accommodation. I could see that the accompanying officials were getting restless. Madam Zhang then mentioned to me that our guest had a train to catch. I replied, 'Please tell him to go and catch it.' She then explained that protocol is that he could not leave until we had left. I quickly got Xuelin and we said goodbye jumped in the car and left. Xuelin had to arrange for someone to go back quietly and finish paying our bill later.

Protocol was much in evidence at the end of the day too. We were hosted by the vice president of the Shandong Province Red Cross Society for a farewell dinner, as we would be crossing into Jiangsu the next day. We had been in Shandong for nearly four weeks and we had got to know members of the local team very well indeed—Li Nan and Liu were less friends and more family by the time we came to say goodbye.

The formalities of the Chinese dinner table are quite sophisticated compared to the informality which governs most meals in the West. The principal host sits at the round table facing the door or the kitchen so they can direct the waiters and waitresses and see other guests arriving. The most honoured guest sits to their right. The second host sits opposite them and the second most honoured guest sits to their right. The rest of the seats are filled accordingly with occasional polite and friendly disputes as a guest may seek to place a fellow guest in a more honoured place at the table.

Once the table seating is concluded, the principal host will make the first of three short toasts. After each toast the guest will stand and go round to touch glasses with each other. Even in this action status is all important: The less senior of the two people clinking glasses must touch their glass slightly lower than the lip on the more senior person's glass. There is often again a playful polite exchange as people of similar status may try to lower their glass to show greater honour and the other guest will respond likewise. Every Chinese table has a carousel revolving glass tray on which food is placed. It is acceptable that after a number of toasts, just simply to tap the carousel.

After the principal host had given their three toasts, I went to try and respond before getting a familiar stare across the table from Xuelin saying more eloquently than words ever could, 'Don't you dare!' Later she explained that if I spoke as the guest and proposed a toast that would mean that the meal would be finished, but we had hardly started. There were three more toasts from the second toast and then after the sliced melon had been served, Xuelin smiled and raised her glass from across the table and I knew it was time for me to propose a toast after which there would be the exchange of small gifts and finally photographs.

After navigating the higher points of Chinese protocol from breakfast through to dinner, navigating the traffic and road crossings of the S344 seemed much easier and far less dangerous.

August 31 Day 36
Jiangsu Province

Route: Tai'erzhuang, Zaozhuang, Shandong Province – Pizhou, Xuzhou, Jiangsu Province
Today walked: 23.70 miles / 38.20 km
Total walked: 570.60 miles / 918.80 km

This was a multiple landmark day. We crossed the Grand Canal from Tai'erzhuang into Jiangsu Province. It was an emotional time to say goodbye to our Red Cross team from Shandong and the volunteers who had walked with us through Zaozhuang. It was also a time to meet the new team. We had about thirty minutes of farewells/greetings and photographs just across the bridge.

I had slightly held up proceedings because I was captivated by the Grand Canal and especially a shipyard under the bridge where three new barges were under construction. I come from Tyneside, which was known for its shipbuilding prowess, and that sight of welders at work on rusty steel decks is one which resonates with my soul. Shipbuilding is one of those strategic industries which all developing countries try to project through feeding them subsidised military orders, then through nationalisation, but ultimately the jobs go because they can be built much cheaper elsewhere. In the case of Tyneside it was the rise of South Korean shipbuilders that led to our demise, but then we switched to offshore oil rigs and so some of the skills were kept. After the oil rigs came the offshore wind farms and next? A quick fact check reveals that most of the world's new ships are built in North East Asia (41% in South Korea, 29% in Japan and 24% in China---

that leaves just 6% shared between the rest of the world).

As we walked along the road towards Pizhou, it was not shipbuilding but farming which again dominated the landscape and the roadside. This area was renowned for the production of garlic, which made for an interesting smell along the road. I was able to talk with some of the farmers and discuss garlic farming and what makes a good garlic, etc. A top quality garlic, so I discovered, has an unbroken skin over the segments and has a slight red/purple tinge in the colour. It is this colouring which is indicative of extra flavour and attracts a premium price. Most of the garlic produced at the farm we talked with was for export markets with the largest market being Brazil. I know the price of garlic at our local Sainsbury's on Wilton Road, London, is about 50p (5 yuan). I mentioned this to the farmer who laughed and collected up ten of his best garlic cloves and said that was what 5 yuan would buy you from him. It is another interesting comment on globalisation that 5p in Pizhou becomes 50p in London; where does the 45p go? I ask and the farmer says he has no idea either, but I think he deserves more of it.

Just as we are about to finish the day of walking, there is an extra surprise as Madam Zhang and Xuelin direct me into a school playground where there is a full dress rehearsal for a traditional folk play. The costumes are amazing and the music created an atmosphere that you felt had not changed for centuries. Children surrounded the school yard with their parents and were absolutely captivated by the story, which as usual involved goodies and baddies, and after a lot of chasing about the goodies win in the end. It was wonderful.

This was raw cultural exchange. So much of what happens in culture in the UK has become professionalised but this was all put on by local garlic farmers to celebrate the end of the harvest. There were no lottery or local authority grants or sponsorship by local companies. This was just a community coming together to celebrate its history and culture. Every aspect of the play was home-produced: There was a family who had specialised for generations in making costumes, another that had specialised in making the masks, another family specialised in painting the masks, others specialised in music. It seemed that the homemade ingredients added to the sense that this was authentic culture. I loved every single minute of it ... this was the real China I had come to see.

September 1 Day 37
Hope House—Pizhou

Xuzhou, Jiangsu Province
A Day Off

Today was a day I will never forget. We went to visit Hope House, a school/clinic in Pizhou caring for children with disabilities both physical and mental (learning difficulties as we refer to them in the UK). The House has been supported by many organisations including the Red Cross and the Norwegian Agency for Development Cooperation (NORAD). It is not difficult to see why. It is a place of hope and transformation.

To see children with disabilities evokes a special empathy in parents and, in my case, grandparents. These are not remote distant people, these are children and they could be any of our children. Being an older man, it is quite normal for children to refer to you grandpa in China. But this time when they did, my eyes would well up as I would see my grandson Matthew in their faces.

Hope House began in the 1990s in response to a flood in the area which resulted in disease, I am guessing something like Typhoid. The result was a large number of children who lost limbs. There was a crisis and a local man decided to provide a solution—Hope House. The founder focused particularly on the benefits of sport for children with disabilities in building health, strength and confidence.

We first visited a treatment room for small children with brain injuries and then visited rooms where extensive physiotherapy was being performed on small children for twenty minutes at a time. We stood by one girl, about two or three, as she had her ankles and knee joints rotated. She looked up and smiled at us as if to say 'It's okay—it looks worse than it feels.' I was so humbled by her courage.

In the next room there was a small stepping machine. One of the boys, about five, was stepping on the machine whilst facing the wall so he could concentrate. When we all arrived, his face lit up and he wanted to show us how he could do the big steps—he struggled up one side and down the other—and again, and again, and again, and again each time to loud cheers. His physiotherapist politely suggested we might like to leave, as he simply wouldn't stop while we were there and he really shouldn't do more than one of the big set of steps in each session. What energy for life.

We live in a society which often celebrates victimhood as a badge of honour. Everybody, it seems, is a victim of something or someone and we are encouraged to respond to that person through the circumstance of which they are a victim. We are encouraged to draw up examples from our own lives in which we might too have been victims of something. The life-limiting message is that your circumstance is not your fault, it is the fault of someone or something else and so your family and society should devote itself to compensating you for your suffering. Yet here were young children with almost unspeakable disabilities and yet their faces were full of joy and hope. They may have been victims of circumstance but rather than wallow in self-pity for which they would be fully entitled, they became victors over those circumstances.

Sport was a major theme. Rather than wrap the children in cotton wool to protect them, the founder of Hope House wanted them to encourage them to get involved in competitive sport. From this one small school in Pizhou they produced 12 gold medal and 2 silver medal winners at the London 2012 Paralympic Games and are hoping to do even better in Rio. Table tennis is their speciality.

After a short introduction to the school in the boardroom, I was invited to write a message to the school. I was so moved by what I had seen I went on to three pages of the record book, but my most heartfelt message was that whilst the school had a deserved reputation for producing great sporting champions, everyone I had met that day was a champion, be it the child, the physiotherapist, the parent or grandparent or administrator. They were 'champions' for the hope they inspired in us all.

Our final visit was to a classroom where we were to present 170 new Thermos flasks from the Red Cross with some of the monies raised so far from the walk—one for each child. When we arrived, a young girl of about five stood up and welcomed us in excellent English. They then sang the traditional Chinese folk song *What a Beautiful Jasmine Flower* which they had learned especially for us—just perhaps because I had let slip earlier in the walk that it was a favourite of Xuelin and mine and had been sung at our wedding. At the end of the song I was invited to say something and I was just lost for words, or should I say, any words I said could not have adequately conveyed the feelings I had at that moment.

Hope House has had a profound impact upon us, and Xuelin and I are so grateful for the opportunity to have seen this for ourselves, to witness such courage, such optimism, such devotion, such beauty and such hunger for life. Our desire is that the Spirit of Hope will continue to inspire us and others for many years to come.

September 2 Day 38
Peace & Sport

Route: Xinhezhen, Pizhou, Xuzhou – Border of Suqian
Today walked: 20.50 miles / 33.10 km
Total walked: 591.10 miles / 951.90 km

It was a quiet day …. Xuelin and Madam Zhang had gone back to Beijing for the 70th Anniversary Parade.

We finished the 20.5 mile walk by 5 p.m. and I took the opportunity to have a relaxed walk in the evening sunshine in Shagou Lake Metasequoia Park, a short walk from our guest house. I have been struck all the way from Beijing how wonderful the parks are, immaculately maintained. Indeed that goes not just for the parks but all the hedgerows and borders alongside the roads. Labour is cheap, I suppose, but it says something about a community's values as to how it maintains its public spaces.

As I walked through the park alongside the lake with its view across to the temple I noticed a sports area of basketball and badminton courts. The basketball courts were all in full use. I enjoy basketball. My son Matthew was a talented player at college in the USA and later in basketball coaching. I have many happy memories of taking him to games and watching him play and coach.

Watching these games on a Walk for Peace inevitably got me thinking about human nature and the role of sport. Sport is in many ways has become as important as commerce in ordering some human societies. It is not difficult to see why:

First, we must accept that men are by nature competitive and tribal. Players would arrive from work or college and join a game of basketball. It only seemed to take a few minutes to establish a pecking order in team and a ranking of the most and least talented. Players seemed a bit lost as they first entered the game but as soon as they could see who was the most talented player, they seemed to relax, accept their position in the team (tribe) and enjoy the comradery.

Second, the comradeship of the players was low-key but when they started to play against another team, it became intense. It was as if the team was a loose association of individuals when playing between themselves but once there was an opposing team, they formed strong bonds, the joking stopped and they seemed able to sacrifice their own ambitions for the greater success of the team. A few minutes ago these individuals had arrived at the court as friends, but once they had lined up on opposing teams, it was if they were from different countries.

Third, when two very pretty young ladies who had been playing badminton on a neighbouring court finished their game and came across to watch, the effect on the male players was almost instantaneous. Without seeming to ever look in their direction the arrival of the girls seemed to dramatically raise the energy and effort levels of both teams. Tackles became a lot more physical and there was a lot more shouting and arguing as a result. It was as if competition and aggression were being used to show dominance in order to secure a mate. That said, the girls didn't look that impressed by it and soon left, allowing the game to return to its original pace.

The more those in world political and military leadership understand this basic hardwiring at work in and between humans, the more aware we will be of the forces which draw us into war, terrorism and acts of violence. The more these instincts can be worked out on the basketball court, the safer the world will be for us all.

September 3 Day 39
The Big Parade

Route: Border of Suqian – Sucheng District, Suqian
Today walked: 22.50 miles / 36.20 km
Total walked: 613.60 miles / 988.10 km

It was quiet on the roads, as today was the day of the 70th Anniversary Parade in Beijing. It was a major national and international event. For many people it was a national holiday, so they could gather with friends and family and watch the Parade on their TV. The tickets for places at the Parade in Beijing were highly prized, and we were honoured that both Xuelin (overseas Chinese representative of the UK) and Madam Zhang (Red Cross Society of China) had been invited.

We had a long walk ahead of us, but I suggested to the team that we start earlier and then break around 10 a.m. for a couple of hours so we could all watch the parade together. This we did. We were fortunate that the governor of the nearby township of Caiji, Mr. Zhu, invited us to join him at his offices and watch the parade on a large projector screen and endless refills of green tea.

The parade was held in glorious sunshine and blue skies in Tian'anmen Square. We were told that there were 12,000 troops, 500 pieces of military hardware and 200 planes taking part in the parade—it looked more. It was begun with a precision demonstration in marching and drill. It was as if they were robots (and soon they may be), such was the coordination of every step.

It is the ability of individuals to come together to form multi-skilled units, to willingly sacrifice all personal ambition, identity and even life itself for the advancement of the common mission of the group, which has made the human species such an awesome predator. Ironically, of course, history shows it is a skill which has and still is used with greatest potency against other members of its own species.

I am a politician and therefore I was impressed by the words of President Xi Jinping at the beginning of the parade, 'Justice will prevail! Peace will prevail! The people will prevail!' I thought that those words could have been uttered by any of the noticeably absent Western leaders and would have won widespread approval. The subtext of this message was of course—justice, peace and people will only be able to prevail if they have the military strength and organisation to deter acts of aggression such as that which was experienced against China by Japan in World War II. This doesn't make China exceptional, it makes China normal. The fact that today we still have wars taking place around the world tells us that being armed to the teeth can deter conflict, but it can also provoke conflict. Moreover, if you place your national security in weapons alone, you begin to see solutions only through that lens-sidelining diplomacy, law and international institutions.

The parade proceeded perfectly—not a foot out of place. It was led off by veterans of WWII, and it was right that their contribution was recognised. This was very similar to the Victory over Japan (VJ-Day) commemoration which had taken place in London a couple of weeks earlier. The commemoration, rather than celebration, was led by Her Majesty The Queen focused on expressing national thanks and gratitude on to those 71,000 British and Commonwealth casualties in the war against Japan and honouring survivors. There would have been a lot more casualties, of course, had it not been for the courageous action of the Chinese Expeditionary Force in coming to the rescue of the encircled British 1st Burma Division at the Battle of Yenangyaung. All countries have a selective memory when it comes to history. In Britain there was traditional wreath laying at the Cenotaph in Whitehall. A service of remembrance was held in church, where the focus was on sacrifice and reconciliation. Finally, there was a marching display on Horse-guards Parade and fly past of military aircraft. The expression of gratitude for VJ-Day in London and Beijing was different, but it reflected difference in scale of experience—Britain had not been brutally occupied for eight long years. A city the size of Birmingham or Manchester had not seen a massacre of 300,000 of its citizens—men, women and children butchered by the occupying forces as in Nanking/Nanjing.

The end of the parade brought some greater hope with the release of 70,000 doves and thousands of balloons, and a sense of a new beginning lifted the mood. I took this as an unspoken recognition that times had changed—the Japan of today as a democratic market economy is not the same as the militaristic Imperial Japanese Empire of WWII, just as modern Germany is not Nazi Germany of WWII, and to stretch the point a little further, Britain is not the Colonial Britain of the Opium Wars. Countries with long histories inevitably have dark chapters they would prefer to forget.

The parade being over, it was time to get back on the road … to Suqian.

September 4 Day 40
1,000 km in Suqian

Route: Sucheng District – Suyu District, Suqian
Today walked: 26.00 miles / 41.90 km
Total walked: 639.60 miles / 1,030.00 km

Little mysteries continue to be explained on this trip:

Every time Xuelin and I check into a hotel, Xuelin will be on the phone asking reception for the toothbrush and toothpaste. I always find this a little strange. But in China I have discovered that no matter how basic the guest house or hotel, they always provide toothbrush and toothpaste, a comb and a shower cap.

I mentioned in the first week of this blog that I had encountered more 'random acts of kindness' (bottles of water or food) in the first miles in China than I had in the previous 4,500 miles of walking for peace. This experience leads me to challenge my belief that China was different from all the other eighteen countries I had walked through. I reflect that all these examples were in Hebei Province. This is not to ask them to start again, it is simply to say that my thesis, which was 'People are the same all over the world in their approach to strangers.' I believe this still holds—if you smile, they smile back; if you ask for directions, they do their best to help and if you ask for food or accommodation, then they will ask for money. That is nice and as it should be—it is not being Chinese, British or Greek, it is being human.

Another update is that in my five weeks and six hundred miles of walking I have only ever seen one other 'foreigner'—a Western looking man in our hotel in Jinan 300 miles back up the road. Coming from Britain, which is so cosmopolitan, that is quite a surprise. Thinking of China's importance to the global economy, I again find that a surprise.

In order to keep in contact with my two sons during the trip, they have both signed up for WeChat, a Chinese social media app like What's App or FaceTime. I think if I were to point to one thing about the modern world that utterly amazes me every time, it would be that I can sit in a hotel lobby in rural China and have a thirty minute video call with Matt in Texas. I can ask my grandson Matthew about his first few days at school, and he can show me his work. I can then speak and see my other son Alex in Brazil to discuss the latest transfer signings in the premiership, all in perfect quality video. And, it's all for free! How do they do that?

After a long day on the road we arrive into the beautiful and highly sophisticated city of Suqian. It is located on the Yangtze River Delta on the edge of Lake Luoma. It has a rich and distinctive culture, being the birthplace of Xiang Yu (born 232 BC), who at the age of 27 became the Conqueror of Western Chu and Qin and who died at the age of 31. His story is similar to Alexander the Great, who became head of the army in Macedon (modern day Macedonia) at the age of 20 and whose empire extended from Africa to the western reaches of modern China in 320 BC and who died at the age of 32.

That phrase, 'Only the good die young'—I really never understood where it came from. So many great figures from history did die young: Diana, Princess of Wales, JFK, Joan of Arc, Anne Frank, Martin Luther King, Buddy Holly, Bruce Lee, Mozart and Van Gogh, to name a few. Apparently, it was first stated by the Greek Herodutus in 442 BC and then made famous by William Wordsworth in his poem *Excursion—The good die first, And they whose hearts are dry as summer dust / Burn to the socket*—although Wordsworth himself lived on until he was 80. I can only think that in some ways our preserved memory of these people is of their youthful energy and potential cut short. Anyway, I find that the older I get, the less I want to agree with this ….

Oh yes, and Xuelin and Madam Zhang arrived back just in time to celebrate 1,000 km on the walk outside a mushroom factory at Dingzuizhen on the S325 to Huai'an.

September 5 Day 41
International Eco-Quadrathlon Classic

Suqian, Jiangsu Province
A Day Off

Zhao Kai, the vice president of the Red Cross in Jiangsu Province, had received an invitation for me to take part in the opening of the 2015 Suqian Eco-Quadrathlon being held at Lake Luoma and Santai Hill. I didn't know quite what to expect. I didn't know what an 'eco-quadrathlon' was, but it was sport and I saw an opportunity to convey the message of peace through sport so immediately accepted. Special-event shirts for us to wear at the opening ceremony were dropped off at our hotel the evening before, and I was glad I had lost a few pounds on the walk from Beijing so I could squeeze into it.

We arrived at the edge of Lake Luoma and were quite surprised to see a few thousand competitors and officials gathered on the lakeshore. The quadrathlon is made up of cross country running, cycling, swimming and kayaking over a 58 km course. The 'eco' part of the competition was to try and blend competitive sport in with the natural environment. I hadn't really thought about it before, but most sports take part in stadiums, indoor arenas, pools or in city centres. There are not many sports that come easily to mind which seek to use the natural environment as the backdrop and race track-skiing, fishing, hunting, three-day eventing, rally driving and some cycling stages. The limitation is, of course, not just for competitors, it is access for spectators and providing a route accessible for the media.

The point which the Suqian organisers were trying to make was that sport can play a great role in drawing people to explore outdoor spaces. We often say the world is crowded and yet the entire world population of 7 billion standing shoulder to shoulder would be able to stand in the city of Los Angeles (500 sq miles). We have vast open spaces but have chosen largely for economic reasons to concentrate human populations in cities. As the global population expands we are going to need to reverse that industrialisation trend, and with the wide availability of IT and super-fast broadband connectivity, there is no reason why we need to be crammed together in expensive congested and polluted cities.

Along with Wei Guoqiang, Secretary of the CPC Committee in Suqian and Wang Tianqi, the Mayor of Suqian, I was invited to speak to the competitors at the opening ceremony. I struggled to think of what to say but landed on the word 'Eco', which in the Greek original means 'home'. Ecology is literally the study of our home. So an 'eco' sporting event is a sporting event which seeks to promote/study in some way our common home. Most of the time we look at the world politically. Lines drawn on a map, and often disputed, show the boundaries of 200 or so polities on the planet.

Yet national boundaries are a human and legal construct. If you were to look down on the Earth from the International Space Station, there would be very few evidences during the day that humans actually lived there—Suez and Panama canals and the Great Wall of China—so I am told. At night the cities light up, revealing the concentration of human populations, but there is absolutely no giant sign which states 'United Kingdom', 'United States of America' or 'People's Republic of China' or 'Vanuatu'. All nations, cities, mountains, deserts, rivers and oceans merge into one glorious and beautiful planet called Earth—Our home.

Some things nations can do alone, but caring for and maintaining our planet/our home is something that we can only do together. The care of the environment is not of one nation but of all nations. The responsibility for maintaining our home is not the task of one individual or organisation but of all humanity. The 'eco' then is not about you or me, it is about us. The 'eco' will not shape our histories, but our actions today will shape our future. Suqian is on to something very significant here and I hope it continues with it ....

September 6 Day 42
Whatever You Do for the Least ...

Suqian, Jiangsu Province
A Day Off

One of the great things about this walk is working with the Red Cross. It is not just the practical support which they give us but the introductions to meet inspiring people and hear their stories. In my mind I am still thinking about the visit to Hope House in Pizhou, which left a big impression on Xuelin and me. As we arrive into Suqian we are invited to visit the Suqian Welfare Institute, which is similar to Hope House in that they are caring and educating children with severe physical and mental disabilities.

As parents it makes our heart ache that through a lottery of life these children arrive into the world with disabilities. It is natural to look at their disabilities and ask why? But this does not help. Far better to look at their abilities and ask why not? This is the inspiring work taking place each day in Pizhou and Suqian. There is a major difference though:

Whereas the children in Pizhou were surrounded by family who loved and cared for them and brought them to and from Hope House each day, the children in Suqian were orphans. In some cases parents had died, and in others the parents could not cope and placed them in the care of the Welfare Institute. As parents we would not dare judge or criticise another parent whose position we cannot begin to understand. We were at the Institute for an hour but we understand the demands on parents, grandparents and siblings of providing the constant care required.

That said, the effect on the child must be enormous. Not only must they come to terms with their disabilities, but they must do so without the love and support of their family. What overwhelmed us during our visit was that though these children would have every reason to be resentful and bitter, they were instead overflowing with happiness and love.

It is as if god has looked upon them and given them a larger than normal heart and soul, which radiates warmth and love to all those who are privileged to come into contact with them. In discussions with staff and carers it was this golden quality in these young lives which kept them going and wanting to give the children the best possible start in life. But they also have other tasks too …

In addition to caring for the children the Institute seeks to find permanent homes for these children. In one area of the Institute 'Honour Hall' they show photographs of children placed with families all over the world and their life achievements—graduating from college or getting married. I so admired these families for what they had done, not for their own child but for someone else's. I remembered the words of Jesus in the Bible in Matthew's gospel 'Whatever you did for the least of my brothers (children), you did this also for me.'

I always want to believe that people are basically good, although some people point to our daily news stories and disagree. They say that the only rational approach to life is pure self-interest. I disagree and I am in good company: A few weeks ago I walked through the hometown of the great teacher Mencius, a student of Confucius; he used the following illustration to explain this concept. If a child falls into a well, will those who are nearby calculate their actions around self-interest, saying: 'How will this help me if I help?' 'Does the child have wealthy parents who might pay me a reward or powerful parents who might promote me?' No. They rush to the well to help the child because it is in danger and their hearts are moved to want to help. This 'movement of the heart' Mencius called 'compassion' and was his starting point for believing basic goodness of all human beings.

This raises the possibility that the reason why we don't see more of human compassion is because we do not acknowledge and believe in human goodness. On the contrary, our starting point in social media and television news often seems to be that a belief in human badness as the basis of our nature. I would challenge you to go to Suqian Welfare Institute, meet the children, meet the carers, meet the adopting families, and it will show you something that will be sure to change your mind.

September 7 Day 43
Lightning Speed in Suqian

Route: Suyu District – Siyangxian, Suqian
Today walked: 25.50 miles / 41.10 km
Total walked: 665.10 miles / 1,071.10 km

Suqian the place literally means 'overnight'. The 'overnight' refers to the overnight refuge when the Yellow River would overflow, but I would discover another meaning of the word.

Xuelin and I were honoured to be invited for dinner on Sunday with Suqian's Party Secretary Wei and Mayor Wang, whom we had met at the Opening Ceremony of the Eco-Quadrathlon the day before. Both Secretary Wei and Mayor Wang were keen walkers, and they were interested in what further measures could be taken to make Suqian a 'walker-friendly' city.

I sensed a good moment to pitch an idea: Could Suqian become the first place in the world to hold an Annual Walk for Peace? The successful Eco-Quadrathlon event combined sport and the countryside, could they combine peace and the countryside through a Walk for Peace? The immediate response was positive. They mentioned Santai Hill Forest Park as being a possible venue. I said that I hadn't seen the park ….

There was then a long conversation in Chinese between Xuelin and the Mayor, Party Secretary and Zhao Kai, Secretary General of the Red Cross. The result of the discussion was that I could visit the park the next morning at 7:30 a.m. before I started my walk out of Suqian towards Huai'an. What is more, they would like me to plant a tree in the Memorial Forest for International Friendly Exchanges. 'What type of tree would I like to plant?'

I smiled. I could see how I might be able to visit the park but how would they manage to organise a tree planting? It was already 8 p.m. on Sunday evening. 'This is Suqian,' came the reply.

We were back in our room in the hotel and Xuelin got a message about 10 p.m., asking to confirm a proof of the words for the plaque commemorating the planting. Monday morning we set off from the hotel at 7:30 a.m. and arrived at the Forest Park. It was a beautiful morning. Waiting for us at the gate were small golf buggies with a tour guide who told us all about the Park in the five minutes it took us to reach the Memorial Forest. At the forest the Party Secretary and Mayor were already waiting with a group of photographers.

The Party Secretary pointed to two trees and said these were the trees we were going to plant. They were 'sweet-scented Osmanthus trees, the city tree of Suqian and also of Xuelin's hometown and our destination, Hangzhou', came the reply via the translator. We were handed spades and directed to the spot alongside a plaque marking the occasion in both Chinese and English.

I was still getting over the speed that everything was happening when there were some formal photos and then farewells and the Party Secretary, Mayor and entourage were gone. It took about five minutes start to finish.

I was left reflecting on how long this might have taken to organise in the UK? Leaving aside the fact that this was a Sunday evening …. There would be planning approvals, tree health checks, wording approvals for the plaque, the purchase of the trees and spades would need to be put out for public tender following EU procurement rules. Those attending would need to be checked to ensure that they had the appropriate health and safety experience to oversee the planting of a tree. There would be a full risk assessment, first-aid trained individuals on hand, high visibility jackets, protective gloves, footwear, hats and goggles for participants to wear. There would need to be contingency plans in case it was raining.

In Suqian they 'Just Do it.' …. This is why when the EU economy grows at 1% we call it a 'recovery', and when China grows at 7 percent we call it a 'slowdown'.

September 8 Day 44

Red Nails

Route: Siyangxian, Suqian – Huaiyin District, Huai'an
Today walked: 20.60 miles / 33.20 km
Total walked: 685.70 miles / 1,104.30 km

I think one of the first jokes I can remember telling in the schoolyard at Kells Lane School aged six or seven was:

> Q: Why do elephants paint their toe nails red?
> A: So they can hide in cherry trees?

Wait for groans ....

> Q: Have you ever seen an elephant in a cherry tree? (wait for them to say "no")
> A: See, it works then!

I was reminded of this when I sat down to start writing my blog updates today. I confess I don't find the discipline of writing blogs easy—on my days off I just want to sleep. Xuelin thinks sleep is something that happens in the seconds between social media replies on WeChat. The most interesting of all Chinese characteristics to the British is that of being direct, so Xuelin looked up and said, 'Try and make the blog funny. Your blogs are too serious. People don't want to read them.' I reply with my usual ironic, 'Honey, you shouldn't hold back for the sake of my feelings. Tell me what you really think.'

There aren't many laughs in walking 25 miles alongside busy roads day after day in 30 degree plus heat but let me try and find something ... oh yes:

I have been suffering with a highly embarrassing problem for a man over the past few days—pink finger nails. I know our finger nails are meant to be pinkish but this is pink nail varnish colour. I think that it must have come from some 100 yuan I had in my bag when it was raining. But no matter how much I washed the nails the colour wouldn't come out. Concerned I did what we all do in such circumstances I put 'pink nails' into a search engine and one of the entries suggested that this could be a sign of the early onset of kidney disease and that I should see a doctor. I didn't feel unwell though.

Next morning during a drink break I joked about my nails to Madam Zhang, who said she had exactly the same problem and had cut her nails to remove the pink. Xuelin then said that she had found pink spots the same colour in her hair that morning and was worried that it was some kind of infection. Madam Zhang then said, 'This will be from the Opening Ceremony for the Eco-Quadrathlon .... We were all on the stage together and when the Games were officially opened Chinese firecrackers went off over our heads. This is the powder from the firecrackers which had got into our hair.'

Mystery solved. Now, if only we could find some cherry trees to hide in.

September 9 Day 45
It's a Small World in Huai'an

Huai'an, Jiangsu Province
A Day Off

Huai'an is a city of around 5 million people in Jiangsu, standing on the edge of the Grand Canal connecting our start point of Beijing and our destination point of Hangzhou. The canal is a UNESCO World Heritage Site being the longest (1,104 miles) and one of the earliest canals in the world. The oldest sections of the canal were built in the 5th century BC. I know this because we visited the excellent China Water Transport Museum in Huai'an this afternoon. In fact I could tell you a whole lot more from how it was funded (a special levy), to its early uses (military), etc. but I won't, just in case you get the chance to visit the exhibition for yourself.

We crossed the boundary between Suqian and Huai'an yesterday and with it came a now familiar change routine for the Red Cross volunteers who would guide us through their county or city. We must have done around twenty of these handovers by now, and they have developed a ritualistic almost religious process of thanks and photos to the past team and greetings (and photos) with the new team. Sometimes the teams change so fast we don't get to know everyone's names. These people are the backbone of the walk, and they have been planning and preparing for the few days we might be in their city for months.

Invariably the first day is a bit tough as we get to know each other. I always thank them and then tell them that I am sure there are many scenic roads in their wonderful city or county but for me the shortest route is always the most beautiful. I explain that whilst Chinese people's generosity, hospitality and care for guests are qualities admired around the world, on this walk we value simplicity highest of all. The longer we have together, the more we all adapt, which is where Xuelin and Madam Zhang play such a crucial role in communication and team building.

Huai'an is a famous city in China because it is the birthplace of Zhou Enlai, late Premier of the People's Republic of China from 1949 until 1976. Zhou, with his film-star good looks and Western education, was a kind of 'thinking man's revolutionary' a kind of Che Guevara of the East. He served faithfully under Mao Zedong despite threats from the Red Guards during the 'Cultural Revolution'. I confess I knew very little if anything about Zhou Enlai before I arrived in Huai'an; however, this afternoon we also visited the Zhou Enlai Memorial Hall and Exhibition, and so I could tell you a whole lot more, but won't, just in case you get the chance to visit for yourself.

Now here is a good quiz question: What connects Zhou Enlai of the Communist Party of China and Dr. Billy Graham, the American Evangelical Christian Evangelist and spiritual confidant of successive American presidents since Richard Nixon? The answer is that Huai'an was the birthplace of both Zhou Enlai and Ruth Bell Graham, wife of Dr. Billy Graham. Ruth Graham's father was a doctor and medical missionary in the city before they moved to Pyongyang (North Korea), where Ruth went to school at the same Christian School attended by Kim Il Sung, founding president of North Korea. Interesting also, isn't it, that Zhou Enlai was to make his international reputation as the person who opened China up to the West by organising the visit to President Richard Nixon to China in 1972 and the Geneva and Bandung Peace Conferences, which sought to lower Cold War tensions following the Korean War? Dr. Billy Graham's greatest diplomatic success was to help facilitate improved relations between North and South Korea in the early 1990s.

It's a small, small world in Huai'an.

September 10 Day 46
Secretary of the Party Committee in 'Peacetown'

Route: Huaiyin District – Hongzexian, Huai'an
Today walked: 21.60 miles / 34.70 km
Total walked: 707.30 miles / 1,139.00 km

Day 46 and back on the S205, this time heading out of Huai'an. Our visit to Huai'an had been fascinating and I was sorry not to be able to spend more time there. As always, it is the schedule which drives us on. We need to be in Nanjing on September 19. The S205 takes us all the way and road signs had started to appear showing 'Nanjing 215 km' and they were drawing us in.

We were told to expect a VIP visitor who wanted to walk with us, so we stopped for a lunch break in a small town on the S205. A visit to the local shop to get stocked up with some iced green tea, which has now overtaken Coke Zero as the drink of choice on the walk, quickly made us a focus of attention.

English is a compulsory subject in Chinese schools, so it is often children and young people who are most willing to start up a conversation. Two young girls told Xuelin that they had heard that 'There was a foreigner who was walking for peace down their road and they wanted to come and find out more.' Their first question was, 'What did I think of their town?' I guess that would be the most common question on all my walks, as we are all proud of our hometown, but there was a particular reason I would remember this town.

'Welcome to Huai'an, Lord Bates. You have chosen a perfect place to rest, this is Peace Town!' said a tall, elegant man in perfect English with a warm smile. The person greeting me was Dr. Yao Xiaodong, Secretary of the Party committee in Huai'an. It is difficult to convey to a Westerner the importance of the position of Party Secretary in China. Perhaps if you combined the roles of Mayor of London with Commissioner of the Metropolitan Police and added the Bishop of London into the mix for good measure, you might be getting somewhere close. Added to which Huai'an is a second-tier city with a population of five million.

So the fact that Huai'an Party Secretary Yao had travelled back from Beijing to meet us and was dressed in a splendid 'Walk for Peace' T-shirt had our local Red Cross volunteers rubbing their eyes to see if this was really happening. We politicians are a predicable lot and I took it that when we were told that a VIP was coming to walk with us, that meant there would be a few steps and a lot of photographs, but Secretary Yao was with us for the remaining 12 km of the walk.

As we walked and talked I discovered that Secretary Yao had not only visited London many times he had actually had lunch in the House of Lords canteen with our mutual friend Lord Wei. The 'small world' of Huai'an just got a lot smaller. His academic background and early career was in journalism, which was an unusual background for a Party Secretary, as most had worked their way up through administrative roles.

We had a long conversation about the challenges Huai'an was facing in seeking to drive economic growth with and at the same time care for the environment. The whole of the Huai'an area is flat, low lying and is a network of rivers, lakes and canals, which makes it prone to flooding. Living in Huai'an, understanding rising water levels and changing climate patterns is not a debate about science, it is a question of survival. We also spoke about healthcare, and Yao was very keen to learn from the experiences of the National Health Service in the UK, which is as admired in China as it is in the UK.

After our walk and talk he invited us for dinner, where we sampled the local delicacy of crayfish from Hongzehu Lake. I have to confess that the crayfish weren't my favourite memory of Huai'an, but in China they have a phrase which means doing something you don't really want to for a greater good, they say 'I ate/drank/went/walked, etc. for the Revolution.' Well, I did my bit for the revolution. Xuelin did even more by eating some of my share and discretely placing some of her left-over shells on my plate.

Secretary Yao, like myself, was an admirer of Professor Joe Nye, the former Dean of the Kennedy School of Government at Harvard University. Professor Nye had famously advocated greater us of 'soft power' to advance strategic aims. Soft power being things like culture, education, tourism, sport, business, arts as opposed to an over focus on hard power, military, trade blocs, etc. We spoke about China's soft power and how it could be deployed in the future.

Soft power is also, of course, what had brought us together, a Communist and a Conservative politician taking time to walk and talk with each other and appreciate each other's culture a little better as a result. It is interesting, of course, that our memories of places are so often not of the things we see but of the people we meet. The people of Huai'an and Peace Town will endure long and happily in the memory though I hope the crayfish of Hongzehu Lake will endure not quite so long in the stomach.

September 11 Day 47

Address to Students in Jinling Middle School

Route: Hongzexian – Xuyixian, Huai'an
Today walked: 23.00 miles / 37.00 km
Total walked: 730.30 miles / 1,176.00 km

Day 47, still on the S205. Not much to add. Thought I would use this time and space to write a draft for a talk which I have been invited to give in Nanjing on the subject of Culture and Peace:

The theme of my talk is the role of culture in peace-building. A purpose of my walk from Beijing to Nanjing has been to highlight the First Year of UK-China Cultural Exchange: My proposition is that Culture Connects.

To explore this topic adequately we need to understand what we mean by culture. The origin of the word is similar in English, or I should say Latin, to 'agri' culture or farming and that gives us a clue. The meaning of the word culture relates to the process of cultivation, literally 'inhabit, till, care for' of the mind and soul. Culture, it is argued, is what makes us human, a distinctive species. It is the ability to cultivate that space between the ears and around the heart that sets us apart from other animals.

Inherent in this description of culture as cultivation is an assumption that the ground is fertile for culture to develop, and for thousands, perhaps million so years that was not so, but suddenly it seemed to burst onto the scene, expressing itself in cave paintings, music playing, worship, ritual and storytelling. As desperate tribes of nomadic hunter-gathers became cultivators of land and settled into cities, the consolidation of cultures gathered pace.

Today culture touches every part of our lives and world. I have walked seven thousand km through eighteen countries on walks for peace and I haven't yet come across one that does have its own very strong culture in food, language, music, dress, art, drama, religion, traditions, stories and special sites, national sporting heroes, etc. With the advent of film, television and the internet we have seen trends towards a globalisation of culture, and many countries struggle to keep their cultural identity intact because it is so important to the notion of identity, be that regional, ethnic or national. Why?

I would suggest that culture gives us roots, a sense of belonging and answers the question of where we came from. Just as a family home has its own culture—mum's cooking, dad's chair, favourite songs, special photos, favourite clothes, family traditions—they all make us who we are and culture gives us identity. Of course, we cannot expect every family to have exactly the same culture. But rather than being threatened by difference, we should see that our communities are stronger where cultural difference is allowed to flourish for the benefit of all.

That is not always the case. Today our news is filled with wars and conflicts. There are wars happening around the world today. So what went wrong? My suggestion is that disputes begin at a cultural level. They begin by suggesting that one nation's culture is the dominant one and that all others are lesser. On by walks when I speak to people from different countries, I am struck by how they all believe that their people are the most friendly, their food is the most delicious, their ancient leaders are the most heroic or wise, their music is the most melodic, their fighting men are the most courageous, their religion is the most true, their scenery is the most spectacular and so on.

Culture, as I have said, goes to the heart of our human identity, so when people seek to devalue our culture or replace our culture with their own, then they are seeking to devalue or remove our identity, and that provokes a hostile reaction. To illustrate: If you criticise the cooking of your best friends' mother, see how long you will survive as their 'best friend'.

Let me try and explain this another way: We all begin life with the same hardware and operating system, then through family, culture and education we gradually load on different programmes. My computer, with all its files, photos, music, emails, programmes and apps, will be unlike any other but it can connect with any other because the underlying operating system allows it to and encourages it to because culture is about communicating. The more we share culture out of mutual respect, the more we communicate. The more we communicate the less we distrust and the more we respect and understand. The more we have trust and understanding as the basis of human relations, the less we are likely to have conflict. Hence, culture connects and the more we cultivate it, the more we will harvest peace.

September 12 Day 48
Wei Shen Mo—Walk for Peace

Huai'an, Jiangsu Province
A Day Off

As I walk from Beijing to Hangzhou the most frequent comment I get is *Wei shen mo*? or Why? It is a straightforward question but the answers quickly exhaust my limited Chinese vocabulary, so let me try to explain in English:

Why walk? When I was a young boy, I had a map on my bedroom wall and I would imagine how I might walk around the world one day. It was a childhood dream, but it wasn't until I was asked a group of young people in 2009 whom I was encouraging to pursue their dreams why I hadn't pursued mine, that I began to step out. I quickly realised that at the age of nearly fifty I couldn't walk without a clear and compelling purpose. That is because as you get older your body may be weaker but your mind gets stronger. I decided that my purpose would be peace. I also found that when I walked, we could use that as a means to raise money for charities. I have now undertaken major walks every year since 2011 with the support of my wife, Xuelin, and have covered over 8,000 km in eighteen countries, raising over ₤120,000 for charitable causes.

Why peace? There needed to be a strong enough reason for me to walk, and my passion is peace. Our TV news screens and history books are filled with examples of the catastrophic effects when people seek to resolve their differences not through dialogue but through violence. I recall seeing documentary pictures in black and white film of men marching off to war, and I thought what would it take for men to march for peace instead? What would it be like if young men heroically marched off not to die for their country but to live for the world? I still haven't found answers yet but I have found a cause and that cause is peace.

Why China? This is a special year as we mark the 70th anniversary of the end of World War II the most devastating war in human history. China suffered greatly in that war, and the original plan was to walk from Beijing to Nanjing to recognise that terrible suffering. It is also the First Year of the UK-China Cultural Exchange, where we recognise the way in which culture—be it sport, education, fashion or tea—enriches the modern relations between our two countries. Finally, the decision to start the walk in Beijing and end in Hangzhou was because Hangzhou is the home city of Xuelin. As someone observed, 'Michael is walking from Beijing to Nanjing for peace and from Nanjing to Hangzhou for love.' Not a bad summary.

Which charity are you supporting this year? Xuelin and I are delighted to be working closely with the Red Cross Society of China. The Red Cross in China is one of the largest volunteer organisations in the world with over two million people in China who regularly give of their time to support their work, undertaking First Aid training, blood donations, helping struggling families financially and emergency response to disasters. With the Red Cross we have identified two projects in Jiangsu Province which we will be supporting with donations raised on the walk: Hope House School in Pizhou, which provides support for children with physical and mental disabilities, and Suqian Child Welfare Institute, which cares for orphaned children with disabilities. We have visited both schools on the walk and been impressed by the amazing work which they are doing. So far we have raised 160,000 yuan from over 500 donations, and we would love this figure to reach 500,000 yuan by the time we reach Hangzhou on October 6.

What has impressed you most on your walk? I think the things that have really struck me: First is the warmth and kindness of the Chinese people we have met along the way; shepherds minding their flocks of sheep, small traders selling pomegranates, women harvesting water chestnuts in floating bathtubs, road maintenance workers, petrol pump attendants, the outside noodle restaurant, old men playing cards or chess by the roadside, the Red Cross volunteers who come out to walk with me and guide me through their city or county safely. It is invariably ordinary, hard working people whom I come into contact with, and I have been overwhelmed by that experience. The second thing which has impressed me is the natural beauty of China once you get outside the city. The tree-lined rivers and canals. The lakes filled with Lotus flowers. The mountains of Tai'an. The third thing which has impressed me most has been the quality of the surface of the roads. I have walked on a lot of roads, and those in China are as good as or better than any I have walked on in Europe.

What have been the greatest challenges you have faced so far? So far after nearly fifty days we have reached Huai'an in Jiangsu Province, which is 1,100 km from our start point. The greatest challenge has undoubtedly been the weather. Being from the UK, I am used to rain but not to the sun. It has been very hot and humid, so much so that on a number of days we simply had to abandon walking and rest in the shade between 11 a.m. and 3 p.m. I am fifty four years old and not especially fit, so walking in these temperatures just drains every bit of energy I have.

What have been your most memorable experiences? I can think of many in the Taishan Mountains. I walked through a small village called Xingjiatun. There were a group of people sitting around a large old tree and they invited me to come and join them. I sat under the tree that was over five hundred years old and drank cool fresh water from a 700-year-old well. We talked about life in the village and I exchanged stories about life in London. There was lots of fun and laughter. I was told that I was the first Westerner to visit their village in living memory by one of the village elders who was himself 95 years old and a veteran of World War II. We connected through pictures of family and food. Then there was time for photographs and then, as if was a natural as drawing water up from the old well, villagers operated their smart phones and started scanning WeChat bar codes with us so we could exchange the pictures online. It was a picture of a truly global village of which we are all part not by virtue of our nationality but because of our humanity.

September 13 Day 49
'In Vogue' Xuyi

Route: Xuyixian, Huai'an, Jiangsu Province – Tianchang, Chuzhou, Anhui Province
Today walked: 21.50 miles / 34.60 km
Total walked: 751.80 miles / 1,210.60 km

Vogue means 'style' in French and it is the name of the most famous fashion magazine in the world. It was founded in 1892 in America but now has 26 global editions including *Vogue China*. It has given rise to an idiom in English of being 'in Vogue' meaning that something or someone is highly fashionable. Why am I telling you this? Well, today is a day off and I am staying in the Vogue Hotel in Xuyi on the southern edge of Hongzehu Lake and so I am literally 'in Vogue', and my kids would add, 'probably for the first and certainly for the last time in my life'.

The Red Cross volunteers, knowing that I had a hard stretch travelling down from Huai'an and needed to recover for the push to Nanjing, found us a perfect hotel with amazing views across the vast lake. The hotel staff could not have been more kind in their care for us. I was amazed how much they knew about my walk from Beijing. This interest seemed to come from a genuine appreciation that someone would come to walk for peace in their country. They didn't want to charge us for our room, but Xuelin patiently explained that we wanted to personally cover all our accommodation and travel costs on the walk but they would be welcome to make a contribution to the Red Cross. To our amazement overnight they decided to raise funds for the projects we are supporting (Hope House, Pizhou and Suqian

Institute) and presented Xuelin and I with a cheque to the Red Cross for 20,000 yuan (£2,000).

It is very much part of Chinese culture to 'want to please'—it is drawn deep from their Confucian roots. I can't speak for others from the West, but I find our culture is more about people giving space to 'please yourself' rather than going out of your way to 'please others'. An example would be that the chef at the Vogue Hotel wanted to try and find food to serve that his British guest might appreciate—at breakfast I was served Haggis, which is a traditional Scottish dish made of lamb and oats and a knife and fork to eat it with rather than chopsticks. I am not an expert on Haggis but this tasted as perfect as any I have had in Scotland.

For some reason I could never imagine a hotel in Britain serving up Chinese noodles and dumplings with chopsticks for a Chinese walker. The greatest phrase in British hospitality would be to tell the guest where everything is and tell them to help themselves and to 'let them know if there is anything they need'. I have no doubt that many British hotels, if a Chinese guest signed in and said, 'Would there be any chance of having Chinese dumplings with chopsticks?' that they would do their very best to try and accommodate the request, but they wouldn't initiate it for fear of not giving the guest enough space or worst of all appearing to presume what the guest would like.

Xuelin and I discussed the 'Haggis' incident quite a bit and she made the point that in Chinese culture it is not totally true to say that they only want to please, it is just because they have found that they get a greater pleasure from putting others first. I then began to think of my mum, who is a wonderful hostess, she simply cannot do enough for guests. My mum will seldom sit at the table and take time to eat because she will be in the kitchen preparing the next course or washing up. We would often plead with her as a family to sit down and enjoy the meal, to leave the washing and the cooking to us, but she would say that serving us and guests was something that gives her the greatest pleasure.

Perhaps we are not that far apart after all. Perhaps if we all realised that there is a happiness and satisfaction in giving and serving that can never be attained in taking or helping ourselves, then 'putting others first' might become 'in Vogue' and our world might be a better more humane place.

Thank you again, Vogue Hotel, Xuyi, for your generosity of spirit which blessed us, and we hope that will return to bless you twice over.

September 14 Day 50

Sinopec, 1,200 km and Jane Austen

Route: G205 Highway, Tianchang, Anhui Province – Nanjing, Jiangsu Province
Today walked: 23.30 miles / 37.50 km
Total walked: 775.10 miles / 1,248.10 km

One very good group of friends we have enjoyed meeting along the long S205 have been the petrol forecourt attendants at the Sinopec petrol stations. They are always such a cheerful group of young people in their smart blue uniforms who come out to the edge of the forecourt to take pictures of us passing by. It is a strong network, as information quickly passes from one petrol station to the next that we are on our way.

It is a basic rule of walking never to pass a WC (toilet) without paying a visit. I try to observe this rule on my walks and then feel guilty for using their WC without buying something from the shop, so go in for some water or iced tea. As a result I have become a bit of a specialist on petrol station WCs. China is a wonderful place and has so much going for it, but I am still struggling to come to terms with going to the WC in a long communal squat trough. Normally, Xuelin, knowing of my Western sensitivities, will stand guard over the door to give me a bit of space but today even she wasn't able to hold off about 20 men who arrived off a bus trip. They were all smoking and there was no elbow room. I have said too much. Quickly moving on ... as I did ....

Today was a very special day for a number of reasons: First, we marked 1,200 km on the walk. Second, we had to say farewell to our volunteers from Huai'an who had been with us for the past week and done such a great job. Third, it was the fiftieth day of the walk. Fourth, we crossed our fourth province in China on the walk so far, Anhui, in a day. Fifth, we finished at a sign over the S205 which showed for the first time 'Hangzhou–335 km' our destination point. Sixth, we arrived into the Nanjing City area and were greeted by our new Red Cross volunteers who would be with us for the next week.

It is fast approaching two months since we set off from Beijing and over the past few days I have noticed the seasons beginning to change. The crops in the field are less bright green and are turning a mellow yellow. The leaves are beginning to fall from the trees. Change is on the way. It is a poetic time of year, a time of reflection on the summer of opportunities past. Yet with the closing thoughts of the current year, there are just the smallest hints of hopes and dreams for next spring, should we make it through the winter. I love poetry and literature and wish that I could be a poet or an author but know this is a great talent given to but a favoured few, one of whom is Jane Austen.

Jane Austen (1775–1817) was one of our greatest English novelists, most noted for her classic brooding love stories of *Pride & Prejudice* and *Sense & Sensibility*, but in one of her lesser known but her first published work, *Persuasion*, she uses these lines to describe autumn. Having slightly lowered the tone of this blog by delving too deeply into the hidden world of the roadside bog (WC) I will try to conclude on more fragrant terms with an extract from *Persuasion*:

'Her pleasure in the walk must arise from the exercise and the day, from the view of the last smiles of the year upon the tawny leaves and withered hedges, and from repeating to herself some few of the thousand poetical descriptions extant of autumn—that season of peculiar and inexhaustible influence on the mind of taste and tenderness—that season which has drawn from every poet worthy of being read some attempt at description, or some lines of feeling.'

September 15 Day 51
Hope, Haircuts and Singing Horses

Nanjing, Jiangsu Province
A Day Off

It is a rest day in Luhe, about 40 km north of Nanjing. It is a busy day with a lot to pack in to the blog post, so let me get started:

We have had a documentary team with us since Beijing but today the director visited and wanted to have a substantial sit-down interview with Xuelin and me. We set aside an hour but it lasted one hour and thirty minutes. The real pressure was on Xuelin, who had to interpret the questions and the answers.

One area which the director was keen to press on was what happens when 'Walk for Peace' comes up against militarism, be it in a parade or an exhibition? I respond by saying you respect it because wars and warriors are the most honoured and sacred elements of all human tribal societies. Every tribal grouping believes its warriors are the most courageous, fearless and heroic. Every tribal grouping believes its wars and causes are always the most just. Every tribal grouping believes its enemies are evil, a threat to their way of life and utterly unreasonable. I believe that about Britain. I expect they will believe that about China. Indeed I expect all 196 member states of the UN and numerous other military movements will believe that about their warriors and their causes.

This answer doesn't quite seem to satisfy as the point is well made that China had been humiliated by the Japanese in WWII, and it should be understandable that it wishes to make a statement that it is now of a size and power that it would never allow this to happen again. We agree that when peace goes up against the military, peace will always look weak and cowardly and war will always look strong and courageous. To try and change that you need to undo millions of years of human tribal hard-wiring that sees violence as the means to resolving conflicts. 'So is walking for peace always going to fail?' 'No,' I answered. 'I have hope ....'

After a heavy interview I went for a haircut. The hairdresser was just around the corner from the hotel and had just started in business a few months ago. I have written before about my deep affection for those who step out in business on their own, so I wanted to try and help with advice about how to get customers. He wanted to talk with me about how a Chinese hairdresser can do a good haircut for Westerners because their hair is soft and thin (in my case, very thin) but the Chinese found it very difficult to give a good haircut to a Westerner because the hair is thicker and strong.

I was talking so much (through Xuelin translating again) that I forgot to explain what style I wanted, and what seemed to be taking shape was a kind of Kim Jong Un bouffant. I immediately stopped the business consulting and switched to hair, and we managed to get it back to a Western haircut with Chinese characteristics! Xuelin and female members of the team seemed to like it, so I left him a 50-yuan tip. Xuelin was horrified at my extravagance with the tip and immediately went off the haircut, saying she would expect him to cure my bald patch for that price. Ouch!

Back in the hotel room, on my own, I was pleased to discover the TV had the BBC World Service channel. On screen was an episode of 'Hard Talk' where Stephen Sackur was interviewing Aref Ali Nayed, the Libyan Ambassador to the United Arab Emirates and a key player in the post-Gaddafi internal conflict negotiations. In that impatient and slightly sneering way in which the British and Americans often interview people for whom English is not their first language, the host quoted back to Aref Ali Nayed his remarks when last on the programme, in which he spoke in the wake of the Arab Spring that 'Libya was now on a path to peace, prosperity, and democracy ...' Sackur pressed him 'Why did you get it so wrong?' His reply 'I always have hope ....'

The story is told of a prisoner about to be executed but who tells the king that he can teach his prize horse to sing for his birthday in nine months' time. Intrigued, the king postpones his execution and the prisoner sets to work. After three months his cellmate says, 'This is stupid. You know the horse can't sing.' 'Okay,' replies the prisoner, 'but if I didn't say I could do it, I would have been dead three months ago, and who knows over the next six months, the king may die, the horse may die, or, ...' 'Or what?' asks the cellmate, 'or, the horse might sing.' Hope keeps us alive ....

I guess Ambassador Aref Ali Nayed and I are on the same page ... so when you are scrolling through your social media news feed and see amazing video from Libyan desert of horse singing *Give Peace a Chance* remember you read it here first.

September 16 Day 52
Nanjing in Sight

Route: Tianchang, Chuzhou, Anhui Province – Liuhe District, Nanjing, Jiangsu Province
Today walked: 23.60 miles / 37.90 km
Total walked: 798.70 miles / 1,286.00 km

Back on the road again, but not the S205, which is undergoing repairs, so I am directed to follow the X203. I am so glad we did. It was a beautiful road full of interesting twists and turns, changes in scenery and small towns and villages to walk through. There was a noticeable increase in the affluence off the main highway. This was a commuter zone for Nanjing, where families could enjoy gentle hills, lakes and clear blue skies away from the metropolis—I guess if they could afford it, that is.

The weather was beginning to turn now. After the summer growth the crops were being collected in for harvest. It seemed that every available roadside space was spread with wheat being gently raked to dry in the sun before being packed in sacks and sent to market. There is a beauty and simplicity about rural life, especially arable crops. There are obvious seasons: You start at first light and finish when the sun goes down. You work hard in good weather and learn to rest in bad weather. You plant a seed, add sun and water, let nature take its course and then reap a harvest. I am sure that there is more to it than that, but sometimes modern life in the cities can be so complex because we lose sight of what we are doing and why. With modern communications and air conditioned offices, work is 24/7 and 365 days a year. In return we seem at times unable to see any evidence of a harvest in return for our labours.

After a serene walk, the best since my walk along the Pomegranate Way, I arrive back at the hotel and open my email. As usual, a whole wave of complexity floods into my Inbox from back home. Everything is urgent, decisions need to be taken in hours. I work long into the early morning to respond and when the last email was sent, I drift off to sleep, my laptop still open, with envious thoughts of those farmers along the X203.

September 17 Day 53
'Bridge Over the River Yangtze'

Route: Liuhe District – North Yangtze River Bridge, Nanjing
Today walked: 19.80 miles / 31.80 km
Total walked: 818.50 miles / 1,317.80 km

On September 17 (Day 53, Thursday) we set off from Luhe in the direction of Nanjing. We were not going to cross the Yangtze River today. I was a bit disappointed, as I always get a burst of energy when there is a major city to arrive in. As always there was a reason for stopping short of the Bridge over the River Yangtze: The Bridge has a very special significance in Chinese history and we were to cross it at 10 a.m. on Friday, 18 September—not before (for reasons which I will explain tomorrow).

The additional reason to delay was that we were to be joined by Madam Hao (Linna), who is Vice Chairman of the Red Cross Society in China and a great friend and supporter of our walk. Madam Hao was also bringing with her Wang Jiyan who is a very famous and successful businessman and founder of Phoenix Satellite TV. It was hinted by Madam Zhang (Ming) that he may have some good news for us on the fundraising side.

Xuelin reminded me over breakfast that I tend to overfocus on the challenge of the walk and forget the wider mission of the walk: We are here to raise funds for important causes through the Red Cross, such as Hope House; we are here to spread the message of peace and reconciliation as we mark the 70th Anniversary of the end of World War II; we are here to draw attention to the First Year of the UK-China Cultural

Exchange.

Because of this wider mission it will mean that we will not always take the most direct route for the walk; that we need to give time to explain our mission to potential donors; that I need to keep my blogs, social media sites up to date; that I need to take time to talk to the journalists and the media and that I need to engage with the young Red Cross Volunteers from each town/city/district who come out and join me for a few hours on the walk as we pass through their area.

I confess that I find the walking itself enough of a challenge at age 54, but I am grateful for Xuelin reminding me that it is not the walk itself which is the purpose, it is the mission which is purpose, and the walk is a means to fulfilling that purpose. Never lose sight of the mission was her message. I pondered as I walked that famous scene from the epic movie, *Bridge over the River Kwai* directed by David Lean ....

The movie is about the use of British prisoners of war by Japanese captors to construct a bridge over a river on the Burma-Siam (Thailand) railway, which as being constructed to bring supplies and re-inforcements to the Japanese front line in the war. The British prisoners are under the 'command' of Lieutenant Colonel Nicholson, played by Alec Guinness. They were being appallingly treated by their captors, dying of disease and malnutrition. In order to secure better treatment and conditions for his men, he agrees to build the best bridge he can.

The British prisoners perform an incredible feat of engineering in building the bridge, earning the respect even of their Japanese captors. The closing scene is of Colonel Nicholson looking with immense pride at the finished bridge and admiring the incredible work of his men in creating it. The train whistle blows in the distance as the first Japanese troop train is approaching to cross the new bridge. Then Nicholson notices wires leading to explosives which have been placed there by British and American special forces who had been tasked with destroying the bridge, and the train that was about to cross.

Rather than do his best to support the special forces by concealing their plan to blow the bridge Nicholson alerts the Japanese guards and tries to stop them. To him the Bridge represented a way of protecting his men from the brutal and inhumane treatment of their captors and maintaining the morale of the prisoners he was responsible for. It had given them purpose and pride in the darkness of their captivity. Yet in doing so, Nicholson had lost sight of the greater mission—to defeat the enemy. It is a classic human dilemma brilliantly exposed by David Lean. In the final scene Nicholson comes to his senses and, fatally wounded, detonates the explosives on the bridge himself.

To invoke the memory of the Bridge over the River Kwai in order to explain why we delayed our crossing of the Bridge over the River Yangtze is, of course, ridiculous, but it is a timely reminder to me that in 'what' we are doing we must never lose sight of 'why' we are doing it.

September 18 Day 54
Crossing a Bridge of History

Route: towards the Yangtze River Bridge, Nanjing
Today walked: 8.80 miles / 14.20 km
Total walked: 827.30 miles / 1,332.00 km

Day 54 we set off from north Nanjing to walk towards the Yangtze River Bridge, revived by my first visit to a Starbucks coffee shop in weeks. There is a much larger group than usual joining us for the crossing of this iconic bridge. Added significance is given to the walk as we time our departure so that we arrive on the Bridge at 10 a.m. on Friday, 18 September—this is a moment of national reflection, as its marks the anniversary of the Japanese invasion of China in 1931.

The bridge is a huge structure carrying cars and also a railway, but the vast natural expanse of the Yangtze River keeps the man-made structure strangely in proportion. The bridge is a symbol of national pride, as it was the first which China built itself. Before that infrastructure had normally been built and partly funded by the Soviet Union. It was opened in 1968 and Xuelin recalls her father bringing her to see the 'wonder of the modern world' and having her picture taken there when she was 8 years old. We try to find the spot of the photo to re-create it.

Enormous 'workers struggle' sculptures guard the four corners of the bridge. The bridge carries 80,000 vehicles a day but there is also narrow footpath in each direction which the few pedestrians must share with the many motorscooters. It is not for the faint hearted—the hand rails on the side of the bridge don't seem that high, and one bump from a passing scooter might send you over the edge. There is, therefore, some relief when the air-raid sirens sound three times to signal the buildup to the 10 a.m. moment of observance, and the traffic stops. We pause and reflect. A few moments later and the horns are sounding again and we are being bumped from side to side of the footpath by the scooters and bikes.

History in China, as elsewhere, is not perfectly coherent. I ask why it is that we are marking 1931 as the start of the Japanese invasion rather than 1937, which other exhibitions and memorials refer to. It was explained that the War against the Japanese Aggression began in 1937 but the Japanese Invasion happened in 1931.

Still not very clear, but I don't want my hosts to feel uncomfortable and realise that the intervening six years may be a 'missing chunk' from Chinese history. It is a bit like trying to find the chapter in British history textbooks on the abdication of King Edward VIII and his visits to Adolf Hitler as the Duke of Windsor in the 1930s ... let's not go there but rather get to Winston Churchill and the Battle of Britain as quickly as possible.

Later research in history, just for the record, told me that in the early days of the war, China was a divided country. Chiang Kai-shek had formed a nationalist Government—the Kuomintang (KMT), but his dictatorial regime was opposed by Mao Zedong's Communists (Communist Party of China, or CPC). Civil War erupted between the Communists and Nationalists—the period of Mao's 'Long March'—after the CPC was expelled from the KMT-led government.

In 1931 Japan, spotting the internal Chinese distraction, made a grab for the northeast region of China called Manchuria. The KMT official strategy was to secure control of China against its internal enemy (CPC) first. This meant the Japanese met virtually no resistance to their invasion and gradually expanded from Manchuria to Shanghai and Taiwan. It wasn't until pressure from Stalin and Western democracies on the KMT and CPC to unite and fight back against Japan that resulted in the Xi'an Agreement in

1937 that the war against the Japanese occupation began.

The war with Japan ended with VJ Day in 1945 in which the CPC-KMT China was allies with Russia, Britain and America. Not long after the end of WWII and the defeat of Japan, the agreement which had ended the Chinese Civil War in 1937, unravelled. The Civil War between the KMT and CPC resumed but the now vastly superior strength of the CPC People's Liberation Army led to defeat for the KMT in 1949. The CPC declared the People's Republic of China on October 1, 1949. The KMT was forced to retreat to Taiwan along with around 2 million of its members. Today the CPC is a ruling Party in the People's Republic of China and the KMT is the largest part of the ruling government in Taiwan (which they call the Republic of China), which is known as part of China.

September 19 Day 55
Walking Through the Darkness into the Light

Nanjing, Jiangsu Province
A Day Off

It was our first full day in Nanjing. Nanjing is known throughout the world for the atrocities which happened here in what has known as the 'Rape of Nanking'. Following its capture by invading Imperial Japanese troops on December 13, 1937 there followed what can perhaps be described as a mass 'slaughter of the innocence'.

In the space of six weeks of madness Japanese troops butchered about 300,000 unarmed men, women and children with beheadings, shootings and the burial of people alive in mass graves. In addition there were at least 20,000 recorded rapes. The horrific accounts are recorded in the Memorial Hall of the Victims of the Nanjing Massacre.

It was right that this memorial to the horror and inhumanity of war should be our first visit on a 'Walk for Peace'. How can you possibly begin to teach about the value of peace until you have examined thoroughly the true cost of war?

The site of the museum was built on some of the mass graves. Like other museums of genocide around the world, such as Yad Vashem in Jerusalem, the architects have effectively used dark subterranean spaces to covey the feeling that you are physically descending into the darkest places of humanity. In the Memorial Hall are etched the names of many of the victims. I look at the names as think of them not as iron characters listed on a wall but rather as sons, daughters, mothers, fathers ….

This is what happens in war, people lose sight of the human value of a person. Once you cease to see someone as human first, a moral equivalent, then mass slaughter becomes as impersonal as the slaughter of animals in an abattoir. Victor Frankl, a survivor of the holocaust at Auswitch, would explain that the German guards would strip new arrivals of all clothes, shave their heads, take their identity cards and tattoo a name on their arses. From then on they were a number not a name and the evil became easier to commit.

I don't want to detail the atrocities recorded; they were deeply disturbing and those wishing to find out more of what went on can research online or visit for themselves. I want to say something about how I felt. Truthfully angry! How could humans do this to other humans? It seems to me that evil is when we cease to have empathy, to show any feelings for the victims of our actions.

There needs, however, to be great care that we do not respond in the same way in taking away the humanity of the perpetrators of these crimes. The Japanese soldiers who had competitions with each other to see how many people they could behead in a day were no less human than those they were slaughtering. To say that this tells us what the soldiers of one nation are capable of is to miss the point and to run the risk of it happening again. The message of the museum is that this is what humans are capable of. Nelson Mandela said, 'When we dehumanise our opponents we abandon the possibility of peacefully resolving our differences.' I was reminded also of the words of Alexander Solzenitsyn in Gulag Archipeligo:

'Gradually it was disclosed to me that the line separating good and evil passes not through states, nor between classes, nor between political parties either—but right through every human heart—and through all human hearts. This line shifts. Inside us, it oscillates with the years. And even within hearts overwhelmed by evil, one small bridgehead of good is retained. And even in the best of all hearts, there remains … an unuprooted small corner of evil.'

As if to underscore this, I came to one unexpected part of the exhibition dedicated to a German, John Rabe, who was the director of Siemens in China, which was headquartered in Nanjing in 1937, as it was then the capital of China. Seeing and being horrified at the first-hand account of the unfolding massacre in December 1937, Rabe opened his home to refugees—it quickly became home and refuge to 600 people. Then with others, including American missionaries and academics, they proposed the establishment of an International Safety Zone for refugees in a 4-square-km area of the city.

Why the Japanese were willing even to consider a request from John Rabe? (Reread the Solzenitsyn quote at this point.) Because, like Oscar Schindler in Poland, who saved thousands of Jews, Rabe was a member of the Nazi Party. Rabe had written to Adolf Hitler personally to draw his attention to what was happening and urge him to put pressure on Japan, a member of the Axis Powers (along with Italy). The Japanese reluctantly agreed to the request, and the Red Cross provided humanitarian aid to some 250,000 people in the Zone. These 250,000 people would have almost certainly been slaughtered along with others had the zone not existed.

After the war was over, Rabe returned to Germany and was arrested by the British and denounced for his Nazi membership. He lost his permit to work in the British Zone. He then had to undergo an extensive denazification process during which time he couldn't work and used all his savings. Rabe and his family lived in a one-room apartment kept going only by a monthly food parcel sent by the Communist Party officials in Nanjing. He died in poverty in 1950.

I was wrestling with so many different competing thoughts of what I had seen in the exhibition. I needed time to reflect on them, but as I was about to exit the museum, I was led to a table where there was a large open red book in which my hosts invited me to record a message. Cameras and dignitaries gathered round to see what I would say. I knew this was sacred ground for the Chinese. It was sacred ground for humanity also. After pausing for a few seconds, I picked up the marker pen and wrote:

'Walk for Peace. To be able to make peace with the present we must first make peace with the past. This exhibition shows not only what evil humans are capable of but also what good—I am thinking here of John Rabe and the International Safety Zone. In the past the city of Nanjing has been associated in the mind of the world with an act of unspeakable brutality. My hope and prayer is that in the future it will become known around the world as a place of peace and reconciliation. The journey to that place must take us through the dark corridors of this museum and then out into the light beyond. I have walked this journey with you. Michael Bates 19/9/15'

September 20 Day 56
Donations Breakthrough

Nanjing, Jiangsu Province
A Day Off

I have mentioned frequently that there were three objectives: First, to complete the walk, and so far we are ahead of schedule in reaching Nanjing with around 300 km to go. Second, to spread the message of Walk for Peace, which is that peace is possible if we work for it and realise that we are all human first—having had the opportunity to share this message with hundreds of young people along the way either directly or indirectly through this blog and social media. I think this objective is being reached. We have still two weeks to go. The final objective has been to raise funds in China and in the UK for projects we have identified with the Red Cross—Xuelin set us an ambitious target of raising £50,000 or 500,000 yuan and for most of the walk we have been stuck around £10,000 or 100,000 yuan.

Xuelin is an amazing businesswoman, and once she sets an objective she isn't going to miss it. In many ways this is why we are a good team in these walks. I am a hopeless fundraiser. I hate asking for money. But I can walk and when I set myself an objective for walking, to this point, I have always hit it or exceeded it no matter what obstacles are placed in my way. Xuelin is not a great walker but she is a fantastic fundraiser.

I suppose the key to good fundraising, like good walking, is to have a clear purpose. Probably at the beginning of the walk when we were generally raising funds for projects to be identified, people felt that they wanted to know where their hard-earned money was going before they parted with it. That is why when we identified the first two projects, Hope House in Pizhou, which works with children with physical and mental disabilities, and the Suqian Orphanage for Children, we found a more receptive mood for donations.

Xuelin is an active member of the Zhejiang University Alumni, and the alumni have been tremendous supporters of the walk throughout our journey. Today Zhejiang University and Jiangsu Alumni organised a walk with over 120 people coming along to support the Walk for Peace and walk with us around the ancient walls of Nanjing. In addition the alumni created a specific bar code so that alumni in the group could donate via WeChat or mobile phone. This innovation raised 120,000 yuan from 600 people making donations from 1 yuan to 1,000 yuan.

Xuelin was contacted by a friend in the UK, Julia Wang, who runs a successful international student internship scheme. Julia came up with the idea of getting young people to take part in an 'Apprentice' style competition to raise funds for the Red Cross projects identified through our walk. Over 200 people applied and Julia selected 30 from Nanjing to undertake the challenge. The young people were divided into six teams, and each team was given 500 yuan and one week to try and increase that amount. It was a fantastic project, and when we met the students at the end of the week-long activity and they presented us with a cheque for 30,000 yuan (£3,000), we were inspired by their commitment and grateful.

Also in Nanjing we were joined by three local companies who came together through the Red Cross and Wang Jiyan of Phoenix television to present us with a cheque for 150,000 yuan (£15,000).

So far donations have come from over 1,000 people, which is important because the more people who engage in the walk through walking a few miles with us, donating their money no matter how much or little, or by reading these blogs, then the message is being spread.

In the UK there is a website which collects donations in a tax-efficient way for UK taxpayers, and those funds go to the British Red Cross. So far that site has collected Ł4,300 (43,000 yuan).

With a struggling start to the fundraising through the efforts of hundreds of people and the work of Xuelin, the total funds raised so far are 460,000 yuan (Ł46,000), which when added to the Ł4,300 in the UK, takes us just over our target for the walk. It is an amazing response and the funds will make a real difference in many children's lives. Of course, Xuelin being Xuelin, is not for stopping there and there is a possibility that we might be able to do even better than this by the time we reach Hangzhou to conclude the walk on October 5.

On behalf of Xuelin and I and the Red Cross in China and Britain, can we thank everyone who has contributed to this amazing result so far.

September 21 Day 57
Nanjing Declaration

Nanjing, Jiangsu Province
A Day Off

It is Monday 21, September the United Nations International Day of Peace. I am in Nanjing and I want to pitch an idea to see if there might be a response.

Preamble: Xuelin and I have been deeply moved by our encounters with young people here in Nanjing. On Saturday we attended an event with around 30 young people who had volunteered for a 'Charity Apprentice' competition to raise funds for Walk for Peace. On Sunday around 120 young people turned out with Zhejiang University Alumni to 'Walk for Peace' around the ancient walls of Nanjing. Today we were at Jinling Middle School for a talk to around 150 students, followed by a football match. Ever since we left Beijing 57 days ago we have been accompanied on the walk by different groups of local Red Cross Volunteers. Young people have always energised me with their 'can do' and 'change the world' attitude. It was young people in Newcastle in 2009 who first challenged me to start walking. They continue to be a source of inspiration. So when asked by some of those young people and a young journalist at this morning's press conference whether 'Walk for Peace' had any plans to leave some kind of legacy organisation from the walk that could continue to 'Walk' and to 'Work' for Peace we thought about this very carefully.

The idea of an organisation had not crossed my mind. My thoughts with Xuelin as I finish this walk are turning to the walk in 2016, which we are planning to mark the Olympic Truce for the Rio 2016 Games. I walk alone. Xuelin and I have developed a very efficient mechanism for planning a walk, doing the walk and raising funds for the nominated good cause. Organisations scare me. They are full of committees, bureaucracies, territorial arguments, inflated egos and internal squabbles. I started walking because I wanted to break out of sterile politics and do something direct to make a difference. That said, what if other people share my frustrations and are seeking a vehicle through which they too can make a difference for good? Could we not help them? Should we not help them?

It is late at night. I have a long day of walking out of Nanjing tomorrow but I want to draft an idea on this day in this place for these young people to see if it resonates and if doesn't, how could it be changed to ensure that it did?

Concept: To create a youth organisation that provides a channel for people to explore cultural differences and to think and act about peace and understanding locally, nationally and internationally.

Aim: To build peace through an international public diplomacy network around connecting cultures and enrich individual's experience and knowledge.

Idea: A group in Nanjing called PAX (the Latin word for Peace) and standing for 'Peace through Cultural Exchange'.

Overarching principles: Enjoyment, excellence, education, respect, service, accessibility and achievement.

Definition:

The origin of the word is similar in English, or I should say Latin, to 'agri' culture or farming and that gives us a clue. The meaning of the word culture relates to the process of cultivation, literally 'inhabit, till, care for' of the mind and soul. Culture, it is argued, is what makes us human, a distinctive species. It is the ability to cultivate that space between the ears and around the heart that sets us apart from other animals.

Inherent in this description of culture as cultivation is an assumption that the ground is fertile for culture to develop and for thousands, perhaps million of years that was not so but suddenly it seemed to burst onto the scene expressing itself in cave paintings, music playing, worship, customs, dress, ritual and storytelling. Culture for the purposes of this proposal is taken to mean:

Education, Sport, Art, Music, Drama, Religion, Dance, Philosophy, Literature, Food, History, Film, Fashion and Language.

Structure:

PAX would be a franchise which is awarded by the Walk for Peace Foundation, following a bid by a group from a particular city or district which complies with the criteria set out by the Foundation.

Membership would be open to everyone from the age of 16.

There could be no discrimination on any grounds.

Members would be encouraged to make activities accessible to those with physical and mental disabilities.

Each city/town level PAX branch would be called a 'Missio'. There could only be one Mission in each city though it is possible that in very large cities consulates could be opened to cater for particular specialism and localities.

The Mission would be comprised of members and officers copied from diplomatic ranks and headed by a PAX Ambassador. They would be supported by Chargé d'affaires, Minister, Minister Counsellor, Counsellor, First Secretary, Second Secretary, Third Secretary, Attaché and Assistant Attaché.

There would be four 'Divisions' of activities, each led by an officer: Arts, Education, Philosophy, and Sport. Each Mission would be invited to nominate a particular Division as a 'Major' or a 'Specialism'.

For PAX to work it must avoid being drawn into the political arena. PAX is about being respectful and seeking to understand and connect with different cultures, not to change them. Each mission must be prepared to respect the host political and legal system which is operating in their area.

To reduce bureaucracy wherever possible organisation and

communication should be done through social media.

The purpose of PAX is not to promote one culture as superior over another. It starts from the position that we are all: Human first. That we are all of equal value. That our cultural identity is a reflection of our particular upbringing, education and experience. Our cultural identity is unique to us. That does not mean it should not be open to question through PAX events, but the questioning must be to seek to understand rather than challenge.

Activities:

Each PAX Mission would need to organise events and issue short reports online to give details of activities on:

April 6—United Nations International Day for Sport Development & Peace

September 21—United Nations Day for International Peace

The start of the Olympic truce for both Winter and Summer Games.

There would be an annual General Assembly Meeting for each Mission to receive reports on activities, present awards, and appoint officers.

There would be an annual Walk for Peace.

It addition ….

It would be envisaged that a Mission would be based around activities rather than bureaucracies. In other words, the purpose of the mission is to promote peace through cultural exchange. Examples might include:

Members sharing in a social setting their own unique cultural identity;

Sporting competitions between members and with other groups or organisations;

Learning from students experiences who have studied overseas or foreign students or teachers attending local schools or universities;

Visits to historic sites, museums, locations that might assist in understanding some new aspect of culture;

Attending or organising concerts with different styles of dance or music;

Lectures on particular aspects of philosophy of other ideas;

Talks by diplomats, officials and business people from other regions or countries;

Marking or exploring major religious festivals or places of worship;

Film nights showing world cinema movies followed by discussion;

Awards:

PAX would promote a system of lifelong service and lifelong learning. The Walk for Peace Foundation would draw up and oversee the judging of award programmes and competitions. Awards will be meritocratic as will promotion of officers—it's not who you are but what you do that counts.

In today's global world businesses, organisations and educational institutions are all looking for young people who are culturally aware and sensitive. PAX could provide a means for demonstrating to those organisations a commitment on the part of the member to engage and explore at a cultural level.

How could this be improved to make it more effective in enriching your cultural experience and promoting peace and goodwill to all peoples?

September 22 Day 58
Thoughts on Professor Bates

Route: Gulou District – Jiangning District, Nanjing
Today walked: 25.10 miles / 40.30 km
Total walked: 852.40 miles / 1,372.30 km

It was a tough start to the walk today. The football match at Jinling Middle School the previous evening had left me feeling aches and pains in muscles I hadn't known existed. All the team members arrived in the hotel foyer at 8 a.m., limping or trying to stretch out the cramps. Of course, it always hurts more when you lose, and our 3–0 defeat to the young Jinling School was not a fair reflection of the game—it should have been 7–0!

We hobbled our way through the city centre of Nanjing and then out into the prosperous suburbs. In one of those great miracles which I have never experienced before, we arrived at the 20 km mark and a planned stop for lunch, and there was a Starbucks! I feel Starbucks is my spiritual home. My favourite Starbucks is at the junction of 48th and Park Avenue in Manhattan. It was the Starbucks I first called 'home', as it was closest to the office where I frequently worked when in New York with Oxford Analytica, whose HQ was 230 Park Avenue. I even had a special seat where I could see the top of the Chrysler Building. They knew my name and my order and played jazz. Well, Jinling in Nanjing might not be quite there but they played jazz, so half-way.

As I drank my Grande Skinny Latte and listened to the legend that is John Coltrane, my mind went back to a visit I had made with Xuelin to the home of John Rabe, who was the Seimens Manager in Nanjing at the time of the Japanese invasion and who first chaired the International Safety Zone, which saved over 250,000 lives. We visited the home and the museum on our first day in Nanjing but there were too many people with us for the small house with a remarkable history, and so Xuelin arranged for me to go back the following morning for a private visit with Mr. Yang Shanyou, who is the Curator of the museum and a member of faculty at Nanjing University, which manages the museum.

Mr. Yang was very surprised to see that we had come back again and wanted to show us some displays for Miner Searle Bates, who was a history professor at Nanjing University and had not only worked with John Rabe to establish the International Safety Zone in Nanjing but in 1939 took over its chairmanship. Mr. Yang thought that my interest may be because Professor Bates had played such a significant role in the Zone. I was sorry to disappoint him. Professor Bates was an American Christian missionary who came to Nanjing with the YMCA in 1920. He was a graduate of Yale, Oxford and Harvard but felt called by god to serve the people of China, which he did for thirty years until 1950.

The more I read about him the more I grew in admiration. There were many records of him. On more than one occasion he had pistols pointed at his head as he intervened to protect women who were being molested by occupying troops. There is nothing passive about being a pacifist. Professor Bates documented the atrocities being committed in Nanjing, and his evidence was crucial in bringing the perpetrators to justice in the Tokyo and Nanjing War Trials.

There were two quotes which were carried in the displays and which struck a chord of admiration: First, 'Peace of Earth and Goodwill to All Men' and then 'Religious faith is believing that good things are worth doing for their own sake even in a world that seems overpoweringly evil. I remain assured in hard experience that neither by national guns nor by national gods will mankind be saved, but only by the genuine regard for all members of the human family.'

This second quote had a great effect on me. It is one thing for me as someone who has never been confronted with the true horrors of war and only had my values of peace tested by the occasional blister rather than the face of death, to express to the belief that we are all human first and encourage people to seek peace and goodwill. Yet here was a man who had had those beliefs tested to the extreme at a time of incredible danger and inhumanity and he upheld their truth and value as a bright light not through the words but through his actions.

Peace heroes, unlike war heroes, seldom merit medals, statues or public adulation, but I was grateful for Seimens, John Rabe House and Nanjing University for keeping these precious memories of John Rabe and Professor Bates alive to demonstrate that 'The light shines in the darkness and the darkness has not overcome it' (John 1:5).

September 23 Day 59
The Voice of Youth

Route: Jiangning District – Lishuixian, Nanjing
Today walked: 25.70 miles / 41.30 km
Total walked: 878.10 miles / 1,413.60 km

The second day walking out of Nanjing and we are still in the suburbs. Walking through suburbs is a slog. There isn't the excitement of the city/town centres nor the beauty of the countryside and rural life. There isn't a great deal to write about or celebrate apart from passing the 1,400-km mile marker.

My thoughts turn back to Nanjing and especially to the young people I met at the Nanjing Memorial Museum who had worked so hard to raise funds for the Red Cross projects. One of the young people spoke for the group as a welcome and Xuelin took a picture of the speech as it was written and delivered in both Chinese and English. Often we are told what young people think or believe, but we don't often get the chance to hear it from them themselves, but here are the words of one young person in China:

Dear Lord Bates, my young friends,

This is the 70th anniversary of the end of the Second World War, which is also an important time when Lord Bates attends the commemorative activity with our young people in the Memorial Hall of the Victims of the Nanjing Massacre. When Lord Bates and his wife travelled tirelessly thousands of miles to China to spread the thought of peace, we shall not forget the bloodshed and humiliation behind this episode in our country's history.

Looking back on those turbulent days we admire the courage of our national heroes who fought and shed blood for our country in battlefields. We also can't forget the spirit of the 56 nationalities united against the enemy as one and we can't forget that over 300,000 compatriots were killed in our homeland. How shocking the past is. They are reminding us not to forget the national humiliation. These shall serve as alarm bell that reminds us not to forget our national humiliation.

Seventy years have passed, we, the Chinese young people, still engrave the great dedication of the martyrs who sacrificed for the country and faced death unflinchingly. We bear this history in mind and we cherish peace more than ever. At this moment we propose to our young friends as follows:

Remember history and don't forget national humiliation. Let's learn that history together, let's remember the precious experience which the tough times taught us, better construct our great country and strive to realise the great dream of the great rejuvenation of China!

Cherish peace, remember our obligations. Peace and development are the themes of this age and also in common wish of people worldwide. The peaceful society where we are currently living is not easily come by. We shall remember our obligations to bravely bear the responsibility of society and country. Do not let history repeat itself to help vulnerable groups, to spread justice and make the olive branch of peace never fade.

Live plainly, work hard and be eager to learn. The hardship of yesterday makes the prosperity of today. As a Chinese young person we shall not abandon our traditions, although the material conditions become better and the society more stable. We shall be hardworking, thrifty and eager to learn.

Stick to your dreams, be motivated by practice sincerely. Young people shall have dreams and practice sincerely to become a useful person! We dare to dream and we fight with strong minds. Thus, we can get what we want in our old age without regret. We are neither afraid of hardships nor the long journey because we clearly know we shall see success after these untold hardships and sufferings. In the current society full of temptation of power and money, we cannot be enslaved. We shall strive for our dreams to lay a foundation for the future.

We wish you could stick to your dreams and realise your ambitions and get what you truly want. Let's remember history together and cherish peace. Let's put this enthusiasm into action, strive for the development of the Chinese nation, peace of the world and build a beautiful homeland for everyone.

I think it is very important that we let the words of this young person be allowed to stand on their own so that we, adults, perhaps from other countries or cultures, might try and understand the sincere thoughts and hopes which lie behind their composition.

September 24 Day 60
Back to Beijing

Beijing
A Day Off

We found ourselves a few days ahead of schedule on account of having saved time by taking to S205 route from Huai'an to Nanjing rather than the eastern side of Gaoyou Lake to Yangzhou on our way to Nanjing. It was a decision which was greeted by surprise by our friends in the Jiangsu Red Cross, as Yangzhou is an 'amazingly beautiful city'—which I am sure it is—but saving 10 miles is an 'amazingly beautiful thought' at this stage of the journey.

Having taken the more direct route and freed up a few extra days, I was looking forward to using them to leisurely get up to date with blogs and emails. No chance. Not when Xuelin is driving the fundraising and activity around the walk. These are three good days to be spent productively. Xuelin arranged an extremely busy round of meetings, interviews and events back in Beijing. When Xuelin told me the programme on the High Speed Train journey from Lishui station to Beijing, I began to think that the east coast route to Yangzhou didn't seem too bad after all.

Our first meeting off the train was with Lin Jun, head of All-China Federation of Returned Overseas Chinese. Lin has a very busy job, as he is responsible for 50 million plus overseas Chinese, and it is one which involves seemingly endless travel—he was leaving for Indonesia immediately after our meeting.

The list of where Overseas Chinese are located makes interesting reading. Many are obvious, such as neighbouring Thailand (9.32 million), Malaysia (6.96 million), Indonesia (2.8 million) and Myanmar (1.6 million), and Singapore, Philippines, Cambodia and Vietnam also have significant populations. During the Chinese Civil War there were very large movements of the defeated Nationalist government (Kuomintang) to such countries and regions as Singapore, Malaysia, Indonesia and the Philippines as well as, of course, to Taiwan.

Some are less obvious—the United States has the third highest number of ethnic Chinese (3.7 million); many travelled there in the 19th century to help build railways and support gold mines. Also, Canada has 1.5 million, many of whom were invited to come following the Hong Kong handover. Peru has 1.3 million ethnic Chinese—not sure how or why but would be interested to learn more. In Europe France has the largest Chinese population (700,000) with the UK second (466,000). The fastest growing overseas Chinese communities are in Africa and in Eastern Russia, especially the port city of Vladivostock.

It is good to keep in touch with Diasporas because they remind us that great population migrations are nothing new. They have happened down through the centuries as a result of wars or famines and will continue to do so, as it is a basic human instinct to move in order to secure food, safety and a better future for themselves and their families. That is what millions of British people did as they travelled to America, Canada, Australia, New Zealand and southern Africa in centuries past. Australia remains the top destination for Britain (207,000) emigrating abroad, then the United States (72,000) and Spain (52,000).

As if often the case with very busy people, they have an air of quiet calm about them. It might be very different in the outer office, but Lin is very interested in our walk and for the reasons which lie behind it. He is an educated and thoughtful man, I am guessing around sixty, and skilled in calligraphy and even makes fine teapots just in case I didn't feel inadequate already. He is wise and broad-minded, as travel often makes you. It was Mark Twain who remarked, 'Travel is fatal to prejudice, bigotry, and narrow-mindedness.' In the course of conversation he offers some advice; in Chinese culture this is unusual as they don't want to offend the guest, but I think he judged that I, and if not me then certainly our translator (Xuelin) might be open to it. 'You should think of doing shorter walks in more places.' I think this may be a frequent conversation topic between Xuelin and me as we conclude this walk and start to think of the next one.

After some more media interviews we were invited to a British Chamber of Commerce/China British Business Council dinner for a visiting British parliamentary delegation. This has been a big week in China for the British, as a high-level delegation of government ministers led by the Chancellor of the Exchequer, George Osborne, arrived in China to promote British trade. The Chancellor set the UK the target of becoming China's second largest trading partner after the United States and spoke of a Golden Decade of trade relations. These are exciting times indeed. It is so much more productive for the world when nations trade goods rather than accusations.

The hosts invited me to say a few words about my experiences on my walk to the largely business audience. Peace, hope and walking a 1,000 miles for charity perhaps don't come naturally to an audience perhaps more concerned with the Shanghai Stock Exchange, so I followed my father's advice on preaching, 'If you don't strike oil after five minutes stop boring and sit down.' (Note to translators—this is wordplay, as to drill an oil well you bore. If someone is disinterested in what you are saying, then you may be said to be boring.) I think I sat down in two minutes actually, but Xuelin and I had a few very interesting conversations afterwards, one very significant, which just goes to show you should never pre-judge people.

September 25 Day 61
The Importance of Communication

Beijing
A Day Off

Today was a day set aside purely for interviews: Some in our hotel and one which required us to travel to east Beijing and the incredible new HQ of Phoenix television near Chaoyang Park. The building looks from the outside like a giant doughnut, but everything about the building is designed for a purpose—the flowing curves of its glass and steel facade capture rainwater which is recycled for use in the building. The partial arches around the base allow the optimum flow of air through the structure to assist natural cooling.

Xuelin trained as an architect so this was special treat for her and she had many questions. The original remit or specification to the famous Beijing Institute for Architectural Design was 'Un-forbidden Office' after the Forbidden City of Beijing. This was to be a building which said to the staff and to the world not 'keep out' but 'come in'. Architecture so often reflects the underlying philosophy and self-confidence of an economy.

In the past China has made good use of prestigious firms of foreign architects such as Herzog & de Meuron's 'Birds Nest Stadium' or Norman Foster's Beijing International Airport. The Phoenix media centre is a bit of a statement that 'Hey we can do this for ourselves' (and at a fraction of the cost). It is an amazing building and we enjoy exploring its wide open spaces.

It was not just for the architecture that we came; it was because Phoenix television had taken a long interest in the walk and in my previous walks through their operations in London. They have a weekly programme called *Charity China* and they were to feature Walk for Peace and our partners on the walk, Red Cross Society of China.

A key part of any modern charity fundraising activity is media. It is not that the media drives donations but when the charity has appeared on the media it seems to give a verification of its aims and objectives. This is certainly what Xuelin has found as she has built up the WeChat and WeiBo platforms, which have helped generate a significant portion of the donations to date. It is very difficult to do this because, of course, there are so many worthy causes and yet a limited number of media outlets to carry them.

That is why charities increasingly look to celebrities to endorse their activities. One step by Angelina Jolie in the UK or Yao Chen in China in support of a cause can raise more than a thousand miles by an unknown politician. So the very fact that Phoenix, CCTV, *China Daily* and *Beijing Evening Daily* and the *Beijing News* have been so interested in our walk so far is a great encouragement which is translated each day into real donations for good causes through the Red Cross.

One other benefit of having a series of interviews on days off is that in the past when TV crews have travelled out to walk with us, they have found me absolutely exhausted by the demands simply of walking 40 km in a day, and therefore I am washed out by the end of the day when they want to talk with me. As we take time out to engage with the journalists on this trip, Xuelin and I find their line of questions interesting and really helpful in learning not only how to convey what we are doing but why we are doing it. The Latin word for communication is not from a root word which is about speaking or writing in a didactic (lecturing) way, it is from a word which means 'sharing', which suggests that both the viewer, interviewer and the interviewee should end up being better informed when good communication takes place.

September 26 Day 62
Rock the Boat

Beijing
A Day Off

It was an early start to make our way out to Daoxiang Lake on the northern edge of Beijing. It is the new centre for Asian Rowing being located in a vast area of rivers and lakes sheltered by mountains and two leading Chinese universities, Peking University and Tsinghua University, which supply a steady flower of rowing talent. Asian Rowing has received new impetus since leading Chinese entrepreneur Wang Shi took on a leading role.

Wang Shi is something of a legend in China. He is chairman of China's largest real estate development company, China Vanke. Wang is recognised as one of the leading figures in China's economic opening up. He is someone who has also promoted ethical business principles holding to 'no bribery' and 'no more than 25% profit policy'. He still managed to build a vast business empire. He is a quietly spoken and studious man but one who wants to be judged by his actions rather than his words. He has climbed Qomolangma twice (breaking the age record for the oldest Chinese mountaineer to reach the summit at the age of 59 in 2010). He has trekked to the North and South Poles and moves between boardroom and classroom effortlessly, undertaking research studies at Oxford and Harvard.

Needless to say of someone so eminent in so many fields, he didn't have a clue who I was but fortunately knew and respected Xuelin. They are members of the same WeChat group. Through the group he read some of my blog entries and wanted to support us. Following an exchange of emails and late-night telephone calls and in the lightning fast Chinese way that things can happen in China, we were invited to attend the launch of Asian Rowing's new home and take part in a special charity event called 'Rock & Row for Peace' which Wang and his team had organised to promote the Walk for Peace. First there was a little challenge to overcome ….

In the flurry of calls and emails somewhere Xuelin asked me, 'Have you ever rowed?' I replied of course, thinking of Saltwell Park Lake as a child and a couple of times at Oxford and Durham when studying at university. By rowing I meant 'sat in a boat with a couple of oars and a couple of beers and ideally a couple of girls'. By rowing Chairman Wang's team meant one of those eight-man boats you see in the Olympics or the Oxford Cambridge Boat Race. We arrived at the launch site, each of us oblivious to the misunderstanding between us—which was about to become apparent.

The speeches went well. We cut the ribbon—that went well. I was then introduced to my teammates—from Deep Dive, who had just returned from intensive training in Cambridge, England—that went well but they did all seem to be half my age, half my weight and 10 times my fitness. Then we were introduced to the boat—my heart sank, I didn't think I would be able to keep my backside in the boat never mind on the small sliding seat. I tried to manage expectations by saying, 'I normally row with two oars,' 'Oh you mean sculling?' came the reply 'Did I?' I thought to myself. I was then asked whether I preferred stroke or boweside? They were speaking perfect English but it was a foreign language. 'What number do you want?' asked another, I said '4' with confidence—I had at least figured out by then that there were eight seats so four would put me somewhere not too obvious in the middle.

The Deep Dive team was going to be racing Wang's team. They stripped down to the rowing kit, all skin tight like a cyclists, to show off their perfectly defined muscle groups. I had thought this was a row around a lake so hadn't bothered to bring any sports kit—I was there in my trousers, black leather shoes and Walk for Truce T-shirt. I called Xuelin over to explain the problems and her response was a smile and getting me a pair of hotel slippers from our baggage in the car. Okay, so now I didn't have leather shoes but I was still lifting an 8-man boat and we were walking to the river bank—all I could think of was, at what point do I drop out? Knowing that the 'Rock for Peace' special event was to come later I wanted to show willing and at least try. After all how difficult could it really be?

    I got in, or more accurately, was lowered into the boat; as soon as I landed in P4 I started hearing 'Steady the boat' calls. The boat was so narrow and sleek it felt as if you were sitting on top of the water and the slightest tip you felt would bring water over the side. As we pushed off from the quay—I felt actually quite scared. My feet were too big to fit in the built-in shoes on the boat so I had no grip. It seemed every time I went to even touch the oar beside me, I would get a 'steady the boat' shout. Teammates who had been saying how thrilled they were to have me on the team on land now out on the water were beginning to have mutinous murmurings about 'Whose bright idea was this to take this useless sack of potatoes out on the water?' I kept my oar blade flat on the water as it seemed the best way to steady the boat and avoid a Deep Dive. I begin to think of a great book title called 'If you want to walk on water you need to get out of the boat …' it seemed as if either I or my teammates were soon going to put that faith to the test.

    We set off up the river to take our positions for the race. I tried a few strokes, but they resulted in a steady boat shout again so I was told to just stop. We made our way up past the spectators and the press gallery and I could hear Xuelin shouting 'Why aren't you rowing?' I didn't want to say anything in case I got another 'steady the boat' shout. We got to the head of the river and were joined by a professional umpire on a launch. He wanted to check that I was okay. When I said I think it might be better if I left the boat and he told me that this would mean climbing onto his launch mid-river, I decided that the safest option was probably to try and stay in the boat. They then decided that if I didn't row and the seat behind me didn't row then we would keep balance. So we were off. Soon my teammates were happy we were going down the river quicker with six rowers than we came up with eight. That is the importance of balance in rowing so I discovered.

We arrived back at the landing platform and I have never been more grateful to see dry land. The fact that we had made it back without sinking covered all the personal embarrassment I felt with my fellow team members—well at least until I made it back to the Club House for a rather quiet breakfast. Chairman Wang was characteristically gracious and philosophical. We then had the 'Rock and Row for Peace' event, which was really fun with competing really teams on rowing machines with progress on a big screen. It raised a lot of interest in the Walk for Peace, probably mostly around thinking how can a man so unfit, who cannot even get into a boat by himself never mind row could ever walk 1,000 miles. Well, that as they say is another story which I am still trying to write ….

September 27 Day 63
Moon Festival

Route: Lishuixian, Nanjing – Liyang, Changzhou
Today walked: 25.30 miles / 40.70 km
Total walked: 903.40 miles / 1,454.30 km

It had been a punishing and humiliating day out on the river in Beijing. The rowing action is very different from the walking action and therefore I was already seizing up around my shoulders. We arrived back at Lishui Station on Saturday evening, but were met by our wonderful and faithful friends from the Jiangsu Red Cross. We have been together for almost a month now as we travelled across this great province, and their patience and kindness has been a constant inspiration for Xuelin and me.

The way in which the rest-day breaks had fallen meant that we were scheduled to walk on Moon Festival, or the Mid-Autumn Festival, one of the most important family days, according to China's lunar year. It is perhaps not quite Christmas in the Western sense—that would be Chinese New Year—but it is certainly Thanksgiving in the US or perhaps Easter in the UK. We felt very sad for the small core team that they were missing their families in order to support us on the walk, but just as we were thinking how we could thank them, they produced a big box of moon cakes for us. It was typical of their generosity of spirit that they would think of us missing our families on Moon Festival rather than them missing theirs.

Moon or Mid-Autumn Festival has been celebrated in China for thousands of years—records go back to 2000 BC but Moon Worship was common even before then. It is traditionally composed of three elements: gathering of friends, family and, of course, the harvest; Thanksgiving for friends, family and harvest and prayer for partners, babies, good health and a good future. The most famous gift in China's mainland is moon cake with its moon-shaped lotus-bean centre. Often they are piled in groups of thirteen or cut into thirteen to symbolise the thirteen months of the lunar calendar.

Next morning it was moon cake for breakfast and greetings of *Zhong qiu jie kuai le* (Happy Mid-Autumn Festival), which I kept confusing with *Sheng ri kuai le* which is Happy Birthday. Anyway no one seemed to mind and we set about the task for the day, which was a long walk from just past Lishui to before Liyang. The road was good but all my joints were aching from the rowing experience the day before.

One other thing which we had picked up, I suspect from the long (4.5 hour) train journey, was a cold. Xuelin had it worst but it was also building up in me. In the evening we went in search of pharmacists and different remedies. One thing China has is an infinite variety of medicines or herbal remedies. They are mostly herbal-based. They are all quite cheap so the approach seems to be buying a few and see which one works for you. I picked out Bamyl just because it was made by AstraZeneca, which I had heard of. We went back to our room and mixed various potions before trying to get to sleep.

Normally, I am fairly relaxed about minor illnesses on the basis that they will just work their way out of the system in time. That was not really an option on the walk. We were now into the last seven days and only had two days for rest. We need to arrive in Hangzhou on Monday, 5th October and specifically at 5 p.m. There was no space for a 3–4 day illness. I began to regret spending three days in Beijing and cutting our time so close. The news also carried reports that the tail of Typhoon Dujuan would land around where we are on Monday evening. I don't know what we did to offend the Moon but I would now like to officially apologise on behalf of the team. It won't happen again. *Sheng ri kuai le*!

September 28 Day 64
Route Perspectives and Teapots in Yixing

Route: Liyang, Changzhou – Yixing, Wuxi
Today walked: 26.20 miles / 42.20 km
Total walked: 929.60 miles / 1,496.50 km

We continued along the G104 through the south of Jiangsu Province, heading in the direction of the great Taihu Lake. Madam Zhang had been back in Beijing for a few days working on aspects of the final stages of the trip and the mechanics for directing funds to chosen causes. Liyang is on the high-speed rail line, so she was able to return almost direct to the hotel. It was good to have her back with us. Every good team needs a good leader and we are blessed to have Madam Zhang.

Xuelin had been down with a heavy cold although I have found that in Xuelin's case 'illness' means that she only works for 15 hours a day rather than the usual 20. Of all the 'medicines' that Xuelin thinks are aiding her recovery, top of the list are 'Hall's Mentholyptus' I mention that these are British-made candy, not medicine, but she looks at me as if to say, 'So what, if it works?'

Anyway we spend about half the day in Liyang and then cross the border into Yixing for the second half. We are joined by a second television crew who had come from Beijing with Madam Zhang having secured Red Cross approval to cover the walk for a short promotional video about British-Chinese relations—I am on my best behavior (as always, of course).

A new district means a new map. Why is it when you open a map, you immediately find five men appear from nowhere and start pointing different locations on it and arguing? The debates are mostly about competing views of what the route should be: There are those who think safety first and want to stick to wide roads with good bike/walking lanes; there are those who want the most scenic route—to show me a great temple, museum, battlefield, or other place of historic interest. Meanwhile, Xuelin and I observed the debate and simply want to find the shortest possible path between where we are and where we need to get to.

Routes are, of course, a question of perspective. If you love your town and city, and most people do, then you want a visitor to see all the amazing places there are. If you are sitting in a car following the walk, then that scenic route that takes you over a mountain pass via a beautiful temple with spectacular views over a lake sounds just perfect. Then, of course, if you have been walking for sixty-five days, if every bone and joint in body is aching and crying out for you to stop, if you have visited 101 'amazing sites' already on your journey, then all you want is to get to the next hotel, shower and get to bed as soon as possible.

If that means walking barefoot over a high speed rail track, blindfold through a motorway tunnel, crossing a ravine on a trapeze wire, or walking past the main entrance to the Taj Mahal at sunset without missing a step, then you have my current perspective. Madam Zhang arrives at the communal map-reading exercise: 'Ah, Lord, Yixing is very famous for teapots. We can take a detour here and visit the factory of one of grandmasters' of Chinese teapot-making.' I reply, 'Excellent suggestion Madam Zhang' and obediently walk on.

September 29 Day 65
A Tale of Two Dreams

Wuxi, Jiangsu Province
A Day Off

The term 'Chinese Dream' has become very popular in China since 2013 when it was promoted by President Xi Jinping in a series of speeches on Chinese socialist building. It sounded like the American Dream which we are more familiar with in the West—that ideal that 'All men are created equal and have the right to life, liberty and the pursuit of happiness.'

President Xi said that the Chinese Dream was about 'national rejuvenation, improvement of people's livelihoods, prosperity, construction of a better society and a strengthened military'. He said that young people should 'dare to dream, work assiduously to fulfill the dreams and contribute to the revitalisation of the nation'.

This was interesting background to a deep question which I was asked by an interviewer 'How would you compare the Chinese and the British Dreams?' The first problem, which I probably need to return to, was that I wasn't aware that there was a concept of the 'British Dream'. The British culture tends to be very practical, class-based and suspicious of sentimental terms like dreams—in this respect I am not culturally British, as I love the idea of dreams. My life has been shaped by my dreams.

I begin my answer by saying that in Britain if you asked young people what their dream was, then they might say to be a famous footballer if they were boys or a famous pop singer if they were girls. The problem starts here because I don't believe that is their dream—it was someone else's. I believe that people have very deep and unique personal dreams for their lives, but they are scared of attracting the ridicule and mockery of their friends by sharing them, so they choose 'social-media acceptable' and ready-made flat-packed dreams instead. It is such a waste of their hidden talent and their personal dream, which were meant to inspire and illuminate the world.

If there is a weakness in the British or Western dream, then it is perhaps that it is too individualistic and focused on the spin off benefits of a dream realised, such as fame, money or power. A good society is one which encourages people to discover and develop their unique talents, gifts and dreams not just for themselves but for benefit of us all.

So how does this compare to the Chinese dream? The short answer is that I am not very sure. Xuelin would be a better person to ask. That said, here is my best attempt at an answer. In some ways Chinese young people I meet display similar characteristics to their Western counterparts in the sense that they may often describe their dream as being something which might win the approval of others, chiefly their parents, such as studying hard and winning a place at a prestigious university. Chinese young people are more collective and less individualistic than their Western counterparts, which is to be expected given the cultural difference reflected in their history and underlying philosophy. Therefore, instinctively Chinese young people might think not only what does this dream mean for me and what does it mean for my family and my country? President Xi perfectly captures this thinking in his description of the Chinese Dream mentioned earlier. One final difference with Chinese and British dreams is that failure is a huge shame in Chinese culture and can sometimes mean that people don't want to take risks; in American and Britain perhaps the greatest failure would be in not having a go.

I was left thinking that perhaps it is less productive to focus on how Chinese and British dreams might differ and more constructive to think about how they are similar. If the composition of dreams is similar, then I would observe that the reasons why dreams fail are common to both also.

First, people select their dreams too early. In order to discover your unique gifts and talents, you need to have experiences which bring them out. This is a kind of pyramid theory because you can only build a pyramid as high as the base is wide. The broader the base the higher you can build. A good piece of advice for a young person is to experience more: Don't just try one sport, try as many as possible before you chose the one you are naturally gifted at. Don't choose one subject to major in but try many to discover where you are strongest. Travel and explore more. Try and have a broader circle of friends who have different interests and passions. Read more. Connect more.

Second, start with the end in mind. Imagine you are looking back at the end of your life. Ask yourself, what does success look like? What does life look like once I have achieved my dream?

Third, examine your motivation. Motivation is everything. Ask yourself not only what is my dream but why do I want it?

Fourth, build a team of friends around you who are dream-builders not dream-killers. I am fifty-four but I have a group of four trusted friends whom I have known for over twenty five years. We meet together regularly to offer advice and encourage each other. It is important to have people who will tell you the honest truth, whom know you and care for you.

Fifth, don't give your dream to other people to pour cold water on or tell you why it won't work. They should be focused on realising their dream, so don't allow them to undermine yours. Often people are negative about someone else's dream not because they think you might fail but because they fear most you might succeed!

Sixth, concentrate on developing your strengths, don't waste time on your weaknesses. It is normal for us to focus on our weaknesses, what skills we haven't got, and forget to develop the skills you have. We compare our weaknesses to other people's strengths and conclude we are inferior to them. The best way to help your weaknesses is to focus on developing your strengths.

Finally, dreams are not time-limited. As long as we are breathing, then so is the dream within us. It is sometimes said that 'education is wasted on the young' by which they mean that the older we get the more we value education and can place it in the context of life experience. So it is with dreams; sometimes they can be wasted on the young who think success in life is guaranteed and that they will live forever. If they could meet the person who has known the failure of a business, failure in a relationship, or ill-health, then they would be different. You can't learn experience in a classroom, it is part of life and needs to lived and learned as we go along. For this reason it might be that the best people to realise a dream are those who are old. They may be physically weaker but they are emotionally, intellectually and spiritually stronger. You are never too old to be the person you might have been. Why not test this, by starting today.

September 30 Day 66
China Growing Taller and Getting Deeper

Route: Yixing, Wuxi, Jiangsu Province – Changxingxian, Huzhou, Zhejiang Province
Today walked: 28.30 miles / 45.50 km
Total walked: 957.90 miles / 1,542.00 km

Back on the G104 for our final day in Jiangsu Province. I will miss the Red Cross team who has been with us over the last 25 days. We have become good friends.

Professionally, I have long taken an interest in trends over events. The argument goes that the world changes gradually and sometimes imperceivably to our event-obsessed media. Truth is not found in the dot of one event but in the joining together of many dots to observe a trend. All along my journey from Beijing I had discovered lots of dots in the form of new temples being built on mountain tops or prayer towers, parks and pagodas. I think it is a trend showing a desire to rediscover the deep philosophical and spiritual history of the country.

Those roots have not always been encouraged. Sometimes they have been deliberately torn up, as in the early stages of the 'Cultural Revolution', but now there is a growing desire to rediscover the vast wealth of history of the great peoples of China. It is ironic that it was an obsessive adherence to the works of Marx, a German philosopher, which turned the Red Guards against their own history and culture.

The great opening up of China economically has been taking place since 1984, but the deepening of China is something that is seldom written about but is, I believe, something of significance that should be discussed more. I would be as positive about the deepening of Chinese society as I would be about its opening up. Religion and philosophy are part of man's search for meaning. They are what make us human—that desire to see the material world in a spiritual context. Every civilisation in the world through history has a religious or philosophical system. They give us our moral codes; our rites of passage and provide us with a belief of where we came from, why, and where we are going to.

China has a rich history from which to draw inspiration for the modern soul. Confucianism, Taoism, and Legalism as well as adapted imports such as Zen Buddhism—to name but a few. When the history of five thousand years of scholarship, literature, and architecture were dismissed, the Chinese society was chopping at its own roots. To deny our history and culture is a sign of insecurity, to embrace it is a sign of strength. Now these roots are being rediscovered and invited to take their rightful place in modern China, and the society will be more stable, the branches better nourished and able to produce even better fruit.

October 1 Day 67
It's a Small, Small World in Zhejiang

Route: Changxingxian – Downtown, Huzhou
Today walked: 23.90 miles / 38.40 km
Total walked: 981.80 miles / 1,580.40 km

A spectacular view of the Taihu Lake greeted us from the G104 as we crossed the border from Jiangsu to Zhejiang. Taihu Lake is the third largest freshwater lake in China. It is a good reminder that the natural environment is a key driver in the development of civilisation. There is a reason why early civilisation flourished on the Yangtze River Delta rather than in the Gobi Desert. It is because of the abundance of fresh water, the fertile flat lands for crops and a large network of lakes and rivers connecting to the sea for navigation and trade. It is also the reason why control of the lands was fiercely contested.

We set off down the G104 and it was then suggested we take a more scenic route down the edge of Taihu Lake. The weather wasn't great, blustery with light rain, but the lake still looked majestic. Also rather than marching along being sprayed by heavy lorries, we were on a glorious cycle path and footpath which ran around the edge of the lake. Everywhere I have been in China I have noticed how extraordinarily well kept the hedges and borders were alongside the road. Along the edge of Taihu Lake these borders were turned into an art form, absolutely beautiful. I think the 20 km stretch of Taihu Lake down to Huzhou must be the best cycle path in the world, and it is inspiring for walkers too.

I paused for a short break during a heavy downpour in a bus shelter. As I sat drinking my water, a lady wearing a Union Jack T-shirt approached holding an iPhone. I thought that she might want a picture with this strange Westerner but she was wanting me to look at the phone. I smiled and looked and there was a picture of me on the terrace of the House of Lords with a young man; I didn't recognise him immediately. Madam Zhang appeared and helped to translate. This lady was Li Huizi, a well known Huzhou artist. The boy in the photo was Mali Wei Qi, who is her son, studying in London and currently working as part of Xuelin's team translating these blogs into Chinese every day. What a small world!

Li Huizi had put her talents to great use by designing a picture based on our walk, which I had used often without fully appreciating the artist. In addition to the work of Li Huizi and her son, she had also come with a very generous donation to the Red Cross projects we are supporting through the walk. And as if that wasn't a great enough contribution to Walk for Peace from this one family, she then joined me for the remaining 25 km of the day's walk. It is so encouraging to meet such people and to see their commitment to our common cause.

The meeting also reminded us of the incredible work being down back in London and here in China every day to take these blogs and translate them into Chinese. I know that my use of some terms often challenges their abilities to the limit, but Xuelin tells me that the quality of their work is absolutely outstanding, and we are so grateful to them.

October 2 Day 68
It's not the Critic that Counts + PS & PPS

Huzhou, Zhejiang Province
A Day Off

It is a rest day in Huzhou as we prepare for the final three-day push to the finish line in Hangzhou, around 100 km away. It is a beautiful day and a beautiful stay at the New Century Hotel. With its range of Western TV channels I am able to catch up on lots of the sports news from the Rugby World Cup. In Britain, like so many areas of life, sport tends to be loosely divided along class lines. Rugby Union-like cricket tends to be a middle-class sport whilst Rugby League and football are more working class.

The division really stems from school, as it tended to be the private schools or the state schools in affluent areas which would play rugby in the winter and cricket in the summer. At my state school in a working class area of Tyneside, they played football in winter, summer, spring and morning, noon and night. Why am I saying this? Well, part as a little cultural exchange but really because at the moment England is hosting the Rugby Union World Cup, and things aren't going too well. England was defeated by fellow Brits. Wales and now must win against Australia (the favourites) to stay in the competition.

I follow football rather than rugby, but when the national team is competing, whether it is in the four-man bobsleigh or synchronised swimming, I want them to win and do well. I was watching a string of commentators giving their 'expert analysis' with the benefit of slow motion replays, of where England is going wrong and what it needs to do to win the game against Australia on Saturday. I don't think there was a member of the England team, including the bus driver and the lady who washes the shorts and irons the shirts, who escaped criticism for their performance against Wales.

Criticism hurts. Often we can hardly remember the numerous encouraging things that are said about us, but we never forget a word of criticism. Why is this? Well, basically it is because we are all a bit insecure and need approval. But the other reason is that the minute you get off the sofa or out of the stands and set foot on the pitch, you will become a target for criticism. If you can't handle criticism, then your place is back on the sofa with a beer in one hand and the remote control in the other.

Critics know they have power because we are all sensitive to criticism. So, the film critic gives an unfavourable review to a new movie, but he or she has never acted, directed or written a screenplay. The art critic dismisses the latest work of an artist and yet has never painted. The commentator criticises the actions of officials but could he or she have done better? Aristotle summed this up perfectly in 350 BC when he wrote: 'Criticism is something we can avoid easily by saying nothing, doing nothing, and being nothing.'

Theodore Roosevelt, the 26th President of the United States, who came in for his fair share of criticism said,

> It is not the critic who counts; not the man who points out how the strong man stumbles, or where the doer of deeds could have done them better. The credit belongs to the man who is actually in the arena, whose face is marred by dust and sweat and blood; who strives valiantly; who errs, who comes short again and again, because there is not effort without error and shortcomings; but who does actually strive to do the deeds; who knows the great enthusiasms, the great devotions, who spends himself in a worthy cause, who at the best knows in the end the triumph of high achievement, and who at the worst, if he fails, at least he fails while daring

greatly, so that his place shall never be with those cold and timid souls who neither know victory nor defeat.

So, as the England rugby team walk out into the area again in London on Saturday in front of a packed Twickenham with 82,000 spectators after the game, no player will waste a second thinking of the critics. They are there on the pitch marred by dust, sweat and blood. Which player would swap that spine-tingling opportunity to sit up in the stands with a lukewarm coffee and a soggy sausage roll to commentate on the performance of others? Life is not meant to be a spectator sport. It is meant to be lived out in the centre of the arena where the voice of the critics is drowned out by the thrill of the game.

For those Chinese friends who have yet to discover the joys of rugby (although there is a Chinese National Rugby team—currently ranked 66th in the world—one place above England—only joking!) should watch the movie *Invictus* directed by Clint Eastwood and starring Morgan Freeman and Matt Damon. The title of the movie is based on a famous poem by W. E. Henley of the same name. In order to lift the spirits of my home team ahead of the clash against Australia, I will leave you with two short verses from the epic poem:

> In the fell clutch of circumstance
> I have not winced nor cried aloud.
> Under the bludgeonings of chance
> My head is bloody, but unbowed.
>
> It matters not how strait the gate,
> How charged with punishments the scroll,
> I am the master of my fate,
> I am the captain of my soul.

Come on England!

P.S. —Postscripts (P.S.) are a useful tool when writing about fast-moving events. I am afraid my stirring words did not reach the England rugby dressing room in time, for they were soundly beaten by Australia, 33 to 13 and are now out of the World Cup, which they are hosting. My point, I think, still holds in that: It is the true joy of life to be out in the arena covered in sweat and mud giving your all even when you are being thrashed by the Aussies than it is to be a mere spectator, or worse, a commentator.

P.P.S. —Now I am getting confused here, is a PPS a postscript to a PS? Or, should this be a new PS? Don't criticizse me if I make the wrong choice. The afterthought was that when I had written the blog, Xuelin read it and remarked that in China self-criticism was encouraged and then went on to criticise me for not mentioning it. Xuelin is, of course, right, the best form of criticism is that which comes from within because you are more likely to act upon it. I should also say that there are some people in this world who will instinctively want the very best for you and will offer selfless advice without any agenda other than your personal happiness—these people are called—'your parents'. Listen to them.

October 3 Day 69
Personal Safety?

Route: Downtown – Deqingxian, Huzhou
Today walked: 27.90 miles / 45.00 km
Total walked: 1,009.70 miles / 1,625.40 km

It was my own fault—I was so excited at seeing a Starbucks across the road from our hotel in Huzhou that I walked out into the road when I thought the traffic had stopped and a motor scooter came around the blind-side of a truck and almost took us both out.

It was a close call but on arrival in the heavenly tranquility that is Starbucks I reflected on how rare an instance this had been on my walk in China and how safe I had felt on the journey. I recalled a conversation I had had last year about my proposed journey with someone who had cycled from Qingdao to Beijing. He said that it was dangerous enough being on a bike but on foot on busy roads I just 'wouldn't survive'.

Well, I don't want to tempt fate but so far he is wrong, very wrong. In fact as I have walked along the roads in the daytime and around the town and village centres in the evening I have felt very safe. China is an orderly and respectful society. At times it may look a bit chaotic on the surface but there is a strong moral code, and if that fails to restrain then there is a real fear of authority.

On most of my walks I am alone and therefore from a safety point of view, you might think quite vulnerable especially when you can be seen to be carrying all your worldly possessions in your rucksack including cash, cards, iPhone, camera, passport and computer. I once remember being given a stern briefing by a British Embassy security adviser in Sarajevo; he estimated that I was walking around with at least a 1,000 euro in easily realisable cash/items on my back which can make you a bit of a target, especially to drug addicts.

I am not blasé when it comes to personal safety. I do not like to walk in dusk or dark or in very heavy rain. I like to walk facing the oncoming traffic so that I can eyeball the driver to see if he/she is aware of me. That said, in China you must walk 'with the direction of traffic' but also most of the time I was walking with other people, so we created a greater presence on the road.

When I am walking around towns and cities at night, I try to stick to well-lit areas. When I do come across suspicious groups or individuals, then I always avoid eye contact. Eye contact is critical to conflict in the animal kingdom because making eye contact with a human or animal can be seen as threatening. Also humans (perhaps all animals do this) use eye contact as a means of weighing up the weakness/strength of someone whom they might attack; avoid eye contact and you at least create a doubt in their mind over your capabilities to defend yourself if attacked.

I have walked through 18 countries on my walks to date and China is as safe as any and more safe than most. I wanted to test this perception out in numbers, so I went to check out the international ranking of countries by murder/homicide rates and this seemed to confirm my instinct about China. With a rate of murders per 100,000 of population of 1.0, that puts it amongst the lowest rates in the world—188th out of 218. The rate is the same as the UK (190th) and France (191st).

To show just how relatively those countries are, it is worth noting that India, with a murder rate of 3.5 per 100,000, the United States is 111th with a murder rate of 4.7 (compared to 1.0 in China), the Philippines is 8.8 per 100,000, Russia is 9.2, South Africa is 31, Jamaica 39.3, Venezuela is 53.7 and Honduras is 90.4.

To show just how bad the murder rate is in countries like Honduras,

Venezuela, Jamaica and South Africa, then consider the murder rate in Iraq is 8.8 per 100,000 population and Afghanistan is 6.5.

Most countries with high violent crime rates are those in which there is a drug trade or other form of organised crime and high levels of alcoholism. People addicted to drugs will do anything to get their next fix. People under the influence of drugs or excessive alcohol lose their sense of inbuilt personal restraint. People involved in gang cultures will do almost anything to retain the respect of other gang members.

The fact that China has relatively low rates of violent crime might be due to the fact that it has managed to control the driving forces behind crime. It takes a very tough stance, of course, and the fact that China executed over 550 prisoners (2014), which is the largest number of executions in the world—twice as many as Iran and the United States—was 35. Of course, I am switching statistical methods to make a point here—when expressed in executions per 1 million population, it falls to 10th.

The Chinese people might fairly point to the fact that every 1.0 per 100,000 rise in the murder rate is 13,410 innocent people who are killed per year compared to 550 executed. However, I have always been opposed to the death penalty because I believe that life is sacred and no one has the right to take it away; because courts can make mistakes—we frequently receive reports that new evidence has been found which prove someone convicted of a murder is innocent—it is bad enough that someone may have been deprived of his or her liberty for 10 or 15 years but they can be released—not so if they were executed; my third reason is that I believe in personal redemption. I believe that basically good people in a moment of madness can do bad things, but they are capable of facing up to the evil they have done and working for the remainder of their lives (albeit mostly in prison) to try and make amends.

Those doubting this latter point might read or watch Victor Hugo's *Les Miserables* and reflect on the encounter between Jean Valjean and Bishop Myriel. (I choose Victor Hugo because he is a highly respected figure in China. He was one of the few Western thinkers at the time to call the burning and looting of the Old Summer Palace in Beijing in 1860 by Anglo-French forces an act of 'barbarism', which on reflection was probably an understatement).

October 4 Day 70

Mrs. Wu's Question Goes to the Heart of the Matter

Route: Deqingxian, Huzhou – Yuhang District, Hangzhou
Today walked: 26.30 miles / 42.30 km
Total walked: 1,036.00 miles / 1,667.70 km

It was raining hard during the day as we set off from Donglinzhen and followed a path along a riverbank which became progressively more muddy. The grips on the soles of my new walking shoes in Beijing have been completely worn down by the walk, so I was slipping around like a ballerina, or more like an elephant on roller skates. This slowed progress and with only one day to go. At lunchtime we had only done 12 km and we should have done 18 km.

Xuelin did not want me to miss the target point for Day 70, which was Renhezhen. Her reasons were not only that we did not want to leave more than 35 km to do on the final day but also because she wanted us be able to stay at her home and have dinner with her mother and brother-in-law. We had a bit of a debate with rain-soaked maps as to which was the best route into Hangzhou—the river or the high speed rail line? The railline won and it proved to be a good decision as it brought us into Renhezhen at 5 p.m.

It was wonderful to walk through the door of Xuelin's mum's beautiful home. It is one of my favourite places on the planet. It is an oasis of green in a sea of concrete. The wonderful array of trees and flowers in the garden attracts birds from far and wide. You are woken up with a wonderful dawn chorus. I think birdsong is the most beautiful music in the world for its melody and the fact that it is from living creatures communicating with each other live.

I am proud to be a son-in-law of Hangzhou and proud Mrs. Wu is my mother-in-law. She is always so cheerful, gives me a hug and then pats my stomach and asks how my Chinese is coming along. Fortunately, on the walk I have managed to pick up about fifty new phrases or words, which I spill out in random fashion to try and impress her. Sadly, my attempts seem to produce more laughter than admiration.

A beautiful dinner is prepared and enjoyed. As the plates are being cleared away, Mrs. Wu looked at me with sadness in her eyes and spoke at some length. I asked Xuelin what her mum had said and her response surprised me, 'My mum said, why do you trade your life for this walk? Your health is the most important thing; why would you risk it for this walk? Why put yourself through such hardship when you should be enjoying this time of life?' Mrs. Wu and her daughter have a habit of being direct, but even so this caught me off guard.

I had just slipped and slogged 42.3 km in the driving rain. I didn't enjoy one bit of it. I just wanted to finish. The fact that my shorts and shirt were soaked by the rain meant that I got friction burns in sensitive places and could only half sit on the seat at the dining room table. I feel guilty to say this, but I was tired and fed-up and Mrs. Wu perhaps sensed this and asked the obvious question. Why?

I am in politics and am privileged to be a member of the UK Parliament and also to serve as a minister in the UK government. I regard these positions as both an incredible honour and heavy responsibility to serve my country and my party. I do my best but politics is at times like wading through treacle to get things done—this probably says less about the political process in the UK and more about my lack of skill and ability within it. Walking therefore to me is kind of direct action. At the end of each day I can see distance travelled on a map, funds raised for charity online and opportunities to understand and share thoughts through conversations and blogs.

Moreover, the areas which you are required to focus on in the political arena are not necessarily the ones for which you have a burning passion. My passion is peace.

I became exposed to the world and the roots of conflict through an incredible seven years as Director of Consultancy & Research at Oxford Analytica www.oxan.com. This continued for two years of doctoral research at Durham University into ethics and foreign policy which I failed to complete (insert: guilt). I continue to read and research extensively in this area. I believe we are on the verge of exposing the male lust for violence and the human glorification of war for what it is a primeval animal instinct. Its roots lie more in anthropology and tribal culture than in politics. Its antidotes are in the realms of competitive sport, education, cultural exchange and international systems of justice.

My core theory is that 'we are all the same'; there is good and evil in the world but it is not out there, it is in us. There are differences in culture, language and religion but these are explained not by some divine plan but by simple accident of birth and our tribal roots. The more we see each other as human first and our adopted culture second, the less we will distrust, the less we will feel threatened by difference, the less we will feel superior or inferior, and the more we may seek to resolve disputes through agreed systems of justice based on the fundamental principle of the equal value, worth, rights and responsibilities of each and every human being.

It sounds so improbable—a world without war? Yet I feel like some fifteenth century explorer who senses in his bones there is a Northwest Passage between the Pacific and Atlantic oceans but lacks the evidence to prove it. At some point you just want to stop analysing the maps and get in a boat and go and find it. Well, for me walking is 'getting in the boat'. In each country I walk through, eighteen so far, what strikes me most are not our differences, which are trivial, entirely cultural and massively overstated, but our similarities, which are vast, awe-inspiring and largely unexplored.

I have yet to prove this theory or win an argument on its central premise, even amongst high school students, let alone political colleagues. I don't have the intellect or the words to even make the case, let alone win the argument, so I let my walk be my talk and hope.

October 5 Day 71
Crossing the Finishing Line

Route: Yuhang District – Zhejiang University, Hangzhou
Today walked: 21.70 miles / 35.00 km
Total walked: 1,057.70 miles / 1,702.70 km

The final day. Did I think it would ever come? In the plan it was meant to be a rather symbolic walk of 10 km on to the campus of Zhejiang University, but slower progress over the past few days meant that I still had 35 km to walk.

Xuelin and Madam Zhang were in a whirlwind of activity organising the closing ceremony, meeting points for people who wanted to come out and join us for a few miles on the final day, meeting points for press and media who were wanting to cover the final stages of the walk or present us with donations for the charitable causes. Apart from signing T-shirts, writing thank you notes and posing for photographs, all I had to concern myself with was walking 35 km.

Within a couple of hours we were walking under the G2501 ring-road and into the city of Hangzhou. Hangzhou is one of the most beautiful and prosperous cities in China. It has a population of over 21 million. It is surrounded by hills and mountains which produce some of the finest and most expensive tea (Dragon well or longjing) in China and it was the centre of the silk trade. It is a city focused around the West Lake, which is a magnet for tourism and led Marco Polo to describe the city as the 'Venice of the East', and as if that weren't enough praise, he added (in Italian of course). 'Hangzhou is the finest and most splendid city in the world.' Its location on the Yangtze River Delta and at the southern end of the Grand Canal connecting it to Beijing added to its commercial and trading appeal and from there its wealth.

Today it retains those physical strengths, and it has also become a technology centre because of the leading universities and great living conditions and is the home to the Alibaba Group, one of the largest tech companies in the world. The prosperity is very obvious from the western luxury cars, high fashions, huge Gucci & Luis Vuitton stores and flats with lake views that cost more than flats in London and New York.

When Xuelin and I had originally thought of a route for a walk in China, we had thought of following the Grand Canal through its entire length but then found that in many places there was no road or footpath to travel along. So when we came into the city, we quickly joined the footpath along the Jinghang Canal stretch of the Grand Canal and followed it down about 10 km to West Lake Plaza. The footpath along the canal was amazing although the falling leaves and wet conditions made it quite challenging in places.

By now I was in top gear, walking with the end in sight and was probably doing 6 km per hour. So much so that Xuelin had to come and tell us to slow down because they weren't expecting us to arrive at the university campus until 4:30 p.m. and because of the rain they had needed to move the ceremony indoors.

Not needing much persuading to stop at a Starbucks, we sat down and checked the mileage on my pedometers. I carry two iPhones, both with the same app (Moves), which I can then cross-check to record an accurate distance. The apps were showing that I was going to finish having done 1,698 km, and so we decided that as we had time instead of taking the direct route down Shuguang Road, we would walk around the edge of West Lake and this would take us just over 1,700 km. It was a good idea but this was National Holiday week and even in the rain the narrow paths and bridges around the lake were packed with tourists, which slowed us up a bit, but it was a good strategy all round.

Suddenly the crowds drifted away as we walked up from the West Lake up Yugu Road and through the famous Hangzhou Botanical Gardens. I was joined by Madam Zhang and Xuelin for the final couple of kilometers, which was what I wanted, for without them then this walk simply would not have happened. The number of Red Cross volunteers, Zhejiang University alumni, friends and supporters was now around 30–40 though I couldn't quite see the end of the group.

I wanted Xuelin to choose the end point of the walk in Hangzhou. Madam Zhang was right, this was a Walk for Peace from Beijing to Nanjing and a Walk for Love from Nanjing to Hangzhou. My partner in both walks is Xuelin. We met through my first walk for peace in 2011 and this is not just my passion, it is ours. Xuelin was a student of architectural design at Zhejiang University—Yuquan Campus for seven years, competing two degrees before coming to London to work in architectural practice.

For Xuelin her association with Zhejiang University is a very special one. She is president of the Alumni in the UK. Zhejiang is one of China's top-tier universities, usually coming in third in league tables just behind Peking and Tsinghua. So Zhejiang University was the end point of the walk and the Temple of Heaven was the start.

As we approached the campus entrance, we saw a huge number of umbrellas and thought perhaps there had been an accident but as we got closer it became clear they were there for us. We walked up to the finish line together to loud cheers and then after a short pause I pushed through the red ribbon marking the end of the walk. Students stepped forward with bouquets of flowers. Officials came to offer their congratulations. Everyone wanted a photo and we were only happy to oblige. It was a truly memorable homecoming. I felt incredibly proud to be a 'son-in law' of this great city, university and very proud of my wife.

That wasn't quite it though ….

After the photos people started heading to main hall for the formal welcome ceremony. With great organisation Xuelin had booked a room at a hotel next door where I could go for a shower and change of clothes. As we went in the room I sat on the chair and Xuelin and I just looked at each other and smiled. It was like the scene you see when a Formula One race is over and the winners go into the small room to put on their official caps and get weighed. Words are few. The race is over—no words are necessary.

Ten minutes later and we are back on the university campus and ushered into a formal seated area with what seemed like a couple of hundred people seated in front of a large Walk for Peace banner. Madam Zhang, our host for the ceremony, project director from the Red Cross, constant companion on the walk and friend had everything organised to the last detail.

There were kind and generous speeches from Wu Jing, Vice Chairman of the Zhejiang Provincial Committee of the CPPCC, and Madam Hao Linna, deputy head of the Red Cross Society of China, who had been with us at the start and visited us in Nanjing and was now here at the close. There were welcomes from the Dean and Secretary of the university committee of the Communist Party of China (CPC). Most important of all we were able to hand over the first cheque for ₤50,000 (500,000 yuan) to Hope House, Pizhou, the Suqien Orphanage and Zhejiang Elderly Care. The leaders of these organisations had all made the journey down to receive the cheque, which made the presentation all the more special.

The total of pledges came to ₤70,000 (700,000 yuan) but in good accounting style the Red Cross wanted to make sure the monies had been received before they were distributed. There was also ₤5,706 which had been collected for the British Red Cross through the JustGiving site in the UK. The Red Cross had covered all its costs for the walk centrally so that all the funds raised could go to the causes we identified, a wonderful gesture and, of course, Xuelin and I had covered all our costs personally also. Our hope is that the total may increase still further in the days to come.

In my remarks I added our thanks to Madam Zhang for her inspirational work as the project team leader. We were blessed to have her with us and it had been a privilege to get to know her. I also thanked those who had walked with us—over 700, and those who had donated to the charitable causes—over 1,000. I thanked the 20 Red Cross teams who had guided us through their city, district or province. I thanked the Zhejiang Alumni, the support team back in London who had done such an amazing job of translating these blogs in record time and the documentary team from CCTV who had followed us all the way from Beijing.

I had one final message and that was for those in the audience and in the media who had listened to the generous tributes which had been made. I was worried that they might take this as being about me being special, which is to miss the point. The point is that we are all special and capable of doing truly amazing things. It matters not your age, your education, your social or professional status, your health, and your wealth. If we follow our passion, focus on what we have rather than what we have not, and have the courage to take the first step, then we can all achieve extraordinary things. If you think that is far-fetched, then perhaps you should take a trip to Pizhou and Hope House, and you will meet people with severe disabilities whose focus is not on limitations of their wheelchair but on their dreams of achieving Paralympic gold medals in Rio de Janeiro. If you want a lesson in inspiration, forget about me, celebrate them and do something yourself—today.

Homecoming Reflection

London, The UK

I was expecting a few friends, but we arrived at the New Imperial on Lisle Street, Chinatown to find a room packed with 70 well-wishers and decked out with welcome home banners and a large screen scrolling pictures from the walk. I got quite a lump in my throat. Xuelin smiled; she was in on the surprise, but it was as much recognition of her achievement as mine.

The event was the work of the Zhejiang UK Association, our dear friends Ping Huang and her committee. I have stopped asking how the Chinese people seem capable of putting on the most complex, professional events at incredibly short notice.

Xuelin and I took our place at a table and were amazed to see so many leading figures from the UK Chinese community: C. T. Tang OBE, Chairman of the Chinatown Association and owner of the New Imperial, who had been our first donor to the Red Cross; Chinese community leader Dr. Shan and his wife, Sherry; Counselor General Fei and Counselor Li from the Chinese Embassy; Christine Li from the British China Project; Charlie Wang, Chairman of the Chinese Finance Association; Zhu Mingming, President of the UK Chinese Business Association, and even Mr. Hung Ng MBE, President of the Association for the Promotion of Chinese Education, had travelled down from Newcastle especially.

Ping Huang told us that all the places had gone in a couple of days and there were actually more who wanted to be there. There was something more than mere geography which seemed to have touched the hearts of the Chinese community in the UK about our walk this year. Often I know they feel that they are often forgotten or taken for granted. There are around 600,000 British Chinese in the UK, about 1% of the population. It is one of the oldest ethnic communities in the UK with its origins in maritime trade in the nineteenth centuries in London and Liverpool.

The British Chinese make a positive contribution to the UK society. They are rightly proud of both their Chinese roots and their British identity. It is very rare to see Chinese involved in crime or stirring up community divisions; their children are the highest achievers by ethnic group in education, their grandparents are amongst the lowest users of the NHS due to their healthy lifestyles and entrepreneurship, and hard work is in their DNA. I know that because they keep a low profile (except at Chinese New Year) and because they aren't to be found airing grievances in the media, the British Chinese often feel taken for granted. It seemed therefore that this 'crazy fellow Brit' taking time to get to know their ancestral country and culture was something they genuinely appreciated.

Normally when I speak I see eyes glazing over with utter boredom after three minutes but I spoke for twenty minutes and they seemed to still be interested—music to a politician's soul!

What were my standout reflections?

- The quality of the infrastructure.
- The vastness of the rural spaces in between urban zones.
- The cheerfulness and kindness of ordinary people.
- The speed with which things can happen.
- The incredible beauty of the countryside, mountains, lakes and rivers.
- The rediscovery of ancient Chinese culture and philosophy which is underway.
- The real affection of Chinese people for the UK.

- The centrality of children in Chinese society and their passion for education.
- The inter-generational strength of Chinese society.
- The innocence of Chinese society and their sentimentality rather than cynicism.
- The pain and suffering of the Chinese during World War II.
- The generosity of the Chinese people—over 99% of donors and donations to the Red Cross charities were Chinese people.

I closed my remarks with a personal tribute to Xuelin, without whom I simply would not have been able to embark on such an expedition. I recalled that on our final night Zhejiang University had put on a banquet for us which was attended by about 120 alumni and faculty from the university. At the end of the evening the Dean produced a special gift for Xuelin; it was her confidential report and score card over the seven years of study. There was only one occasion when her grades fell below 90%—she was described as an 'outstanding student with great promise'. I concluded by saying that I hope they felt that she had realised their ambition for her but from what I had seen, I believed she is capable of even more, a bit like China itself.

附录一

麦克·贝茨勋爵 2011—2016 年徒步回顾

2016 年
阿根廷·布宜诺斯艾利斯—巴西·里约热内卢
为奥林匹克休战徒步

【时间】

4月6日（联合国运动和平发展日）—7月29日（里约奥运会奥林匹克休战启动日）。

历时 115 天。

【路线】

阿根廷·布宜诺斯艾利斯—巴西·里约热内卢。

途经 4 个国家：阿根廷、乌拉圭、巴拉圭以及巴西。

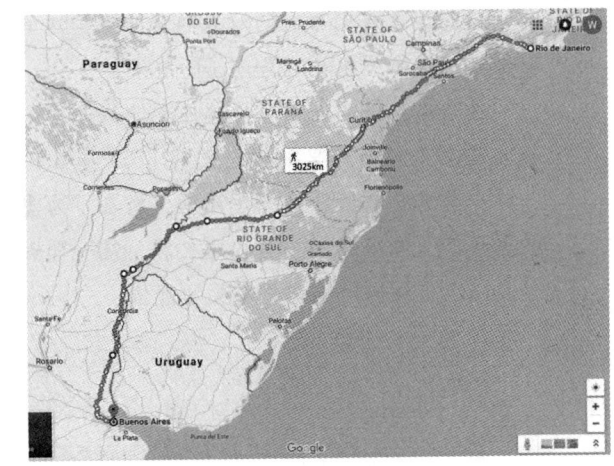

【距离】

3025 公里 (1880 英里)。

【成就】

募集了超过 26 万英镑善款捐给联合国儿童基金会。

【政要来信】

国际奥林匹克委员会主席托马斯·巴赫的来信

敬爱的贝茨勋爵：

　　愿好运与勇气一直伴随着您的"为奥林匹克休战徒步"之旅！我了解到您的这次徒步路程漫长，但我期盼您接下来的每一步都会通过传播奥林匹克体育精神为人类构建更加和平美好的世界添砖加瓦。衷心感谢您为传播奥林匹克休战的和平理念做出的贡献！

　　奥林匹克休战精神所象征的包容、团结和和平理念体现了全人类的共同价值。由于体育是体现人类存在并且达到普遍规律的唯一领域，因此体育的特殊性表现在它将奥林匹克休战精神付诸了实践。不管在世界何处，体育的规则适用于每一个人。这些规则是在体现人类共同价值观并精确解读了我们共同的人性的基础上构建的。因此，体育常常被当作全世界人民的文化交流与沟通的桥梁。

　　感谢您为提高人们对奥林匹克休战这一古老传统的认知的倡议！从布宜诺斯艾利斯到里约热内卢的1750英里的徒步路程，和所有的旅程一样，都需要从迈开第一步开始。您在"为奥林匹克休战徒步"中宣扬的奥林匹克休战精神——构建包容、统一与和平的世界——恰恰是当今世界比以往任何时候都更需要的价值。

　　此致
敬意

托马斯·巴赫
2016年3月10日

INTERNATIONAL
OLYMPIC
COMMITTEE

The President

Lord Michael Bates
The Rt Hon the Lord Bates
Minister of State
The Home Office
2 Marsham Street
London
SW1P 4DF
Great Britain

Lausanne, 10 March 2016

Dear Lord Bates,

As you set out on the Walk for Peace, I wish you good luck and fortitude on your journey. You have a long walk ahead of you, but it is my hope that every step along the way will be a step towards building a peaceful and better world through sport and the Olympic ideal. Thank you for spreading the message of peace that the Olympic Truce represents.

The Olympic Truce stands for the common human values of tolerance, solidarity and peace. Sport is in a unique position to put the spirit of the Olympic Truce into practise because sport is the only area of human existence that has achieved universal law. Regardless of where in the world we practise sport, the rules are the same and apply to everyone. They are based on universal values that define our common humanity. In this way, sport is always about building bridges between people and cultures.

Thank you for your initiative to raise awareness for this noble ancient tradition of the Olympic Truce. Like all journeys, walking the 1,750 miles from Buenos Aires to Rio de Janeiro also begins with a single step. With your Walk for Peace, you are carrying the spirit of the Olympic Truce into a world that needs the values of tolerance, solidarity and peace more than ever before.

Yours sincerely

Thomas A.C

Château de Vidy, 1007 Lausanne, Switzerland | Tel. +41 21 621 6111 | Fax +41 21 621 6216 | www.olympic.org

英国时任首相卡梅伦的来信

麦克惠鉴：

在阁下决意辞去现任政府职务，为宣传联合国奥林匹克休战精神以及为联合国儿童基金会募集善款而即将奔赴南美开展单人徒步行走之际，我谨对您在任职期间所做的贡献表示感谢！对您而言，辞职必定是艰难的抉择。但此项善举发自内心，我理解您投身公益的愿望，并向您致以最真诚的祝福。

借此机会，我想对您在国会的工作及迄今做出的巨大贡献表示敬意。您在国务大臣这一现职中的表现得到了高度评价，相信您的贡献必将为国会及上议院同人所称颂并久久怀念。我尤其感谢您在上议院主持诸如《现代奴隶法案》《精神药品法案》以及最近的《移民法案》等重要政府立法工作时所做出的努力；您作为国务大臣，代表内政部在上议院中发声、回应问题等，日常工作同样卓有成效。

我同时非常感谢多年来您对保守党的付出和贡献。您此前担任保守党副主席以及北方局的领袖人物，始终以饱满的热情和奉献精神投身工作。身为我们之中最为忠心耿耿、恪尽职守的成员，您应当为自己在政府和我们党的工作中取得的成绩感到自豪。

此次布宜诺斯艾利斯至里约热内卢的单人徒步之旅，将是一项富有成效的倡议，与您的2012年伦敦奥林匹克休战行动相互呼应并具有同等重要的意义。面对这次巨大挑战，衷心祝愿您一切顺利。

最后，再次感谢您对保守党和政府所做出的贡献！谨以此函向您的奥林匹克休战宣传活动致以我最诚挚的祝愿，祝您一路平安，徒步成功！

此祝
行安

戴维
2016年3月18日

10 DOWNING STREET
LONDON SW1A 2AA

THE PRIME MINISTER

18 March 2016

Dear Michael,

I wanted to take this opportunity to write and thank you for your Ministerial service, following your decision to step down from the Government to undertake a solo-walk across South America in support of the UN Olympic truce and to raise funds for UNICEF – a cause so close to your heart. It must have been a very tough decision to decide to stand down – and a deeply personal one – but I understand completely your wish to pursue this venture and you do so with my warmest blessing.

In particular, I would like to pay tribute to your parliamentary service, and your outstanding contribution to date. Your most recent work as Minister of State at the Home Office has been hugely valued and I have no doubt that your input will be greatly missed across the department, as well as by colleagues across the House. I am immensely grateful for your efforts in steering many important pieces of government legislation through the House of Lords, including the Modern Slavery Bill, the Psychoactive Substances Bill and, most recently, the Immigration Bill. This, in addition to your routine work as our Minister of State, taking questions and representing the Home Office in the House of Lords so effectively.

I am also immensely grateful for your hard work and service to the Conservative Party over so many years. Having previously played a leading role on the Northern Board and served as Deputy Party Chairman, you have always brought great passion and commitment to your work. You have been such a loyal and dedicated colleague throughout, and – whether it be for the Government or our party – you can be extremely proud of all that you have achieved.

英国女王的来信

尊敬的贝茨勋爵：

　　感谢您在 3 月 23 日给克里斯托弗·盖德爵士的信中告知女王陛下，您将辞去在英国政府中的部长职位。

　　我已经将您的信呈交女王陛下阅览，她对您的来信表示衷心感谢。得知为了宣传奥林匹克休战精神，以及为联合国儿童基金会筹款以帮助战火中的儿童，您将从布宜诺斯艾利斯单人徒步到里约热内卢，全程 2000 英里 (3000 公里)，女王陛下借此信祝您一切顺利。

　　随信附上女王陛下最诚挚的祝福。

　　您真诚的，

萨曼莎·科恩
女王私人助理
2016 年 4 月 18 日

BUCKINGHAM PALACE

18th April, 2016.

Dear Lord Bates,

Thank you for your letter of 23rd March, addressed to Sir Christopher Geidt, informing The Queen that you have stepped down from your role as a Minister in Her Majesty's Government.

I have shown your letter to The Queen who was grateful to be kept informed and wishes you all the best for your 2000 mile solo-walk from Buenos Aires to Rio de Janeiro to raise awareness for the 2016 Olympic truce and to raise funds for Unicef's 'Children in Danger' initiative.

This letter comes with Her Majesty's warmest good wishes.

Yours sincerely,

Samantha Cohen
Assistant Private Secretary to The Queen

The Rt. Hon. Lord Bates of Langburgh

联合国秘书长潘基文的来信

敬爱的贝茨勋爵：

　　首先热烈祝贺您最近从2018年青奥会主办城市布宜诺斯艾利斯到2016年奥运会及残奥会主办城市里约热内卢的"为奥林匹克休战徒步"之旅。我清楚记得，我们于2011年在日内瓦联合国欧洲总部会见，一起见证了联合国大会通过的2012年伦敦奥运会奥林匹克休战协议，那一次，您与您的太太雪琳正徒步行进在从希腊奥林匹亚至伦敦的征途上。

　　您以实际行动对奥林匹克休战协议以及联合国大会第70届会议通过的第四项决议做出贡献，即"通过体育和奥林匹克理想，创造更加美好、和平的世界"，对此我深为赞赏。体育是实现教育、健康、可持续发展以及和平的重要手段。这一点也继续体现在日前发布的联合国《2030年可持续发展议程》中，旨在建立和平、包容的世界。

　　您此次徒步对于各成员国发扬奥林匹克休战精神，促进各个国家及其人民之间开展对话、增进互相理解是个积极倡导。我钦佩您的勇气和奉献，而且我深知，您太太的支持是不可或缺的。

　　最后，请再次接受我最诚挚的祝愿，祝您顺利完成余下的征程，并向您一直以来为世界和平做出的努力表示衷心感谢！

此致
敬礼

潘基文
2016年6月30日

THE SECRETARY-GENERAL

30 June 2016

Dear Lord Bates,

Congratulations on your latest Walk for the Olympic Truce, from Buenos Aires, host city for the 2018 Youth Summer Olympic Games, to Rio de Janeiro, host city of the 2016 Olympic and Paralympic Games. I fondly recall meeting you in Geneva in 2011, when the London 2012 Olympic Truce was adopted by the General Assembly. At the time you and your wife, Xuelin, were in the middle of a prodigious trek from Olympia to London.

I thoroughly commend your dedication to the Truce and your contribution to the implementation of the United Nations General Assembly resolution 70/4, 'Building a peaceful and better world through sport and the Olympic ideal'. Sport is a powerful tool for education, health, sustainable development and peace. This has most recently been recognized in the newly adopted 2030 Agenda for Sustainable Development, which aims to promote peaceful and inclusive societies.

Your current walk is a wonderful initiative to encourage the observance of the Olympic Truce and to advocate for dialogue and mutual understanding among people and nations. I admire your commitment and fortitude, and that of your wife, whose support is, I know, indispensable.

Please accept my very best wishes for a successful conclusion to your latest walk, and my sincere gratitude for your continued efforts on behalf of world peace.

Yours sincerely,

BAN Ki-moon

The Right Honourable Lord Bates of Langburgh
House of Lords
London

2015 年
中国·北京—中国·杭州
为和平徒步

【时间】

7月27日(2012年伦敦奥运会三周年)—10月5日。

历时71天。

【路线】

中国·北京—中国·杭州。

途经6省。

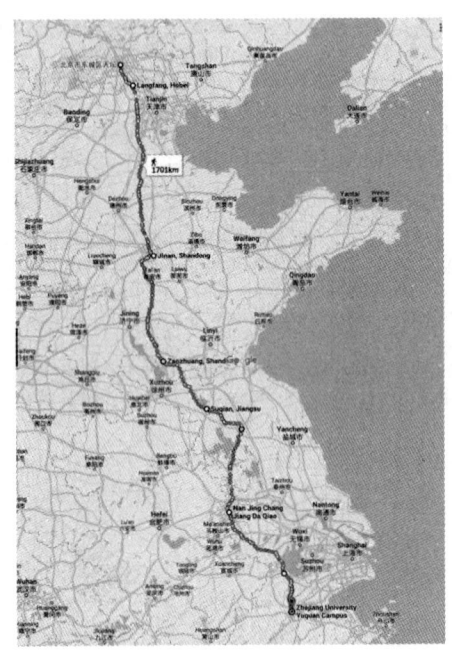

【距离】

1702.7公里(1057.7英里)。

【成就】

募集了9万英镑善款捐给红十字会推荐的沿途慈善项目。

2014 年
英国·伦敦—德国·柏林
为和平徒步

【时间】

8月4日—9月27日。

历时54天。

【路线】

英国·伦敦(纪念"一战"100周年)—德国·柏林。

途经5个国家(包括"一战"战场,1914年圣诞节休战区域以及前东德与西德曾经的边界)。

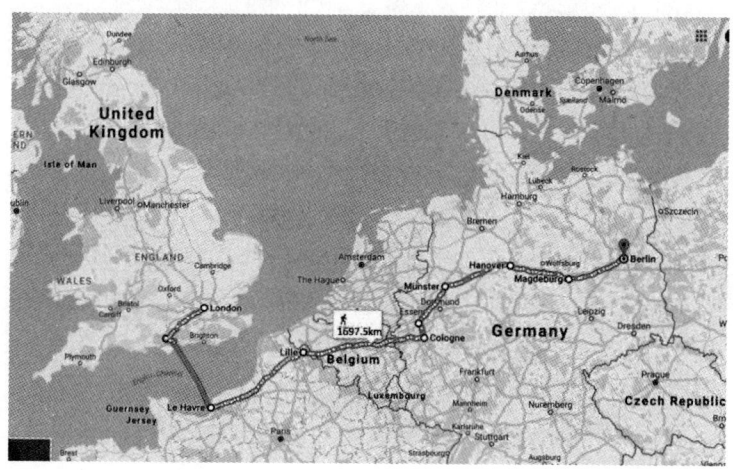

【距离】

1697.5公里(1054.8英里)。

【成就】

募集了4万英镑善款捐给德国和平村慈善机构用于帮助战乱地区儿童的救援工作。

2013年
英国·伦敦—英国·德里
为叙利亚儿童徒步

【时间】

7月27日（伦敦奥运会一周年）—9月9日。

历时35天。

【路线】

英国·伦敦—英国·德里。

途经爱尔兰共和国。

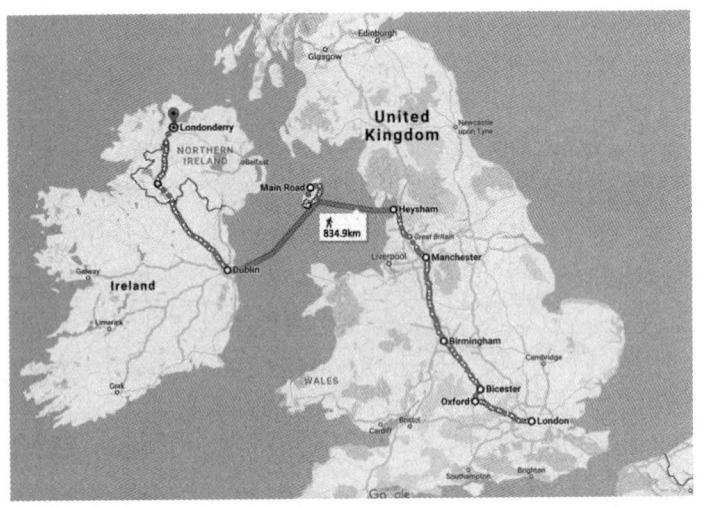

【距离】

834.9公里 (518.8 英里)。

【成就】

募集了5万英镑善款捐给拯救儿童基金会用于帮助叙利亚儿童。

2011—2012 年
希腊·奥林匹亚—英国·伦敦
为奥林匹克休战徒步

【时间】

2011 年 4 月 22 日—2012 年 2 月 15 日。

历时 300 天。

【路线】

希腊·奥林匹亚—英国·伦敦。

途经 14 个国家。

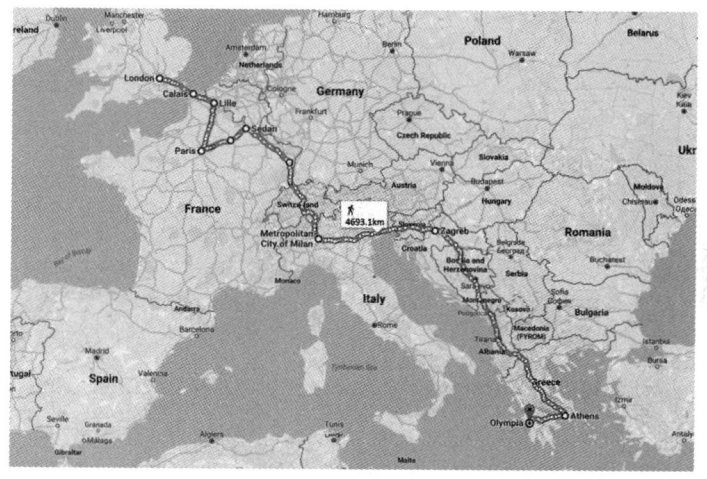

【距离】

4693.1 公里 (2916.2 英里)。

【成就】

在阿尔巴尼亚·地拉那、克罗地亚·斯普利特、斯洛文尼亚·卢布尔雅那、意大利·罗马、意大利·米兰、法国·巴黎以及英国·伦敦与当地人一同进行奥林匹克休战徒步。

附录二

2015年"为和平徒步"捐款名单（部分）*

慈善学徒	Bates Family	Ou Zhang	毕敏
国际学生实习计划	Becky Bao	Phoebe & Lily	边莎莎
杭州海邦留学联盟	Bella Zou	Rob & Di Parsons	卞东辉
杭州花家山庄	Binwei Lu	Rongrong	蔡传强
江苏大众书局图书文化有限公司	Couple Bates	Silvia Ding	蔡赐河
江苏龙虎网信息科技股份有限公司	Daibin	Simon Li	蔡建华
江苏泗州饭店有限公司	David Bates	Stephen Bates	蔡文男
经济分会	Dr. Christina Zhang	Tim, Ben & Ruth	曹春霞
伦敦华埠商会	Felix Xia	Water Hu	曹庆峰
南京观睿文化传播有限公司	George Li	Weijian Qi	曹庆华
上海快鹿投资集团	Gerry Langley	William Wu	常春藤
协和华东	Grace Gu	Xun Liu	常惠刚
英国华商报	Huali Tang	Yammi	常雷
英中经济文化促进会	Hui Huang & Luke Jackson	Yuhong	车鉴
永兴特钢	Jachi Xiong	Zhenyu Yan	陈安
浙江汇华房地产开发有限公司	Jayne Douglass	Zhong Wang	陈波
浙江建工房地产开发集团	Jihou Zheng	安飞东	陈超平
浙江康吉尔有限公司	Joanna Zhong	安宏娟	陈成振
浙江省对外服务公司	John & Liz	安志鹏	陈聪
浙江省对外交流服务中心	Laura Wang	白建军	陈琮文
浙江省发展侨务事业基金会	Linda Xiong	白小龙	陈大玲
浙江省海外交流协会	Longfellow Liu	包天钦	陈东
Al. Neil & Dan	Michael Liu	包铁民	陈峰烽
Alex Ge	Mr. & Mrs. Emmanuel de Stoppani	包玉龙	陈国良
Arthur & Catherine Bates		北贝乐	陈海东

---

* 受篇幅所限，仅列出捐款数额50元以上的团体和个人，其他600多位捐款者在此不一一列出。
捐款名单由麦克·贝茨勋爵夫妇提供。

陈昊	陈颖	范红梅	顾建华	侯谨谦
陈昊男	陈映烈	范建勇	顾秾	胡斌
陈洪	陈余宽	范俊	顾庆新	胡桂萍
陈焕耀	陈远青	范瑞坤	顾叶仁	胡娟红
陈辉	陈灼声	范铁	顾迎化	胡倩
陈基细	程厚博	方柏山	关频杰	胡永群
陈佳	程华九	方侃	关炆奇	黄冰
陈健勇	程一峰	方向	冠一	黄兵
陈杰	池清 & 金岳亨	方元弟	贵体谦	黄浩忠
陈金妹	池毓修	芳菲	郭建涛	黄建刚
陈静宜	迟婧彦	冯国震	郭洁瑜	黄乐夫
陈军	迟乃河	冯建	郭力杰	黄萌
陈坤林	迟志强	冯美兰	郭年明	黄咪咪
陈兰	崔军	冯善忠	郭强	黄伟
陈临江	崔丽娟	付艾伦	郭尉	黄新建
陈旻	崔亚涛	付峰	郭跃	黄馨
陈敏	代建国	付维幸	哈里森	黄秀玉
陈明新	戴立	傅明	海丽曼	黄宣武
陈慕燕	戴润昌	傅赛凤	海燕	黄晔
陈七	单声博士 & 单秋桂林	傅蔚冈	寒静	霍法如
陈谦	稻谷	傅献玉	韩方敏	姬乐乐
陈秋香	邓宝金	傅振球	韩鹏飞	季建芳
陈荣	邓君剑	高洪凯	杭剑平	家慧
陈瑞华	邓明	高玲玲	郝林娜	简崇军
陈上荣	邓柱廷	高翔	何洪杭	建云
陈仕平	狄玲	高艳红	何玲玲	江南雨
陈习龄	刁杰明	郜俊林	何明耿	姜际春
陈小钦	丁德坤	葛爱玲	何素	姜若萍
陈晓敏	丁维娜	龚魏	贺慧娟	姜晓玲
陈秀荣	董成舟	龚向阳	贺湘	蒋晨
陈学英	董慧芬	顾炳元	洪钢	蒋盈盈
陈艺敏	杜玉娟	顾红	洪冀宁	焦健

金朝龙	李建勇	郦菊红	刘姝娟	罗卿平
金剑辉	李剑	连德江	刘顺美	罗贤强
金王来	李健	梁剑	刘小华	马宝山
金伟钰	李金荣	梁齐洋	刘晓华	马福荣
金永辉	李娟	梁月山	刘新	马嘉
津红	李军	廖慧兰	刘新元	马可奥勒留
靖长华	李立枝	廖秀琴	刘鑫	马丽
瞿莹	李林	廖亦铭	刘亚明	马列
康胜燕	李芒＆房艾玫	林本诚	刘彦斌	马秋梅
柯砾	李孟波	林波波	刘艳林	马文博
孔剑	李孟迁	林超	刘胤宏	马月红
孔庆秀	李仁杰	林国荣	刘颖	毛峰
来镇	李韧	林航	刘永兵	毛力军
赖彩琳	李少方	林孔周	刘永淼	毛永锋
赖国宾	李绍林	林莉	刘芸芸	毛玉龙
赖小平	李唯佳	林理德	龙奕	毛植成
兰俭	李熙琳	林美银	楼晔	冒荔
兰蔻	李相君	林明植	卢霖	梅月华
乐辉	李欣安	林年成	卢晓丽	孟惠强
雷赛平	李欣然	林年青	卢溢华	孟庆霞
莉莉	李秀生	林钦	鲁祖统	缪峰
李宝平	李旭辉	林群欣	陆其清	缪斯纯
李潺	李雪刚	林维贵	路映虹	缪艳萍
李春高	李伊平	林伟斌	璐璐	穆欣
李道升	李怡琨	林宜利	吕博涵	倪小辉
李德宏	李永彤	凌云	吕宏丽	宁志威
李芳	李育青	刘常芳	吕洪凤	欧玉星
李根	李昱	刘贵赟	吕建生	潘广儒
李汉进	李昭明	刘红丽	吕丽丽	潘家驹
李浩	李真驹	刘卉	吕任东	潘乐郡
李卉子	厉春莲	刘键	罗嘉羽	潘勤敏
李嘉连	厉秀华	刘鹏忠	罗琦	潘晓涵

潘旭华	石坚	王斌	王小丽	吴敏芳
潘仰知	寿培平	王炳辉	王晓杰	吴奇
彭少剑	舒晓华	王泊雅	王晓霞	吴清秀
戚华婧	宋舒	王昌南 & 黄萍	王昕坤	吴思齐
钱萃阳	苏玲燕 & 董丹申	王朝辉	王鑫	吴燕
钱华峰	苏伟志	王聃	王星	吴一心
钱晓辉	苏云芝	王东明	王旭明	吴雨霞
钱昱	孙宝频	王广宇	王怡发	吴玉光
秦保红	孙斌	王浩飞	王艺霏	吴跃玲
邱意淳	孙红艳	王红果	王渊	伍善雄
裘建军	孙威	王继利	王云汛	奚灵平
裘健	孙晓丹	王家厚	王中杰	夏小虎
任德豹	孙幸福	王嘉宏	韦臻	项秀英
任国才	孙志祥	王建华	魏德毅	项秀玉
任浩	谭艳玲	王建杰	魏静	肖焕跃 & 肖杨
任小鸿	汤政	王建利	魏忠东	肖珺
阮锡长	唐谦一家	王进学	温红媚	肖立程
邵建波	陶锦辉	王京辉	温起	肖奇凤
邵子睿	田长桉	王兰英	温兴建	肖茜
沈丹凤	田力	王莉	文江	肖炜
沈德魁	田明	王璐璐	翁纪远	谢斌
沈国强	田征	王梦迪	翁岚	谢东奎
沈鸿霞	佟帅	王民	翁茜	谢漾
沈骏	童志锋	王强	翁绳飞	忻立靖
沈琦明	万萍	王清	吴超英	辛斌
沈文平	汪博	王全爱	吴晨	辛承军
沈晓安	汪建文	王权	吴丹花	熊亚伟
沈毅	汪可雯	王荣娟	吴海伦	熊永华
盛国辉	汪荣勋	王若凡	吴建滨	徐琛凤
施建基	汪胜忠	王书恺	吴建忠	徐道睦
施建日	汪雪琴	王滔	吴剑	徐惠忠
施小伟	王峥	王伟	吴晶	徐坚真

徐璐	叶楠	袁九根	张君豪	张政平
徐强	叶佩善	袁云贵	张磊	张志华
徐秀香	叶青	曾剑琴	张力	张智颖
徐旭昶	叶青青	曾莉娜	张立	章利勇
徐燕	叶素珍	曾灵敏	张立峰	赵滨
徐燕峰	叶学强	曾肖微	张丽丽	赵承良
徐正安	叶学群	曾云	张美凤	赵国卫
许蓓	叶竹民	曾子	张明	赵凯
许德钦	叶子	翟永泉	张鹏	赵克强
许伟良	宜卓	詹雪梅	张巧巧	赵倩
许旭波	易才拾	占福文	张巧中	赵琴
许雅香	因扎东	张必来	张锐	赵胜男
薛建君	殷杰	张兵	张尚鑫	赵顺禄
薛世文	殷茵	张灿燕	张少琴	赵卫
闫志纯	应黎灿	张潮	张维仁	赵晓村
严求真	应泉	张岱	张伟	赵学法
严永军	永军	张典	张文德	赵志强
严振羽	游鸿强	张东平	张文军	珍珍
羊大雄	游淑淋	张光和	张祥荣	郑碧玲
杨国忠	于丽颖	张国权	张小帆	郑炳克
杨海	于佩	张菡	张小颖	郑光
杨建光	于燕如	张红娟	张绪军	郑惠茹
杨金坤	余爱钦	张红军	张阳	郑慧
杨柳	余彩霞	张虎	张养发	郑培强
杨晓敏	余春桂	张晖	张烨坤	郑霞意
杨耀宇	余良珍	张嘉显	张伊	郑在峰
杨玉龙	余少华	张建农	张颐	周絃光
杨振岗	余晚晚	张建平	张轶龙	周佳
杨忠红	俞祁平	张杰	张崟	周俭
姚桂海	宇山	张金萱	张瑛俏	周建文
姚军	袁芳	张飔	张媛	周科
叶龙海	袁慧光	张娟	张振新	周莉

周明	周妍	朱黎	朱雪昌	庄克服
周奇鹏	周颖	朱力克	朱禺	庄文元
周琦	周愉飞	朱南松＆杨荔雯	朱悦	卓建方
周淑颖	周宇	朱世哲	朱跃龙	卓旭东
周维	周跃武	朱巍	竺涛	左廷福
周宵飞	朱海红	朱卫平	祝建武	
周雪琴	朱恺	朱小久	祝敏	

后 记

旅行中，我们不免会随身携带一个文化包袱。这个塑造我们世界观的文化包袱，决定我们对我们所看到的事和遇到的人做出何种判断。

我选择三个月游历中国的模式非同寻常，那就是徒步旅行。这是我做的一项沿京杭大运河徒步行走的慈善活动，两地相距大约1600公里。这次活动得到了我妻子的支持，而且中国红十字会的几个朋友还主动为我作导游。这并不是我的第一次慈善行走，而是第四次。我们已经走过18个国家，到2016年，从阿根廷首都布宜诺斯艾利斯到巴西的里约热内卢，我们穿行国家的数字已上升至23个。当你徒步行走时，你需要与你经过地方的人密切接触，寻找食物、水、住所，同时寻求行进方向的建议。

卸下身上沉重的文化包袱，我从北京的天坛出发，享受未来71天完全沉浸于这个国家的独特机会。以前出发时，最多也就是一些家人和朋友来为我们送行，可这次却来了大约150人。中国民众、政府官员和媒体记者似乎真的被我们打动了，一个"疯狂的外国人"会选择踏上这样的征途，简直是不可思议。人们想把串珠和鲜花作为礼物送给我们。几个小铃铛被人挂在了我的帆布背包上，不求什么回报，只为回来时能获得一张照片留念。

这是我第一次看到的真正意义上的中国，也是给我留下最刻骨铭心印象的一次。来自最近一项YouGov民意调查，数据显示中国人是世界上最乐观的人，有41%的中国人回答说他们认为世界正在变得越来越好，而33%的人回答说世界变得越来越糟；在英国只有 4% 的人认为世界正在变得越来越好，而 65% 的人认为世界变得越来越糟。我意识到如果要准确地观察真正的中国，我就需要换个镜头，抛弃玩世不恭和悲观情绪，变得情感丰富而且积极乐观。

在曲阜，孔子的故里和安息地，我要探索儒家思想在当代中国的影响究竟有多深。社会阶层、政治秩序和和睦共处的概念塑造了中国文化，就像希腊哲学和基督教所构建出西方文明那样。根是文化、民族或家庭给我们的一种身份和归属感，是社会稳定和发展不可或缺的，这是一个显著的特点。我在徒步中注意到许多地方的寺庙和古建筑得以重建，人们在重拾历史。

这种历史感、社会秩序、责任和和谐渗透在各个方面：你坐在哪儿吃东西，你吃什么，你见什么人，你受到何种礼遇。西方文化，尤其是英美国家，强调个人潜能和自我愉悦，而中国文化的出发点则更倾向于你对家庭和社会的责任感，以及能否令他人愉悦。这里，我不是在做价值观判定，只是简单地观察。这些文化存在着，并且形成了我们看待世界和我们自己的方式。

夏日炎热而漫长，行走一天后，我们常常会在傍晚溜进当地的城镇或村子，享受一顿热气腾腾的面条或水饺。当地那种安宁祥和的气氛给我留下了深刻的印象。我相信中国也有犯罪和酗酒的问题，但我在公共场所还从来没有遇到过。各家各户其乐融融地聚集在广场上，有人用儿童车或踏板车推着孩子们走来走去，男人玩棋牌，女人跳广场舞，大家喝着茶，一幅太平盛景。

这种情感、责任和义务的融合没有哪儿能比家庭体现得更为淋漓尽致了，特别是他们对孩子的态度。在中国人眼中，儿女比天大。我发现在中国的农村和乡镇很少能见到小孩独处，他们总是被家里上上下下的亲人们簇拥着，是众人关注的焦点。

我们知道孩子的早期教育是多么重要。而中国孩子所接受的启蒙教育真是令人难以置信，随后的教育体系也渗透着此类元素。在这样的教育体系中，令人满意的课堂纪律和责任观念能够培养出毕恭毕敬、勤勉顺从的学生，从而培养出毕恭毕敬、勤勉顺从的好公民。徒步中国期间，我看到这一现象被成千上万种方式演绎着。这不仅成为一个值得赞美的理由，而且不经意间解释了中国社会的强大和稳定。

经济合作与发展组织（OECD）在 65 个国家和地区实施了国际学生评估项目（PISA），上海在数学、科学和阅读方面高居榜首，而美国和英国则仅处于大约25或30名左右的位置。这不啻为一个了不起的成就，而更让人为之赞叹的是，它竟然是由一个人均GDP仅列世界第72位的国家取得的！中国的全球化进程正是通过教育实现的。

这种优秀的教育成绩还反映在中国留学生人数大幅增长上。中国留学生占世界留学生总人数的三分之一。在英国，2014—2015年，大学录取中国学生达89540人，独居各国榜首。

对中国人来说，教育是一种民族情怀。在农村的小镇里，你会看到新学校如雨后春笋般不断地涌现。中国国内大学的排名直线上升，而且70%～80%的海外留学生如今选择回国就业。中国学生在世界顶尖大学中占据的比例很高，这是一份不可思议的知识资本储备，势必会在中国未来几十年的发展中派上用场。

在"分享经济增长的成果"这一点上，值得注意的是，为提高所有中国人的生活水平，中国付出了巨大努力。在我走过的地方，绝大多数财富被重新分配，用以改善普通人的生活状况。

徒步中国期间，各村各镇，崭新的马路和基建设施不时地映入眼帘，有的人正在忙着盖新房，有的人已经搬进了新家。那里正在兴建新的学校和医院，还有公共配套设施。人们与我攀谈时常常会谈及自己生活水平发生的巨大改善。

中国是人类历史上脱贫人数最多的国家，有6.8亿中国人脱离了贫困！联合国千年发展目标全球减贫成就里，中国占四分之三。中国的极端贫穷人口比率从1980年的84%下降至现在的10%。对于那些亟盼减少贫困、兴建公共基础设施和改善生活机遇的国家而言，中国无疑是一个鲜活的成功案例。

中国的景色秀美宜人，特别是当你远离大都市，那如画般的旖旎风光绝对会让你流连忘返。在长达千余公里的徒步行走中，我会一连几天穿行在种植单一作物的农田中，例如大枣、大蒜、石榴、荸荠，当然还有橘子。我会跟途中遇到的农民和劳作者攀谈，了解一些耕作过程和市场行情。这是一片远离快节奏发展和熙攘喧嚣都市的秀丽景色。

徒步旅行，真是参观一个国家基础设施的好途径。中国的基础设施给人留下深刻印象。我走过的地方，路面标准极高。护栏、排水设施和路肩都经过精心维护，各村负责各自范围内的维护工作，仿佛在相互竞争，看谁的维护工作做得最好。公路，尤其是我徒步经过的地方公路，仅仅是中国基础设施奇迹的一个掠影罢了。

据麦肯锡咨询公司报告显示，中国的基础设施年支出已经超过了美国和欧盟。中国拥有世界上最大的高速铁路网——截止 2016 年已达到约 2 万公里，是欧洲已建或在建高速铁路总长度的两倍左右。自 2007 年以来，中国机场的数量增加了 62%，高速公路总长增加了 157%，集装箱码头的数量增加了 132%。

从 2008 年北京奥运会暨残奥会到 2016 年杭州 G20 峰会这段时间，英国年均经济增长率为 +0.92%，在七国集团中高居榜首。而中国的年均 GDP 增长率为 8.54%，同前 25 年的平均增长率惊人一致。作为当今世界第二大经济体，中国仅在年度增长量上便可与荷兰整个国内的 GDP 旗鼓相当，且高于瑞士。评论家们仍会提及"中国经济增长放缓"。在中国，8.54% 被称为"增长放缓"，而在欧洲，不到 1% 却被称为"经济复苏"。

美国高盛公司首席经济师吉姆·奥尼尔（Jim O'Neil）在他 2001 年写的一篇文章中界定了令人振奋的世界"新型工业经济体"——巴西、俄罗斯、印度、中国和南非，即"金砖五国"。这 5 个经济体的人口占世界总人口的一半。有人提出，由于金砖五国处于相似的发展阶段，它们的经济增长率也大致相同，然而事实并非如此。我们知道，中国从北京奥运会到杭州 G20 峰会期间（2008—2016 年）的年均增长率为 8.54%，相比之下，印度仅为 2.2%，巴西为 2.04%，南非为 1.9%，俄罗斯为 0.98%。这些事实进一步说明，要解释中国的卓越成就，我们应该看得更加深远一些。

除了重视教育、热衷基础建设，我们还应提及另外一个中国特色，这便是勤劳！一个炎热的傍晚，我邂逅了一位在宿迁郊区耙路堤的 85 岁老者。我问这是不是他自家的地。他满脸疑惑地予以否认。我问他为何要从事这么繁重的工作，他回答说"工作有益身心健康"。这份劳动热情以及"崇高生活有劳有逸"的信仰，皆深深植根于中国文化中。

我在离开北京 71 天后到达杭州。杭州是个人才荟萃的城市，但在我看来，其中最杰出的当属我的妻子李雪琳。我们最初计划的徒步路线是从北京到南京，却提前几周完成了任务，于是在妻子的建议下徒步前往杭州。我们徒步经过了 6 个省份，上百个村庄和城市，一路上邂逅了数不清的男女老少。

我上次来华时经常待在北京、上海和杭州这样的大都市，而这次，我的目的是寻找中国的真面目。我知道，它藏匿于国际化大都市之外。我并非是在寻找希尔顿（Hilton）在经典小说《消失的地平线》中描写的乌托邦之梦——神秘的"香格里拉"。同我们国家一样，中国也有自己的问题和矛盾，乌托邦压根就不存在。但有人说过，穿别人的鞋子走上一英里，才能感同身受，了解对方世界的本色。我穿着自己的鞋，却在他们的土地上足足走了一千多公里！

真是一个无与伦比的机会。在我的旅程中，即便是遇到生活极度贫困的人，在他们的身上也能感受到善良和慷慨的品质，这让我感慨万分，从而改变了我对这个国家及其百姓生活所持有的旧观念。我很荣幸能够生活在英国这个奇妙之邦，我可以诚实地说我热爱自己的祖国，但我们若能虚心学习他人之长，肯定能够取得突破。中国十分敬重和迷恋英国这个小小岛国及其取得的令世界感叹的成就。中国人有意学习英国的教育、商业、创意产业和国民医疗保健制度。我确信，如果我的英国同胞们能够以同样方式审视中国的成功及其文化，我们必将取得更大的成就。我们对于中国的看法也许仍然会受到自己文化包袱中的那些偏见所蒙蔽。首届中英文化交流年以及我的徒步"真实中国"之旅，似乎是一个检验我们旧观念及理由的绝佳时机。不妨扪心自问：我们如何才能通过文化交流和相互尊重，汲取两种文化之精华，让它们精益求精？

Conclusion

The problem with travel is the cultural baggage we bring with us. The cultural baggage that shapes our worldview and by which we form judgements of the places we see and the people we meet. The cultural baggage which is neatly packed for us by social elites from second-hand sources to save us the trouble our 'little minds' have in figuring things out for ourselves. But what if that baggage was lost in transition and you needed enter the country embracing its people the way you found them rather than the way you have been told you should find them? This I did in China during 2015, the official First UK-China Year of Cultural Exchange. This book tells you what I found.

My chosen mode of getting around on my three-month visit to China was an unusual one—walking. I was undertaking a charity walk from Beijing to Hangzhou, roughly following the Grand Canal connecting the two cities and extending some 1,000 miles. I was supported by my wife, and friends from the Red Cross would be my guides. This was not my first long walk for charity; it was our fourth. We had walked through 18 countries—now 23, having walked from Buenos Aires to Rio de Janeiro in 2016. When you walk, you need to engage with the communities you walk through in a real way—seeking food, water, shelter and advice on directions.

Breaking free from my heavy cultural baggage and with an opportunity to fully immerse myself in the country over the next 71 days, I set off from the Temple of Heaven in Beijing. On previous walks there would perhaps be a handful of family and friends coming out to see us off, but for this walk we had around 150. Chinese people, officials and media seemed genuinely touched that a 'crazy foreigner' would choose to embark upon such an expedition. People wanted to give us gifts of beads, flowers. Small bells were attached to my rucksack with only a photo requested in return.

This was perhaps the first and most striking impression of the real China I encountered—it is deeply sentimental, nostalgic and believing of the best. British culture, at least in metropolitan elite circles, is much more cynical. This finding was backed up by a recent YouGov Opinion Poll which found that the Chinese were the most optimistic people in the world, with 41% responding to say they thought that the world was getting better and 33% responding to say it was getting worse; the figures for Britain were that only 4% thought the world was getting better and 65% thought it was getting worse. I realised that if I were to accurately view the real China, then I needed to change the lens I was observing it through from cynical and pessimistic to sentimental and optimistic. Not to do so would be akin to trying to understand the meaning of Chinese characters using the Latin alphabet.

In Qufu, the home and final resting place of Confucius, I was to discover how deep the roots of the philosophy/religion of Confucianism go in modern China. The concepts of social hierarchy, political order and harmonious living give Chinese culture its shape and form every bit as much as Greek philosophy and the Christian religion have formed Western civilisation. It has not always been so. In the Cultural Revolution there was an attempt to eradicate social and cultural history, with catastrophic effect. Roots, be they cultural, national or familial, give us a sense of identity and belonging which is necessary for social stability and growth. It was a notable feature of my walk to note how, in many, many places, temples and ancient buildings were being rebuilt and history was being re-embraced as the Chinese rediscovered their history—incredible history not just over the past 70 but over the previous 5,000 years.

This sense of history, social order, duty and harmony permeates everything from where you sit to eat to what you eat, whom you meet, how you are received. Whereas Western culture, especially Anglo-American, places a strong emphasis on the potential of the individual and pleasing oneself, Chinese culture would have its starting point closer to your obligations to your family and wider community and pleasing others. Here I am not making a value judgement, just simply observing that they exist and shape the way we see the world and ourselves in it.

In the evenings after a long, hot day walking, we would often walk out into the local town or village to have some fresh noodles or dumplings. I was struck by how safe and unthreatening the atmosphere was. I am sure that China has its problems with crime and excessive drinking, but it was not visible in the public places I saw. The market squares were full of families—young children being pushed around in toy cars or scooters, men playing board games, women doing synchronized dancing and everyone drinking tea.

Nowhere do these combinations of sentimentality, duty and obligation come together more powerfully than in the home and in particular in their attitudes to children. Children are the centre of the universe for the Chinese. I used to think this was because of the 'one child' policy, now relaxed to 'two children', but I began to realise that this ran far deeper. I noticed that in villages and towns you rarely saw children alone, but instead they were surrounded by immediate and extended family—the constant focus of attention.

We know how important early-years development is for children. In China children receive an incredible head start. This then feeds through into the education system, where the sense of order in the classroom and duty to please others leads to respectful, compliant and industrious students who in turn grow up to become respectful, compliant and industrious citizens. I saw this expressed in a thousand different ways on my travels through China, and it became not just a reason for admiration but also an underlying explanation for the strength and stability of Chinese society.

The Programme for International Student Assessment (PISA), undertaken by the OECD in 65 countries/regions, finds Shanghai, China, first in maths and science and reading, with the USA and the UK ranking in the mid-20s or early 30s. What makes this performance all the more remarkable is that it is produced in a country that is still ranked only 72nd in the world in terms of nominal GDP per capita. China is not just manufacturing its way in the world, it is developing itself through education.

This strong academic performance is reflected in a vast growth in the number of students studying overseas, accounting for one-third of the total overseas student numbers around the world. In the UK there were 89,540 Chinese students enrolled at universities (2014–2015), more than any other country. The next largest cohort was from India,18,320 students, and in the United States,16,895 students.

These numbers are interesting for a number of reasons. First, British universities are acknowledged as being, after the United States, the best in the world. Hence, the academic requirements required for entry into those universities will again be amongst the highest in the world. The Chinese are meeting those standards in ever-increasing numbers—and studying in a foreign language. Next, given that the costs of being a foreign student in the UK or the US are extraordinarily high, it reveals not just the wealth of parents sending children to study abroad but also their desire to sacrifice all they have to give their child the best education possible.

Education for the Chinese is a national obsession. In small towns in rural areas you would see new schools springup as the Chinese leadership 'shares the proceeds of economic growth', to coin a phrase. Their domestic universities are surging up the international rankings. What is more, 70–80% of graduates now return to China as 'turtles', as they are known, because they see their best career prospects at home. The high proportion of Chinese students studying at the world's leading universities is an incredible reserve of intellectual capital which will be deployed to develop China in the decades ahead.

On this theme of 'sharing the proceeds of growth', it is notable that huge efforts are made to raise the standard of living for all Chinese. In many economies that have grown fast, the profits have been skimmed off by the political leadership and deployed in Swiss and British bank accounts and properties. The result is that great divides open up between rich and poor, which become a festering sore of social injustice. I don't know the extent to which 'skimming' has happened in China, but it is very clear to see how the vast majority of wealth has been redistributed to raise the conditions of ordinary people in the areas which I was walking through.

In every village you would see not only new roads and infrastructure but new homes being built or occupied and new schools and hospitals being built and utility connections. The people I spoke to were often speaking of the great improvements in their lives, which is unusual in developing countries, where talk is often of wasteful schemes and corrupt officials.

At this point my cultural baggage would be telling me that these people were oppressed and simply concealing the truth, but that can't be so. I was walking a route over which I was in complete control. A route that would vary randomly through villages and towns and stopping to meet people when and where I wanted. China has lifted more people out of poverty than any country in human history—680 million. Three-quarters of the reduction in poverty identified by the United Nations under the Global Millennium Development Goals was achieved by China alone. Its extreme poverty rate has been reduced from 84% in 1980 to 10% now. For those passionate about reducing poverty, public infrastructure and improving life chances, China must surely be a glowing example on a scale of the Industrial Revolution in the UK.

The landscape of China is beautiful, especially when you escape the big cities. On my walk of a thousand miles I would guess about one hundred miles out of the thousand would have been urban or industrial and the rest rural and agricultural. I would walk for days through farms dedicated to growing one particular crop such as dates, garlic, pomegranates, water chestnutsor Mandarin oranges—of course. I would get to talk to the farmers and the workers and understand something about the farming process and prices at market on the way. It was a scene that was far from the fast-paced development, hustle and bustle of the metropolitan areas.

One day I was climbing in the Taishan Mountains. It was a hot August day and we arrived in a small village—Xingjiatun. There was a great tree offering shade from the midday sun and seats underneath. We sat down and villagers came out to talk. They told me the tree was 500 years old and the well beside it was 700 years old. They drew cold water out of the well to refresh me and even a treat of cool watermelon which had been kept in the well. It was a scene from where time had stood still.

As we talked, I asked how many foreign visitors they had had to their village. The answer surprised me—I was the first. To record this historic moment we asked if we could take a picture with the villagers. The Chinese love photographs so they didn't need much persuading as we crowded together under the great tree. I felt perhaps I should explain what a camera was or a phone. What happened next was took me by complete surprise.

After the photo was taken, young and old pulled out their own smart phones and started asking for individual pictures and scanning QS codes so they could share pictures on WeChat and WeiBo. It was a seamless integration of the ancient and modern worlds existing side by side in harmony. Made possible because telecom coverage and wifi access is just part of the critical infrastructure which has been built in all parts of the country and which has become indispensable to young and old alike.

Walking is a good way to see national infrastructure. In my walks I have certainly seen the good, the bad and the ugly. Infrastructure in China is impressive. The road surfaces I walked along were of an extremely high standard. The hedges, gutters and verges were meticulously maintained— each village took responsibility for looking after its section, and there seemed to be competition as to who could maintain it best. Roads, especially the local roads I was walking on, are only one small part of the infrastructure miracle in China.

According to McKinsey & Company management consultants, China has now overtaken the United States and the European Union in terms of annual cash spent on infrastructure. It shows China has the largest high-speed rail network in the world—some 20,000 km as of 2016. That is about twice the total High Speed Rail in Europe either built or currently under construction. It compares to 108 km of HSR track we have in the UK. Moreover, by the time the UK expands its HSR network by a further

225 km (HSR2) in 2026, China will have built a further 18,000 km. Even with this scale of development in China, there is still a need to book tickets well in advance, such is the demand. It is not just rail which is seeing rapid expansion. Since 2007 China has seen a 62% increase in the number of airports, a 157% increase in the length of expressways and a 132% increase in the number of container terminals.

Not surprisingly with such epic development of infrastructure in China, its civil engineers and construction companies have become in demand around the world. The return on capital employed in infrastructure is notoriously long term, which can often make governments struggling with short-term election cycles shy away from long-term commitments. China is spared such limits on its thinking and instead sets its sights on 2049 and the centenary of the founding of the People's Republic, by which time it expects to be the leading economy in the world. Few would now doubt that it is on track to achieve this with time to spare. This was not always the case.

I recalled making visits to China in the early years of the new century while working for a respected firm of political and economic analysts. We would look at the extraordinary pace of growth that had occurred in China between 1991 and 2001 and how it had continued despite the 1997 Asian Financial Crisis and the bursting of the 'Dot.com Bubble' in 2000. We looked ahead and concluded that China's economic growth was simply 'unsustainable' and that it would require a massive correction to asset prices, which in turn could trigger social and political upheaval.

So, when the rest of the world watched awestruck by the quality of the Beijing Olympic Games, economists and political commentators were scratching their heads and wondering how China seemed to be rewriting the economic rule book. Far from crashing, the Chinese economy had quickened its pace of growth from 8.3% in 2001 to 14.2% in 2007.

To be fair, not all commentators got it so hopelessly wrong. Thomas Friedman, in his classic 2008 *New York Times* op-ed, 'The Biblical Seven Years', suggested that China had outperformed the United States because it had not been diverted into costly though necessary military conflicts. He also made the cultural observation on the source of the Chinese economic miracle, stating: 'And, I repeat, they got all this not by discovering oil. They got it by digging inside themselves.' This was a courageous statement by a Western liberal commentator, as it went against the grain of accepted cultural stereotypes of the time, and he was widely criticised for it.

Well, that was 2008. The Games were over and soon we all thought so would be the Chinese 'economic miracle'. The first sign came as economic data suggested that the Chinese economic growth was slowing down from its peak of 14.2% in 2007 to 9.6% in 2008, but this was soon realised not be a reflection of problems with asset prices or the banking system in China but rather in the West. What happened over the next four years was the greatest economic crisis in the West since the Great Depression. Its effects are still being felt as Western governments come to terms with high levels of national debt and consumer debt and banks seek to repair their balance sheets.

During the period between the Beijing Olympic & Paralympic Games and this year's G20 Meetings in Hangzhou (2008–2016), UK annual economic growth averaged +0.92% per annum—the best in the G7 economies; in China average annual growth in GDP was 8.54%, remarkably in line with average growth rates over the preceding 25 years. Just the annual growth of China, now the second largest economy in the world, is the equivalent to the entire GDP of the Netherlands and greater than that of Switzerland. Still, commentators will refer to the 'Chinese economic slowdown'. In China growth of 8.54% is called a 'slowdown' whilst growth of less than 1% in Europe is called a 'recovery'—time to check that baggage again.

The chief economist of Goldman Sachs, Jim O'Neil, wrote a paper identifying the exciting 'newly industrialising economies' of the world in 2001—Brazil, Russia, India, China and South Africa—which became known by the acronym 'BRICS'. Together, these five economies accounted for half the world's population. It was suggested that growth rates would be roughly similar, as each country was at a similar stage of development, and yet that was not the case. We know that average growth rate in China was 8.54% per annum between the Beijing Olympics and the Hangzhou G20 (2008 and 2016), but the comparative average figures were 2.2% per annum for India, 2.04% per annum for Brazil, 1.9% per annum in South Africa and 0.98% per annum for Russia. This adds to the suggestion that to explain the extraordinary performance of China, we need to look deeper.

There is one other Chinese characteristic which we should mention in addition to education: a passion for infrastructure and love of technology because it is, I believe, fundamental to understanding how all these elements are bound together to explain their exceptional success. Hard work. There is a culture of a belief in the nobleness of workand the duty of work. I recall at the end of a long, hot day meeting an elderly man raking a roadside embankment outside Suqianin the early evening. I asked him how old he was—he said he was 85. I asked him if this was his land or his job. He looked puzzled and said 'No.' I asked why therefore he was doing such a demanding task and his reply was 'Work is good for you.' This passion and belief in work as being as critical to noble living as resting runs deep in Chinese culture. Work is literally worshipped whether it is in the classroom, one the factory floor or on a roadside in Suqian.

Seventy-one days after leaving Beijing I arrived in Hangzhou, the birthplace of many great people, the greatest of which, in my view, is Xuelin Li, my wife. The original walk was planned between Beijing (the northern capital) and Nanjing (the southern capital), but we had arrived a couple of weeks early and so I was persuaded by Xuelin to walk on to Hangzhou. We walked through six provinces, hundreds of villages and cities, and met thousands of people along the way.

When I had visited China before, I had often stayed within the major cities of Beijing, Shanghai and Hangzhou, but I had come in search of the real China, and I knew that this would lie outside the main cosmopolitan centres. I wasn't searching for a mythical 'Shangri-la', a Utopian dream from Hilton's classic 'Lost Horizon' novel. China has its problems and inconsistencies like the rest of us. It is certainly no Utopia. But it is said that to begin to understand someone else's world, you need to walk a mile in their shoes. Well, I may have brought my own shoes but I had walked over a 1,000 miles on their roads.

It was an amazing privilege. I was overwhelmed by the kindness and generosity, especially of its poorest people that I met. It transformed my understanding of this country and the lives of its people. I am privileged to live in another amazing country, Britain. Without getting too uncharacteristically sentimental, I can honestly say that I love my country, but I believe we can still do better, especially if we are prepared learn from others. The Chinese have a deep respect and fascination with Britain and what this small island has managed to achieve in the world. The Chinese want to learn from British education, business, creative industries, National Health Service. I am convinced that my fellow countrymen and women could achieve even greater things if they were to view China's successes and culture in the same way. Our view of China may still be obscured by those preconceptions packed for us in our cultural baggage. The First Year of UK-China Cultural Exchange and my walk through the 'real China' would seem a very good time to examine what we are packing and why. And ask ourselves the question as to how through cultural exchange and mutual respect we use the best of each culture to strengthen both.

图书在版编目（CIP）数据

徒步中国：爱与和平的信仰征途：汉英对照／（英）麦克·贝茨勋爵(Lord Michael Bates) 著；李雪琳·贝茨勋爵夫人(Lady Xuelin Li Bates) 等译. —— 北京：新世界出版社，2016.10
 ISBN 978-7-5104-6029-6

Ⅰ.①徒… Ⅱ.①麦…②李… Ⅲ.①日记—作品集—英国—现代—汉、英 Ⅳ.①I561.65

中国版本图书馆CIP数据核字(2016) 第250490号

Walk for Peace
徒步中国——爱与和平的信仰征途

策划协调：张　明
作　　者：麦克·贝茨勋爵
翻　　译：李雪琳·贝茨勋爵夫人 等
责任编辑：李莎莎
装帧设计：贺玉婷
责任印制：李一鸣　黄厚清
出版发行：新世界出版社
社　　址：北京市西城区百万庄大街24号（100037）
发 行 部：(010)6899 5968　　(010)6899 8705（传真）
总 编 室：(010)6899 5424　　(010)6832 6679（传真）
网　　址：http://www.nwp.cn
　　　　　http://www.nwp.com.cn
版 权 部：+8610 6899 6306
版权部电子信箱：nwpcd@sina.com
印　　刷：三河市骏杰印刷有限公司
经　　销：新华书店
开　　本：787mm×1092mm　1/16
字　　数：407千字　印张：27.5
版　　次：2016年10月第1版　2016年10月第1次印刷
书　　号：ISBN 978-7-5104-6029-6
定　　价：68.00元

版权所有，侵权必究
凡购本社图书，如有缺页、倒页、脱页等印装错误，可随时退换。
客服电话：(010)6899 8638